Spanish

Manual

Correct Conjug. **DATE DUE**
and Regional Use

Alfredo González Hermoso

PASSPORT BOOKS
NTC/Contemporary Publishing Group

JUL 2001

Library of Congress Cataloging-in-Publication Data

González Hermoso, A.
    Spanish verb manual: 5,000 verbs, correct conjugations and regional use/
Alfredo González Hermoso.
        p.   cm.
    ISBN 0-8442-1346-2
    1. Spanish language—Verb.   2. Spanish language—Verb—Tables. I. Title.
PC4271.G63   1999
468.2'421—dc21   99-29909
                                                                                  CIP
                                                                                  Rev.

Cover design by Amy Yu Ng

Definitions of regional verb usage by Diccionario de la Lengua
Española de la R.A.E. (Real Academia de la Lengua Española)

English language adaptation by Raymond Hundley, Ph.D.

Interior illustrations by Ángeles San José

Revisions of regional verb usage by Víctor Barrionuevo (Argentina), María Teresa
Rivera (Bolivian Embassy), Antonio Vergara (Chile), Elizabeth Weber (Colombian
Embassy), Felipe Lázaro (Cuba), María Amor López (Ecuadorian Embassy),
Rafael Hernández (El Salvadorian Embassy), Karla Acuña (Guatemalan Embassy),
Iris Ponce (Honduran Embassy), Leonora Moreleón and Natalia Moreleón (Mexico),
Donald Castillo (Nicaraguan Embassy), Flor María Arauz (Panamanian Embassy),
Alcidiades González Delvalle (Paraguayan Embassy), Patricia Jahncke (Peru),
Daniel Duarte (Embassy of the Dominican Republic), Sara Tcharkhetian (River
Plate), Thomas Rübens (Uruguay), Tomás Onaindía (Venezuela)

This edition first published in 1999 by Passport Books
A division of NTC/Contemporary Publishing Group, Inc.
4255 West Touhy Avenue, Lincolnwood (Chicago), Illinois 60646–1975 U.S.A.
© EDELSA Grupo Didascalia S.A. 1996, 1997
© A. González Hermoso 1996, 1997
English adaptation © 1999 by NTC/Contemporary Publishing
Group, Inc.
International Standard Book Number: 0-8442-1346-2
99 00 01 02 03 04 TCP 18 17 16 15 14 13 12 11 10 9 8 7 6 5 4 3 2 1

CONTENTS

INTRODUCTION

The **Spanish Verb Manual** facilitates fast, accurate use of the most common verbs in modern Spanish. It gives a general introduction to the use of verbs in Spanish and also provides unique information on the regional use of Spanish verbs throughout Latin America.

1. The first section is marked with a **g** (for *grammar*) and presents a practical summary of the grammatical system of the Spanish verb.

Basic indicators are provided that will help students recognize the tense of verbs they encounter, as well as make it easy to form correct verb tenses themselves. Irregular verb forms (including spelling and accent changes) are presented according to the standard categories used by Spanish language experts.

This section also includes a simplified comparison between each Spanish tense and the corresponding tense(s) in English.

2. The second section is marked with a **t** (for *tables*) and presents 82 tables of verb conjugations that serve as models for the conjugation of the more than 5,000 verbs identified in this book.

Tables 1–4 present the standard auxiliary (helping) verbs (*haber, tener, ser, estar*). Table 81 is the model for verbs conjugated in the passive voice, and Table 82, the model for verbs conjugated in the reflexive.

The verbs are organized according to the last two letters (endings) in their infinitive form. Tables 5–23 contain the models for verbs ending in **-ar**; Tables 24–50 contain the models for verbs ending in **-er**; and Tables 51–80 contain the models for verbs ending in **-ir**.

Within each group, the regular model for that ending begins the group: 5, *cantar;* 24, *beber;* and 51, *vivir.* The models for verbs that have spelling or accent changes are introduced after the regular forms. Following these, all other verbs are classified as irregular verbs. Where applicable, irregular verbs that are defective or exhibit stem changes are noted in their heading.

In the tables, the roots and the parts of the verb that do not undergo changes have been marked in bold type; the irregularities have been marked in red ink; and the endings and compound tenses have been left in regular type.

3. The third section is marked with a **v** (for *verb index*) and contains an extensive alphabetical listing of the most common verbs in the Spanish language, together with a basic English translation.

Verbs that are only used in participle form are not included. A large number of verbs in Spanish can either be used reflexively or non-reflexively. In the verb index, only those verbs that are exclusively conjugated in the reflexive form are marked as reflexives. To answer any question regarding the conjugation of a verb that is used reflexively, see Table 82 on page 112.

Next to the verb and its English translation, the name and number of its corresponding model table are indicated. To the right of the Spanish verb, there may be a footnote reference number, which means that this verb requires additional explanatory information (see pages 173–74). Irregular verbs are marked with an asterisk (*) before them.

4. The fourth section is marked with a **p** (for *prepositions*) and contains an alphabetical list of the most common verbs in Spanish along with the prepositions and prepositional phrases most commonly used with each verb.

A rigorous process of selection has been employed to eliminate prepositions that the verb *does not need* and to select only those prepositions and prepositional phrases that native speakers, in their spontaneous use of the language, would have no doubt about attributing to a certain verb. The examples are simple and, when it is possible or necessary, they attempt to come close to the actual usage of the verb. For that reason, many of the examples are idiomatic expressions.

5. The fifth section is marked with an **e** (for *expressions*) and contains a selection of 93 verbs with almost 300 idiomatic expressions that use these verbs.

This section represents very informal language use and even includes some idiomatic expressions used in *street talk*. It seemed wise to indicate (with an *F*) those expressions which are very familiar or informal and should only be used in very informal, colloquial contexts.

Similar expressions are presented in parallel form, along with an equivalent English translation, and other observations about the expression, such as its literal meaning (in italics), its vulgarity and *machismo*. Finally, some expressions are comically illustrated in order to demonstrate the sometimes absurd starting point of their meaning.

6. The sixth section is marked **r** (for *regional use*) and contains an alphabetical list of verbs used in different regions of Latin America, along with an explanation of their meaning (in English) with an original translation of the *Real Academia de la Lengua Española*. In some cases, a brief clarification is also included along with the meaning provided. Next to the explanation, the text presents the name and number of the verb's model for conjugation in the verb tables.

7. Finally, an appendix contains a brief grammatical summary of the regional distinctions that affect the use of verbs. The main aspect emphasized here is the *voseo* (use of *vos*), which is a special feature of Spanish in Latin America.

THE PUBLISHERS

the grammatical system of the verb in Spanish

1 Conjugation in Spanish: classification of verbs

In Spanish, verbs are divided into three groups according to the ending of their infinitives:

> **First conjugation:** infinitive ending in **-AR**: *Cantar*.
>
> **Second conjugation:** infinitive ending in **-ER**: *Beber*.
>
> **Third conjugation:** infinitive ending in **-IR**: *Vivir*.

2 Basic information about Spanish verbs

A. THE FORM OF THE VERB

● The Spanish verb is made up of three parts: the **stem** (or root), the **tense indicator**, and the **personal ending**.

Example:

am - ába - mos

stem   tense indicator   personal ending
(imperfect indicative)   (1st person plural)

● The form of the verb can be **personal** if the person is specified, or **impersonal** if it is not.

• There are six persons to the verb: **three singular** and **three plural**.

SINGULAR	**1st** (yo) **2nd** (tú) **3rd** (él/ella/usted)		**PLURAL**	**1st** (nosotros) **2nd** (vosotros) **3rd** (ellos/ellas/ustedes)

• Throughout Latin America, **vosotros** has been replaced by **ustedes**; and in certain regions, **vos** has replaced **tú** (see Appendix, pages 284–288).

• In Spanish, unlike other languages, it is not necessary to say (or write) the personal pronoun in front of the verb form. Therefore, in this text, they will only be used after the verb forms that indicate commands (the **imperative**), since traditionally they are used with that form.

grammatical system

● The **impersonal forms** of the verb (which do not indicate person) are the following three: **infinitive**, **gerund**, and **participle**.

● Verbs are also classified as either **simple** or **compound**. The compound verbs use the auxiliary verb **HABER** (*Table 1*, page 28) for their formation.

B. MOODS

● There are three verbal moods: 1. **Indicative**, 2. **Subjunctive**, and 3. **Imperative**.

● The mood of a verb indicates the attitude of the speaker toward the action of the verb.

• The **indicative mood** is more objective, expressing facts, observations, descriptions, and narrations—*what is.*

• The **subjunctive mood** is more subjective, expressing doubt, desire, emotion, and uncertainty—*what may, might, or ought to be.*
   The subjunctive mood is used much more extensively in Spanish than in English. In Spanish, it is almost impossible to communicate thoughts, convictions, doubts, and emotions without using the subjunctive.

• The **imperative mood** is used to express commands, requests, warnings, and invitations.

● Within each mood, there are **tenses**.

C. TENSES

● The tenses are, essentially, **present**, **past**, and **future**. However, within the past tense, for example, there are several tenses **with different names**.

• The verbs can be formed in **simple** or **compound** forms (depending upon whether or not they use the auxiliary verb **HABER**).

• The following chart (page 11) presents the three moods of the verb and the tenses that exist in each mood. The tenses are shown as they appear throughout the *Verb Tables* section: grouped by mood and structure (simple or compound) and called by their Spanish name. In parentheses, the chart also indicates the name(s) by which these tenses are commonly known in English.

• The chart on pages 12–13 then provides the English equivalents of each Spanish tense *by meaning*. In this simplified guide, example sentences illustrate the tense(s) that are usually required in English to create the corresponding sense or translation.

MODO INDICATIVO (Indicative mood)

Simple tenses	**PRESENTE** (present) **CONDICIONAL** **SIMPLE** (conditional)	**PRETÉRITO** **IMPERFECTO** (imperfect)	**PRETÉRITO** **INDEFINIDO**[1] (preterite *or* preterit)	**FUTURO** **IMPERFECTO**[2] (future)
Compound tenses	**PRETÉRITO** **PERFECTO**[3] (present perfect) **CONDICIONAL** **COMPUESTO** (conditional perfect)	**PRETÉRITO** **PLUSCUAMPERFECTO** (past perfect *or* pluperfect)	**PRETÉRITO ANTERIOR** (past anterior *or* preterite perfect)	**FUTURO** **PERFECTO**[4] (future perfect)

MODO SUBJUNTIVO (Subjunctive mood)

Simple tenses	**PRESENTE** (present)	**PRETÉRITO** **IMPERFECTO** (imperfect)	**FUTURO** **IMPERFECTO**[5] (future)
Compound tenses	**PRETÉRITO** **PERFECTO** (present perfect)	**PRETÉRITO** **PLUSCUAMPERFECTO** (past perfect *or* pluperfect)	**FUTURO** **PERFECTO**[6] (future perfect)

MODO IMPERATIVO (Imperative mood)

Simple tenses	**PRESENTE** (present)

– Notes:

• The following tenses have alternative names: [1]**pretérito indefinido = perfecto simple;** [2,5]**futuro imperfecto = futuro (simple);** [3]**pretérito perfecto = perfecto compuesto;** [4,6]**futuro perfecto = futuro compuesto**. We have used the former options, which are the more traditional ones, in order to differentiate the tenses more clearly.

• The two future tenses of the subjunctive mood[5,6] are used very little. They belong to a language style that is very sophisticated, technical, and archaic.

• For each simple tense, there is a corresponding compound tense, formed from HABER in the same simple tense + the past participle of the relevant verb.

• The **impersonal forms** can also be either **simple** or **compound**, as indicated below:

FORMAS NO PERSONALES (Impersonal forms)

Simple forms:	INFINITIVO (infinitive)	GERUNDIO (gerund)	PARTICIPIO (past participle)
Compound forms:	INFINITIVO	GERUNDIO	

SPANISH TENSES AND THEIR ENGLISH EQUIVALENTS

MODO INDICATIVO

PRESENTE	PRETÉRITO IMPERFECTO	PRETÉRITO INDEFINIDO	FUTURO IMPERFECTO
Escribo una carta. **Present** or **Present Progressive** I write a letter. I am writing a letter.	*El almorzaba cuando llegaron. Siempre caminábamos al parque cada sábado.* **Past Progressive or "used" + Infinitive** (for habitual or repeated past action) He was eating lunch when they arrived. We always used to walk to the park every Saturday.	*Hablé con ella ayer.* **Simple Past** I spoke with her yesterday.	*Hablaré con ella mañana.* **Future** I will/shall speak to her tomorrow.

PRETÉRITO PERFECTO	PRETÉRITO PLUSCUAMPERFECTO	PRETÉRITO ANTERIOR	FUTURO PERFECTO
He trabajado mucho hoy. **Present Perfect** I have worked a great deal today.	*Ella había salido cuando nosotros llegamos.* **Past Perfect (Pluperfect)** She had left when we arrived.	*Cuando ellos llegaron, él ya hubo estado allí por tres horas.* **Past Perfect (Pluperfect)** When they arrived, he had already been there for three hours.	*Habré terminado la tarea antes de que llegue la profesora.* **Future Perfect** I will have finished the homework assignment before the professor arrives.

CONDICIONAL SIMPLE	CONDICIONAL COMPUESTO
Me gustaría hacerlo, pero no puedo. **Simple Conditional** I would like to do it, but I can't.	*Si ella hubiera sido justa, lo habría despedido.* **Conditional Perfect** If she had been fair, she would have fired him.

MODO SUBJUNTIVO

PRESENTE

Quiero que entiendas.
Infinitive is often used (no present subjunctive in English).
I want you to understand.

PRETÉRITO PERFECTO

Espero que ella haya visto la llave en el piso.
Present Perfect
I hope that she has seen the key on the floor.

PRETÉRITO IMPERFECTO

Yo quería que ella te invitara.
Si yo fuera rey, lo haría. (contrary-to-fact)
Infinitive is often used. **Past Subjunctive** is rarely used in English (only for contrary-to-fact).
I wanted her to invite you.
If I were king, I would do it. (English subjunctive)

PRETÉRITO PLUSCUAMPERFECTO

Si yo hubiera/hubiese estado aquí, él no te habría atacado.
Past Perfect (Pluperfect)
If I had been here, he would not have attacked you.

FUTURO IMPERFECTO

Adonde fueres, haz lo que vieres.
(has almost disappeared from spoken Spanish)
Present Indicative (sometimes "should" is added in English to convey what may happen in the future, e.g. *Should the legislature decide...*)
Wherever you go, do as you see.

FUTURO PERFECTO

Mañana sabremos lo que la Asamblea hubiere decidido.
Future Perfect
Tomorrow we will know that the Assembly will have decided.

MODO IMPERATIVO

PRESENTE DE IMPERATIVO

Escríbalo/Escríbelo
Imperative (command form)
Write it!

FORMAS NO PERSONALES

INFINITIVO

Voy a vender juguetes.
Nadar es fácil.
Infinitive or **Gerund**
I am going to sell toys.
Swimming is easy.

INFINITIVO COMPUESTO

Al no haber visto otra alternativa, decidimos venderlo.
Perfect Infinitive or **Gerund**
Upon not having seen any other alternative, we decided to sell it.

GERUNDIO

Estoy hablando.
Present Participle (in the progressive tenses)
I am speaking.

GERUNDIO COMPUESTO

Habiendo engañado al pueblo, el ladrón se fugó en la noche.
Past Perfect Participle
Having deceived the people, the thief ran away in the night.

PARTICIPIO

He terminado el trabajo.
Past Participle (in the perfect tenses)
I have finished the work.

grammatical system

D. VOICE

● The **active voice** is used to express cases in which the subject **does the action of the verb**.

● The **passive voice** describes situations in which **the action of the verb is done *to* the subject** (the subject **receives** the action of the verb).

• The passive voice is formed in every tense with the auxiliary verb **SER**. For example:

ACTIVE VOICE:	PASSIVE VOICE:
José *lava* el carro cada sábado.	El carro *es lavado* por José cada sábado.
Joe **washes** the car every Saturday.	The car **is washed** by Joe every Saturday.
Juan le *tiró* la pelota a María.	La pelota le *fue tirada* a María por Juan.
John **threw** the ball to Mary.	The ball **was thrown** to Mary by John.

__3__ Regular conjugations

INTRODUCTION

In the *Verb Tables* section, three regular verb models are given:

-ar	:	5	*cantar*	(page 33)
-er	:	24	*beber*	(page 51)
-ir	:	51	*vivir*	(page 79)

Each of these verbs opens a section containing other verbs that have the same ending, regardless of any changes in spelling, accents, or irregularities of vowels or consonants.

Note: The large number of Spanish verbs ending in **-ear** are completely regular and are conjugated like *cantar* (*Table 5*, page 33). The student merely has to remember that the final **-e** of the stem is never lost in any time or person.

Example: *Telefonear*   – 1st pers. sing. pres. ind.: *telefoneo*
                     – 3rd pers. pl. pres. subj.: *telefoneen*
                     – 1st pers. sing. preterite: *telefoneé*

FORMATION OF SIMPLE TENSES

- Formed using the stem of the verb:	the present tenses (indicative, subjunctive, imperative); imperfect indicative; preterite; gerund; and participle.
- Formed using the infinitive:	future and conditional indicative.
- Formed using the 3rd person plural preterite (removing the **-ron** ending):	imperfect and future subjunctive.

grammatical system

Comments

● The imperative mood only has two forms that are unique to it:

1. The second person singular, which corresponds (except in certain irregular verbs) to the second person of the present indicative, removing the **-s** from the ending:

$$\text{(tú) cantas} \longrightarrow \textit{\textbf{canta tú}}$$

2. The second person plural, which is formed by replacing the final **-r** of the infinitive with **-d**:

$$\text{cantar} \longrightarrow \textit{\textbf{cantad vosotros/as}}$$

● The other forms used by the imperative mood actually belong to the present subjunctive:

Present Subjunctive		Imperative	
(él/ella/usted)	cante	*cante*	*él/ella/usted*
(nosotros/as)	cantemos	*cantemos*	*nosotros/as*
(ellos/ellas/ustedes)	canten	*canten*	*ellos/ellas/ustedes*

In the table on page 16, you will find the endings that are used to conjugate regular verbs in the simple tenses. Remember that **stem** refers to the infinitive with the *-ar*, *-er* or *-ir* ending removed. Example: *mantener → **manten** (stem)*.

Also, note the way in which the tenses build on one another:

1. The **presente de subjuntivo** (present subjunctive) takes the first person singular indicative, drops the *-o*, and adds the "opposite" ending (that is, *-ar* verbs use *-e* endings, and *-er/-ir* verbs use *-a* endings).

2. The **imperfecto de subjuntivo** (imperfect subjunctive) takes the third person plural of the preterite, removes the ending *-ron*, and adds the *-ra* endings (*-ra, -ras, -ra, -ramos, -rais, -ran*).

The **imperfecto de subjuntivo** also has an alternative *-se* ending form, which is used primarily in writing of a sophisticated or antiquated style.

The **futuro de subjuntivo** (future subjunctive) also uses the third person plural of the preterite, adding the *-re* endings (*-re, -res, -re, -remos, -reis, -ren*).

3. The **futuro de indicativo** (future indicative) and **condicional** (conditional) are both based on the infinitive of the verb:

futuro de indicativo = full infinitive + *-é, -ás, -á -emos, -éis, -án*
condicional = full infinitive + *-ía, -ías, -ía, -íamos, íais, ían*

15

g

THE FORMATION OF SIMPLE TENSES FOR REGULAR VERBS

-ar

	Pres. de indicativo (stem +)	Imperativo (stem +)	Pres. de subjuntivo (stem +)	Imperf. de indicativo (stem +)	Pretérito indefinido (stem +)
	- o		- e	- aba	- é
	- as	- a	- es	- abas	- aste
	- a	- e	- e	- aba	- ó
	- amos	- emos	- emos	- ábamos	- amos
	- áis	- ad	- éis	- abais	- asteis
	- an	- en	- en	- aban	- a ron

Gerundio: stem + - ando Participio: stem + - ado

-er

	Pres. de indicativo (stem +)	Imperativo (stem +)	Pres. de subjuntivo (stem +)	Imperf. de indicativo (stem +)	Pretérito indefinido (stem +)
	- o		- a	- ía	- í
	- es	- e	- as	- ías	- iste
	- e	- a	- a	- ía	- ió
	- emos	- amos	- amos	- íamos	- imos
	- éis	- ed	- áis	- íais	- isteis
	- en	- an	- an	- ían	- ie ron

Gerundio: stem + - iendo Participio: stem + - ido

-ir

	Pres. de indicativo (stem +)	Imperativo (stem +)	Pres. de subjuntivo (stem +)
	- o		- a
	- es	- e	- as
	- e	- a	- a
	- imos	- amos	- amos
	- ís	- id	- áis
	- en	- an	- an

Shared tenses (apply to -ar, -er, -ir)

Imperfecto de subjuntivo:
- ra or - se
- ras or - ses
- ra or - se
- ramos or - semos
- rais or - seis
- ran or - sen

Futuro de subjuntivo:
- re, - res, - re, - remos, - reis, - ren

Futuro de indicativo (infinitive +):
- é, - ás, - á, - emos, - éis, - án

Condicional (infinitive +):
- ía, - ías, - ía, - íamos, - íais, - ían

FORMATION OF COMPOUND TENSES

The **compound tenses** of the verb are formed through the use of the appropriate tense of the verb **HABER** (*Table 1*, page 28) plus the past participle. For every compound tense, there is a corresponding simple tense from which it is formed. For example:

Pretérito perfecto de indicativo (present perfect indicative) of *escribir:*
  Presente de indicativo (present indicative) of *haber*
+ **Participio** (past participle) of *escribir*
= *he escrito, has escrito, ha escrito,* etc.

Pretérito pluscuamperfecto de subjuntivo (past perfect subjunctive) of *decir:*
  Pretérito imperfecto de subjuntivo (imperfect subjunctive) of *haber*
+ **Participio** (past participle) of *decir*
= *hubiera dicho, hubieras dicho, hubiera dicho,* etc.

4 Irregular conjugations

The irregularities of Spanish verb conjugation affect the stem of the verbs and are either vocalic (**vowel stem changes**) or consonantal (**consonant stem changes**). Verbs that change a consonant before final **-e** or **-o** in order to retain their original sound are not considered as *irregular* in this section. They are treated in the discussion on spelling changes in section 6, page 229.

There are some verbs that are irregular, but that also have spelling changes; we will refer to them merely as *irregular* in order to simplify the categories.

VOWEL STEM CHANGES

Verbs with a diphthong stem change E → IE

-ar: **Pensar**, *Table 13*, page 41.

These verbs follow this irregular formation: *acertar, apretar, arrendar, atravesar, calentar, cegar, cerrar, comenzar, concertar, confesar, desconcertar, despertar, desterrar,* **empezar** (*Table 15*, page 43), *encerrar, encomendar, enmendar, enterrar, fregar, gobernar, helar, manifestar, merendar,* **negar** (*Table 14*, page 42), *nevar, pensar, plegar, quebrar, recalentar, recomendar, recomenzar, regar, renegar, reventar, segar, sembrar, sentar, sosegar, temblar, tentar, tropezar,* etc.

grammatical system

-er. **Perder**, *Table 29*, page 58.

These verbs follow this irregular formation: *ascender, atender, condescender, defender, desatender, desentenderse, encender, entender, extender,* **querer** (*Table 42*, page 71), *sobre(e)ntender, tender, tra(n)scender,* etc.

-ir. **Discernir**, *Table 66*, page 96.

These verbs follow this irregular formation: *concernir, cernir,* etc.

Verbs with a diphthong stem change O → UE

-ar. **Contar**, *Table 16*, page 44.

These verbs follow this irregular formation: *acordar, acostar, almorzar, apostar, aprobar,* **avergonzar** (*Table 20*, page 48), *colar, colgar, comprobar, concordar, consolar, costar, degollar, demostrar, desacordar, desaprobar, descolgar, descontar, despoblar, encontrar, esforzarse,* **forzar** (*Table 19*, page 47), *mostrar, poblar, probar, recontar, recordar, reforzar, renovar, repoblar, reprobar, resonar, revolcar, rodar,* **rogar** (*Table 18*, page 46), *sobrevolar, soldar, soltar, sonar, soñar, tostar, volar, volcar,* etc.

-er. **Mover**, *Table 30*, page 59.

These verbs follow this irregular formation: *absolver, cocer, conmover, desenvolver, devolver, disolver, doler, escocer, llover, moler, morder, oler*,* **poder** (*Table 40*, page 69), *promover, recocer, remorder, remover, resolver, retorcer, soler, torcer, volver,* etc.

* The verb **oler** has an unusual conjugation: *huelo, hueles, huele, olemos, oléis, huelen.*

Verbs with a diphthong stem change E → IE and a stem change E → I

-ir. **Sentir**, *Table 65*, page 95.

These verbs follow this irregular formation: *adherir, advertir, arrepentirse, conferir, consentir, convertir, deferir, desmentir, diferir, digerir, disentir, divertir, herir, hervir, inferir, ingerir, injerir, invertir, malherir, mentir, pervertir, preferir, proferir, referir, resentir, sugerir, tra(n)sferir,* etc.

Verbs with a diphthong stem change O → UE and a stem change O → U

-ir. **Dormir**, *Table 68*, page 98.

Also following this irregular formation: *morir* (and its irregular participle is **mue rto**).

Verbs with a stem change E → I

-ir: **Pedir**, *Table 60*, page 90.

These verbs follow this irregular formation: *competir, concebir, conseguir,* **corregir** (*Table 61*, page 90), *derretir, despedir, desteñir, desvestir, elegir, embestir, expedir, freír, gemir, impedir, investir, medir, perseguir, proseguir, reelegir, regir,* **reír** (*Table 63*, page 93), *rendir, reñir, repetir, revestir,* **seguir** (*Table 62*, page 92), *servir, sonreír, travestir, vestir,* etc.

Verbs with a stem change I → IE

-ir: **Adquirir**, *Table 67*, page 97.

This verb follows this irregular formation: *inquirir.*

Verbs with a stem change U → UE

-ar: **Jugar**, *Table 21*, page 49.

CONSONANT STEM CHANGES

Verbs ending in -ACER, -ECER, -OCER, and -UCIR with a stem change C → ZC before O or A

A large number of verbs follow this irregular formation: *abastecer, aborrecer, agradecer, aparecer, apetecer, carecer, compadecer, complacer,* **conocer** (*Table 32*, page 61), *convalecer, crecer, desagradecer, desaparecer, desconocer, desfavorecer, deslucir, desmerecer, desobedecer, embellecer, empobrecer, enriquecer, enrojecer, enternecer, entristecer, envejecer, establecer, estremecer, favorecer, florecer, fortalecer,* **lucir** (*Table 70*, page 100), *merecer,* **nacer** (*Table 31*, page 60), **obedecer** (*Table 33*, page 62), *ofrecer, padecer, parecer, permanecer, pertenecer, reaparecer, rejuvenecer, relucir, renacer, restablecer,* etc.

Exceptions: **hacer** (*Table 37*, page 66) and verbs derived from *hacer,* **cocer** (*cuezo, Table 34*, page 63), *escocerse (me escuezo), recocer (recuezo), mecer (mezo).*

grammatical system

Verbs ending in -DUCIR with a stem change C → ZC before A or O. Preterite tense verbs ending in -DUJE

-**ir**: **Traducir**, *Table 69*, page 99.

These verbs follow this irregular formation: *conducir, deducir, inducir, introducir, producir, reconducir, reducir, reproducir, seducir,* etc.

Verbs ending in -UIR with stem changes I → Y before A, E, O

-**ir**: **Concluir**, *Table 59*, page 89.

These verbs follow this irregular formation: *afluir, atribuir, autodestruir, concluir, confluir, constituir, construir, contribuir, destituir, destruir, diluir, disminuir, distribuir, excluir, huir, incluir, influir, instituir, instruir, obstruir, prostituir, reconstituir, reconstruir, restituir, retribuir, su(b)stituir,* etc.

5 Defective verbs

● These verbs are referred to as "defective" because they do not have all their forms, whether tenses or persons. They are verbs, therefore, that are incomplete.

Examples of defective verbs: *soler, Table 46,* page 75.
abolir, Table 71, page 101.

● There are defective verbs that are only conjugated in third person singular and plural (except for the imperative) and in the infinitive (simple and compound). They are sometimes referred to as **third-person verbs**.

Examples of third-person defective verbs include: *acaecer, acontecer, atañer, concernir, incumbir.*

In a certain sense, verbs such as *placer, yacer,* and *gustar* (in the construction "*me gusta*") are also considered to be third-person verbs.

● There are defective verbs that in their literal meaning (not figurative) are only conjugated in the third person singular (except in imperative) and in the infinitive (simple and compound). These are sometimes referred to as **one-person verbs**. The largest group of these verbs is composed of those that are related to time and atmospheric conditions.

Examples of atmospheric one-person verbs: *amanecer, anochecer, atardecer, chispear, clarear, diluviar, granizar, helar, llover, lloviznar, nevar, oscurecer, relampaguear, tronar, ventar.*

● Other verbs can also act as one-person verbs, according to their context in the sentence, especially those that express the occurrence of events.

Examples: *bastar, caber, constar, convenir, faltar, holgar, ocurrir, parecer, sobrar, suceder, urgir.*

6 Spelling and accent changes

Some verbs, regular or irregular, make spelling changes in certain forms in order to preserve the pronunciation of the sound of the final consonant of their stem. Other verbs alter the position of their accented syllables.

CONSONANT SPELLING CHANGES

Verbs ending in:	change:	before:
-car	c → qu	e

-ar: **Atacar**, *Table 7*, page 35.

These verbs follow this change: *abarcar, acercar, aparcar, arrancar, atrancar, desatascar, roncar,* etc.

Verbs ending in:	change:	before:
-cer	c → z	a, o
-cir		

-er: **Vencer**, *Table 26*, page 55.
-ir: **Esparcir**, *Table 54*, page 84.

Verbs that follow this pattern include: *convencer, ejercer, torcer,* **cocer** (*Table 34,* page 61), *escocer, mecer, recocer, resarcir, uncir, zurcir,* etc.

Verbs ending in:	change:	before:
-gar	g → gu	e

-ar: **Pagar**, *Table 6*, page 34.

The following verbs conform to the above pattern: *ahogar, colgar, pegar, regar,* etc.

grammatical system

Verbs ending in:	change:	before:
-ger and **-gir**	**g → j**	**a, o**

-er: **Coger**, *Table 25*, page 54.
-ir: **Corregir**, *Table 61*, page 91.

Verbs that follow this pattern include: *acoger, emerger, encoger, escoger, proteger, recoger*, as well as *afligir, elegir, exigir, fingir, preelegir, reelegir, regir, restringir, surgir*, etc.

Verbs ending in:	change:	before:
-zar	**z → c**	**e**

-ar: **Cruzar**, *Table 8*, page 36.

Verbs that contain this change include: *abrazar, almorzar, empezar, rebozar, rezar*, etc.

VOWEL SPELLING CHANGES

These refer to verbs that **change i → y**, *and* those that **drop i and u**.

Verbs ending in:	change:	before:
-eer	**i → y**	third persons preterite, derived tenses, and gerund

-er: **Leer**, *Table 28*, page 57. (This verb is traditionally categorized as irregular.)

Verbs following this modification include: *creer, poseer, proveer, releer*, etc.

Verbs ending in:	drop the:	before:
-guir	**u**	**a, o**

-ir: **Seguir**, *Table 62*, page 92.

Verbs that undergo this change include: *conseguir, extinguir, perseguir, proseguir*, etc.

Verbs ending in:	drop the:	in:
-eír, -ñer, -ñir, -ullir	last **i**	third persons preterite, derived tenses, and gerund

The following verbs follow this change: *freír*, **reír** (*Table 63*, page 93), *sonreír*, etc.; *atañer*, **tañer** (*Table 27*, page 56), etc.; *desteñir*, *estreñir*, **bruñir** (*Table 58*, page 88), *reñir*, etc.; *bullir*, *escabullirse*, **mullir** (*Table 57*, page 87), *zambullir*, etc.

ACCENT CHANGES

We will look at two of the many groups of Spanish verbs that undergo changes in their accentuation during conjugation.

Verbs ending in -iar

There are two kinds of verbs that end in **-iar**.

Those verbs that do not accent the **i** in the diphthong **io** do not take a written accent mark.

• Example: **Cambiar**

Verbs following this pattern are: *abreviar, acariciar, copiar, estudiar, rumiar,* etc.

Other verbs accent the **i** of the diphthong **io**, forming two syllables and, therefore, do take a written accent mark:

-ar: **Desviar**, *Table 9*, page 37.

Verbs following this pattern are: *averiar, confiar, guiar, variar,* etc.

Verbs ending in -uar

These verbs accent the **u** of the diphthong **ua**, forming two syllables.

-ar: **Actuar**, *Table 10*, page 38.

Verbs following this pattern are: *acentuar, adecuar,* etc.

Note: In order to complete the presentation of spelling changes, we include the verbs that end in **-guar**. These verbs add the diaeresis to the **u** to form **ü** before an **e**.

-ar: **Averiguar**, *Table 11*, page 39.

Verbs following this pattern are: *aguar, amortiguar, apaciguar, atestiguar, menguar, santiguarse,* etc.

grammatical system

7 Auxiliary verbs

In Spanish, there are four extensively used verbs called **auxiliary verbs**: **HABER, TENER, SER,** and **ESTAR**.

● Unlike other languages that only have one verb to express ownership and to form the compound tenses, Spanish has two:

HABER (*Table 1*, page 28).

• We stated above that **HABER** is used to form the compound tenses for all verbs.

• The participle conjugated with **HABER** is invariable (does not change).

Example: *Las chicas se han **ido** de paseo.*

• The participle in compound tenses can never be separated from the auxiliary verb (**HABER**) by any word.

Example: ***He comido*** *bien* and not ***He*** *bien* ***comido***.

• It can also be used as an impersonal verb with the meaning of *exist*, and is used in the present, past, and future indicative, always in the third person singular.

Examples: ***Hay*** *un problema;* ***hay*** *problemas;* ***ha habido*** *problemas.*

TENER (*Table 2*, page 29).

• This is the appropriate verb to express ownership in Spanish and is therefore used a great deal.

● Unlike other languages (such as English) that only have one verb to express the passive voice and the progressive tenses, Spanish has two:

SER (*Table 3*, page 30).

• We have already pointed out that **ser** is used to form all the conjugations of the passive voice in Spanish.

• A representative verb conjugated in the passive voice is presented in *Table 81*, page 111, as a model for all transitive verbs, which are the only verbs that permit conjugation in the passive voice. For example:

*El perro **fue bañado** por la niña.*	*The dog **was bathed** by the girl.*
*La bicicleta **fue reparada** ayer.*	*The bicycle **was repaired** yesterday.*

ESTAR (*Table 4*, page 31).

• The verb ***estar*** is used to form the **progressive tenses**, which are built using the conjugation of ***estar*** + **a present participle** (gerundio), with the meaning of action that is or was ongoing.

• The progressive tenses correspond to the basic verb tenses: present, imperfect, preterite, future, conditional (indicative); and the present, imperfect, and future (subjunctive), using those tenses to conjugate ***estar***. This form is used a great deal in Spanish.

Examples:
present progressive
    Esta niña ***está creciendo*** *mucho.*   *This girl is **growing** a lot.*
imperfect progressive
    Estaba oyendo *música.*   ***I was listening** to music.*
preterite progressive
    Estuvimos jugando *hasta que salimos.* ***We were playing** until we went out.*
future progressive
    A estas horas ya ***estará viniendo**.*   *At this time he/she **will be coming**.*

Note: The participle conjugated with **SER** and **ESTAR** must always agree with the subject.

Examples:
    Los bosques ***fueron devastados***   *The woods **were devastated** by fires.*
    por los incendios.
    Los bancos ***estaban abiertos*** *a esas*   *The banks **were open** at that time.*
    horas.

8   Reflexive verbs

The conjugation known as reflexive is formed with the **reflexive pronoun + a verb conjugated in the active voice**, following the model found in *Table 82*, page 112.

It is important to remember that in Spanish a large number of verbs can function as reflexives or non-reflexives. The difference is a question of meaning, not grammatical form. For that reason, we have not indicated that a verb in the Verb List is reflexive if it can also be used non-reflexively.

grammatical system

Examples:

*Ella **se bañó** rápidamente.*
*La madre **bañó** a su hija.*

*She **took a bath** quickly.*
*The mother **bathed** her daughter.*

*El joven se **levantó** temprano.*
*La señora **levantó** pesas ayer.*

*The young man **got up** early.*
*The lady **lifted** weights yesterday.*

However, verbs that only accept a reflexive use or exclusively use the reflexive form in all of their uses have been marked as such by including the reflexive pronoun ***se*** at the end of the verb (for example, ***endeudarse***).

verb tables

model conjugations

model verb tables

1. HABER AUXILIARY

HAVE

MODO INDICATIVO

PRESENTE	PRETÉRITO IMPERFECTO	PRETÉRITO INDEFINIDO (1)	FUTURO IMPERFECTO
he	**hab** ía	hube	habré
has	**hab** ías	hubiste	habrás
ha	**hab** ía	hubo	habrá
hemos	**hab** íamos	hubimos	habremos
hab éis	**hab** íais	hubisteis	habréis
han	**hab** ían	hubieron	habrán

PRETÉRITO PERFECTO		PRETÉRITO PLUSCUAMPERFECTO		PRETÉRITO ANTERIOR		FUTURO PERFECTO	
he	habido	había	habido	hube	habido	habré	habido
has	habido	habías	habido	hubiste	habido	habrás	habido
ha	habido	había	habido	hubo	habido	habrá	habido
hemos	habido	habíamos	habido	hubimos	habido	habremos	habido
habéis	habido	habíais	habido	hubisteis	habido	habréis	habido
han	habido	habían	habido	hubieron	habido	habrán	habido

CONDICIONAL SIMPLE	CONDICIONAL COMPUESTO	
habría	habría	habido
habrías	habrías	habido
habría	habría	habido
habríamos	habríamos	habido
habríais	habríais	habido
habrían	habrían	habido

MODO SUBJUNTIVO

PRESENTE	PRETÉRITO IMPERFECTO			FUTURO IMPERFECTO (2)
haya	hubiera	or	hubiese	hubiere
hayas	hubieras	or	hubieses	hubieres
haya	hubiera	or	hubiese	hubiere
hayamos	hubiéramos	or	hubiésemos	hubiéremos
hayáis	hubierais	or	hubieseis	hubiereis
hayan	hubieran	or	hubiesen	hubieren

PRETÉRITO PERFECTO		PRETÉRITO PLUSCUAMPERFECTO				FUTURO PERFECTO (3)	
haya	habido	hubiera	or	hubiese	habido	hubiere	habido
hayas	habido	hubieras	or	hubieses	habido	hubieres	habido
haya	habido	hubiera	or	hubiese	habido	hubiere	habido
hayamos	habido	hubiéramos	or	hubiésemos	habido	hubiéremos	habido
hayáis	habido	hubierais	or	hubieseis	habido	hubiereis	habido
hayan	habido	hubieran	or	hubiesen	habido	hubieren	habido

MODO IMPERATIVO

FORMAS NO PERSONALES

PRESENTE	
he	tú
haya	él/ella/usted
hayamos	nosotros/as
hab ed	vosotros/as
hayan	ellos/ellas/ustedes

FORMAS SIMPLES

INFINITIVO	GERUNDIO	PARTICIPIO
haber	**hab** iendo	**hab** ido

FORMAS COMPUESTAS

INFINITIVO	GERUNDIO
haber habido	habiendo habido

(1) or Perfecto simple. (2), (3) rarely used.

2. TENER AUXILIARY — HOLD, HAVE

MODO INDICATIVO

PRESENTE	PRETÉRITO IMPERFECTO	PRETÉRITO INDEFINIDO (1)	FUTURO IMPERFECTO
tengo	ten ía	tuve	tendré
tienes	ten ías	tuviste	tendrás
tiene	ten ía	tuvo	tendrá
ten emos	ten íamos	tuvimos	tendremos
ten éis	ten íais	tuvisteis	tendréis
tienen	ten ían	tuvieron	tendrán

PRETÉRITO PERFECTO	PRETÉRITO PLUSCUAMPERFECTO	PRETÉRITO ANTERIOR	FUTURO PERFECTO
he tenido	había tenido	hube tenido	habré tenido
has tenido	habías tenido	hubiste tenido	habrás tenido
ha tenido	había tenido	hubo tenido	habrá tenido
hemos tenido	habíamos tenido	hubimos tenido	habremos tenido
habéis tenido	habíais tenido	hubisteis tenido	habréis tenido
han tenido	habían tenido	hubieron tenido	habrán tenido

CONDICIONAL SIMPLE	CONDICIONAL COMPUESTO
tendría	habría tenido
tendrías	habrías tenido
tendría	habría tenido
tendríamos	habríamos tenido
tendríais	habríais tenido
tendrían	habrían tenido

MODO SUBJUNTIVO

PRESENTE	PRETÉRITO IMPERFECTO	FUTURO IMPERFECTO (2)
tenga	tuviera or tuviese	tuviere
tengas	tuvieras or tuvieses	tuvieres
tenga	tuviera or tuviese	tuviere
tengamos	tuviéramos or tuviésemos	tuviéremos
tengáis	tuvierais or tuvieseis	tuviereis
tengan	tuvieran or tuviesen	tuvieren

PRETÉRITO PERFECTO	PRETÉRITO PLUSCUAMPERFECTO	FUTURO PERFECTO (3)
haya tenido	hubiera or hubiese tenido	hubiere tenido
hayas tenido	hubieras or hubieses tenido	hubieres tenido
haya tenido	hubiera or hubiese tenido	hubiere tenido
hayamos tenido	hubiéramos or hubiésemos tenido	hubiéremos tenido
hayáis tenido	hubierais or hubieseis tenido	hubiereis tenido
hayan tenido	hubieran or hubiesen tenido	hubieren tenido

MODO IMPERATIVO

PRESENTE	
ten	tú
tenga	él/ella/usted
tengamos	nosotros/as
ten ed	vosotros/as
tengan	ellos/ellas/ustedes

FORMAS NO PERSONALES

FORMAS SIMPLES

INFINITIVO	GERUNDIO	PARTICIPIO
tener	ten iendo	ten ido

FORMAS COMPUESTAS

INFINITIVO	GERUNDIO
haber tenido	habiendo tenido

(1) or Perfecto simple. (2), (3) rarely used.

model verb tables

MODO INDICATIVO

PRESENTE	PRETÉRITO IMPERFECTO	PRETÉRITO INDEFINIDO (1)	FUTURO IMPERFECTO
soy	era	fui	ser é
eres	eras	fuiste	ser ás
es	era	fue	ser á
somos	éramos	fuimos	ser emos
sois	erais	fuisteis	ser éis
son	eran	fueron	ser án

PRETÉRITO PERFECTO		PRETÉRITO PLUSCUAMPERFECTO		PRETÉRITO ANTERIOR		FUTURO PERFECTO	
he	sido	había	sido	hube	sido	habré	sido
has	sido	habías	sido	hubiste	sido	habrás	sido
ha	sido	había	sido	hubo	sido	habrá	sido
hemos	sido	habíamos	sido	hubimos	sido	habremos	sido
habéis	sido	habíais	sido	hubisteis	sido	habréis	sido
han	sido	habían	sido	hubieron	sido	habrán	sido

CONDICIONAL SIMPLE	CONDICIONAL COMPUESTO	
ser ía	habría	sido
ser ías	habrías	sido
ser ía	habría	sido
ser íamos	habríamos	sido
ser íais	habríais	sido
ser ían	habrían	sido

MODO SUBJUNTIVO

PRESENTE	PRETÉRITO IMPERFECTO			FUTURO IMPERFECTO (2)
sea	fuera	or	fuese	fuere
seas	fueras	or	fueses	fueres
sea	fuera	or	fuese	fuere
seamos	fuéramos	or	fuésemos	fuéremos
seáis	fuerais	or	fueseis	fuereis
sean	fueran	or	fuesen	fueren

PRETÉRITO PERFECTO		PRETÉRITO PLUSCUAMPERFECTO				FUTURO PERFECTO (3)	
haya	sido	hubiera	or	hubiese	sido	hubiere	sido
hayas	sido	hubieras	or	hubieses	sido	hubieres	sido
haya	sido	hubiera	or	hubiese	sido	hubiere	sido
hayamos	sido	hubiéramos	or	hubiésemos	sido	hubiéremos	sido
hayáis	sido	hubierais	or	hubieseis	sido	hubiereis	sido
hayan	sido	hubieran	or	hubiesen	sido	hubieren	sido

MODO IMPERATIVO

PRESENTE

sé	tú
sea	él/ella/usted
seamos	nosotros/as
s ed	vosotros/as
sean	ellos/ellas/ustedes

FORMAS NO PERSONALES

FORMAS SIMPLES

INFINITIVO	GERUNDIO	PARTICIPIO
ser	siendo	sido

FORMAS COMPUESTAS

INFINITIVO	GERUNDIO
haber sido	habiendo sido

(1) or Perfecto simple. (2), (3) rarely used.

model verb tables

4. ESTAR AUXILIARY

BE

MODO INDICATIVO

PRESENTE	PRETÉRITO IMPERFECTO	PRETÉRITO INDEFINIDO (1)	FUTURO IMPERFECTO
estoy	est aba	estuve	estar é
est ás	est abas	estuviste	estar ás
est á	est aba	estuvo	estar á
est amos	est ábamos	estuvimos	estar emos
est áis	est abais	estuvisteis	estar éis
est án	est aban	estuvieron	estar án

PRETÉRITO PERFECTO	PRETÉRITO PLUSCUAMPERFECTO	PRETÉRITO ANTERIOR	FUTURO PERFECTO
he estado	había estado	hube estado	habré estado
has estado	habías estado	hubiste estado	habrás estado
ha estado	había estado	hubo estado	habrá estado
hemos estado	habíamos estado	hubimos estado	habremos estado
habéis estado	habíais estado	hubisteis estado	habréis estado
han estado	habían estado	hubieron estado	habrán estado

CONDICIONAL SIMPLE	CONDICIONAL COMPUESTO
estar ía	habría estado
estar ías	habrías estado
estar ía	habría estado
estar íamos	habríamos estado
estar íais	habríais estado
estar ían	habrían estado

MODO SUBJUNTIVO

PRESENTE	PRETÉRITO IMPERFECTO	FUTURO IMPERFECTO (2)
est é	estuviera or estuviese	estuviere
est és	estuvieras or estuvieses	estuvieres
est é	estuviera or estuviese	estuviere
est emos	estuviéramos or estuviésemos	estuviéremos
est éis	estuvierais or estuvieseis	estuviereis
est én	estuvieran or estuviesen	estuvieren

PRETÉRITO PERFECTO	PRETÉRITO PLUSCUAMPERFECTO	FUTURO PERFECTO (3)
haya estado	hubiera or hubiese estado	hubiere estado
hayas estado	hubieras or hubieses estado	hubieres estado
haya estado	hubiera or hubiese estado	hubiere estado
hayamos estado	hubiéramos or hubiésemos estado	hubiéremos estado
hayáis estado	hubierais or hubieseis estado	hubiereis estado
hayan estado	hubieran or hubiesen estado	hubieren estado

MODO IMPERATIVO

PRESENTE

est á	tú
est é	él/ella/usted
est emos	nosotros/as
est ad	vosotros/as
est én	ellos/ellas/ustedes

FORMAS NO PERSONALES

FORMAS SIMPLES

INFINITIVO	GERUNDIO	PARTICIPIO
estar	est ando	est ado

FORMAS COMPUESTAS

INFINITIVO	GERUNDIO
haber estado	habiendo estado

(1) or Perfecto simple. (2), (3) rarely used.

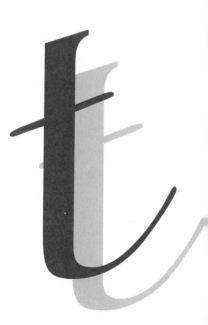

5. CANTAR
6. pagar
7. atacar
8. cruzar
9. desviar
10. actuar
11. averiguar
12. maullar
13. pensar
14. negar
15. empezar
16. contar
17. trocar
18. rogar
19. forzar
20. avergonzar
21. jugar
22. andar
23. dar

5. CANTAR REGULAR

MODO INDICATIVO

PRESENTE	PRETÉRITO IMPERFECTO	PRETÉRITO INDEFINIDO (1)	FUTURO IMPERFECTO
cant o	cant aba	cant é	cantar é
cant as	cant abas	cant aste	cantar ás
cant a	cant aba	cant ó	cantar á
cant amos	cant ábamos	cant amos	cantar emos
cant áis	cant abais	cant asteis	cantar éis
cant an	cant aban	cant aron	cantar án

PRETÉRITO PERFECTO		PRETÉRITO PLUSCUAMPERFECTO		PRETÉRITO ANTERIOR		FUTURO PERFECTO	
he	cantado	había	cantado	hube	cantado	habré	cantado
has	cantado	habías	cantado	hubiste	cantado	habrás	cantado
ha	cantado	había	cantado	hubo	cantado	habrá	cantado
hemos	cantado	habíamos	cantado	hubimos	cantado	habremos	cantado
habéis	cantado	habíais	cantado	hubisteis	cantado	habréis	cantado
han	cantado	habían	cantado	hubieron	cantado	habrán	cantado

CONDICIONAL SIMPLE	CONDICIONAL COMPUESTO	
cantar ía	habría	cantado
cantar ías	habrías	cantado
cantar ía	habría	cantado
cantar íamos	habríamos	cantado
cantar íais	habríais	cantado
cantar ían	habrían	cantado

MODO SUBJUNTIVO

PRESENTE	PRETÉRITO IMPERFECTO			FUTURO IMPERFECTO (2)
cant e	cant ara	or	cant ase	cant are
cant es	cant aras	or	cant ases	cant ares
cant e	cant ara	or	cant ase	cant are
cant emos	cant áramos	or	cant ásemos	cant áremos
cant éis	cant arais	or	cant aseis	cant areis
cant en	cant aran	or	cant asen	cant aren

PRETÉRITO PERFECTO		PRETÉRITO PLUSCUAMPERFECTO			FUTURO PERFECTO (3)	
haya	cantado	hubiera	or hubiese	cantado	hubiere	cantado
hayas	cantado	hubieras	or hubieses	cantado	hubieres	cantado
haya	cantado	hubiera	or hubiese	cantado	hubiere	cantado
hayamos	cantado	hubiéramos	or hubiésemos	cantado	hubiéremos	cantado
hayáis	cantado	hubierais	or hubieseis	cantado	hubiereis	cantado
hayan	cantado	hubieran	or hubiesen	cantado	hubieren	cantado

MODO IMPERATIVO

FORMAS NO PERSONALES

PRESENTE

cant a	tú
cant e	él/ella/usted
cant emos	nosotros/as
cant ad	vosotros/as
cant en	ellos/ellas/ustedes

FORMAS SIMPLES

INFINITIVO	GERUNDIO	PARTICIPIO
cantar	cant ando	cant ado

FORMAS COMPUESTAS

INFINITIVO	GERUNDIO
haber cantado	habiendo cantado

(1) or Perfecto simple. (2), (3) rarely used.

model verb tables

6. PAGAR SPELLING CHANGE (g → gu)

PAY

MODO INDICATIVO

PRESENTE	PRETÉRITO IMPERFECTO	PRETÉRITO INDEFINIDO (1)	FUTURO IMPERFECTO
pag o	pag aba	pagué	pagar é
pag as	pag abas	pag aste	pagar ás
pag a	pag aba	pag ó	pagar á
pag amos	pag ábamos	pag amos	pagar emos
pag áis	pag abais	pag asteis	pagar éis
pag an	pag aban	pag aron	pagar án

PRETÉRITO PERFECTO		PRETÉRITO PLUSCUAMPERFECTO		PRETÉRITO ANTERIOR		FUTURO PERFECTO	
he	pagado	había	pagado	hube	pagado	habré	pagado
has	pagado	habías	pagado	hubiste	pagado	habrás	pagado
ha	pagado	había	pagado	hubo	pagado	habrá	pagado
hemos	pagado	habíamos	pagado	hubimos	pagado	habremos	pagado
habéis	pagado	habíais	pagado	hubisteis	pagado	habréis	pagado
han	pagado	habían	pagado	hubieron	pagado	habrán	pagado

CONDICIONAL SIMPLE	CONDICIONAL COMPUESTO	
pagar ía	habría	pagado
pagar ías	habrías	pagado
pagar ía	habría	pagado
pagar íamos	habríamos	pagado
pagar íais	habríais	pagado
pagar ían	habrían	pagado

MODO SUBJUNTIVO

PRESENTE	PRETÉRITO IMPERFECTO		FUTURO IMPERFECTO (2)
pague	pag ara	or pag ase	pag are
pagues	pag aras	or pag ases	pag ares
pague	pag ara	or pag ase	pag are
paguemos	pag áramos	or pag ásemos	pag áremos
paguéis	pag arais	or pag aseis	pag areis
paguen	pag aran	or pag asen	pag aren

PRETÉRITO PERFECTO		PRETÉRITO PLUSCUAMPERFECTO			FUTURO PERFECTO (3)	
haya	pagado	hubiera	or hubiese	pagado	hubiere	pagado
hayas	pagado	hubieras	or hubieses	pagado	hubieres	pagado
haya	pagado	hubiera	or hubiese	pagado	hubiere	pagado
hayamos	pagado	hubiéramos	or hubiésemos	pagado	hubiéremos	pagado
hayáis	pagado	hubierais	or hubieseis	pagado	hubiereis	pagado
hayan	pagado	hubieran	or hubiesen	pagado	hubieren	pagado

MODO IMPERATIVO

PRESENTE

pag a	tú
pague	él/ella/usted
paguemos	nosotros/as
pag ad	vosotros/as
paguen	ellos/ellas/ustedes

FORMAS NO PERSONALES

FORMAS SIMPLES

INFINITIVO	GERUNDIO	PARTICIPIO
pagar	pag ando	pag ado

FORMAS COMPUESTAS

INFINITIVO	GERUNDIO
haber pagado	habiendo pagado

(1) or Perfecto simple. (2), (3) rarely used.

7. ATACAR SPELLING CHANGE (c → qu) — *ATTACK*

MODO INDICATIVO			
PRESENTE	**PRETÉRITO IMPERFECTO**	**PRETÉRITO INDEFINIDO (1)**	**FUTURO IMPERFECTO**
atac o	**atac** aba	ataqué	**atacar** é
atac as	**atac** abas	**atac** aste	**atacar** ás
atac a	**atac** aba	**atac** ó	**atacar** á
atac amos	**atac** ábamos	**atac** amos	**atacar** emos
atac áis	**atac** abais	**atac** asteis	**atacar** éis
atac an	**atac** aban	**atac** aron	**atacar** án

PRETÉRITO PERFECTO		**PRETÉRITO PLUSCUAMPERFECTO**		**PRETÉRITO ANTERIOR**		**FUTURO PERFECTO**	
he	atacado	había	atacado	hube	atacado	habré	atacado
has	atacado	habías	atacado	hubiste	atacado	habrás	atacado
ha	atacado	había	atacado	hubo	atacado	habrá	atacado
hemos	atacado	habíamos	atacado	hubimos	atacado	habremos	atacado
habéis	atacado	habíais	atacado	hubisteis	atacado	habréis	atacado
han	atacado	habían	atacado	hubieron	atacado	habrán	atacado

CONDICIONAL SIMPLE	CONDICIONAL COMPUESTO	
atacar ía	habría	atacado
atacar ías	habrías	atacado
atacar ía	habría	atacado
atacar íamos	habríamos	atacado
atacar íais	habríais	atacado
atacar ían	habrían	atacado

MODO SUBJUNTIVO		
PRESENTE	**PRETÉRITO IMPERFECTO**	**FUTURO IMPERFECTO (2)**
ataque	**atac** ara *or* **atac** ase	**atac** are
ataques	**atac** aras *or* **atac** ases	**atac** ares
ataque	**atac** ara *or* **atac** ase	**atac** are
ataquemos	**atac** áramos *or* **atac** ásemos	**atac** áremos
ataquéis	**atac** arais *or* **atac** aseis	**atac** areis
ataquen	**atac** aran *or* **atac** asen	**atac** aren

PRETÉRITO PERFECTO		**PRETÉRITO PLUSCUAMPERFECTO**			**FUTURO PERFECTO (3)**	
haya	atacado	hubiera *or*	hubiese	atacado	hubiere	atacado
hayas	atacado	hubieras *or*	hubieses	atacado	hubieres	atacado
haya	atacado	hubiera *or*	hubiese	atacado	hubiere	atacado
hayamos	atacado	hubiéramos *or*	hubiésemos	atacado	hubiéremos	atacado
hayáis	atacado	hubierais *or*	hubieseis	atacado	hubiereis	atacado
hayan	atacado	hubieran *or*	hubiesen	atacado	hubieren	atacado

MODO IMPERATIVO	FORMAS NO PERSONALES

PRESENTE

ataca	tú
ataque	él/ella/usted
ataquemos	nosotros/as
atacad	vosotros/as
ataquen	ellos/ellas/ustedes

FORMAS SIMPLES

INFINITIVO	GERUNDIO	PARTICIPIO
atacar	**atac** ando	**atac** ado

FORMAS COMPUESTAS

INFINITIVO	GERUNDIO
haber atacado	habiendo atacado

(1) or Perfecto simple. (2), (3) rarely used.

model verb tables

8. CRUZAR SPELLING CHANGE (z → c)

CROSS

MODO INDICATIVO

PRESENTE	PRETÉRITO IMPERFECTO	PRETÉRITO INDEFINIDO (1)	FUTURO IMPERFECTO
cruz o	**cruz** aba	cruce	**cruzar** é
cruz as	**cruz** abas	**cruz** aste	**cruzar** ás
cruz a	**cruz** aba	**cruz** ó	**cruzar** á
cruz amos	**cruz** ábamos	**cruz** amos	**cruzar** emos
cruz áis	**cruz** abais	**cruz** asteis	**cruzar** éis
cruz an	**cruz** aban	**cruz** aron	**cruzar** án

PRETÉRITO PERFECTO	PRETÉRITO PLUSCUAMPERFECTO	PRETÉRITO ANTERIOR	FUTURO PERFECTO
he cruzado	había cruzado	hube cruzado	habré cruzado
has cruzado	habías cruzado	hubiste cruzado	habrás cruzado
ha cruzado	había cruzado	hubo cruzado	habrá cruzado
hemos cruzado	habíamos cruzado	hubimos cruzado	habremos cruzado
habéis cruzado	habíais cruzado	hubisteis cruzado	habréis cruzado
han cruzado	habían cruzado	hubieron cruzado	habrán cruzado

CONDICIONAL SIMPLE	CONDICIONAL COMPUESTO
cruzar ía	habría cruzado
cruzar ías	habrías cruzado
cruzar ía	habría cruzado
cruzar íamos	habríamos cruzado
cruzar íais	habríais cruzado
cruzar ían	habrían cruzado

MODO SUBJUNTIVO

PRESENTE	PRETÉRITO IMPERFECTO		FUTURO IMPERFECTO (2)
cruce	**cruz** ara	*or* **cruz** ase	**cruz** are
cruces	**cruz** aras	*or* **cruz** ases	**cruz** ares
cruce	**cruz** ara	*or* **cruz** ase	**cruz** are
crucemos	**cruz** áramos	*or* **cruz** ásemos	**cruz** áremos
crucéis	**cruz** arais	*or* **cruz** aseis	**cruz** areis
crucen	**cruz** aran	*or* **cruz** asen	**cruz** aren

PRETÉRITO PERFECTO	PRETÉRITO PLUSCUAMPERFECTO		FUTURO PERFECTO (3)
haya cruzado	hubiera *or* hubiese cruzado		hubiere cruzado
hayas cruzado	hubieras *or* hubieses cruzado		hubieres cruzado
haya cruzado	hubiera *or* hubiese cruzado		hubiere cruzado
hayamos cruzado	hubiéramos *or* hubiésemos cruzado		hubiéremos cruzado
hayáis cruzado	hubierais *or* hubieseis cruzado		hubiereis cruzado
hayan cruzado	hubieran *or* hubiesen cruzado		hubieren cruzado

MODO IMPERATIVO

FORMAS NO PERSONALES

PRESENTE

cruz a	tú
cruce	él/ella/usted
crucemos	nosotros/as
cruz ad	vosotros/as
crucen	ellos/ellas/ustedes

FORMAS SIMPLES

INFINITIVO	GERUNDIO	PARTICIPIO
cruzar	**cruz** ando	**cruz** ado

FORMAS COMPUESTAS

INFINITIVO	GERUNDIO
haber cruzado	habiendo cruzado

(1) or Perfecto simple. (2), (3) rarely used.

model verb tables

9. DESVIAR ACCENT CHANGE (i → í) *DEVIATE*

MODO INDICATIVO

PRESENTE	PRETÉRITO IMPERFECTO	PRETÉRITO INDEFINIDO (1)	FUTURO IMPERFECTO
desvío	desvi aba	desvi é	desviar é
desvías	desvi abas	desvi aste	desviar ás
desvía	desvi aba	desvi ó	desviar á
desvi amos	desvi ábamos	desvi amos	desviar emos
desvi áis	desvi abais	desvi asteis	desviar éis
desvían	desvi aban	desvi aron	desviar án

PRETÉRITO PERFECTO	PRETÉRITO PLUSCUAMPERFECTO	PRETÉRITO ANTERIOR	FUTURO PERFECTO
he desviado	había desviado	hube desviado	habré desviado
has desviado	habías desviado	hubiste desviado	habrás desviado
ha desviado	había desviado	hubo desviado	habrá desviado
hemos desviado	habíamos desviado	hubimos desviado	habremos desviado
habéis desviado	habíais desviado	hubisteis desviado	habréis desviado
han desviado	habían desviado	hubieron desviado	habrán desviado

CONDICIONAL SIMPLE

desviar ía	
desviar ías	
desviar ía	
desviar íamos	
desviar íais	
desviar ían	

CONDICIONAL COMPUESTO

habría desviado	
habrías desviado	
habría desviado	
habríamos desviado	
habríais desviado	
habrían desviado	

MODO SUBJUNTIVO

PRESENTE	PRETÉRITO IMPERFECTO	FUTURO IMPERFECTO (2)
desvíe	desvi ara or desvi ase	desvi are
desvíes	desvi aras or desvi ases	desvi ares
desvíe	desvi ara or desvi ase	desvi are
desvi emos	desvi áramos or desvi ásemos	desvi áremos
desvi éis	desvi arais or desvi aseis	desvi areis
desvíen	desvi aran or desvi asen	desvi aren

PRETÉRITO PERFECTO	PRETÉRITO PLUSCUAMPERFECTO	FUTURO PERFECTO (3)
haya desviado	hubiera or hubiese desviado	hubiere desviado
hayas desviado	hubieras or hubieses desviado	hubieres desviado
haya desviado	hubiera or hubiese desviado	hubiere desviado
hayamos desviado	hubiéramos or hubiésemos desviado	hubiéremos desviado
hayáis desviado	hubierais or hubieseis desviado	hubiereis desviado
hayan desviado	hubieran or hubiesen desviado	hubieren desviado

MODO IMPERATIVO

PRESENTE

desvía	tú
desvíe	él/ella/usted
desvi emos	nosotros/as
desvi ad	vosotros/as
desvíen	ellos/ellas/ustedes

FORMAS NO PERSONALES

FORMAS SIMPLES

INFINITIVO	GERUNDIO	PARTICIPIO
desviar	desvi ando	desvi ado

FORMAS COMPUESTAS

INFINITIVO	GERUNDIO
haber desviado	habiendo desviado

(1) or Perfecto simple. (2), (3) rarely used.

model verb tables

10. ACTUAR ACCENT CHANGE (u → ú)

ACT

MODO INDICATIVO

PRESENTE	PRETÉRITO IMPERFECTO	PRETÉRITO INDEFINIDO (1)	FUTURO IMPERFECTO
actúo	actu aba	actu é	actuar é
actúas	actu abas	actu aste	actuar ás
actúa	actu aba	actu ó	actuar á
actu amos	actu ábamos	actu amos	actuar emos
actu áis	actu abais	actu asteis	actuar éis
actúan	actu aban	actu aron	actuar án

PRETÉRITO PERFECTO	PRETÉRITO PLUSCUAMPERFECTO	PRETÉRITO ANTERIOR	FUTURO PERFECTO
he actuado	había actuado	hube actuado	habré actuado
has actuado	habías actuado	hubiste actuado	habrás actuado
ha actuado	había actuado	hubo actuado	habrá actuado
hemos actuado	habíamos actuado	hubimos actuado	habremos actuado
habéis actuado	habíais actuado	hubisteis actuado	habréis actuado
han actuado	habían actuado	hubieron actuado	habrán actuado

CONDICIONAL SIMPLE	CONDICIONAL COMPUESTO
actuar ía	habría actuado
actuar ías	habrías actuado
actuar ía	habría actuado
actuar íamos	habríamos actuado
actuar íais	habríais actuado
actuar ían	habrían actuado

MODO SUBJUNTIVO

PRESENTE	PRETÉRITO IMPERFECTO		FUTURO IMPERFECTO (2)
actúe	actu ara	or actu ase	actu are
actúes	actu aras	or actu ases	actu ares
actúe	actu ara	or actu ase	actu are
actu emos	actu áramos	or actu ásemos	actu áremos
actu éis	actu arais	or actu aseis	actu areis
actúen	actu aran	or actu asen	actu aren

PRETÉRITO PERFECTO	PRETÉRITO PLUSCUAMPERFECTO		FUTURO PERFECTO (3)
haya actuado	hubiera or hubiese actuado		hubiere actuado
hayas actuado	hubieras or hubieses actuado		hubieres actuado
haya actuado	hubiera or hubiese actuado		hubiere actuado
hayamos actuado	hubiéramos or hubiésemos actuado		hubiéremos actuado
hayáis actuado	hubierais or hubieseis actuado		hubiereis actuado
hayan actuado	hubieran or hubiesen actuado		hubieren actuado

MODO IMPERATIVO

FORMAS NO PERSONALES

PRESENTE	
actúa	tú
actúe	él/ella/usted
actu emos	nosotros/as
actu ad	vosotros/as
actúen	ellos/ellas/ustedes

FORMAS SIMPLES

INFINITIVO	GERUNDIO	PARTICIPIO
actuar	actu ando	actu ado

FORMAS COMPUESTAS

INFINITIVO	GERUNDIO
haber actuado	habiendo actuado

(1) or Perfecto simple. (2), (3) rarely used.

model verb tables

```
MODO INDICATIVO
```

PRESENTE	PRETÉRITO IMPERFECTO	PRETÉRITO INDEFINIDO (1)	FUTURO IMPERFECTO
averigu o	averigu aba	averigüé	averiguar é
averigu as	averigu abas	averigu aste	averiguar ás
averigu a	averigu aba	averigu ó	averiguar á
averigu amos	averigu ábamos	averigu amos	averiguar emos
averigu áis	averigu abais	averigu asteis	averiguar éis
averigu an	averigu aban	averigu aron	averiguar án

PRETÉRITO PERFECTO		PRETÉRITO PLUSCUAMPERFECTO		PRETÉRITO ANTERIOR		FUTURO PERFECTO	
he	averiguado	había	averiguado	hube	averiguado	habré	averiguado
has	averiguado	habías	averiguado	hubiste	averiguado	habrás	averiguado
ha	averiguado	había	averiguado	hubo	averiguado	habrá	averiguado
hemos	averiguado	habíamos	averiguado	hubimos	averiguado	habremos	averiguado
habéis	averiguado	habíais	averiguado	hubisteis	averiguado	habréis	averiguado
han	averiguado	habían	averiguado	hubieron	averiguado	habrán	averiguado

CONDICIONAL SIMPLE **CONDICIONAL COMPUESTO**

averiguar ía	habría	averiguado
averiguar ías	habrías	averiguado
averiguar ía	habría	averiguado
averiguar íamos	habríamos	averiguado
averiguar íais	habríais	averiguado
averiguar ían	habrían	averiguado

```
MODO SUBJUNTIVO
```

PRESENTE	PRETÉRITO IMPERFECTO		FUTURO IMPERFECTO (2)
averigüe	averigu ara	or averigu ase	averigu are
averigües	averigu aras	or averigu ases	averigu ares
averigüe	averigu ara	or averigu ase	averigu are
averigüemos	averigu áramos	or averigu ásemos	averigu áremos
averigüéis	averigu arais	or averigu aseis	averigu areis
averigüen	averigu aran	or averigu asen	averigu aren

PRETÉRITO PERFECTO		PRETÉRITO PLUSCUAMPERFECTO			FUTURO PERFECTO (3)	
haya	averiguado	hubiera	or hubiese	averiguado	hubiere	averiguado
hayas	averiguado	hubieras	or hubieses	averiguado	hubieres	averiguado
haya	averiguado	hubiera	or hubiese	averiguado	hubiere	averiguado
hayamos	averiguado	hubiéramos	or hubiésemos	averiguado	hubiéremos	averiguado
hayáis	averiguado	hubierais	or hubieseis	averiguado	hubiereis	averiguado
hayan	averiguado	hubieran	or hubiesen	averiguado	hubieren	averiguado

```
MODO IMPERATIVO          FORMAS NO PERSONALES
```

PRESENTE

averigua	tú
averigüe	él/ella/usted
averigüemos	nosotros/as
averigu ad	vosotros/as
averigüen	ellos/ellas/ustedes

FORMAS SIMPLES

INFINITIVO	GERUNDIO	PARTICIPIO
averiguar	averigu ando	averigu ado

FORMAS COMPUESTAS

INFINITIVO	GERUNDIO
haber averiguado	habiendo averiguado

(1) or Perfecto simple. (2), (3) rarely used.

model verb tables

12. MAULLAR ACCENT CHANGE (u → ú)

MEOW

MODO INDICATIVO

PRESENTE	PRETÉRITO IMPERFECTO	PRETÉRITO INDEFINIDO (1)	FUTURO IMPERFECTO
maúllo	maull aba	maull é	maullar é
maúllas	maull abas	maull aste	maullar ás
maúlla	maull aba	maull ó	maullar á
maull amos	maull ábamos	maull amos	maullar emos
maull áis	maull abais	maull asteis	maullar éis
maúllan	maull aban	maull aron	maullar án

PRETÉRITO PERFECTO		PRETÉRITO PLUSCUAMPERFECTO		PRETÉRITO ANTERIOR		FUTURO PERFECTO	
he	maullado	había	maullado	hube	maullado	habré	maullado
has	maullado	habías	maullado	hubiste	maullado	habrás	maullado
ha	maullado	había	maullado	hubo	maullado	habrá	maullado
hemos	maullado	habíamos	maullado	hubimos	maullado	habremos	maullado
habéis	maullado	habíais	maullado	hubisteis	maullado	habréis	maullado
han	maullado	habían	maullado	hubieron	maullado	habrán	maullado

CONDICIONAL SIMPLE

maullar ía	
maullar ías	
maullar ía	
maullar íamos	
maullar íais	
maullar ían	

CONDICIONAL COMPUESTO

habría	maullado
habrías	maullado
habría	maullado
habríamos	maullado
habríais	maullado
habrían	maullado

MODO SUBJUNTIVO

PRESENTE	PRETÉRITO IMPERFECTO			FUTURO IMPERFECTO (2)
maúlle	maull ara	or	maull ase	maull are
maúlles	maull aras	or	maull ases	maull ares
maúlle	maull ara	or	maull ase	maull are
maull emos	maull áramos	or	maull ásemos	maull áremos
maull éis	maull arais	or	maull aseis	maull areis
maúllen	maull aran	or	maull asen	maull aren

PRETÉRITO PERFECTO		PRETÉRITO PLUSCUAMPERFECTO				FUTURO PERFECTO (3)	
haya	maullado	hubiera	or	hubiese	maullado	hubiere	maullado
hayas	maullado	hubieras	or	hubieses	maullado	hubieres	maullado
haya	maullado	hubiera	or	hubiese	maullado	hubiere	maullado
hayamos	maullado	hubiéramos	or	hubiésemos	maullado	hubiéremos	maullado
hayáis	maullado	hubierais	or	hubieseis	maullado	hubiereis	maullado
hayan	maullado	hubieran	or	hubiesen	maullado	hubieren	maullado

MODO IMPERATIVO

PRESENTE

maúlla	tú
maúlle	él/ella/usted
maull emos	nosotros/as
maull ad	vosotros/as
maúllen	ellos/ellas/ustedes

FORMAS NO PERSONALES

FORMAS SIMPLES

INFINITIVO	GERUNDIO	PARTICIPIO
maullar	maull ando	maull ado

FORMAS COMPUESTAS

INFINITIVO	GERUNDIO
haber maullado	habiendo maullado

(1) or Perfecto simple. (2), (3) rarely used.

model verb tables

13. PENSAR IRREGULAR (stem change e → ie)   *THINK*

MODO INDICATIVO

PRESENTE	PRETÉRITO IMPERFECTO	PRETÉRITO INDEFINIDO (1)	FUTURO IMPERFECTO
pienso	**pens** aba	**pens** é	**pensar** é
piensas	**pens** abas	**pens** aste	**pensar** ás
piensa	**pens** aba	**pens** ó	**pensar** á
pens amos	**pens** ábamos	**pens** amos	**pensar** emos
pens áis	**pens** abais	**pens** asteis	**pensar** éis
piensan	**pens** aban	**pens** aron	**pensar** án

PRETÉRITO PERFECTO	PRETÉRITO PLUSCUAMPERFECTO	PRETÉRITO ANTERIOR	FUTURO PERFECTO
he pensado	había pensado	hube pensado	habré pensado
has pensado	habías pensado	hubiste pensado	habrás pensado
ha pensado	había pensado	hubo pensado	habrá pensado
hemos pensado	habíamos pensado	hubimos pensado	habremos pensado
habéis pensado	habíais pensado	hubisteis pensado	habréis pensado
han pensado	habían pensado	hubieron pensado	habrán pensado

CONDICIONAL SIMPLE	CONDICIONAL COMPUESTO
pensar ía	habría pensado
pensar ías	habrías pensado
pensar ía	habría pensado
pensar íamos	habríamos pensado
pensar íais	habríais pensado
pensar ían	habrían pensado

MODO SUBJUNTIVO

PRESENTE	PRETÉRITO IMPERFECTO		FUTURO IMPERFECTO (2)
piense	**pens** ara	*or* **pens** ase	**pens** are
pienses	**pens** aras	*or* **pens** ases	**pens** ares
piense	**pens** ara	*or* **pens** ase	**pens** are
pens emos	**pens** áramos	*or* **pens** ásemos	**pens** áremos
pens éis	**pens** arais	*or* **pens** aseis	**pens** areis
piensen	**pens** aran	*or* **pens** asen	**pens** aren

PRETÉRITO PERFECTO	PRETÉRITO PLUSCUAMPERFECTO		FUTURO PERFECTO (3)
haya pensado	hubiera	*or* hubiese pensado	hubiere pensado
hayas pensado	hubieras	*or* hubieses pensado	hubieres pensado
haya pensado	hubiera	*or* hubiese pensado	hubiere pensado
hayamos pensado	hubiéramos	*or* hubiésemos pensado	hubiéremos pensado
hayáis pensado	hubierais	*or* hubieseis pensado	hubiereis pensado
hayan pensado	hubieran	*or* hubiesen pensado	hubieren pensado

MODO IMPERATIVO

FORMAS NO PERSONALES

PRESENTE

FORMAS SIMPLES

piensa	tú
piense	él/ella/usted
pens emos	nosotros/as
pens ad	vosotros/as
piensen	ellos/ellas/ustedes

INFINITIVO	GERUNDIO	PARTICIPIO
pensar	**pens** ando	**pens** ado

FORMAS COMPUESTAS

INFINITIVO	GERUNDIO
haber pensado	habiendo pensando

(1) or Perfecto simple. (2), (3) rarely used.

model verb tables

14. NEGAR IRREGULAR (stem change e → ie + spelling change g → gu) *DENY, REFUSE*

MODO INDICATIVO

PRESENTE	PRETÉRITO IMPERFECTO	PRETÉRITO INDEFINIDO (1)	FUTURO IMPERFECTO
niego	neg aba	negué	negar é
niegas	neg abas	neg aste	negar ás
niega	neg aba	neg ó	negar á
neg amos	neg ábamos	neg amos	negar emos
neg áis	neg abais	neg asteis	negar éis
niegan	neg aban	neg aron	negar án

PRETÉRITO PERFECTO	PRETÉRITO PLUSCUAMPERFECTO	PRETÉRITO ANTERIOR	FUTURO PERFECTO
he negado	había negado	hube negado	habré negado
has negado	habías negado	hubiste negado	habrás negado
ha negado	había negado	hubo negado	habrá negado
hemos negado	habíamos negado	hubimos negado	habremos negado
habéis negado	habíais negado	hubisteis negado	habréis negado
han negado	habían negado	hubieron negado	habrán negado

CONDICIONAL SIMPLE	CONDICIONAL COMPUESTO
negar ía	habría negado
negar ías	habrías negado
negar ía	habría negado
negar íamos	habríamos negado
negar íais	habríais negado
negar ían	habrían negado

MODO SUBJUNTIVO

PRESENTE	PRETÉRITO IMPERFECTO		FUTURO IMPERFECTO (2)
niegue	neg ara	*or* neg ase	neg are
niegues	neg aras	*or* neg ases	neg ares
niegue	neg ara	*or* neg ase	neg are
neguemos	neg áramos	*or* neg ásemos	neg áremos
neguéis	neg arais	*or* neg aseis	neg areis
nieguen	neg aran	*or* neg asen	neg aren

PRETÉRITO PERFECTO	PRETÉRITO PLUSCUAMPERFECTO		FUTURO PERFECTO (3)
haya negado	hubiera *or* hubiese negado		hubiere negado
hayas negado	hubieras *or* hubieses negado		hubieres negado
haya negado	hubiera *or* hubiese negado		hubiere negado
hayamos negado	hubiéramos *or* hubiésemos negado		hubiéremos negado
hayáis negado	hubierais *or* hubieseis negado		hubiereis negado
hayan negado	hubieran *or* hubiesen negado		hubieren negado

MODO IMPERATIVO

PRESENTE

niega	tú
niegue	él/ella/usted
neguemos	nosotros/as
neg ad	vosotros/as
nieguen	ellos/ellas/ustedes

FORMAS NO PERSONALES

FORMAS SIMPLES

INFINITIVO	GERUNDIO	PARTICIPIO
negar	neg ando	neg ado

FORMAS COMPUESTAS

INFINITIVO	GERUNDIO
haber negado	habiendo negado

(1) or Perfecto simple. (2), (3) rarely used.

15. EMPEZAR IRREGULAR (stem change e → ie + spelling change z → c) BEGIN

MODO INDICATIVO

PRESENTE	PRETÉRITO IMPERFECTO	PRETÉRITO INDEFINIDO (1)	FUTURO IMPERFECTO
empiezo	empez aba	empecé	empezar é
empiezas	empez abas	empez aste	empezar ás
empieza	empez aba	empez ó	empezar á
empez amos	empez ábamos	empez amos	empezar emos
empez áis	empez abais	empez asteis	empezar éis
empiezan	empez aban	empez aron	empezar án

PRETÉRITO PERFECTO	PRETÉRITO PLUSCUAMPERFECTO	PRETÉRITO ANTERIOR	FUTURO PERFECTO
he empezado	había empezado	hube empezado	habré empezado
has empezado	habías empezado	hubiste empezado	habrás empezado
ha empezado	había empezado	hubo empezado	habrá empezado
hemos empezado	habíamos empezado	hubimos empezado	habremos empezado
habéis empezado	habíais empezado	hubisteis empezado	habréis empezado
han empezado	habían empezado	hubieron empezado	habrán empezado

CONDICIONAL SIMPLE	CONDICIONAL COMPUESTO
empezar ía	habría empezado
empezar ías	habrías empezado
empezar ía	habría empezado
empezar íamos	habríamos empezado
empezar íais	habríais empezado
empezar ían	habrían empezado

MODO SUBJUNTIVO

PRESENTE	PRETÉRITO IMPERFECTO		FUTURO IMPERFECTO (2)
empiece	empez ara	or empez ase	empez are
empieces	empez aras	or empez ases	empez ares
empiece	empez ara	or empez ase	empez are
empecemos	empez áramos	or empez ásemos	empez áremos
empecéis	empez arais	or empez aseis	empez areis
empiecen	empez aran	or empez asen	empez aren

PRETÉRITO PERFECTO	PRETÉRITO PLUSCUAMPERFECTO		FUTURO PERFECTO (3)
haya empezado	hubiera empezado	or hubiese empezado	hubiere empezado
hayas empezado	hubieras empezado	or hubieses empezado	hubieres empezado
haya empezado	hubiera empezado	or hubiese empezado	hubiere empezado
hayamos empezado	hubiéramos empezado	or hubiésemos empezado	hubiéremos empezado
hayáis empezado	hubierais empezado	or hubieseis empezado	hubiereis empezado
hayan empezado	hubieran empezado	or hubiesen empezado	hubieren empezado

MODO IMPERATIVO | FORMAS NO PERSONALES

PRESENTE	
empieza	tú
empiece	él/ella/usted
empecemos	nosotros/as
empez ad	vosotros/as
empiecen	ellos/ellas/ustedes

FORMAS SIMPLES

INFINITIVO	GERUNDIO	PARTICIPIO
empezar	empez ando	empez ado

FORMAS COMPUESTAS

INFINITIVO	GERUNDIO
haber empezado	habiendo empezado

(1) or Perfecto simple. (2), (3) rarely used.

model verb tables

16. CONTAR IRREGULAR (stem change o → ue)

COUNT, RELATE

MODO INDICATIVO

PRESENTE	PRETÉRITO IMPERFECTO	PRETÉRITO INDEFINIDO (1)	FUTURO IMPERFECTO
cuento	cont aba	cont é	contar é
cuentas	cont abas	cont aste	contar ás
cuenta	cont aba	cont ó	contar á
cont amos	cont ábamos	cont amos	contar emos
cont áis	cont abais	cont asteis	contar éis
cuentan	cont aban	cont aron	contar án

PRETÉRITO PERFECTO		PRETÉRITO PLUSCUAMPERFECTO		PRETÉRITO ANTERIOR		FUTURO PERFECTO	
he	contado	había	contado	hube	contado	habré	contado
has	contado	habías	contado	hubiste	contado	habrás	contado
ha	contado	había	contado	hubo	contado	habrá	contado
hemos	contado	habíamos	contado	hubimos	contado	habremos	contado
habéis	contado	habíais	contado	hubisteis	contado	habréis	contado
han	contado	habían	contado	hubieron	contado	habrán	contado

CONDICIONAL SIMPLE

contar ía	
contar ías	
contar ía	
contar íamos	
contar íais	
contar ían	

CONDICIONAL COMPUESTO

habría	contado
habrías	contado
habría	contado
habríamos	contado
habríais	contado
habrían	contado

MODO SUBJUNTIVO

PRESENTE	PRETÉRITO IMPERFECTO		FUTURO IMPERFECTO (2)
cuente	cont ara	or cont ase	cont are
cuentes	cont aras	or cont ases	cont ares
cuente	cont ara	or cont ase	cont are
cont emos	cont áramos	or cont ásemos	cont áremos
cont éis	cont arais	or cont aseis	cont areis
cuenten	cont aran	or cont asen	cont aren

PRETÉRITO PERFECTO		PRETÉRITO PLUSCUAMPERFECTO			FUTURO PERFECTO (3)	
haya	contado	hubiera	or hubiese	contado	hubiere	contado
hayas	contado	hubieras	or hubieses	contado	hubieres	contado
haya	contado	hubiera	or hubiese	contado	hubiere	contado
hayamos	contado	hubiéramos	or hubiésemos	contado	hubiéremos	contado
hayáis	contado	hubierais	or hubieseis	contado	hubiereis	contado
hayan	contado	hubieran	or hubiesen	contado	hubieren	contado

MODO IMPERATIVO

PRESENTE

cuenta	tú
cuente	él/ella/usted
cont emos	nosotros/as
cont ad	vosotros/as
cuenten	ellos/ellas/ustedes

FORMAS NO PERSONALES

FORMAS SIMPLES

INFINITIVO	GERUNDIO	PARTICIPIO
contar	cont ando	cont ado

FORMAS COMPUESTAS

INFINITIVO	GERUNDIO
haber contado	habiendo contado

(1) or Perfecto simple. (2), (3) rarely used.

model verb tables

17. TROCAR IRREGULAR (stem change o → ue + spelling change c → qu) *EXCHANGE*

MODO INDICATIVO

PRESENTE	PRETÉRITO IMPERFECTO	PRETÉRITO INDEFINIDO (1)	FUTURO IMPERFECTO
trueco	troc aba	troqué	trocar é
truecas	troc abas	troc aste	trocar ás
trueca	troc aba	troc ó	trocar á
troc amos	troc ábamos	troc amos	trocar emos
troc áis	troc abais	troc asteis	trocar éis
truecan	troc aban	troc aron	trocar án

PRETÉRITO PERFECTO		PRETÉRITO PLUSCUAMPERFECTO		PRETÉRITO ANTERIOR		FUTURO PERFECTO	
he	trocado	había	trocado	hube	trocado	habré	trocado
has	trocado	habías	trocado	hubiste	trocado	habrás	trocado
ha	trocado	había	trocado	hubo	trocado	habrá	trocado
hemos	trocado	habíamos	trocado	hubimos	trocado	habremos	trocado
habéis	trocado	habíais	trocado	hubisteis	trocado	habréis	trocado
han	trocado	habían	trocado	hubieron	trocado	habrán	trocado

CONDICIONAL SIMPLE

trocar ía	
trocar ías	
trocar ía	
trocar íamos	
trocar íais	
trocar ían	

CONDICIONAL COMPUESTO

habría	trocado
habrías	trocado
habría	trocado
habríamos	trocado
habríais	trocado
habrían	trocado

MODO SUBJUNTIVO

PRESENTE	PRETÉRITO IMPERFECTO		FUTURO IMPERFECTO (2)
trueque	troc ara	*or* troc ase	troc are
trueques	troc aras	*or* troc ases	troc ares
trueque	troc ara	*or* troc ase	troc are
troquemos	troc áramos	*or* troc ásemos	troc áremos
troquéis	troc arais	*or* troc aseis	troc areis
truequen	troc aran	*or* troc asen	troc aren

PRETÉRITO PERFECTO		PRETÉRITO PLUSCUAMPERFECTO			FUTURO PERFECTO (3)	
haya	trocado	hubiera	*or* hubiese	trocado	hubiere	trocado
hayas	trocado	hubieras	*or* hubieses	trocado	hubieres	trocado
haya	trocado	hubiera	*or* hubiese	trocado	hubiere	trocado
hayamos	trocado	hubiéramos	*or* hubiésemos	trocado	hubiéremos	trocado
hayáis	trocado	hubierais	*or* hubieseis	trocado	hubiereis	trocado
hayan	trocado	hubieran	*or* hubiesen	trocado	hubieren	trocado

MODO IMPERATIVO

PRESENTE

trueca	tú
trueque	él/ella/usted
troquemos	nosotros/as
troc ad	vosotros/as
truequen	ellos/ellas/ustedes

FORMAS NO PERSONALES

FORMAS SIMPLES

INFINITIVO	GERUNDIO	PARTICIPIO
trocar	troc ando	troc ado

FORMAS COMPUESTAS

INFINITIVO	GERUNDIO
haber trocado	habiendo trocado

(1) or Perfecto simple. (2), (3) rarely used.

model verb tables

18. ROGAR IRREGULAR (stem change o → ue + spelling change g → gu) *BEG*

MODO INDICATIVO

PRESENTE	PRETÉRITO IMPERFECTO	PRETÉRITO INDEFINIDO (1)	FUTURO IMPERFECTO
ruego	**rog** aba	rogué	**rogar** é
ruegas	**rog** abas	**rog** aste	**rogar** ás
ruega	**rog** aba	**rog** ó	**rogar** á
rog amos	**rog** ábamos	**rog** amos	**rogar** emos
rog áis	**rog** abais	**rog** asteis	**rogar** éis
ruegan	**rog** aban	**rog** aron	**rogar** án

PRETÉRITO PERFECTO	PRETÉRITO PLUSCUAMPERFECTO	PRETÉRITO ANTERIOR	FUTURO PERFECTO
he rogado	había rogado	hube rogado	habré rogado
has rogado	habías rogado	hubiste rogado	habrás rogado
ha rogado	había rogado	hubo rogado	habrá rogado
hemos rogado	habíamos rogado	hubimos rogado	habremos rogado
habéis rogado	habíais rogado	hubisteis rogado	habréis rogado
han rogado	habían rogado	hubieron rogado	habrán rogado

CONDICIONAL SIMPLE	CONDICIONAL COMPUESTO
rogar ía	habría rogado
rogar ías	habrías rogado
rogar ía	habría rogado
rogar íamos	habríamos rogado
rogar íais	habríais rogado
rogar ían	habrían rogado

MODO SUBJUNTIVO

PRESENTE	PRETÉRITO IMPERFECTO		FUTURO IMPERFECTO (2)
ruegue	**rog** ara	or **rog** ase	**rog** are
ruegues	**rog** aras	or **rog** ases	**rog** ares
ruegue	**rog** ara	or **rog** ase	**rog** are
roguemos	**rog** áramos	or **rog** ásemos	**rog** áremos
roguéis	**rog** arais	or **rog** aseis	**rog** areis
rueguen	**rog** aran	or **rog** asen	**rog** aren

PRETÉRITO PERFECTO	PRETÉRITO PLUSCUAMPERFECTO		FUTURO PERFECTO (3)
haya rogado	hubiera or hubiese rogado		hubiere rogado
hayas rogado	hubieras or hubieses rogado		hubieres rogado
haya rogado	hubiera or hubiese rogado		hubiere rogado
hayamos rogado	hubiéramos or hubiésemos rogado		hubiéremos rogado
hayáis rogado	hubierais or hubieseis rogado		hubiereis rogado
hayan rogado	hubieran or hubiesen rogado		hubieren rogado

MODO IMPERATIVO

PRESENTE

ruega	tú
ruegue	él/ella/usted
roguemos	nosotros/as
rog ad	vosotros/as
rueguen	ellos/ellas/ustedes

FORMAS NO PERSONALES

FORMAS SIMPLES

INFINITIVO	GERUNDIO	PARTICIPIO
rogar	**rog** ando	**rog** ado

FORMAS COMPUESTAS

INFINITIVO	GERUNDIO
haber rogado	habiendo rogado

(1) or Perfecto simple. (2), (3) rarely used.

model verb tables

19. FORZAR IRREGULAR (stem change o → ue + spelling change z → c) *FORCE*

MODO INDICATIVO

PRESENTE	PRETÉRITO IMPERFECTO	PRETÉRITO INDEFINIDO (1)	FUTURO IMPERFECTO
fuerzo	forz aba	forcé	forzar é
fuerzas	forz abas	forz aste	forzar ás
fuerza	forz aba	forz ó	forzar á
forz amos	forz ábamos	forz amos	forzar emos
forz áis	forz abais	forz asteis	forzar éis
fuerzan	forz aban	forz aron	forzar án

PRETÉRITO PERFECTO	PRETÉRITO PLUSCUAMPERFECTO	PRETÉRITO ANTERIOR	FUTURO PERFECTO
he forzado	había forzado	hube forzado	habré forzado
has forzado	habías forzado	hubiste forzado	habrás forzado
ha forzado	había forzado	hubo forzado	habrá forzado
hemos forzado	habíamos forzado	hubimos forzado	habremos forzado
habéis forzado	habíais forzado	hubisteis forzado	habréis forzado
han forzado	habían forzado	hubieron forzado	habrán forzado

CONDICIONAL SIMPLE	CONDICIONAL COMPUESTO
forzar ía	habría forzado
forzar ías	habrías forzado
forzar ía	habría forzado
forzar íamos	habríamos forzado
forzar íais	habríais forzado
forzar ían	habrían forzado

MODO SUBJUNTIVO

PRESENTE	PRETÉRITO IMPERFECTO		FUTURO IMPERFECTO (2)
fuerce	forz ara	or forz ase	forz are
fuerces	forz aras	or forz ases	forz ares
fuerce	forz ara	or forz ase	forz are
forcemos	forz áramos	or forz ásemos	forz áremos
forcéis	forz arais	or forz aseis	forz areis
fuercen	forz aran	or forz asen	forz aren

PRETÉRITO PERFECTO	PRETÉRITO PLUSCUAMPERFECTO		FUTURO PERFECTO (3)
haya forzado	hubiera	or hubiese forzado	hubiere forzado
hayas forzado	hubieras	or hubieses forzado	hubieres forzado
haya forzado	hubiera	or hubiese forzado	hubiere forzado
hayamos forzado	hubiéramos	or hubiésemos forzado	hubiéremos forzado
hayáis forzado	hubierais	or hubieseis forzado	hubiereis forzado
hayan forzado	hubieran	or hubiesen forzado	hubieren forzado

MODO IMPERATIVO

PRESENTE

fuerza	tú
fuerce	él/ella/usted
forcemos	nosotros/as
forz ad	vosotros/as
fuercen	ellos/ellas/ustedes

FORMAS NO PERSONALES

FORMAS SIMPLES

INFINITIVO	GERUNDIO	PARTICIPIO
forzar	forz ando	forz ado

FORMAS COMPUESTAS

INFINITIVO	GERUNDIO
haber forzado	habiendo forzado

(1) or Perfecto simple. (2), (3) rarely used.

model verb tables

20. AVERGONZAR IRREGULAR (stem change o → ue + accent change u → ü) *SHAME*

MODO INDICATIVO

PRESENTE	PRETÉRITO IMPERFECTO	PRETÉRITO INDEFINIDO (1)	FUTURO IMPERFECTO
avergüenzo	avergonz aba	avergoncé	avergonzar é
avergüenzas	avergonz abas	avergonz aste	avergonzar ás
avergüenza	avergonz aba	avergonz ó	avergonzar á
avergonz amos	avergonz ábamos	avergonz amos	avergonzar emos
avergonz áis	avergonz abais	avergonz asteis	avergonzar éis
avergüenzan	avergonz aban	avergonz aron	avergonzar án

PRETÉRITO PERFECTO		PRETÉRITO PLUSCUAMPERFECTO		PRETÉRITO ANTERIOR		FUTURO PERFECTO	
he	avergonzado	había	avergonzado	hube	avergonzado	habré	avergonzado
has	avergonzado	habías	avergonzado	hubiste	avergonzado	habrás	avergonzado
ha	avergonzado	había	avergonzado	hubo	avergonzado	habrá	avergonzado
hemos	avergonzado	habíamos	avergonzado	hubimos	avergonzado	habremos	avergonzado
habéis	avergonzado	habíais	avergonzado	hubisteis	avergonzado	habréis	avergonzado
han	avergonzado	habían	avergonzado	hubieron	avergonzado	habrán	avergonzado

CONDICIONAL SIMPLE

CONDICIONAL SIMPLE	CONDICIONAL COMPUESTO	
avergonzar ía	habría	avergonzado
avergonzar ías	habrías	avergonzado
avergonzar ía	habría	avergonzado
avergonzar íamos	habríamos	avergonzado
avergonzar íais	habríais	avergonzado
avergonzar ían	habrían	avergonzado

MODO SUBJUNTIVO

PRESENTE	PRETÉRITO IMPERFECTO		FUTURO IMPERFECTO (2)
avergüence	avergonz ara	*or* avergonz ase	avergonz are
avergüences	avergonz aras	*or* avergonz ases	avergonz ares
avergüence	avergonz ara	*or* avergonz ase	avergonz are
avergoncemos	avergonz áramos	*or* avergonz ásemos	avergonz áremos
avergoncéis	avergonz arais	*or* avergonz aseis	avergonz areis
avergüencen	avergonz aran	*or* avergonz asen	avergonz aren

PRETÉRITO PERFECTO		PRETÉRITO PLUSCUAMPERFECTO			FUTURO PERFECTO (3)	
haya	avergonzado	hubiera	*or* hubiese	avergonzado	hubiere	avergonzado
hayas	avergonzado	hubieras	*or* hubieses	avergonzado	hubieres	avergonzado
haya	avergonzado	hubiera	*or* hubiese	avergonzado	hubiere	avergonzado
hayamos	avergonzado	hubiéramos	*or* hubiésemos	avergonzado	hubiéremos	avergonzado
hayáis	avergonzado	hubierais	*or* hubieseis	avergonzado	hubiereis	avergonzado
hayan	avergonzado	hubieran	*or* hubiesen	avergonzado	hubieren	avergonzado

MODO IMPERATIVO

FORMAS NO PERSONALES

PRESENTE

avergüenza	tú
avergüence	él/ella/usted
avergoncemos	nosotros/as
avergonz ad	vosotros/as
avergüencen	ellos/ellas/ustedes

FORMAS SIMPLES

INFINITIVO	GERUNDIO	PARTICIPIO
avergonzar	avergonz ando	avergonz ado

FORMAS COMPUESTAS

INFINITIVO	GERUNDIO
haber avergonzado	habiendo avergonzado

(1) or Perfecto simple. (2), (3) rarely used.

21. JUGAR IRREGULAR (stem change u → ue + spelling change g → gu)   *PLAY*

MODO INDICATIVO

PRESENTE	PRETÉRITO IMPERFECTO	PRETÉRITO INDEFINIDO (1)	FUTURO IMPERFECTO
juego	jug aba	jugué	jugar é
juegas	jug abas	jug aste	jugar ás
juega	jug aba	jug ó	jugar á
jug amos	jug ábamos	jug amos	jugar emos
jug áis	jug abais	jug asteis	jugar éis
juegan	jug aban	jug aron	jugar án

PRETÉRITO PERFECTO	PRETÉRITO PLUSCUAMPERFECTO	PRETÉRITO ANTERIOR	FUTURO PERFECTO
he jugado	había jugado	hube jugado	habré jugado
has jugado	habías jugado	hubiste jugado	habrás jugado
ha jugado	había jugado	hubo jugado	habrá jugado
hemos jugado	habíamos jugado	hubimos jugado	habremos jugado
habéis jugado	habíais jugado	hubisteis jugado	habréis jugado
han jugado	habían jugado	hubieron jugado	habrán jugado

CONDICIONAL SIMPLE	CONDICIONAL COMPUESTO
jugar ía	habría jugado
jugar ías	habrías jugado
jugar ía	habría jugado
jugar íamos	habríamos jugado
jugar íais	habríais jugado
jugar ían	habrían jugado

MODO SUBJUNTIVO

PRESENTE	PRETÉRITO IMPERFECTO	FUTURO IMPERFECTO (2)
juegue	jug ara or jug ase	jug are
juegues	jug aras or jug ases	jug ares
juegue	jug ara or jug ase	jug are
juguemos	jug áramos or jug ásemos	jug áremos
juguéis	jug arais or jug aseis	jug areis
jueguen	jug aran or jug asen	jug aren

PRETÉRITO PERFECTO	PRETÉRITO PLUSCUAMPERFECTO	FUTURO PERFECTO (3)
haya jugado	hubiera or hubiese jugado	hubiere jugado
hayas jugado	hubieras or hubieses jugado	hubieres jugado
haya jugado	hubiera or hubiese jugado	hubiere jugado
hayamos jugado	hubiéramos or hubiésemos jugado	hubiéremos jugado
hayáis jugado	hubierais or hubieseis jugado	hubiereis jugado
hayan jugado	hubieran or hubiesen jugado	hubieren jugado

MODO IMPERATIVO

PRESENTE

juega	tú
juegue	él/ella/usted
juguemos	nosotros/as
jug ad	vosotros/as
jueguen	ellos/ellas/ustedes

FORMAS NO PERSONALES

FORMAS SIMPLES

INFINITIVO	GERUNDIO	PARTICIPIO
jugar	jug ando	jug ado

FORMAS COMPUESTAS

INFINITIVO	GERUNDIO
haber jugado	habiendo jugado

(1) or Perfecto simple. (2), (3) rarely used.

model verb tables

22. ANDAR IRREGULAR

WALK

MODO INDICATIVO

PRESENTE	PRETÉRITO IMPERFECTO	PRETÉRITO INDEFINIDO (1)	FUTURO IMPERFECTO
and o	and aba	anduve	andar é
and as	and abas	anduviste	andar ás
and a	and aba	anduvo	andar á
and amos	and ábamos	anduvimos	andar emos
and áis	and abais	anduvisteis	andar éis
and an	and aban	anduvieron	andar án

PRETÉRITO PERFECTO		PRETÉRITO PLUSCUAMPERFECTO		PRETÉRITO ANTERIOR		FUTURO PERFECTO	
he	andado	había	andado	hube	andado	habré	andado
has	andado	habías	andado	hubiste	andado	habrás	andado
ha	andado	había	andado	hubo	andado	habrá	andado
hemos	andado	habíamos	andado	hubimos	andado	habremos	andado
habéis	andado	habíais	andado	hubisteis	andado	habréis	andado
han	andado	habían	andado	hubieron	andado	habrán	andado

CONDICIONAL SIMPLE

	CONDICIONAL COMPUESTO	
andar ía	habría	andado
andar ías	habrías	andado
andar ía	habría	andado
andar íamos	habríamos	andado
andar íais	habríais	andado
andar ían	habrían	andado

MODO SUBJUNTIVO

PRESENTE	PRETÉRITO IMPERFECTO			FUTURO IMPERFECTO (2)
and e	anduviera	or	anduviese	anduviere
and es	anduvieras	or	anduvieses	anduvieres
and e	anduviera	or	anduviese	anduviere
and emos	anduviéramos	or	anduviésemos	anduviéremos
and éis	anduvierais	or	anduvieseis	anduviereis
and en	anduvieran	or	anduviesen	anduvieren

PRETÉRITO PERFECTO		PRETÉRITO PLUSCUAMPERFECTO				FUTURO PERFECTO (3)	
haya	andado	hubiera	or	hubiese	andado	hubiere	andado
hayas	andado	hubieras	or	hubieses	andado	hubieres	andado
haya	andado	hubiera	or	hubiese	andado	hubiere	andado
hayamos	andado	hubiéramos	or	hubiésemos	andado	hubiéremos	andado
hayáis	andado	hubierais	or	hubieseis	andado	hubiereis	andado
hayan	andado	hubieran	or	hubiesen	andado	hubieren	andado

MODO IMPERATIVO

FORMAS NO PERSONALES

PRESENTE

and a	tú
and e	él/ella/usted
and emos	nosotros/as
and ad	vosotros/as
and en	ellos/ellas/ustedes

FORMAS SIMPLES

INFINITIVO	GERUNDIO	PARTICIPIO
andar	and ando	and ado

FORMAS COMPUESTAS

INFINITIVO	GERUNDIO
haber andado	habiendo andado

(1) or Perfecto simple. (2), (3) rarely used.

23. DAR IRREGULAR

MODO INDICATIVO

PRESENTE	PRETÉRITO IMPERFECTO	PRETÉRITO INDEFINIDO (1)	FUTURO IMPERFECTO
doy	d aba	di	dar é
d as	d abas	diste	dar ás
d a	d aba	dio	dar á
d amos	d ábamos	dimos	dar emos
d ais	d abais	disteis	dar éis
d an	d aban	dieron	dar án

PRETÉRITO PERFECTO	PRETÉRITO PLUSCUAMPERFECTO	PRETÉRITO ANTERIOR	FUTURO PERFECTO
he dado	había dado	hube dado	habré dado
has dado	habías dado	hubiste dado	habrás dado
ha dado	había dado	hubo dado	habrá dado
hemos dado	habíamos dado	hubimos dado	habremos dado
habéis dado	habíais dado	hubisteis dado	habréis dado
han dado	habían dado	hubieron dado	habrán dado

CONDICIONAL SIMPLE	CONDICIONAL COMPUESTO
dar ía	habría dado
dar ías	habrías dado
dar ía	habría dado
dar íamos	habríamos dado
dar íais	habríais dado
dar ían	habrían dado

MODO SUBJUNTIVO

PRESENTE	PRETÉRITO IMPERFECTO		FUTURO IMPERFECTO (2)
dé	diera	or diese	diere
d es	dieras	or dieses	dieres
dé	diera	or diese	diere
d emos	diéramos	or diésemos	diéremos
d eis	dierais	or dieseis	diereis
d en	dieran	or diesen	dieren

PRETÉRITO PERFECTO	PRETÉRITO PLUSCUAMPERFECTO		FUTURO PERFECTO (3)
haya dado	hubiera	or hubiese dado	hubiere dado
hayas dado	hubieras	or hubieses dado	hubieres dado
haya dado	hubiera	or hubiese dado	hubiere dado
hayamos dado	hubiéramos	or hubiésemos dado	hubiéremos dado
hayáis dado	hubierais	or hubieseis dado	hubiereis dado
hayan dado	hubieran	or hubiesen dado	hubieren dado

MODO IMPERATIVO

PRESENTE

d a	tú
dé	él/ella/usted
d emos	nosotros/as
d ad	vosotros/as
d en	ellos/ellas/ustedes

FORMAS NO PERSONALES

FORMAS SIMPLES

INFINITIVO	GERUNDIO	PARTICIPIO
dar	d ando	d ado

FORMAS COMPUESTAS

INFINITIVO	GERUNDIO
haber dado	habiendo dado

(1) or Perfecto simple. (2), (3) rarely used.

24. BEBER
25. coger
26. vencer
27. tañer
28. leer
29. perder
30. mover
31. nacer
32. conocer
33. obedecer
34. cocer
35. caber
36. caer
37. hacer
38. oler
39. placer
40. poder
41. poner
42. querer
43. roer
44. saber
45. satisfacer
46. soler
47. traer
48. valer
49. ver
50. yacer

24. BEBER REGULAR   *DRINK*

MODO INDICATIVO

PRESENTE	PRETÉRITO IMPERFECTO	PRETÉRITO INDEFINIDO (1)	FUTURO IMPERFECTO
beb o	beb ía	beb í	beber é
beb es	beb ías	beb iste	beber ás
beb e	beb ía	beb ió	beber á
beb emos	beb íamos	beb imos	beber emos
beb éis	beb íais	beb isteis	beber éis
beb en	beb ían	beb ieron	beber án

PRETÉRITO PERFECTO	PRETÉRITO PLUSCUAMPERFECTO	PRETÉRITO ANTERIOR	FUTURO PERFECTO
he bebido	había bebido	hube bebido	habré bebido
has bebido	habías bebido	hubiste bebido	habrás bebido
ha bebido	había bebido	hubo bebido	habrá bebido
hemos bebido	habíamos bebido	hubimos bebido	habremos bebido
habéis bebido	habíais bebido	hubisteis bebido	habréis bebido
han bebido	habían bebido	hubieron bebido	habrán bebido

CONDICIONAL SIMPLE

	CONDICIONAL COMPUESTO
beber ía	habría bebido
beber ías	habrías bebido
beber ía	habría bebido
beber íamos	habríamos bebido
beber íais	habríais bebido
beber ían	habrían bebido

MODO SUBJUNTIVO

PRESENTE	PRETÉRITO IMPERFECTO		FUTURO IMPERFECTO (2)
beb a	beb iera	or beb iese	beb iere
beb as	beb ieras	or beb ieses	beb ieres
beb a	beb iera	or beb iese	beb iere
beb amos	beb iéramos	or beb iésemos	beb iéremos
beb áis	beb ierais	or beb ieseis	beb iereis
beb an	beb ieran	or beb iesen	beb ieren

PRETÉRITO PERFECTO	PRETÉRITO PLUSCUAMPERFECTO		FUTURO PERFECTO (3)
haya bebido	hubiera or hubiese bebido		hubiere bebido
hayas bebido	hubieras or hubieses bebido		hubieres bebido
haya bebido	hubiera or hubiese bebido		hubiere bebido
hayamos bebido	hubiéramos or hubiésemos bebido		hubiéremos bebido
hayáis bebido	hubierais or hubieseis bebido		hubiereis bebido
hayan bebido	hubieran or hubiesen bebido		hubieren bebido

MODO IMPERATIVO

PRESENTE

beb e	tú
beb a	él/ella/usted
beb amos	nosotros/as
beb ed	vosotros/as
beb an	ellos/ellas/ustedes

FORMAS NO PERSONALES

FORMAS SIMPLES

INFINITIVO	GERUNDIO	PARTICIPIO
beber	beb iendo	beb ido

FORMAS COMPUESTAS

INFINITIVO	GERUNDIO
haber bebido	habiendo bebido

(1) or Perfecto simple. (2), (3) rarely used.

model verb tables

25. COGER SPELLING CHANGE (g → j)   *CATCH, SEIZE*

MODO INDICATIVO

PRESENTE	PRETÉRITO IMPERFECTO	PRETÉRITO INDEFINIDO (1)	FUTURO IMPERFECTO
cojo	cog ía	cog í	coger é
cog es	cog ías	cog iste	coger ás
cog e	cog ía	cog ió	coger á
cog emos	cog íamos	cog imos	coger emos
cog éis	cog íais	cog isteis	coger éis
cog en	cog ían	cog ieron	coger án

PRETÉRITO PERFECTO		PRETÉRITO PLUSCUAMPERFECTO		PRETÉRITO ANTERIOR		FUTURO PERFECTO	
he	cogido	había	cogido	hube	cogido	habré	cogido
has	cogido	habías	cogido	hubiste	cogido	habrás	cogido
ha	cogido	había	cogido	hubo	cogido	habrá	cogido
hemos	cogido	habíamos	cogido	hubimos	cogido	habremos	cogido
habéis	cogido	habíais	cogido	hubisteis	cogido	habréis	cogido
han	cogido	habían	cogido	hubieron	cogido	habrán	cogido

CONDICIONAL SIMPLE / CONDICIONAL COMPUESTO

CONDICIONAL SIMPLE	CONDICIONAL COMPUESTO	
coger ía	habría	cogido
coger ías	habrías	cogido
coger ía	habría	cogido
coger íamos	habríamos	cogido
coger íais	habríais	cogido
coger ían	habrían	cogido

MODO SUBJUNTIVO

PRESENTE	PRETÉRITO IMPERFECTO			FUTURO IMPERFECTO (2)
coja	cog iera	or	cog iese	cog iere
cojas	cog ieras	or	cog ieses	cog ieres
coja	cog iera	or	cog iese	cog iere
cojamos	cog iéramos	or	cog iésemos	cog iéremos
cojáis	cog ierais	or	cog ieseis	cog iereis
cojan	cog ieran	or	cog iesen	cog ieren

PRETÉRITO PERFECTO		PRETÉRITO PLUSCUAMPERFECTO				FUTURO PERFECTO (3)	
haya	cogido	hubiera	or	hubiese	cogido	hubiere	cogido
hayas	cogido	hubieras	or	hubieses	cogido	hubieres	cogido
haya	cogido	hubiera	or	hubiese	cogido	hubiere	cogido
hayamos	cogido	hubiéramos	or	hubiésemos	cogido	hubiéremos	cogido
hayáis	cogido	hubierais	or	hubieseis	cogido	hubiereis	cogido
hayan	cogido	hubieran	or	hubiesen	cogido	hubieren	cogido

MODO IMPERATIVO / FORMAS NO PERSONALES

PRESENTE

cog e	tú
coja	él/ella/usted
cojamos	nosotros/as
cog ed	vosotros/as
cojan	ellos/ellas/ustedes

FORMAS NO PERSONALES

FORMAS SIMPLES

INFINITIVO	GERUNDIO	PARTICIPIO
coger	cog iendo	cog ido

FORMAS COMPUESTAS

INFINITIVO	GERUNDIO
haber cogido	habiendo cogido

(1) or Perfecto simple. (2), (3) rarely used.

model verb tables

26. VENCER SPELLING CHANGE (c → z)   *DEFEAT*

MODO INDICATIVO

PRESENTE	PRETÉRITO IMPERFECTO	PRETÉRITO INDEFINIDO (1)	FUTURO IMPERFECTO
venzo	venc ía	venc í	vencer é
venc es	venc ías	venc iste	vencer ás
venc e	venc ía	venc ió	vencer á
venc emos	venc íamos	venc imos	vencer emos
venc éis	venc íais	venc isteis	vencer éis
venc en	venc ían	venc ieron	vencer án

PRETÉRITO PERFECTO	PRETÉRITO PLUSCUAMPERFECTO	PRETÉRITO ANTERIOR	FUTURO PERFECTO
he vencido	había vencido	hube vencido	habré vencido
has vencido	habías vencido	hubiste vencido	habrás vencido
ha vencido	había vencido	hubo vencido	habrá vencido
hemos vencido	habíamos vencido	hubimos vencido	habremos vencido
habéis vencido	habíais vencido	hubisteis vencido	habréis vencido
han vencido	habían vencido	hubieron vencido	habrán vencido

CONDICIONAL SIMPLE	CONDICIONAL COMPUESTO
vencer ía	habría vencido
vencer ías	habrías vencido
vencer ía	habría vencido
vencer íamos	habríamos vencido
vencer íais	habríais vencido
vencer ían	habrían vencido

MODO SUBJUNTIVO

PRESENTE	PRETÉRITO IMPERFECTO		FUTURO IMPERFECTO (2)
venza	venc iera	or venc iese	venc iere
venzas	venc ieras	or venc ieses	venc ieres
venza	venc iera	or venc iese	venc iere
venzamos	venc iéramos	or venc iésemos	venc iéremos
venzáis	venc ierais	or venc ieseis	venc iereis
venzan	venc ieran	or venc iesen	venc ieren

PRETÉRITO PERFECTO	PRETÉRITO PLUSCUAMPERFECTO		FUTURO PERFECTO (3)
haya vencido	hubiera	or hubiese vencido	hubiere vencido
hayas vencido	hubieras	or hubieses vencido	hubieres vencido
haya vencido	hubiera	or hubiese vencido	hubiere vencido
hayamos vencido	hubiéramos	or hubiésemos vencido	hubiéremos vencido
hayáis vencido	hubierais	or hubieseis vencido	hubiereis vencido
hayan vencido	hubieran	or hubiesen vencido	hubieren vencido

MODO IMPERATIVO

PRESENTE

venc e	tú
venza	él/ella/usted
venzamos	nosotros/as
venc ed	vosotros/as
venzan	ellos/ellas/ustedes

FORMAS NO PERSONALES

FORMAS SIMPLES

INFINITIVO	GERUNDIO	PARTICIPIO
vencer	venc iendo	venc ido

FORMAS COMPUESTAS

INFINITIVO	GERUNDIO
haber vencido	habiendo vencido

(1) or Perfecto simple. (2), (3) rarely used.

Spanish Verb Manual

model verb tables

27. TAÑER SPELLING CHANGE

PLAY (INSTRUMENT)

MODO INDICATIVO

PRESENTE	PRETÉRITO IMPERFECTO	PRETÉRITO INDEFINIDO (1)	FUTURO IMPERFECTO
tañ o	tañ ía	tañ í	tañer é
tañ es	tañ ías	tañ iste	tañer ás
tañ e	tañ ía	tañó	tañer á
tañ emos	tañ íamos	tañ imos	tañer emos
tañ éis	tañ íais	tañ isteis	tañer éis
tañ en	tañ ían	tañeron	tañer án

PRETÉRITO PERFECTO		PRETÉRITO PLUSCUAMPERFECTO		PRETÉRITO ANTERIOR		FUTURO PERFECTO	
he	tañido	había	tañido	hube	tañido	habré	tañido
has	tañido	habías	tañido	hubiste	tañido	habrás	tañido
ha	tañido	había	tañido	hubo	tañido	habrá	tañido
hemos	tañido	habíamos	tañido	hubimos	tañido	habremos	tañido
habéis	tañido	habíais	tañido	hubisteis	tañido	habréis	tañido
han	tañido	habían	tañido	hubieron	tañido	habrán	tañido

CONDICIONAL SIMPLE

CONDICIONAL COMPUESTO

tañer ía		habría	tañido
tañer ías		habrías	tañido
tañer ía		habría	tañido
tañer íamos		habríamos	tañido
tañer íais		habríais	tañido
tañer ían		habrían	tañido

MODO SUBJUNTIVO

PRESENTE	PRETÉRITO IMPERFECTO			FUTURO IMPERFECTO (2)
tañ a	tañera	or	tañese	tañere
tañ as	tañeras	or	tañeses	tañeres
tañ a	tañera	or	tañese	tañere
tañ amos	tañéramos	or	tañésemos	tañéremos
tañ áis	tañerais	or	tañeseis	tañereis
tañ an	tañeran	or	tañesen	tañeren

PRETÉRITO PERFECTO		PRETÉRITO PLUSCUAMPERFECTO				FUTURO PERFECTO (3)	
haya	tañido	hubiera	or	hubiese	tañido	hubiere	tañido
hayas	tañido	hubieras	or	hubieses	tañido	hubieres	tañido
haya	tañido	hubiera	or	hubiese	tañido	hubiere	tañido
hayamos	tañido	hubiéramos	or	hubiésemos	tañido	hubiéremos	tañido
hayáis	tañido	hubierais	or	hubieseis	tañido	hubiereis	tañido
hayan	tañido	hubieran	or	hubiesen	tañido	hubieren	tañido

MODO IMPERATIVO

FORMAS NO PERSONALES

PRESENTE

FORMAS SIMPLES

tañ e	tú
tañ a	él/ella/usted
tañ amos	nosotros/as
tañ ed	vosotros/as
tañ an	ellos/ellas/ustedes

INFINITIVO	GERUNDIO	PARTICIPIO
tañer	tañendo	tañ ido

FORMAS COMPUESTAS

INFINITIVO	GERUNDIO
haber tañido	habiendo tañido

(1) or Perfecto simple. (2), (3) rarely used.

model verb tables

MODO INDICATIVO

PRESENTE	PRETÉRITO IMPERFECTO	PRETÉRITO INDEFINIDO (1)	FUTURO IMPERFECTO
le o	le ía	le í	leer é
le es	le ías	leíste	leer ás
le e	le ía	leyó	leer á
le emos	le íamos	leímos	leer emos
le éis	le íais	leísteis	leer éis
le en	le ían	leyeron	leer án

PRETÉRITO PERFECTO		PRETÉRITO PLUSCUAMPERFECTO		PRETÉRITO ANTERIOR		FUTURO PERFECTO	
he	leído	había	leído	hube	leído	habré	leído
has	leído	habías	leído	hubiste	leído	habrás	leído
ha	leído	había	leído	hubo	leído	habrá	leído
hemos	leído	habíamos	leído	hubimos	leído	habremos	leído
habéis	leído	habíais	leído	hubisteis	leído	habréis	leído
han	leído	habían	leído	hubieron	leído	habrán	leído

CONDICIONAL SIMPLE	CONDICIONAL COMPUESTO	
leer ía	habría	leído
leer ías	habrías	leído
leer ía	habría	leído
leer íamos	habríamos	leído
leer íais	habríais	leído
leer ían	habrían	leído

MODO SUBJUNTIVO

PRESENTE	PRETÉRITO IMPERFECTO			FUTURO IMPERFECTO (2)
le a	leyera	or	leyese	leyere
le as	leyeras	or	leyeses	leyeres
le a	leyera	or	leyese	leyere
le amos	leyéramos	or	leyésemos	leyéremos
le áis	leyerais	or	leyeseis	leyereis
le an	leyeran	or	leyesen	leyeren

PRETÉRITO PERFECTO		PRETÉRITO PLUSCUAMPERFECTO				FUTURO PERFECTO (3)	
haya	leído	hubiera	or hubiese	leído		hubiere	leído
hayas	leído	hubieras	or hubieses	leído		hubieres	leído
haya	leído	hubiera	or hubiese	leído		hubiere	leído
hayamos	leído	hubiéramos	or hubiésemos	leído		hubiéremos	leído
hayáis	leído	hubierais	or hubieseis	leído		hubiereis	leído
hayan	leído	hubieran	or hubiesen	leído		hubieren	leído

MODO IMPERATIVO

PRESENTE

le e	tú
le a	él/ella/usted
le amos	nosotros/as
le ed	vosotros/as
le an	ellos/ellas/ustedes

FORMAS NO PERSONALES

FORMAS SIMPLES

INFINITIVO	GERUNDIO	PARTICIPIO
leer	leyendo	leído

FORMAS COMPUESTAS

INFINITIVO	GERUNDIO
haber leído	habiendo leído

(1) or Perfecto simple. (2), (3) rarely used.

model verb tables

29. PERDER IRREGULAR (stem change e → ie)   *LOSE, MISS*

MODO INDICATIVO

PRESENTE	PRETÉRITO IMPERFECTO	PRETÉRITO INDEFINIDO (1)	FUTURO IMPERFECTO
pierdo	perd ía	perd í	perder é
pierdes	perd ías	perd iste	perder ás
pierde	perd ía	perd ió	perder á
perd emos	perd íamos	perd imos	perder emos
perd éis	perd íais	perd isteis	perder éis
pierden	perd ían	perd ieron	perder án

PRETÉRITO PERFECTO		PRETÉRITO PLUSCUAMPERFECTO		PRETÉRITO ANTERIOR		FUTURO PERFECTO	
he	perdido	había	perdido	hube	perdido	habré	perdido
has	perdido	habías	perdido	hubiste	perdido	habrás	perdido
ha	perdido	había	perdido	hubo	perdido	habrá	perdido
hemos	perdido	habíamos	perdido	hubimos	perdido	habremos	perdido
habéis	perdido	habíais	perdido	hubisteis	perdido	habréis	perdido
han	perdido	habían	perdido	hubieron	perdido	habrán	perdido

CONDICIONAL SIMPLE   CONDICIONAL COMPUESTO

perder ía	habría	perdido
perder ías	habrías	perdido
perder ía	habría	perdido
perder íamos	habríamos	perdido
perder íais	habríais	perdido
perder ían	habrían	perdido

MODO SUBJUNTIVO

PRESENTE	PRETÉRITO IMPERFECTO		FUTURO IMPERFECTO (2)
pierda	perd iera	*or* perd iese	perd iere
pierdas	perd ieras	*or* perd ieses	perd ieres
pierda	perd iera	*or* perd iese	perd iere
perd amos	perd iéramos	*or* perd iésemos	perd iéremos
perd áis	perd ierais	*or* perd ieseis	perd iereis
pierdan	perd ieran	*or* perd iesen	perd ieren

PRETÉRITO PERFECTO		PRETÉRITO PLUSCUAMPERFECTO			FUTURO PERFECTO (3)	
haya	perdido	hubiera	*or* hubiese	perdido	hubiere	perdido
hayas	perdido	hubieras	*or* hubieses	perdido	hubieres	perdido
haya	perdido	hubiera	*or* hubiese	perdido	hubiere	perdido
hayamos	perdido	hubiéramos	*or* hubiésemos	perdido	hubiéremos	perdido
hayáis	perdido	hubierais	*or* hubieseis	perdido	hubiereis	perdido
hayan	perdido	hubieran	*or* hubiesen	perdido	hubieren	perdido

MODO IMPERATIVO   FORMAS NO PERSONALES

PRESENTE

pierde	tú
pierda	él/ella/usted
perd amos	nosotros/as
perd ed	vosotros/as
pierdan	ellos/ellas/ustedes

FORMAS SIMPLES

INFINITIVO	GERUNDIO	PARTICIPIO
perder	perd iendo	perd ido

FORMAS COMPUESTAS

INFINITIVO	GERUNDIO
haber perdido	habiendo perdido

(1) or Perfecto simple. (2), (3) rarely used.

30. MOVER IRREGULAR (stem change o → ue)   *MOVE*

MODO INDICATIVO

PRESENTE	PRETÉRITO IMPERFECTO	PRETÉRITO INDEFINIDO (1)	FUTURO IMPERFECTO
muevo	mov ía	mov í	mover é
mueves	mov ías	mov iste	mover ás
mueve	mov ía	mov ió	mover á
mov emos	mov íamos	mov imos	mover emos
mov éis	mov íais	mov isteis	mover éis
mueven	mov ían	mov ieron	mover án

PRETÉRITO PERFECTO		PRETÉRITO PLUSCUAMPERFECTO		PRETÉRITO ANTERIOR		FUTURO PERFECTO	
he	movido	había	movido	hube	movido	habré	movido
has	movido	habías	movido	hubiste	movido	habrás	movido
ha	movido	había	movido	hubo	movido	habrá	movido
hemos	movido	habíamos	movido	hubimos	movido	habremos	movido
habéis	movido	habíais	movido	hubisteis	movido	habréis	movido
han	movido	habían	movido	hubieron	movido	habrán	movido

CONDICIONAL SIMPLE

CONDICIONAL COMPUESTO

mover ía		habría	movido
mover ías		habrías	movido
mover ía		habría	movido
mover íamos		habríamos	movido
mover íais		habríais	movido
mover ían		habrían	movido

MODO SUBJUNTIVO

PRESENTE	PRETÉRITO IMPERFECTO		FUTURO IMPERFECTO (2)
mueva	mov iera	*or* mov iese	mov iere
muevas	mov ieras	*or* mov ieses	mov ieres
mueva	mov iera	*or* mov iese	mov iere
mov amos	mov iéramos	*or* mov iésemos	mov iéremos
mov áis	mov ierais	*or* mov ieseis	mov iereis
muevan	mov ieran	*or* mov iesen	mov ieren

PRETÉRITO PERFECTO		PRETÉRITO PLUSCUAMPERFECTO			FUTURO PERFECTO (3)	
haya	movido	hubiera	*or* hubiese	movido	hubiere	movido
hayas	movido	hubieras	*or* hubieses	movido	hubieres	movido
haya	movido	hubiera	*or* hubiese	movido	hubiere	movido
hayamos	movido	hubiéramos	*or* hubiésemos	movido	hubiéremos	movido
hayáis	movido	hubierais	*or* hubieseis	movido	hubiereis	movido
hayan	movido	hubieran	*or* hubiesen	movido	hubieren	movido

MODO IMPERATIVO	FORMAS NO PERSONALES

PRESENTE

FORMAS SIMPLES

mueve	tú
mueva	él/ella/usted
mov amos	nosotros/as
mov ed	vosotros/as
muevan	ellos/ellas/ustedes

INFINITIVO	GERUNDIO	PARTICIPIO
mover	mov iendo	mov ido

FORMAS COMPUESTAS

INFINITIVO	GERUNDIO
haber movido	habiendo movido

(1) or Perfecto simple. (2), (3) rarely used.

model verb tables

MODO INDICATIVO

PRESENTE	PRETÉRITO IMPERFECTO	PRETÉRITO INDEFINIDO (1)	FUTURO IMPERFECTO
nazco	nac ía	nac í	nacer é
nac es	nac ías	nac iste	nacer ás
nac e	nac ía	nac ió	nacer á
nac emos	nac íamos	nac imos	nacer emos
nac éis	nac íais	nac isteis	nacer éis
nac en	nac ían	nac ieron	nacer án

PRETÉRITO PERFECTO		PRETÉRITO PLUSCUAMPERFECTO		PRETÉRITO ANTERIOR		FUTURO PERFECTO	
he	nacido	había	nacido	hube	nacido	habré	nacido
has	nacido	habías	nacido	hubiste	nacido	habrás	nacido
ha	nacido	había	nacido	hubo	nacido	habrá	nacido
hemos	nacido	habíamos	nacido	hubimos	nacido	habremos	nacido
habéis	nacido	habíais	nacido	hubisteis	nacido	habréis	nacido
han	nacido	habían	nacido	hubieron	nacido	habrán	nacido

CONDICIONAL SIMPLE	CONDICIONAL COMPUESTO	
nacer ía	habría	nacido
nacer ías	habrías	nacido
nacer ía	habría	nacido
nacer íamos	habríamos	nacido
nacer íais	habríais	nacido
nacer ían	habrían	nacido

MODO SUBJUNTIVO

PRESENTE	PRETÉRITO IMPERFECTO		FUTURO IMPERFECTO (2)
nazca	nac iera	or nac iese	nac iere
nazcas	nac ieras	or nac ieses	nac ieres
nazca	nac iera	or nac iese	nac iere
nazcamos	nac iéramos	or nac iésemos	nac iéremos
nazcáis	nac ierais	or nac ieseis	nac iereis
nazcan	nac ieran	or nac iesen	nac ieren

PRETÉRITO PERFECTO		PRETÉRITO PLUSCUAMPERFECTO			FUTURO PERFECTO (3)	
haya	nacido	hubiera	or hubiese	nacido	hubiere	nacido
hayas	nacido	hubieras	or hubieses	nacido	hubieres	nacido
haya	nacido	hubiera	or hubiese	nacido	hubiere	nacido
hayamos	nacido	hubiéramos	or hubiésemos	nacido	hubiéremos	nacido
hayáis	nacido	hubierais	or hubieseis	nacido	hubiereis	nacido
hayan	nacido	hubieran	or hubiesen	nacido	hubieren	nacido

MODO IMPERATIVO

PRESENTE

nac e	tú
nazca	él/ella/usted
nazcamos	nosotros/as
nac ed	vosotros/as
nazcan	ellos/ellas/ustedes

FORMAS NO PERSONALES

FORMAS SIMPLES

INFINITIVO	GERUNDIO	PARTICIPIO
nacer	nac iendo	nac ido

FORMAS COMPUESTAS

INFINITIVO	GERUNDIO
haber nacido	habiendo nacido

(1) or Perfecto simple. (2), (3) rarely used.

model verb tables

32. CONOCER IRREGULAR (stem change c → zc) *KNOW, MEET*

MODO INDICATIVO

PRESENTE	PRETÉRITO IMPERFECTO	PRETÉRITO INDEFINIDO (1)	FUTURO IMPERFECTO
conozco	conoc ía	conoc í	conocer é
conoc es	conoc ías	conoc iste	conocer ás
conoc e	conoc ía	conoc ió	conocer á
conoc emos	conoc íamos	conoc imos	conocer emos
conoc éis	conoc íais	conoc isteis	conocer éis
conoc en	conoc ían	conoc ieron	conocer án

PRETÉRITO PERFECTO	PRETÉRITO PLUSCUAMPERFECTO	PRETÉRITO ANTERIOR	FUTURO PERFECTO
he conocido	había conocido	hube conocido	habré conocido
has conocido	habías conocido	hubiste conocido	habrás conocido
ha conocido	había conocido	hubo conocido	habrá conocido
hemos conocido	habíamos conocido	hubimos conocido	habremos conocido
habéis conocido	habíais conocido	hubisteis conocido	habréis conocido
han conocido	habían conocido	hubieron conocido	habrán conocido

CONDICIONAL SIMPLE	CONDICIONAL COMPUESTO	
conoce ría	habría	conocido
conoce rías	habrías	conocido
conoce ría	habría	conocido
conoce ríamos	habríamos	conocido
conoce ríais	habríais	conocido
conoce rían	habrían	conocido

MODO SUBJUNTIVO

PRESENTE	PRETÉRITO IMPERFECTO		FUTURO IMPERFECTO (2)
conozca	conoc iera	or conoc iese	conoc iere
conozcas	conoc ieras	or conoc ieses	conoc ieres
conozca	conoc iera	or conoc iese	conoc iere
conozcamos	conoc iéramos	or conoc iésemos	conoc iéremos
conozcáis	conoc ierais	or conoc ieseis	conoc iereis
conozcan	conoc ieran	or conoc iesen	conoc ieren

PRETÉRITO PERFECTO	PRETÉRITO PLUSCUAMPERFECTO		FUTURO PERFECTO (3)
haya conocido	hubiera	or hubiese conocido	hubiere conocido
hayas conocido	hubieras	or hubieses conocido	hubieres conocido
haya conocido	hubiera	or hubiese conocido	hubiere conocido
hayamos conocido	hubiéramos	or hubiésemos conocido	hubiéremos conocido
hayáis conocido	hubierais	or hubieseis conocido	hubiereis conocido
hayan conocido	hubieran	or hubiesen conocido	hubieren conocido

MODO IMPERATIVO

PRESENTE

conoc e	tú
conozca	él/ella/usted
conozcamos	nosotros/as
conoc ed	vosotros/as
conozcan	ellos/ellas/ustedes

FORMAS NO PERSONALES

FORMAS SIMPLES

INFINITIVO	GERUNDIO	PARTICIPIO
conocer	conoc iendo	conoc ido

FORMAS COMPUESTAS

INFINITIVO	GERUNDIO
haber conocido	habiendo conocido

(1) or Perfecto simple. (2), (3) rarely used.

—— **61** ——

Spanish Verb Manual

model verb tables

33. OBEDECER IRREGULAR (stem change c → zc) — *OBEY*

MODO INDICATIVO

PRESENTE	PRETÉRITO IMPERFECTO	PRETÉRITO INDEFINIDO (1)	FUTURO IMPERFECTO
obedezco	obedec ía	obedec í	obedecer é
obedec es	obedec ías	obedec iste	obedecer ás
obedec e	obedec ía	obedec ió	obedecer á
obedec emos	obedec íamos	obedec imos	obedecer emos
obedec éis	obedec íais	obedec isteis	obedecer éis
obedec en	obedec ían	obedec ieron	obedecer án

PRETÉRITO PERFECTO		PRETÉRITO PLUSCUAMPERFECTO		PRETÉRITO ANTERIOR		FUTURO PERFECTO	
he	obedecido	había	obedecido	hube	obedecido	habré	obedecido
has	obedecido	habías	obedecido	hubiste	obedecido	habrás	obedecido
ha	obedecido	había	obedecido	hubo	obedecido	habrá	obedecido
hemos	obedecido	habíamos	obedecido	hubimos	obedecido	habremos	obedecido
habéis	obedecido	habíais	obedecido	hubisteis	obedecido	habréis	obedecido
han	obedecido	habían	obedecido	hubieron	obedecido	habrán	obedecido

CONDICIONAL SIMPLE / CONDICIONAL COMPUESTO

CONDICIONAL SIMPLE	CONDICIONAL COMPUESTO	
obedecer ía	habría	obedecido
obedecer ías	habrías	obedecido
obedecer ía	habría	obedecido
obedecer íamos	habríamos	obedecido
obedecer íais	habríais	obedecido
obedecer ían	habrían	obedecido

MODO SUBJUNTIVO

PRESENTE	PRETÉRITO IMPERFECTO		FUTURO IMPERFECTO (2)
obedezca	obedec iera	or obedec iese	obedec iere
obedezcas	obedec ieras	or obedec ieses	obedec ieres
obedezca	obedec iera	or obedec iese	obedec iere
obedezcamos	obedec iéramos	or obedec iésemos	obedec iéremos
obedezcáis	obedec ierais	or obedec ieseis	obedec iereis
obedezcan	obedec ieran	or obedec iesen	obedec ieren

PRETÉRITO PERFECTO		PRETÉRITO PLUSCUAMPERFECTO			FUTURO PERFECTO (3)	
haya	obedecido	hubiera	or hubiese	obedecido	hubiere	obedecido
hayas	obedecido	hubieras	or hubieses	obedecido	hubieres	obedecido
haya	obedecido	hubiera	or hubiese	obedecido	hubiere	obedecido
hayamos	obedecido	hubiéramos	or hubiésemos	obedecido	hubiéremos	obedecido
hayáis	obedecido	hubierais	or hubieseis	obedecido	hubiereis	obedecido
hayan	obedecido	hubieran	or hubiesen	obedecido	hubieren	obedecido

MODO IMPERATIVO

PRESENTE

obedec e	tú
obedezca	él/ella/usted
obedezcamos	nosotros/as
obedec ed	vosotros/as
obedezcan	ellos/ellas/ustedes

FORMAS NO PERSONALES

FORMAS SIMPLES

INFINITIVO	GERUNDIO	PARTICIPIO
obedecer	obedec iendo	obedec ido

FORMAS COMPUESTAS

INFINITIVO	GERUNDIO
haber obedecido	habiendo obedecido

(1) or Perfecto simple. (2), (3) rarely used.

model verb tables

34. COCER IRREGULAR (stem change o → ue + spelling change c → z)   *COOK, BOIL*

MODO INDICATIVO

PRESENTE	PRETÉRITO IMPERFECTO	PRETÉRITO INDEFINIDO (1)	FUTURO IMPERFECTO
cuezo	coc ía	coc í	cocer é
cueces	coc ías	coc iste	cocer ás
cuece	coc ía	coc ió	cocer á
coc emos	coc íamos	coc imos	cocer emos
coc éis	coc íais	coc isteis	cocer éis
cuecen	coc ían	coc ieron	cocer án

PRETÉRITO PERFECTO	PRETÉRITO PLUSCUAMPERFECTO	PRETÉRITO ANTERIOR	FUTURO PERFECTO
he cocido	había cocido	hube cocido	habré cocido
has cocido	habías cocido	hubiste cocido	habrás cocido
ha cocido	había cocido	hubo cocido	habrá cocido
hemos cocido	habíamos cocido	hubimos cocido	habremos cocido
habéis cocido	habíais cocido	hubisteis cocido	habréis cocido
han cocido	habían cocido	hubieron cocido	habrán cocido

CONDICIONAL SIMPLE

cocer ía	
cocer ías	
cocer ía	
cocer íamos	
cocer íais	
cocer ían	

CONDICIONAL COMPUESTO

habría	cocido
habrías	cocido
habría	cocido
habríamos	cocido
habríais	cocido
habrían	cocido

MODO SUBJUNTIVO

PRESENTE	PRETÉRITO IMPERFECTO			FUTURO IMPERFECTO (2)
cueza	coc iera	or	coc iese	coc iere
cuezas	coc ieras	or	coc ieses	coc ieres
cueza	coc iera	or	coc iese	coc iere
cozamos	coc iéramos	or	coc iésemos	coc iéremos
cozáis	coc ierais	or	coc ieseis	coc iereis
cuezan	coc ieran	or	coc iesen	coc ieren

PRETÉRITO PERFECTO	PRETÉRITO PLUSCUAMPERFECTO			FUTURO PERFECTO (3)
haya cocido	hubiera	or	hubiese cocido	hubiere cocido
hayas cocido	hubieras	or	hubieses cocido	hubieres cocido
haya cocido	hubiera	or	hubiese cocido	hubiere cocido
hayamos cocido	hubiéramos	or	hubiésemos cocido	hubiéremos cocido
hayáis cocido	hubierais	or	hubieseis cocido	hubiereis cocido
hayan cocido	hubieran	or	hubiesen cocido	hubieren cocido

MODO IMPERATIVO

PRESENTE

cuece	tú
cueza	él/ella/usted
cozamos	nosotros/as
coc ed	vosotros/as
cuezan	ellos/ellas/ustedes

FORMAS NO PERSONALES

FORMAS SIMPLES

INFINITIVO	GERUNDIO	PARTICIPIO
cocer	coc iendo	coc ido

FORMAS COMPUESTAS

INFINITIVO	GERUNDIO
haber cocido	habiendo cocido

(1) or Perfecto simple. (2), (3) rarely used.

model verb tables

35. CABER IRREGULAR

MODO INDICATIVO

PRESENTE	PRETÉRITO IMPERFECTO	PRETÉRITO INDEFINIDO (1)	FUTURO IMPERFECTO
quepo	cab ía	cupe	cabré
cab es	cab ías	cupiste	cabrás
cab e	cab ía	cupo	cabrá
cab emos	cab íamos	cupimos	cabremos
cab éis	cab íais	cupisteis	cabréis
cab en	cab ían	cupieron	cabrán

PRETÉRITO PERFECTO	PRETÉRITO PLUSCUAMPERFECTO	PRETÉRITO ANTERIOR	FUTURO PERFECTO
he cabido	había cabido	hube cabido	habré cabido
has cabido	habías cabido	hubiste cabido	habrás cabido
ha cabido	había cabido	hubo cabido	habrá cabido
hemos cabido	habíamos cabido	hubimos cabido	habremos cabido
habéis cabido	habíais cabido	hubisteis cabido	habréis cabido
han cabido	habían cabido	hubieron cabido	habrán cabido

CONDICIONAL SIMPLE	CONDICIONAL COMPUESTO
cabría	habría cabido
cabrías	habrías cabido
cabría	habría cabido
cabríamos	habríamos cabido
cabríais	habríais cabido
cabrían	habrían cabido

MODO SUBJUNTIVO

PRESENTE	PRETÉRITO IMPERFECTO		FUTURO IMPERFECTO (2)
quepa	cupiera	or cupiese	cupiere
quepas	cupieras	or cupieses	cupieres
quepa	cupiera	or cupiese	cupiere
quepamos	cupiéramos	or cupiésemos	cupiéremos
quepáis	cupierais	or cupieseis	cupiereis
quepan	cupieran	or cupiesen	cupieren

PRETÉRITO PERFECTO	PRETÉRITO PLUSCUAMPERFECTO		FUTURO PERFECTO (3)
haya cabido	hubiera	or hubiese cabido	hubiere cabido
hayas cabido	hubieras	or hubieses cabido	hubieres cabido
haya cabido	hubiera	or hubiese cabido	hubiere cabido
hayamos cabido	hubiéramos	or hubiésemos cabido	hubiéremos cabido
hayáis cabido	hubierais	or hubieseis cabido	hubiereis cabido
hayan cabido	hubieran	or hubiesen cabido	hubieren cabido

MODO IMPERATIVO

PRESENTE

cab e	tú
quepa	él/ella/usted
quepamos	nosotros/as
cab ed	vosotros/as
quepan	ellos/ellas/ustedes

FORMAS NO PERSONALES

FORMAS SIMPLES

INFINITIVO	GERUNDIO	PARTICIPIO
caber	cab iendo	cab ido

FORMAS COMPUESTAS

INFINITIVO	GERUNDIO
haber cabido	habiendo cabido

(1) or Perfecto simple. (2), (3) rarely used.

36. CAER IRREGULAR

MODO INDICATIVO

PRESENTE	PRETÉRITO IMPERFECTO	PRETÉRITO INDEFINIDO (1)	FUTURO IMPERFECTO
caigo	ca ía	ca í	caer é
ca es	ca ías	caíste	caer ás
ca e	ca ía	cayó	caer á
ca emos	ca íamos	caímos	caer emos
ca éis	ca íais	caísteis	caer éis
ca en	ca ían	cayeron	caer án

PRETÉRITO PERFECTO		PRETÉRITO PLUSCUAMPERFECTO		PRETÉRITO ANTERIOR		FUTURO PERFECTO	
he	caído	había	caído	hube	caído	habré	caído
has	caído	habías	caído	hubiste	caído	habrás	caído
ha	caído	había	caído	hubo	caído	habrá	caído
hemos	caído	habíamos	caído	hubimos	caído	habremos	caído
habéis	caído	habíais	caído	hubisteis	caído	habréis	caído
han	caído	habían	caído	hubieron	caído	habrán	caído

CONDICIONAL SIMPLE

			CONDICIONAL COMPUESTO	
caer ía			habría	caído
caer ías			habrías	caído
caer ía			habría	caído
caer íamos			habríamos	caído
caer íais			habríais	caído
caer ían			habrían	caído

MODO SUBJUNTIVO

PRESENTE	PRETÉRITO IMPERFECTO		FUTURO IMPERFECTO (2)
caiga	cayera	or cayese	cayere
caigas	cayeras	or cayeses	cayeres
caiga	cayera	or cayese	cayere
caigamos	cayéramos	or cayésemos	cayéremos
caigáis	cayerais	or cayeseis	cayereis
caigan	cayeran	or cayesen	cayeren

PRETÉRITO PERFECTO		PRETÉRITO PLUSCUAMPERFECTO			FUTURO PERFECTO (3)	
haya	caído	hubiera	or hubiese	caído	hubiere	caído
hayas	caído	hubieras	or hubieses	caído	hubieres	caído
haya	caído	hubiera	or hubiese	caído	hubiere	caído
hayamos	caído	hubiéramos	or hubiésemos	caído	hubiéremos	caído
hayáis	caído	hubierais	or hubieseis	caído	hubiereis	caído
hayan	caído	hubieran	or hubiesen	caído	hubieren	caído

MODO IMPERATIVO

FORMAS NO PERSONALES

PRESENTE

ca e	tú
caiga	él/ella/usted
caigamos	nosotros/as
ca ed	vosotros/as
caigan	ellos/ellas/ustedes

FORMAS SIMPLES

INFINITIVO	GERUNDIO	PARTICIPIO
caer	cayendo	caído

FORMAS COMPUESTAS

INFINITIVO	GERUNDIO
haber caído	habiendo caído

(1) or Perfecto simple. (2), (3) rarely used.

model verb tables

MODO INDICATIVO

PRESENTE	PRETÉRITO IMPERFECTO	PRETÉRITO INDEFINIDO (1)	FUTURO IMPERFECTO
hago	hac ía	hice	haré
hac es	hac ías	hiciste	harás
hac e	hac ía	hizo	hará
hac emos	hac íamos	hicimos	haremos
hac éis	hac íais	hicisteis	haréis
hac en	hac ían	hicieron	harán

PRETÉRITO PERFECTO		PRETÉRITO PLUSCUAMPERFECTO		PRETÉRITO ANTERIOR		FUTURO PERFECTO	
he	hecho	había	hecho	hube	hecho	habré	hecho
has	hecho	habías	hecho	hubiste	hecho	habrás	hecho
ha	hecho	había	hecho	hubo	hecho	habrá	hecho
hemos	hecho	habíamos	hecho	hubimos	hecho	habremos	hecho
habéis	hecho	habíais	hecho	hubisteis	hecho	habréis	hecho
han	hecho	habían	hecho	hubieron	hecho	habrán	hecho

CONDICIONAL SIMPLE	CONDICIONAL COMPUESTO	
haría	habría	hecho
harías	habrías	hecho
haría	habría	hecho
haríamos	habríamos	hecho
haríais	habríais	hecho
harían	habrían	hecho

MODO SUBJUNTIVO

PRESENTE	PRETÉRITO IMPERFECTO			FUTURO IMPERFECTO (2)
haga	hiciera	or	hiciese	hiciere
hagas	hicieras	or	hicieses	hicieres
haga	hiciera	or	hiciese	hiciere
hagamos	hiciéramos	or	hiciésemos	hiciéremos
hagáis	hicierais	or	hicieseis	hiciereis
hagan	hicieran	or	hiciesen	hicieren

PRETÉRITO PERFECTO		PRETÉRITO PLUSCUAMPERFECTO				FUTURO PERFECTO (3)	
haya	hecho	hubiera	or	hubiese	hecho	hubiere	hecho
hayas	hecho	hubieras	or	hubieses	hecho	hubieres	hecho
haya	hecho	hubiera	or	hubiese	hecho	hubiere	hecho
hayamos	hecho	hubiéramos	or	hubiésemos	hecho	hubiéremos	hecho
hayáis	hecho	hubierais	or	hubieseis	hecho	hubiereis	hecho
hayan	hecho	hubieran	or	hubiesen	hecho	hubieren	hecho

MODO IMPERATIVO

PRESENTE

haz	tú
haga	él/ella/usted
hagamos	nosotros/as
hac ed	vosotros/as
hagan	ellos/ellas/ustedes

FORMAS NO PERSONALES

FORMAS SIMPLES

INFINITIVO	GERUNDIO	PARTICIPIO
hacer	hac iendo	hecho

FORMAS COMPUESTAS

INFINITIVO	GERUNDIO
haber hecho	habiendo hecho

(1) or Perfecto simple. (2), (3) rarely used.

38. OLER IRREGULAR (incl. stem change o → ue)   *SMELL*

MODO INDICATIVO

PRESENTE	PRETÉRITO IMPERFECTO	PRETÉRITO INDEFINIDO (1)	FUTURO IMPERFECTO
huelo	ol ía	ol í	oler é
hueles	ol ías	ol iste	oler ás
huele	ol ía	ol ió	oler á
ol emos	ol íamos	ol imos	oler emos
ol éis	ol íais	ol isteis	oler éis
huelen	ol ían	ol ieron	oler án

PRETÉRITO PERFECTO	PRETÉRITO PLUSCUAMPERFECTO	PRETÉRITO ANTERIOR	FUTURO PERFECTO
he olido	había olido	hube olido	habré olido
has olido	habías olido	hubiste olido	habrás olido
ha olido	había olido	hubo olido	habrá olido
hemos olido	habíamos olido	hubimos olido	habremos olido
habéis olido	habíais olido	hubisteis olido	habréis olido
han olido	habían olido	hubieron olido	habrán olido

CONDICIONAL SIMPLE	CONDICIONAL COMPUESTO
oler ía	habría olido
oler ías	habrías olido
oler ía	habría olido
oler íamos	habríamos olido
oler íais	habríais olido
oler ían	habrían olido

MODO SUBJUNTIVO

PRESENTE	PRETÉRITO IMPERFECTO	FUTURO IMPERFECTO (2)
huela	ol iera *or* ol iese	ol iere
huelas	ol ieras *or* ol ieses	ol ieres
huela	ol iera *or* ol iese	ol iere
ol amos	ol iéramos *or* ol iésemos	ol iéremos
ol áis	ol ierais *or* ol ieseis	ol iereis
huelan	ol ieran *or* ol iesen	ol ieren

PRETÉRITO PERFECTO	PRETÉRITO PLUSCUAMPERFECTO	FUTURO PERFECTO (3)
haya olido	hubiera *or* hubiese olido	hubiere olido
hayas olido	hubieras *or* hubieses olido	hubieres olido
haya olido	hubiera *or* hubiese olido	hubiere olido
hayamos olido	hubiéramos *or* hubiésemos olido	hubiéremos olido
hayáis olido	hubierais *or* hubieseis olido	hubiereis olido
hayan olido	hubieran *or* hubiesen olido	hubieren olido

MODO IMPERATIVO

PRESENTE

huele	tú
huela	él/ella/usted
ol amos	nosotros/as
ol ed	vosotros/as
huelan	ellos/ellas/ustedes

FORMAS NO PERSONALES

FORMAS SIMPLES

INFINITIVO	GERUNDIO	PARTICIPIO
oler	ol iendo	ol ido

FORMAS COMPUESTAS

INFINITIVO	GERUNDIO
haber olido	habiendo olido

(1) or Perfecto simple. (2), (3) rarely used.

model verb tables

MODO INDICATIVO

PRESENTE	PRETÉRITO IMPERFECTO	PRETÉRITO INDEFINIDO (1)	FUTURO IMPERFECTO
plazco	**plac** ía	**plac** í	**placer** é
plac es	**plac** ías	**plac** iste	**placer** ás
plac e	**plac** ía	**plac** ió *or* plugo	**placer** á
plac emos	**plac** íamos	**plac** imos	**placer** emos
plac éis	**plac** íais	**plac** isteis	**placer** éis
plac en	**plac** ían	**plac** ieron *or* pluguieron	**placer** án

PRETÉRITO PERFECTO		PRETÉRITO PLUSCUAMPERFECTO		PRETÉRITO ANTERIOR		FUTURO PERFECTO	
he	placido	había	placido	hube	placido	habré	placido
has	placido	habías	placido	hubiste	placido	habrás	placido
ha	placido	había	placido	hubo	placido	habrá	placido
hemos	placido	habíamos	placido	hubimos	placido	habremos	placido
habéis	placido	habíais	placido	hubisteis	placido	habréis	placido
han	placido	habían	placido	hubieron	placido	habrán	placido

CONDICIONAL SIMPLE	CONDICIONAL COMPUESTO	
placer ía	habría	placido
placer ías	habrías	placido
placer ía	habría	placido
placer íamos	habríamos	placido
placer íais	habríais	placido
placer ían	habrían	placido

MODO SUBJUNTIVO

PRESENTE	PRETÉRITO IMPERFECTO			FUTURO IMPERFECTO (2)
plazca	**plac** iera	*or*	**plac** iese	**plac** iere
plazcas	**plac** ieras	*or*	**plac** ieses	**plac** ieres
plazca *or* plegue	**plac** iera *or* pluguiera	*or*	**plac** iese *or* pluguiese	**plac** iere *or* pluguiere
plazcamos	**plac** iéramos	*or*	**plac** iésemos	**plac** iéremos
plazcáis	**plac** ierais	*or*	**plac** ieseis	**plac** iereis
plazcan	**plac** ieran	*or*	**plac** iesen	**plac** ieren

PRETÉRITO PERFECTO		PRETÉRITO PLUSCUAMPERFECTO			FUTURO PERFECTO (3)	
haya	placido	hubiera	*or* hubiese	placido	hubiere	placido
hayas	placido	hubieras	*or* hubieses	placido	hubieres	placido
haya	placido	hubiera	*or* hubiese	placido	hubiere	placido
hayamos	placido	hubiéramos	*or* hubiésemos	placido	hubiéremos	placido
hayáis	placido	hubierais	*or* hubieseis	placido	hubiereis	placido
hayan	placido	hubieran	*or* hubiesen	placido	hubieren	placido

MODO IMPERATIVO

PRESENTE

plac e	tú
plazca	él/ella/usted
plazcamos	nosotros/as
plac ed	vosotros/as
plazcan	ellos/ellas/ustedes

FORMAS NO PERSONALES

FORMAS SIMPLES

INFINITIVO	GERUNDIO	PARTICIPIO
placer	**plac** iendo	**plac** ido

FORMAS COMPUESTAS

INFINITIVO	GERUNDIO
haber placido	habiendo placido

(1) or Perfecto simple. (2), (3) rarely used.

model verb tables

40. PODER IRREGULAR (incl. stem change o → ue)   *BE ABLE*

MODO INDICATIVO

PRESENTE	PRETÉRITO IMPERFECTO	PRETÉRITO INDEFINIDO (1)	FUTURO IMPERFECTO
puedo	pod ía	pude	podré
puedes	pod ías	pudiste	podrás
puede	pod ía	pudo	podrá
pod emos	pod íamos	pudimos	podremos
pod éis	pod íais	pudisteis	podréis
pueden	pod ían	pudieron	podrán

PRETÉRITO PERFECTO		PRETÉRITO PLUSCUAMPERFECTO		PRETÉRITO ANTERIOR		FUTURO PERFECTO	
he	podido	había	podido	hube	podido	habré	podido
has	podido	habías	podido	hubiste	podido	habrás	podido
ha	podido	había	podido	hubo	podido	habrá	podido
hemos	podido	habíamos	podido	hubimos	podido	habremos	podido
habéis	podido	habíais	podido	hubisteis	podido	habréis	podido
han	podido	habían	podido	hubieron	podido	habrán	podido

CONDICIONAL SIMPLE

	CONDICIONAL COMPUESTO	
podría	habría	podido
podrías	habrías	podido
podría	habría	podido
podríamos	habríamos	podido
podríais	habríais	podido
podrían	habrían	podido

MODO SUBJUNTIVO

PRESENTE	PRETÉRITO IMPERFECTO		FUTURO IMPERFECTO (2)
pueda	pudiera	*or* pudiese	pudiere
puedas	pudieras	*or* pudieses	pudieres
pueda	pudiera	*or* pudiese	pudiere
pod amos	pudiéramos	*or* pudiésemos	pudiéremos
pod áis	pudierais	*or* pudieseis	pudiereis
puedan	pudieran	*or* pudiesen	pudieren

PRETÉRITO PERFECTO		PRETÉRITO PLUSCUAMPERFECTO			FUTURO PERFECTO (3)	
haya	podido	hubiera	*or* hubiese	podido	hubiere	podido
hayas	podido	hubieras	*or* hubieses	podido	hubieres	podido
haya	podido	hubiera	*or* hubiese	podido	hubiere	podido
hayamos	podido	hubiéramos	*or* hubiésemos	podido	hubiéremos	podido
hayáis	podido	hubierais	*or* hubieseis	podido	hubiereis	podido
hayan	podido	hubieran	*or* hubiesen	podido	hubieren	podido

MODO IMPERATIVO

PRESENTE

puede	tú
pueda	él/ella/usted
pod amos	nosotros/as
pod ed	vosotros/as
puedan	ellos/ellas/ustedes

FORMAS NO PERSONALES

FORMAS SIMPLES

INFINITIVO	GERUNDIO	PARTICIPIO
poder	pudiendo	pod ido

FORMAS COMPUESTAS

INFINITIVO	GERUNDIO
haber podido	habiendo podido

(1) or Perfecto simple. (2), (3) rarely used.

Spanish Verb Manual

model verb tables

41. PONER IRREGULAR

PUT, PLACE

MODO INDICATIVO

PRESENTE	PRETÉRITO IMPERFECTO	PRETÉRITO INDEFINIDO (1)	FUTURO IMPERFECTO
pongo	pon ía	puse	pondré
pon es	pon ías	pusiste	pondrás
pon e	pon ía	puso	pondrá
pon emos	pon íamos	pusimos	pondremos
pon éis	pon íais	pusisteis	pondréis
pon en	pon ían	pusieron	pondrán

PRETÉRITO PERFECTO		PRETÉRITO PLUSCUAMPERFECTO		PRETÉRITO ANTERIOR		FUTURO PERFECTO	
he	puesto	había	puesto	hube	puesto	habré	puesto
has	puesto	habías	puesto	hubiste	puesto	habrás	puesto
ha	puesto	había	puesto	hubo	puesto	habrá	puesto
hemos	puesto	habíamos	puesto	hubimos	puesto	habremos	puesto
habéis	puesto	habíais	puesto	hubisteis	puesto	habréis	puesto
han	puesto	habían	puesto	hubieron	puesto	habrán	puesto

CONDICIONAL SIMPLE	CONDICIONAL COMPUESTO	
pondría	habría	puesto
pondrías	habrías	puesto
pondría	habría	puesto
pondríamos	habríamos	puesto
pondríais	habríais	puesto
pondrían	habrían	puesto

MODO SUBJUNTIVO

PRESENTE	PRETÉRITO IMPERFECTO		FUTURO IMPERFECTO (2)
ponga	pusiera	or pusiese	pusiere
pongas	pusieras	or pusieses	pusieres
ponga	pusiera	or pusiese	pusiere
pongamos	pusiéramos	or pusiésemos	pusiéremos
pongáis	pusierais	or pusieseis	pusiereis
pongan	pusieran	or pusiesen	pusieren

PRETÉRITO PERFECTO		PRETÉRITO PLUSCUAMPERFECTO			FUTURO PERFECTO (3)	
haya	puesto	hubiera	or hubiese	puesto	hubiere	puesto
hayas	puesto	hubieras	or hubieses	puesto	hubieres	puesto
haya	puesto	hubiera	or hubiese	puesto	hubiere	puesto
hayamos	puesto	hubiéramos	or hubiésemos	puesto	hubiéremos	puesto
hayáis	puesto	hubierais	or hubieseis	puesto	hubiereis	puesto
hayan	puesto	hubieran	or hubiesen	puesto	hubieren	puesto

MODO IMPERATIVO

FORMAS NO PERSONALES

PRESENTE

FORMAS SIMPLES

pon	tú
ponga	él/ella/usted
pongamos	nosotros/as
pon ed	vosotros/as
pongan	ellos/ellas/ustedes

INFINITIVO	GERUNDIO	PARTICIPIO
poner	pon iendo	puesto

FORMAS COMPUESTAS

INFINITIVO	GERUNDIO
haber puesto	habiendo puesto

(1) or Perfecto simple. (2), (3) rarely used.

model verb tables

42. QUERER IRREGULAR (incl. stem change e → ie)   *WANT, LOVE*

MODO INDICATIVO

PRESENTE	PRETÉRITO IMPERFECTO	PRETÉRITO INDEFINIDO (1)	FUTURO IMPERFECTO
quiero	quer ía	quise	querré
quieres	quer ías	quisiste	querrás
quiere	quer ía	quiso	querrá
quer emos	quer íamos	quisimos	querremos
quer éis	quer íais	quisisteis	querréis
quieren	quer ían	quisieron	querrán

PRETÉRITO PERFECTO	PRETÉRITO PLUSCUAMPERFECTO	PRETÉRITO ANTERIOR	FUTURO PERFECTO
he querido	había querido	hube querido	habré querido
has querido	habías querido	hubiste querido	habrás querido
ha querido	había querido	hubo querido	habrá querido
hemos querido	habíamos querido	hubimos querido	habremos querido
habéis querido	habíais querido	hubisteis querido	habréis querido
han querido	habían querido	hubieron querido	habrán querido

CONDICIONAL SIMPLE

CONDICIONAL COMPUESTO
querría	habría querido
querrías	habrías querido
querría	habría querido
querríamos	habríamos querido
querríais	habríais querido
querrían	habrían querido

MODO SUBJUNTIVO

PRESENTE	PRETÉRITO IMPERFECTO	FUTURO IMPERFECTO (2)
quiera	quisiera *or* quisiese	quisiere
quieras	quisieras *or* quisieses	quisieres
quiera	quisiera *or* quisiese	quisiere
quer amos	quisiéramos *or* quisiésemos	quisiéremos
quer áis	quisierais *or* quisieseis	quisiereis
quieran	quisieran *or* quisiesen	quisieren

PRETÉRITO PERFECTO	PRETÉRITO PLUSCUAMPERFECTO	FUTURO PERFECTO (3)
haya querido	hubiera *or* hubiese querido	hubiere querido
hayas querido	hubieras *or* hubieses querido	hubieres querido
haya querido	hubiera *or* hubiese querido	hubiere querido
hayamos querido	hubiéramos *or* hubiésemos querido	hubiéremos querido
hayáis querido	hubierais *or* hubieseis querido	hubiereis querido
hayan querido	hubieran *or* hubiesen querido	hubieren querido

MODO IMPERATIVO	FORMAS NO PERSONALES

PRESENTE

quiere	tú
quiera	él/ella/usted
quer amos	nosotros/as
quer ed	vosotros/as
quieran	ellos/ellas/ustedes

FORMAS SIMPLES

INFINITIVO	GERUNDIO	PARTICIPIO
querer	quer iendo	quer ido

FORMAS COMPUESTAS

INFINITIVO	GERUNDIO
haber querido	habiendo querido

(1) or Perfecto simple. (2), (3) rarely used.

model verb tables

43. ROER IRREGULAR (incl. stem change o → oi)   *GNAW*

MODO INDICATIVO

PRESENTE	PRETÉRITO IMPERFECTO	PRETÉRITO INDEFINIDO (1)	FUTURO IMPERFECTO
ro o *or* **roigo** *or* **royo**	**ro** ía	**ro** í	**roer** é
ro es	**ro** ías	**ro**íste	**roer** ás
ro e	**ro** ía	**ro**yó	**roer** á
ro emos	**ro** íamos	**ro**ímos	**roer** emos
ro éis	**ro** íais	**ro**ísteis	**roer** éis
ro en	**ro** ían	**ro**yeron	**roer** án

PRETÉRITO PERFECTO	PRETÉRITO PLUSCUAMPERFECTO	PRETÉRITO ANTERIOR	FUTURO PERFECTO
he roído	había roído	hube roído	habré roído
has roído	habías roído	hubiste roído	habrás roído
ha roído	había roído	hubo roído	habrá roído
hemos roído	habíamos roído	hubimos roído	habremos roído
habéis roído	habíais roído	hubisteis roído	habréis roído
han roído	habían roído	hubieron roído	habrán roído

CONDICIONAL SIMPLE	CONDICIONAL COMPUESTO
roer ía	habría roído
roer ías	habrías roído
roer ía	habría roído
roer íamos	habríamos roído
roer íais	habríais roído
roer ían	habrían roído

MODO SUBJUNTIVO

PRESENTE			PRETÉRITO IMPERFECTO		FUTURO IMPERFECTO (2)
ro a *or* **roiga** *or* **roya**			**ro**yera *or* **ro**yese		**ro**yere
ro as *or* **roigas** *or* **royas**			**ro**yeras *or* **ro**yeses		**ro**yeres
ro a *or* **roiga** *or* **roya**			**ro**yera *or* **ro**yese		**ro**yere
ro amos *or* **roigamos** *or* **royamos**			**ro**yéramos *or* **ro**yésemos		**ro**yéremos
ro áis *or* **roigáis** *or* **royáis**			**ro**yerais *or* **ro**yeseis		**ro**yereis
ro an *or* **roigan** *or* **royan**			**ro**yeran *or* **ro**yesen		**ro**yeren

PRETÉRITO PERFECTO	PRETÉRITO PLUSCUAMPERFECTO		FUTURO PERFECTO (3)
haya roído	hubiera *or* hubiese roído		hubiere roído
hayas roído	hubieras *or* hubieses roído		hubieres roído
haya roído	hubiera *or* hubiese roído		hubiere roído
hayamos roído	hubiéramos *or* hubiésemos roído		hubiéremos roído
hayáis roído	hubierais *or* hubieseis roído		hubiereis roído
hayan roído	hubieran *or* hubiesen roído		hubieren roído

MODO IMPERATIVO	FORMAS NO PERSONALES

PRESENTE

FORMAS SIMPLES

ro e	tú
ro a *or* **roiga** *or* **roya**	él/ella/usted
ro amos *or* **roigamos** *or* **royamos**	nosotros/as
ro ed	vosotros/as
ro an *or* **roigan** *or* **royan**	ellos/ellas/ustedes

INFINITIVO	GERUNDIO	PARTICIPIO
roer	royendo	roído

FORMAS COMPUESTAS

INFINITIVO	GERUNDIO
haber roído	habiendo roído

(1) or Perfecto simple. (2), (3) rarely used.

44. SABER IRREGULAR

MODO INDICATIVO

PRESENTE	PRETÉRITO IMPERFECTO	PRETÉRITO INDEFINIDO (1)	FUTURO IMPERFECTO
sé	sab ía	supe	sabré
sab es	sab ías	supiste	sabrás
sab e	sab ía	supo	sabrá
sab emos	sab íamos	supimos	sabremos
sab éis	sab íais	supisteis	sabréis
sab en	sab ían	supieron	sabrán

PRETÉRITO PERFECTO	PRETÉRITO PLUSCUAMPERFECTO	PRETÉRITO ANTERIOR	FUTURO PERFECTO
he sabido	había sabido	hube sabido	habré sabido
has sabido	habías sabido	hubiste sabido	habrás sabido
ha sabido	había sabido	hubo sabido	habrá sabido
hemos sabido	habíamos sabido	hubimos sabido	habremos sabido
habéis sabido	habíais sabido	hubisteis sabido	habréis sabido
han sabido	habían sabido	hubieron sabido	habrán sabido

CONDICIONAL SIMPLE	CONDICIONAL COMPUESTO
sabría	habría sabido
sabrías	habrías sabido
sabría	habría sabido
sabríamos	habríamos sabido
sabríais	habríais sabido
sabrían	habrían sabido

MODO SUBJUNTIVO

PRESENTE	PRETÉRITO IMPERFECTO	FUTURO IMPERFECTO (2)
sepa	supiera or supiese	supiere
sepas	supieras or supieses	supieres
sepa	supiera or supiese	supiere
sepamos	supiéramos or supiésemos	supiéremos
sepáis	supierais or supieseis	supiereis
sepan	supieran or supiesen	supieren

PRETÉRITO PERFECTO	PRETÉRITO PLUSCUAMPERFECTO	FUTURO PERFECTO (3)
haya sabido	hubiera or hubiese sabido	hubiere sabido
hayas sabido	hubieras or hubieses sabido	hubieres sabido
haya sabido	hubiera or hubiese sabido	hubiere sabido
hayamos sabido	hubiéramos or hubiésemos sabido	hubiéremos sabido
hayáis sabido	hubierais or hubieseis sabido	hubiereis sabido
hayan sabido	hubieran or hubiesen sabido	hubieren sabido

MODO IMPERATIVO

PRESENTE

sab e	tú
sepa	él/ella/usted
sepamos	nosotros/as
sab ed	vosotros/as
sepan	ellos/ellas/ustedes

FORMAS NO PERSONALES

FORMAS SIMPLES

INFINITIVO	GERUNDIO	PARTICIPIO
saber	sab iendo	sab ido

FORMAS COMPUESTAS

INFINITIVO	GERUNDIO
haber sabido	habiendo sabido

(1) or Perfecto simple. (2), (3) rarely used.

model verb tables

MODO INDICATIVO

PRESENTE	PRETÉRITO IMPERFECTO	PRETÉRITO INDEFINIDO (1)	FUTURO IMPERFECTO
satisfago	satisfac ía	satisfice	satisfaré
satisfac es	satisfac ías	satisficiste	satisfarás
satisfac e	satisfac ía	satisfizo	satisfará
satisfac emos	satisfac íamos	satisficimos	satisfaremos
satisfac éis	satisfac íais	satisficisteis	satisfaréis
satisfac en	satisfac ían	satisficieron	satisfarán

PRETÉRITO PERFECTO		PRETÉRITO PLUSCUAMPERFECTO		PRETÉRITO ANTERIOR		FUTURO PERFECTO	
he	satisfecho	había	satisfecho	hube	satisfecho	habré	satisfecho
has	satisfecho	habías	satisfecho	hubiste	satisfecho	habrás	satisfecho
ha	satisfecho	había	satisfecho	hubo	satisfecho	habrá	satisfecho
hemos	satisfecho	habíamos	satisfecho	hubimos	satisfecho	habremos	satisfecho
habéis	satisfecho	habíais	satisfecho	hubisteis	satisfecho	habréis	satisfecho
han	satisfecho	habían	satisfecho	hubieron	satisfecho	habrán	satisfecho

CONDICIONAL SIMPLE

satisfaría	
satisfarías	
satisfaría	
satisfaríamos	
satisfaríais	
satisfarían	

CONDICIONAL COMPUESTO

habría	satisfecho
habrías	satisfecho
habría	satisfecho
habríamos	satisfecho
habríais	satisfecho
habrían	satisfecho

MODO SUBJUNTIVO

PRESENTE	PRETÉRITO IMPERFECTO		FUTURO IMPERFECTO (2)
satisfaga	satisficiera	or satisficiese	satisficiere
satisfagas	satisficieras	or satisficieses	satisficieres
satisfaga	satisficiera	or satisficiese	satisficiere
satisfagamos	satisficiéramos	or satisficiésemos	satisficiéremos
satisfagáis	satisficierais	or satisficieseis	satisficiereis
satisfagan	satisficieran	or satisficiesen	satisficieren

PRETÉRITO PERFECTO		PRETÉRITO PLUSCUAMPERFECTO			FUTURO PERFECTO (3)	
haya	satisfecho	hubiera	or hubiese	satisfecho	hubiere	satisfecho
hayas	satisfecho	hubieras	or hubieses	satisfecho	hubieres	satisfecho
haya	satisfecho	hubiera	or hubiese	satisfecho	hubiere	satisfecho
hayamos	satisfecho	hubiéramos	or hubiésemos	satisfecho	hubiéremos	satisfecho
hayáis	satisfecho	hubierais	or hubieseis	satisfecho	hubiereis	satisfecho
hayan	satisfecho	hubieran	or hubiesen	satisfecho	hubieren	satisfecho

MODO IMPERATIVO

PRESENTE

satisfaz *or* satisface	tú
satisfaga	él/ella/usted
satisfagamos	nosotros/as
satisfac ed	vosotros/as
satisfagan	ellos/ellas/ustedes

(1) or Perfecto simple. (2), (3) rarely used.

FORMAS NO PERSONALES

FORMAS SIMPLES

INFINITIVO	GERUNDIO	PARTICIPIO
satisfacer	**satisfac** iendo	satisfecho

FORMAS COMPUESTAS

INFINITIVO	GERUNDIO
haber satisfecho	habiendo satisfecho

46. SOLER IRREGULAR (stem change o → ue and defective)   *BE IN THE HABIT OF*

MODO INDICATIVO

PRESENTE	PRETÉRITO IMPERFECTO	PRETÉRITO INDEFINIDO (1)	FUTURO IMPERFECTO
suelo	sol ía	sol í	—
sueles	sol ías	sol iste	—
suele	sol ía	sol ió	—
sol emos	sol íamos	sol imos	—
sol éis	sol íais	sol isteis	—
suelen	sol ían	sol ieron	—

PRETÉRITO PERFECTO		PRETÉRITO PLUSCUAMPERFECTO		PRETÉRITO ANTERIOR		FUTURO PERFECTO	
—	—	—	—	—	—	—	—
—	—	—	—	—	—	—	—
—	—	—	—	—	—	—	—
—	—	—	—	—	—	—	—
—	—	—	—	—	—	—	—
—	—	—	—	—	—	—	—

CONDICIONAL SIMPLE	CONDICIONAL COMPUESTO	
—	—	—
—	—	—
—	—	—
—	—	—
—	—	—

MODO SUBJUNTIVO

PRESENTE	PRETÉRITO IMPERFECTO		FUTURO IMPERFECTO (2)
suela	sol iera	or sol iese	—
suelas	sol ieras	or sol ieses	—
suela	sol iera	or sol iese	—
sol amos	sol iéramos	or sol iésemos	—
sol áis	sol ierais	or sol ieseis	—
suelan	sol ieran	or sol iesen	—

PRETÉRITO PERFECTO		PRETÉRITO PLUSCUAMPERFECTO			FUTURO PERFECTO (3)	
—	—	—	— —	—	—	—
—	—	—	— —	—	—	—
—	—	—	— —	—	—	—
—	—	—	— —	—	—	—
—	—	—	— —	—	—	—
—	—	—	— —	—	—	—

MODO IMPERATIVO

PRESENTE

—	tú
—	él/ella/usted
—	nosotros/as
—	vosotros/as
—	ellos/ellas/ustedes

FORMAS NO PERSONALES

FORMAS SIMPLES

INFINITIVO	GERUNDIO	PARTICIPIO
soler	—	—

FORMAS COMPUESTAS

INFINITIVO	GERUNDIO
—	—

(1) or Perfecto simple. (2), (3) rarely used.

model verb tables

47. TRAER IRREGULAR

BRING, WEAR

MODO INDICATIVO

PRESENTE	PRETÉRITO IMPERFECTO	PRETÉRITO INDEFINIDO (1)	FUTURO IMPERFECTO
traigo	tra ía	traje	traer é
tra es	tra ías	trajiste	traer ás
tra e	tra ía	trajo	traer á
tra emos	tra íamos	trajimos	traer emos
tra éis	tra íais	trajisteis	traer éis
tra en	tra ían	trajeron	traer án

PRETÉRITO PERFECTO		PRETÉRITO PLUSCUAMPERFECTO		PRETÉRITO ANTERIOR		FUTURO PERFECTO	
he	traído	había	traído	hube	traído	habré	traído
has	traído	habías	traído	hubiste	traído	habrás	traído
ha	traído	había	traído	hubo	traído	habrá	traído
hemos	traído	habíamos	traído	hubimos	traído	habremos	traído
habéis	traído	habíais	traído	hubisteis	traído	habréis	traído
han	traído	habían	traído	hubieron	traído	habrán	traído

CONDICIONAL SIMPLE	CONDICIONAL COMPUESTO	
traer ía	habría	traído
traer ías	habrías	traído
traer ía	habría	traído
traer íamos	habríamos	traído
traer íais	habríais	traído
traer ían	habrían	traído

MODO SUBJUNTIVO

PRESENTE	PRETÉRITO IMPERFECTO		FUTURO IMPERFECTO (2)
traiga	trajera	or trajese	trajere
traigas	trajeras	or trajeses	trajeres
traiga	trajera	or trajese	trajere
traigamos	trajéramos	or trajésemos	trajéremos
traigáis	trajerais	or trajeseis	trajereis
traigan	trajeran	or trajesen	trajeren

PRETÉRITO PERFECTO		PRETÉRITO PLUSCUAMPERFECTO			FUTURO PERFECTO (3)	
haya	traído	hubiera	or hubiese	traído	hubiere	traído
hayas	traído	hubieras	or hubieses	traído	hubieres	traído
haya	traído	hubiera	or hubiese	traído	hubiere	traído
hayamos	traído	hubiéramos	or hubiésemos	traído	hubiéremos	traído
hayáis	traído	hubierais	or hubieseis	traído	hubiereis	traído
hayan	traído	hubieran	or hubiesen	traído	hubieren	traído

MODO IMPERATIVO

FORMAS NO PERSONALES

PRESENTE	
tra e	tú
traiga	él/ella/usted
traigamos	nosotros/as
tra ed	vosotros/as
traigan	ellos/ellas/ustedes

FORMAS SIMPLES

INFINITIVO	GERUNDIO	PARTICIPIO
traer	trayendo	traído

FORMAS COMPUESTAS

INFINITIVO	GERUNDIO
haber traído	habiendo traído

(1) or Perfecto simple. (2), (3) rarely used.

model verb tables

48. VALER IRREGULAR

MODO INDICATIVO

PRESENTE	PRETÉRITO IMPERFECTO	PRETÉRITO INDEFINIDO (1)	FUTURO IMPERFECTO
valgo	val ía	val í	valdré
val es	val ías	val iste	valdrás
val e	val ía	val ió	valdrá
val emos	val íamos	val imos	valdremos
val éis	val íais	val isteis	valdréis
val en	val ían	val ieron	valdrán

PRETÉRITO PERFECTO	PRETÉRITO PLUSCUAMPERFECTO	PRETÉRITO ANTERIOR	FUTURO PERFECTO
he valido	había valido	hube valido	habré valido
has valido	habías valido	hubiste valido	habrás valido
ha valido	había valido	hubo valido	habrá valido
hemos valido	habíamos valido	hubimos valido	habremos valido
habéis valido	habíais valido	hubisteis valido	habréis valido
han valido	habían valido	hubieron valido	habrán valido

CONDICIONAL SIMPLE / CONDICIONAL COMPUESTO

CONDICIONAL SIMPLE	CONDICIONAL COMPUESTO
valdría	habría valido
valdrías	habrías valido
valdría	habría valido
valdríamos	habríamos valido
valdríais	habríais valido
valdrían	habrían valido

MODO SUBJUNTIVO

PRESENTE	PRETÉRITO IMPERFECTO	FUTURO IMPERFECTO (2)
valga	val iera or val iese	val iere
valgas	val ieras or val ieses	val ieres
valga	val iera or val iese	val iere
valgamos	val iéramos or val iésemos	val iéremos
valgáis	val ierais or val ieseis	val iereis
valgan	val ieran or val iesen	val ieren

PRETÉRITO PERFECTO	PRETÉRITO PLUSCUAMPERFECTO	FUTURO PERFECTO (3)
haya valido	hubiera or hubiese valido	hubiere valido
hayas valido	hubieras or hubieses valido	hubieres valido
haya valido	hubiera or hubiese valido	hubiere valido
hayamos valido	hubiéramos or hubiésemos valido	hubiéremos valido
hayáis valido	hubierais or hubieseis valido	hubiereis valido
hayan valido	hubieran or hubiesen valido	hubieren valido

MODO IMPERATIVO

PRESENTE

val e	tú
valga	él/ella/usted
valgamos	nosotros/as
val ed	vosotros/as
valgan	ellos/ellas/ustedes

FORMAS NO PERSONALES

FORMAS SIMPLES

INFINITIVO	GERUNDIO	PARTICIPIO
valer	val iendo	val ido

FORMAS COMPUESTAS

INFINITIVO	GERUNDIO
haber valido	habiendo valido

(1) or Perfecto simple. (2), (3) rarely used.

model verb tables

49. VER IRREGULAR   *SEE, LOOK AT*

MODO INDICATIVO

PRESENTE	PRETÉRITO IMPERFECTO	PRETÉRITO INDEFINIDO (1)	FUTURO IMPERFECTO
ve o	ve ía	vi	ver é
ves	ve ías	viste	ver ás
ve	ve ía	vio	ver á
vemos	ve íamos	vimos	ver emos
veis	ve íais	visteis	ver éis
ven	ve ían	vieron	ver án

PRETÉRITO PERFECTO		PRETÉRITO PLUSCUAMPERFECTO		PRETÉRITO ANTERIOR		FUTURO PERFECTO	
he	visto	había	visto	hube	visto	habré	visto
has	visto	habías	visto	hubiste	visto	habrás	visto
ha	visto	había	visto	hubo	visto	habrá	visto
hemos	visto	habíamos	visto	hubimos	visto	habremos	visto
habéis	visto	habíais	visto	hubisteis	visto	habréis	visto
han	visto	habían	visto	hubieron	visto	habrán	visto

CONDICIONAL SIMPLE	CONDICIONAL COMPUESTO	
ver ía	habría	visto
ver ías	habrías	visto
ver ía	habría	visto
ver íamos	habríamos	visto
ver íais	habríais	visto
ver ían	habrían	visto

MODO SUBJUNTIVO

PRESENTE	PRETÉRITO IMPERFECTO		FUTURO IMPERFECTO (2)
ve a	viera	or viese	viere
ve as	vieras	or vieses	vieres
ve a	viera	or viese	viere
ve amos	viéramos	or viésemos	viéremos
ve áis	vierais	or vieseis	viereis
ve an	vieran	or viesen	vieren

PRETÉRITO PERFECTO		PRETÉRITO PLUSCUAMPERFECTO			FUTURO PERFECTO (3)	
haya	visto	hubiera	or hubiese	visto	hubiere	visto
hayas	visto	hubieras	or hubieses	visto	hubieres	visto
haya	visto	hubiera	or hubiese	visto	hubiere	visto
hayamos	visto	hubiéramos	or hubiésemos	visto	hubiéremos	visto
hayáis	visto	hubierais	or hubieseis	visto	hubiereis	visto
hayan	visto	hubieran	or hubiesen	visto	hubieren	visto

MODO IMPERATIVO

FORMAS NO PERSONALES

PRESENTE	
ve	tú
ve a	él/ella/usted
ve amos	nosotros/as
ved	vosotros/as
ve an	ellos/ellas/ustedes

FORMAS SIMPLES

INFINITIVO	GERUNDIO	PARTICIPIO
ver	viendo	visto

FORMAS COMPUESTAS

INFINITIVO	GERUNDIO
haber visto	habiendo visto

(1) or Perfecto simple. (2), (3) rarely used.

Spanish Verb Manual ———— 78 ————

50. YACER IRREGULAR

BE LYING DOWN

MODO INDICATIVO

PRESENTE	PRETÉRITO IMPERFECTO	PRETÉRITO INDEFINIDO (1)	FUTURO IMPERFECTO
yazco *or* yazgo *or* yago	yac ía	yac í	yacer é
yac es	yac ías	yac iste	yacer ás
yac e	yac ía	yac ió	yacer á
yac emos	yac íamos	yac imos	yacer emos
yac éis	yac íais	yac isteis	yacer éis
yac en	yac ían	yac ieron	yacer án

PRETÉRITO PERFECTO	PRETÉRITO PLUSCUAMPERFECTO	PRETÉRITO ANTERIOR	FUTURO PERFECTO
he yacido	había yacido	hube yacido	habré yacido
has yacido	habías yacido	hubiste yacido	habrás yacido
ha yacido	había yacido	hubo yacido	habrá yacido
hemos yacido	habíamos yacido	hubimos yacido	habremos yacido
habéis yacido	habíais yacido	hubisteis yacido	habréis yacido
han yacido	habían yacido	hubieron yacido	habrán yacido

CONDICIONAL SIMPLE

CONDICIONAL COMPUESTO

CONDICIONAL SIMPLE	CONDICIONAL COMPUESTO
yacería	habría yacido
yacerías	habrías yacido
yacería	habría yacido
yaceríamos	habríamos yacido
yaceríais	habríais yacido
yacerían	habrían yacido

MODO SUBJUNTIVO

PRESENTE			PRETÉRITO IMPERFECTO		FUTURO IMPERFECTO (2)
yazca *or* yazga	*or* yaga	yac iera	*or* yac iese	yac iere
yazcas *or* yazgas	*or* yagas	yac ieras	*or* yac ieses	yac ieres
yazca *or* yazga	*or* yaga	yac iera	*or* yac iese	yac iere
yazcamos *or* yazgamos	*or* yagamos	yac iéramos	*or* yac iésemos	yac iéremos
yazcáis *or* yazgáis	*or* yagáis	yac ierais	*or* yac ieseis	yac iereis
yazcan *or* yazgan	*or* yagan	yac ieran	*or* yac iesen	yac ieren

PRETÉRITO PERFECTO	PRETÉRITO PLUSCUAMPERFECTO		FUTURO PERFECTO (3)
haya yacido	hubiera *or* hubiese	yacido	hubiere yacido
hayas yacido	hubieras *or* hubieses	yacido	hubieres yacido
haya yacido	hubiera *or* hubiese	yacido	hubiere yacido
hayamos yacido	hubiéramos *or* hubiésemos	yacido	hubiéremos yacido
hayáis yacido	hubierais *or* hubieseis	yacido	hubiereis yacido
hayan yacido	hubieran *or* hubiesen	yacido	hubieren yacido

MODO IMPERATIVO

FORMAS NO PERSONALES

PRESENTE

yac e *or* yaz	tú
yazca *or* yazga *or* yaga	él/ella/usted
yazcamos *or* yazgamos *or* yagamos	nosotros/as
yac ed	vosotros/as
yazcan *or* yazgan *or* yagan	ellos/ellas/ustedes

FORMAS SIMPLES

INFINITIVO	GERUNDIO	PARTICIPIO
yacer	yac iendo	yac ido

FORMAS COMPUESTAS

INFINITIVO	GERUNDIO
haber yacido	habiendo yacido

(1) or Perfecto simple. (2), (3) rarely used.

– ire

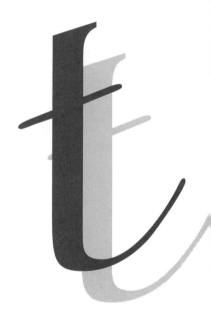

51. VIVIR
52. dirigir
53. distinguir
54. esparcir
55. prohibir
56. reunir
57. mullir
58. bruñir
59. concluir
60. pedir
61. corregir
62. seguir
63. reír
64. teñir
65. sentir
66. discernir
67. adquirir
68. dormir
69. traducir
70. lucir
71. abolir
72. asir
73. bendecir
74. decir
75. delinquir
76. erguir
77. ir
78. oír
79. salir
80. venir

51. VIVIR REGULAR — *LIVE*

MODO INDICATIVO

PRESENTE	PRETÉRITO IMPERFECTO	PRETÉRITO INDEFINIDO (1)	FUTURO IMPERFECTO
viv o	viv ía	viv í	vivir é
viv es	viv ías	viv iste	vivir ás
viv e	viv ía	viv ió	vivir á
viv imos	viv íamos	viv imos	vivir emos
viv ís	viv íais	viv isteis	vivir éis
viv en	viv ían	viv ieron	vivir án

PRETÉRITO PERFECTO		PRETÉRITO PLUSCUAMPERFECTO		PRETÉRITO ANTERIOR		FUTURO PERFECTO	
he	vivido	había	vivido	hube	vivido	habré	vivido
has	vivido	habías	vivido	hubiste	vivido	habrás	vivido
ha	vivido	había	vivido	hubo	vivido	habrá	vivido
hemos	vivido	habíamos	vivido	hubimos	vivido	habremos	vivido
habéis	vivido	habíais	vivido	hubisteis	vivido	habréis	vivido
han	vivido	habían	vivido	hubieron	vivido	habrán	vivido

CONDICIONAL SIMPLE / CONDICIONAL COMPUESTO

CONDICIONAL SIMPLE	CONDICIONAL COMPUESTO	
vivir ía	habría	vivido
vivir ías	habrías	vivido
vivir ía	habría	vivido
vivir íamos	habríamos	vivido
vivir íais	habríais	vivido
vivir ían	habrían	vivido

MODO SUBJUNTIVO

PRESENTE	PRETÉRITO IMPERFECTO		FUTURO IMPERFECTO (2)
viv a	viv iera	or viv iese	viv iere
viv as	viv ieras	or viv ieses	viv ieres
viv a	viv iera	or viv iese	viv iere
viv amos	viv iéramos	or viv iésemos	viv iéremos
viv áis	viv ierais	or viv ieseis	viv iereis
viv an	viv ieran	or viv iesen	viv ieren

PRETÉRITO PERFECTO		PRETÉRITO PLUSCUAMPERFECTO			FUTURO PERFECTO (3)	
haya	vivido	hubiera	or hubiese	vivido	hubiere	vivido
hayas	vivido	hubieras	or hubieses	vivido	hubieres	vivido
haya	vivido	hubiera	or hubiese	vivido	hubiere	vivido
hayamos	vivido	hubiéramos	or hubiésemos	vivido	hubiéremos	vivido
hayáis	vivido	hubierais	or hubieseis	vivido	hubiereis	vivido
hayan	vivido	hubieran	or hubiesen	vivido	hubieren	vivido

MODO IMPERATIVO

PRESENTE

viv e	tú
viv a	él/ella/usted
viv amos	nosotros/as
viv id	vosotros/as
viv an	ellos/ellas/ustedes

FORMAS NO PERSONALES

FORMAS SIMPLES

INFINITIVO	GERUNDIO	PARTICIPIO
vivir	viv iendo	viv ido

FORMAS COMPUESTAS

INFINITIVO	GERUNDIO
haber vivido	habiendo vivido

(1) or Perfecto simple. (2), (3) rarely used.

model verb tables

52. DIRIGIR SPELLING CHANGE (g → j)

DIRECT, ADDRESS

MODO INDICATIVO

PRESENTE	PRETÉRITO IMPERFECTO	PRETÉRITO INDEFINIDO (1)	FUTURO IMPERFECTO
dirijo	dirig ía	dirig í	dirigir é
dirig es	dirig ías	dirig iste	dirigir ás
dirig e	dirig ía	dirig ió	dirigir á
dirig imos	dirig íamos	dirig imos	dirigir emos
dirig ís	dirig íais	dirig isteis	dirigir éis
dirig en	dirig ían	dirig ieron	dirigir án

PRETÉRITO PERFECTO	PRETÉRITO PLUSCUAMPERFECTO	PRETÉRITO ANTERIOR	FUTURO PERFECTO
he dirigido	había dirigido	hube dirigido	habré dirigido
has dirigido	habías dirigido	hubiste dirigido	habrás dirigido
ha dirigido	había dirigido	hubo dirigido	habrá dirigido
hemos dirigido	habíamos dirigido	hubimos dirigido	habremos dirigido
habéis dirigido	habíais dirigido	hubisteis dirigido	habréis dirigido
han dirigido	habían dirigido	hubieron dirigido	habrán dirigido

CONDICIONAL SIMPLE

CONDICIONAL COMPUESTO

CONDICIONAL SIMPLE	CONDICIONAL COMPUESTO	
dirigir ía	habría	dirigido
dirigir ías	habrías	dirigido
dirigir ía	habría	dirigido
dirigir íamos	habríamos	dirigido
dirigir íais	habríais	dirigido
dirigir ían	habrían	dirigido

MODO SUBJUNTIVO

PRESENTE	PRETÉRITO IMPERFECTO		FUTURO IMPERFECTO (2)
dirija	dirig iera	or dirig iese	dirig iere
dirijas	dirig ieras	or dirig ieses	dirig ieres
dirija	dirig iera	or dirig iese	dirig iere
dirijamos	dirig iéramos	or dirig iésemos	dirig iéremos
dirijáis	dirig ierais	or dirig ieseis	dirig iereis
dirijan	dirig ieran	or dirig iesen	dirig ieren

PRETÉRITO PERFECTO	PRETÉRITO PLUSCUAMPERFECTO		FUTURO PERFECTO (3)
haya dirigido	hubiera or hubiese dirigido		hubiere dirigido
hayas dirigido	hubieras or hubieses dirigido		hubieres dirigido
haya dirigido	hubiera or hubiese dirigido		hubiere dirigido
hayamos dirigido	hubiéramos or hubiésemos dirigido		hubiéremos dirigido
hayáis dirigido	hubierais or hubieseis dirigido		hubiereis dirigido
hayan dirigido	hubieran or hubiesen dirigido		hubieren dirigido

MODO IMPERATIVO

FORMAS NO PERSONALES

PRESENTE

dirig e	tú
dirija	él/ella/usted
dirijamos	nosotros/as
dirig id	vosotros/as
dirijan	ellos/ellas/ustedes

FORMAS SIMPLES

INFINITIVO	GERUNDIO	PARTICIPIO
dirigir	dirig iendo	dirig ido

FORMAS COMPUESTAS

INFINITIVO	GERUNDIO
haber dirigido	habiendo dirigido

(1) or Perfecto simple. (2), (3) rarely used.

model verb tables

53. DISTINGUIR SPELLING CHANGE (gu → g) — DISTINGUISH

MODO INDICATIVO

PRESENTE	PRETÉRITO IMPERFECTO	PRETÉRITO INDEFINIDO (1)	FUTURO IMPERFECTO
distingo	distingu ía	distingu í	distinguir é
distingu es	distingu ías	distingu iste	distinguir ás
distingu e	distingu ía	distingu ió	distinguir á
distingu imos	distingu íamos	distingu imos	distinguir emos
distingu ís	distingu íais	distingu isteis	distinguir éis
distingu en	distingu ían	distingu ieron	distinguir án

PRETÉRITO PERFECTO		PRETÉRITO PLUSCUAMPERFECTO		PRETÉRITO ANTERIOR		FUTURO PERFECTO	
he	distinguido	había	distinguido	hube	distinguido	habré	distinguido
has	distinguido	habías	distinguido	hubiste	distinguido	habrás	distinguido
ha	distinguido	había	distinguido	hubo	distinguido	habrá	distinguido
hemos	distinguido	habíamos	distinguido	hubimos	distinguido	habremos	distinguido
habéis	distinguido	habíais	distinguido	hubisteis	distinguido	habréis	distinguido
han	distinguido	habían	distinguido	hubieron	distinguido	habrán	distinguido

CONDICIONAL SIMPLE

distinguir ía
distinguir ías
distinguir ía
distinguir íamos
distinguir íais
distinguir ían

CONDICIONAL COMPUESTO

habría	distinguido
habrías	distinguido
habría	distinguido
habríamos	distinguido
habríais	distinguido
habrían	distinguido

MODO SUBJUNTIVO

PRESENTE	PRETÉRITO IMPERFECTO		FUTURO IMPERFECTO (2)
distinga	distingu iera	or distingu iese	distingu iere
distingas	distingu ieras	or distingu ieses	distingu ieres
distinga	distingu iera	or distingu iese	distingu iere
distingamos	distingu iéramos	or distingu iésemos	distingu iéremos
distingáis	distingu ierais	or distingu ieseis	distingu iereis
distingan	distingu ieran	or distingu iesen	distingu ieren

PRETÉRITO PERFECTO		PRETÉRITO PLUSCUAMPERFECTO			FUTURO PERFECTO (3)	
haya	distinguido	hubiera	or hubiese	distinguido	hubiere	distinguido
hayas	distinguido	hubieras	or hubieses	distinguido	hubieres	distinguido
haya	distinguido	hubiera	or hubiese	distinguido	hubiere	distinguido
hayamos	distinguido	hubiéramos	or hubiésemos	distinguido	hubiéremos	distinguido
hayáis	distinguido	hubierais	or hubieseis	distinguido	hubiereis	distinguido
hayan	distinguido	hubieran	or hubiesen	distinguido	hubieren	distinguido

MODO IMPERATIVO

PRESENTE

distingu e	tú
distinga	él/ella/usted
distingamos	nosotros/as
distingu id	vosotros/as
distingan	ellos/ellas/ustedes

FORMAS NO PERSONALES

FORMAS SIMPLES

INFINITIVO	GERUNDIO	PARTICIPIO
distinguir	distingu iendo	distingu ido

FORMAS COMPUESTAS

INFINITIVO	GERUNDIO
haber distinguido	habiendo distinguido

(1) or Perfecto simple. (2), (3) rarely used.

model verb tables

54. ESPARCIR SPELLING CHANGE (c → z) SCATTER

MODO INDICATIVO			

PRESENTE	PRETÉRITO IMPERFECTO	PRETÉRITO INDEFINIDO (1)	FUTURO IMPERFECTO
esparzo	esparc ía	esparc í	esparcir é
esparc es	esparc ías	esparc iste	esparcir ás
esparc e	esparc ía	esparc ió	esparcir á
esparc emos	esparc íamos	esparc imos	esparcir emos
esparc ís	esparc íais	esparc isteis	esparcir éis
esparc en	esparc ían	esparc ieron	esparcir án

PRETÉRITO PERFECTO		PRETÉRITO PLUSCUAMPERFECTO		PRETÉRITO ANTERIOR		FUTURO PERFECTO	
he	esparcido	había	esparcido	hube	esparcido	habré	esparcido
has	esparcido	habías	esparcido	hubiste	esparcido	habrás	esparcido
ha	esparcido	había	esparcido	hubo	esparcido	habrá	esparcido
hemos	esparcido	habíamos	esparcido	hubimos	esparcido	habremos	esparcido
habéis	esparcido	habíais	esparcido	hubisteis	esparcido	habréis	esparcido
han	esparcido	habían	esparcido	hubieron	esparcido	habrán	esparcido

CONDICIONAL SIMPLE	CONDICIONAL COMPUESTO	
esparcir ía	habría	esparcido
esparcir ías	habrías	esparcido
esparcir ía	habría	esparcido
esparcir íamos	habríamos	esparcido
esparcir íais	habríais	esparcido
esparcir ían	habrían	esparcido

MODO SUBJUNTIVO		

PRESENTE	PRETÉRITO IMPERFECTO			FUTURO IMPERFECTO (2)
esparza	esparc iera	or	esparc iese	esparc iere
esparzas	esparc ieras	or	esparc ieses	esparc ieres
esparza	esparc iera	or	esparc iese	esparc iere
esparzamos	esparc iéramos	or	esparc iésemos	esparc iéremos
esparzáis	esparc ierais	or	esparc ieseis	esparc iereis
esparzan	esparc ieran	or	esparc iesen	esparc ieren

PRETÉRITO PERFECTO		PRETÉRITO PLUSCUAMPERFECTO			FUTURO PERFECTO (3)		
haya	esparcido	hubiera	or	hubiese	esparcido	hubiere	esparcido
hayas	esparcido	hubieras	or	hubieses	esparcido	hubieres	esparcido
haya	esparcido	hubiera	or	hubiese	esparcido	hubiere	esparcido
hayamos	esparcido	hubiéramos	or	hubiésemos	esparcido	hubiéremos	esparcido
hayáis	esparcido	hubierais	or	hubieseis	esparcido	hubiereis	esparcido
hayan	esparcido	hubieran	or	hubiesen	esparcido	hubieren	esparcido

MODO IMPERATIVO	FORMAS NO PERSONALES

PRESENTE

esparc e	tú
esparza	él/ella/usted
esparzamos	nosotros/as
esparc id	vosotros/as
esparzan	ellos/ellas/ustedes

FORMAS SIMPLES

INFINITIVO	GERUNDIO	PARTICIPIO
esparcir	esparc iendo	esparc ido

FORMAS COMPUESTAS

INFINITIVO	GERUNDIO
haber esparcido	habiendo esparcido

(1) or Perfecto simple. (2), (3) rarely used.

55. PROHIBIR ACCENT CHANGE (i → í)   *PROHIBIT*

MODO INDICATIVO

PRESENTE	PRETÉRITO IMPERFECTO	PRETÉRITO INDEFINIDO (1)	FUTURO IMPERFECTO
prohíbo	prohib ía	prohib í	prohibir é
prohíbes	prohib ías	prohib iste	prohibir ás
prohíbe	prohib ía	prohib ió	prohibir á
prohib imos	prohib íamos	prohib imos	prohibir emos
prohib ís	prohib íais	prohib isteis	prohibir éis
prohíben	prohib ían	prohib ieron	prohibir án

PRETÉRITO PERFECTO		PRETÉRITO PLUSCUAMPERFECTO		PRETÉRITO ANTERIOR		FUTURO PERFECTO	
he	prohibido	había	prohibido	hube	prohibido	habré	prohibido
has	prohibido	habías	prohibido	hubiste	prohibido	habrás	prohibido
ha	prohibido	había	prohibido	hubo	prohibido	habrá	prohibido
hemos	prohibido	habíamos	prohibido	hubimos	prohibido	habremos	prohibido
habéis	prohibido	habíais	prohibido	hubisteis	prohibido	habréis	prohibido
han	prohibido	habían	prohibido	hubieron	prohibido	habrán	prohibido

CONDICIONAL SIMPLE

CONDICIONAL COMPUESTO

prohibir ía	habría prohibido
prohibir ías	habrías prohibido
prohibir ía	habría prohibido
prohibir íamos	habríamos prohibido
prohibir íais	habríais prohibido
prohibir ían	habrían prohibido

MODO SUBJUNTIVO

PRESENTE	PRETÉRITO IMPERFECTO		FUTURO IMPERFECTO (2)
prohíba	prohib iera	or prohib iese	prohib iere
prohíbas	prohib ieras	or prohib ieses	prohib ieres
prohíba	prohib iera	or prohib iese	prohib iere
prohib amos	prohib iéramos	or prohib iésemos	prohib iéremos
prohib áis	prohib ierais	or prohib ieseis	prohib iereis
prohíban	prohib ieran	or prohib iesen	prohib ieren

PRETÉRITO PERFECTO		PRETÉRITO PLUSCUAMPERFECTO			FUTURO PERFECTO (3)	
haya	prohibido	hubiera	or hubiese	prohibido	hubiere	prohibido
hayas	prohibido	hubieras	or hubieses	prohibido	hubieres	prohibido
haya	prohibido	hubiera	or hubiese	prohibido	hubiere	prohibido
hayamos	prohibido	hubiéramos	or hubiésemos	prohibido	hubiéremos	prohibido
hayáis	prohibido	hubierais	or hubieseis	prohibido	hubiereis	prohibido
hayan	prohibido	hubieran	or hubiesen	prohibido	hubieren	prohibido

MODO IMPERATIVO

FORMAS NO PERSONALES

PRESENTE

prohíbe	tú
prohíba	él/ella/usted
prohib amos	nosotros/as
prohib id	vosotros/as
prohíban	ellos/ellas/ustedes

FORMAS SIMPLES

INFINITIVO	GERUNDIO	PARTICIPIO
prohibir	prohib iendo	prohib ido

FORMAS COMPUESTAS

INFINITIVO	GERUNDIO
haber prohibido	habiendo prohibido

(1) or Perfecto simple. (2), (3) rarely used.

model verb tables

56. REUNIR ACCENT CHANGE (u → ú)

MODO INDICATIVO

PRESENTE	PRETÉRITO IMPERFECTO	PRETÉRITO INDEFINIDO (1)	FUTURO IMPERFECTO
reúno	reun ía	reun í	reunir é
reúnes	reun ías	reun iste	reunir ás
reúne	reun ía	reun ió	reunir á
reun imos	reun íamos	reun imos	reunir emos
reun ís	reun íais	reun isteis	reunir éis
reúnen	reun ían	reun ieron	reunir án

PRETÉRITO PERFECTO		PRETÉRITO PLUSCUAMPERFECTO		PRETÉRITO ANTERIOR		FUTURO PERFECTO	
he	reunido	había	reunido	hube	reunido	habré	reunido
has	reunido	habías	reunido	hubiste	reunido	habrás	reunido
ha	reunido	había	reunido	hubo	reunido	habrá	reunido
hemos	reunido	habíamos	reunido	hubimos	reunido	habremos	reunido
habéis	reunido	habíais	reunido	hubisteis	reunido	habréis	reunido
han	reunido	habían	reunido	hubieron	reunido	habrán	reunido

CONDICIONAL SIMPLE

CONDICIONAL COMPUESTO

CONDICIONAL SIMPLE	CONDICIONAL COMPUESTO	
reunir ía	habría	reunido
reunir ías	habrías	reunido
reunir ía	habría	reunido
reunir íamos	habríamos	reunido
reunir íais	habríais	reunido
reunir ían	habrían	reunido

MODO SUBJUNTIVO

PRESENTE	PRETÉRITO IMPERFECTO		FUTURO IMPERFECTO (2)
reúna	reun iera	*or* reun iese	reun iere
reúnas	reun ieras	*or* reun ieses	reun ieres
reúna	reun iera	*or* reun iese	reun iere
reun amos	reun iéramos	*or* reun iésemos	reun iéremos
reun áis	reun ierais	*or* reun ieseis	reun iereis
reúnan	reun ieran	*or* reun iesen	reun ieren

PRETÉRITO PERFECTO		PRETÉRITO PLUSCUAMPERFECTO			FUTURO PERFECTO (3)	
haya	reunido	hubiera	*or* hubiese	reunido	hubiere	reunido
hayas	reunido	hubieras	*or* hubieses	reunido	hubieres	reunido
haya	reunido	hubiera	*or* hubiese	reunido	hubiere	reunido
hayamos	reunido	hubiéramos	*or* hubiésemos	reunido	hubiéremos	reunido
hayáis	reunido	hubierais	*or* hubieseis	reunido	hubiereis	reunido
hayan	reunido	hubieran	*or* hubiesen	reunido	hubieren	reunido

MODO IMPERATIVO

FORMAS NO PERSONALES

PRESENTE

reúne	tú
reúna	él/ella/usted
reun amos	nosotros/as
reun id	vosotros/as
reúnan	ellos/ellas/ustedes

FORMAS SIMPLES

INFINITIVO	GERUNDIO	PARTICIPIO
reunir	reun iendo	reun ido

FORMAS COMPUESTAS

INFINITIVO	GERUNDIO
haber reunido	habiendo reunido

(1) or Perfecto simple. (2), (3) rarely used.

57. MULLIR SPELLING CHANGE

FLUFF, BEAT UP

MODO INDICATIVO

PRESENTE	PRETÉRITO IMPERFECTO	PRETÉRITO INDEFINIDO (1)	FUTURO IMPERFECTO
mull o	**mull** ía	**mull** í	**mullir** é
mull es	**mull** ías	**mull** iste	**mullir** ás
mull e	**mull** ía	mulló	**mullir** á
mull imos	**mull** íamos	**mull** imos	**mullir** emos
mull ís	**mull** íais	**mull** isteis	**mullir** éis
mull en	**mull** ían	mulleron	**mullir** án

PRETÉRITO PERFECTO		PRETÉRITO PLUSCUAMPERFECTO		PRETÉRITO ANTERIOR		FUTURO PERFECTO	
he	mullido	había	mullido	hube	mullido	habré	mullido
has	mullido	habías	mullido	hubiste	mullido	habrás	mullido
ha	mullido	había	mullido	hubo	mullido	habrá	mullido
hemos	mullido	habíamos	mullido	hubimos	mullido	habremos	mullido
habéis	mullido	habíais	mullido	hubisteis	mullido	habréis	mullido
han	mullido	habían	mullido	hubieron	mullido	habrán	mullido

CONDICIONAL SIMPLE

	CONDICIONAL COMPUESTO	
mullir ía	habría	mullido
mullir ías	habrías	mullido
mullir ía	habría	mullido
mullir íamos	habríamos	mullido
mullir íais	habríais	mullido
mullir ían	habrían	mullido

MODO SUBJUNTIVO

PRESENTE	PRETÉRITO IMPERFECTO		FUTURO IMPERFECTO (2)
mull a	mullera	*or* **mullese**	mullere
mull as	mulleras	*or* **mulleses**	mulleres
mull a	mullera	*or* **mullese**	mullere
mull amos	mulléramos	*or* **mullésemos**	mulléremos
mull áis	mullerais	*or* **mulleseis**	mullereis
mull an	mulleran	*or* **mullesen**	mulleren

PRETÉRITO PERFECTO		PRETÉRITO PLUSCUAMPERFECTO			FUTURO PERFECTO (3)	
haya	mullido	hubiera	*or* hubiese	mullido	hubiere	mullido
hayas	mullido	hubieras	*or* hubieses	mullido	hubieres	mullido
haya	mullido	hubiera	*or* hubiese	mullido	hubiere	mullido
hayamos	mullido	hubiéramos	*or* hubiésemos	mullido	hubiéremos	mullido
hayáis	mullido	hubierais	*or* hubieseis	mullido	hubiereis	mullido
hayan	mullido	hubieran	*or* hubiesen	mullido	hubieren	mullido

MODO IMPERATIVO

FORMAS NO PERSONALES

PRESENTE

mulle	tú
mulla	él/ella/usted
mullamos	nosotros/as
mullid	vosotros/as
mullan	ellos/ellas/ustedes

FORMAS SIMPLES

INFINITIVO	GERUNDIO	PARTICIPIO
mullir	mullendo	**mull** ido

FORMAS COMPUESTAS

INFINITIVO	GERUNDIO
haber mullido	habiendo mullido

(1) or Perfecto simple. (2), (3) rarely used.

model verb tables

58. BRUÑIR SPELLING CHANGE

POLISH

MODO INDICATIVO

PRESENTE	PRETÉRITO IMPERFECTO	PRETÉRITO INDEFINIDO (1)	FUTURO IMPERFECTO
bruñ o	bruñ ía	bruñ í	bruñir é
bruñ es	bruñ ías	bruñ iste	bruñir ás
bruñ e	bruñ ía	bruñó	bruñir á
bruñ imos	bruñ íamos	bruñ imos	bruñir emos
bruñ ís	bruñ íais	bruñ isteis	bruñir éis
bruñ en	bruñ ían	bruñeron	bruñir án

PRETÉRITO PERFECTO		PRETÉRITO PLUSCUAMPERFECTO		PRETÉRITO ANTERIOR		FUTURO PERFECTO	
he	bruñido	había	bruñido	hube	bruñido	habré	bruñido
has	bruñido	habías	bruñido	hubiste	bruñido	habrás	bruñido
ha	bruñido	había	bruñido	hubo	bruñido	habrá	bruñido
hemos	bruñido	habíamos	bruñido	hubimos	bruñido	habremos	bruñido
habéis	bruñido	habíais	bruñido	hubisteis	bruñido	habréis	bruñido
han	bruñido	habían	bruñido	hubieron	bruñido	habrán	bruñido

CONDICIONAL SIMPLE

	CONDICIONAL COMPUESTO	
bruñir ía	habría	bruñido
bruñir ías	habrías	bruñido
bruñir ía	habría	bruñido
bruñir íamos	habríamos	bruñido
bruñir íais	habríais	bruñido
bruñir ían	habrían	bruñido

MODO SUBJUNTIVO

PRESENTE	PRETÉRITO IMPERFECTO			FUTURO IMPERFECTO (2)
bruñ a	bruñera	*or*	bruñese	bruñere
bruñ as	bruñeras	*or*	bruñeses	bruñeres
bruñ a	bruñera	*or*	bruñese	bruñere
bruñ amos	bruñéramos	*or*	bruñésemos	bruñéremos
bruñ áis	bruñerais	*or*	bruñeseis	bruñereis
bruñ an	bruñeran	*or*	bruñesen	bruñeren

PRETÉRITO PERFECTO		PRETÉRITO PLUSCUAMPERFECTO				FUTURO PERFECTO (3)	
haya	bruñido	hubiera	*or*	hubiese	bruñido	hubiere	bruñido
hayas	bruñido	hubieras	*or*	hubieses	bruñido	hubieres	bruñido
haya	bruñido	hubiera	*or*	hubiese	bruñido	hubiere	bruñido
hayamos	bruñido	hubiéramos	*or*	hubiésemos	bruñido	hubiéremos	bruñido
hayáis	bruñido	hubierais	*or*	hubieseis	bruñido	hubiereis	bruñido
hayan	bruñido	hubieran	*or*	hubiesen	bruñido	hubieren	bruñido

MODO IMPERATIVO

FORMAS NO PERSONALES

PRESENTE	
bruñ e	tú
bruñ a	él/ella/usted
bruñ amos	nosotros/as
bruñ id	vosotros/as
bruñ an	ellos/ellas/ustedes

FORMAS SIMPLES

INFINITIVO	GERUNDIO	PARTICIPIO
bruñir	bruñendo	bruñ ido

FORMAS COMPUESTAS

INFINITIVO	GERUNDIO
haber bruñido	habiendo bruñido

(1) or Perfecto simple. (2), (3) rarely used.

59. CONCLUIR IRREGULAR (stem change i → y)   *FINISH*

MODO INDICATIVO

PRESENTE	PRETÉRITO IMPERFECTO	PRETÉRITO INDEFINIDO (1)	FUTURO IMPERFECTO
concluyo	conclu ía	conclu í	concluir é
concluyes	conclu ías	conclu iste	concluir ás
concluye	conclu ía	concluyó	concluir á
conclu imos	conclu íamos	conclu imos	concluir emos
conclu ís	conclu íais	conclu isteis	concluir éis
concluyen	conclu ían	concluyeron	concluir án

PRETÉRITO PERFECTO		PRETÉRITO PLUSCUAMPERFECTO		PRETÉRITO ANTERIOR		FUTURO PERFECTO	
he	concluido	había	concluido	hube	concluido	habré	concluido
has	concluido	habías	concluido	hubiste	concluido	habrás	concluido
ha	concluido	había	concluido	hubo	concluido	habrá	concluido
hemos	concluido	habíamos	concluido	hubimos	concluido	habremos	concluido
habéis	concluido	habíais	concluido	hubisteis	concluido	habréis	concluido
han	concluido	habían	concluido	hubieron	concluido	habrán	concluido

CONDICIONAL SIMPLE | CONDICIONAL COMPUESTO

CONDICIONAL SIMPLE	CONDICIONAL COMPUESTO	
concluir ía	habría	concluido
concluir ías	habrías	concluido
concluir ía	habría	concluido
concluir íamos	habríamos	concluido
concluir íais	habríais	concluido
concluir ían	habrían	concluido

MODO SUBJUNTIVO

PRESENTE	PRETÉRITO IMPERFECTO		FUTURO IMPERFECTO (2)
concluya	concluyera	or concluyese	concluyere
concluyas	concluyeras	or concluyeses	concluyeres
concluya	concluyera	or concluyese	concluyere
concluyamos	concluyéramos	or concluyésemos	concluyéremos
concluyáis	concluyerais	or concluyeseis	concluyereis
concluyan	concluyeran	or concluyesen	concluyeren

PRETÉRITO PERFECTO		PRETÉRITO PLUSCUAMPERFECTO			FUTURO PERFECTO (3)	
haya	concluido	hubiera	or hubiese	concluido	hubiere	concluido
hayas	concluido	hubieras	or hubieses	concluido	hubieres	concluido
haya	concluido	hubiera	or hubiese	concluido	hubiere	concluido
hayamos	concluido	hubiéramos	or hubiésemos	concluido	hubiéremos	concluido
hayáis	concluido	hubierais	or hubieseis	concluido	hubiereis	concluido
hayan	concluido	hubieran	or hubiesen	concluido	hubieren	concluido

MODO IMPERATIVO | FORMAS NO PERSONALES

PRESENTE

concluye	tú
concluya	él/ella/usted
concluyamos	nosotros/as
conclu id	vosotros/as
concluyan	ellos/ellas/ustedes

FORMAS SIMPLES

INFINITIVO	GERUNDIO	PARTICIPIO
concluir	concluyendo	conclu ido

FORMAS COMPUESTAS

INFINITIVO	GERUNDIO
haber concluido	habiendo concluido

(1) or Perfecto simple. (2), (3) rarely used.

model verb tables

60. PEDIR IRREGULAR (stem change e → i)   ASK FOR, ORDER

MODO INDICATIVO

PRESENTE	PRETÉRITO IMPERFECTO	PRETÉRITO INDEFINIDO (1)	FUTURO IMPERFECTO
pido	ped ía	ped í	pedir é
pides	ped ías	ped iste	pedir ás
pide	ped ía	pidió	pedir á
ped imos	ped íamos	ped imos	pedir emos
ped ís	ped íais	ped isteis	pedir éis
piden	ped ían	pidieron	pedi rán

PRETÉRITO PERFECTO	PRETÉRITO PLUSCUAMPERFECTO	PRETÉRITO ANTERIOR	FUTURO PERFECTO
he pedido	había pedido	hube pedido	habré pedido
has pedido	habías pedido	hubiste pedido	habrás pedido
ha pedido	había pedido	hubo pedido	habrá pedido
hemos pedido	habíamos pedido	hubimos pedido	habremos pedido
habéis pedido	habíais pedido	hubisteis pedido	habréis pedido
han pedido	habían pedido	hubieron pedido	habrán pedido

CONDICIONAL SIMPLE

pedir ía	
pedir ías	
pedir ía	
pedir íamos	
pedir íais	
pedir ían	

CONDICIONAL COMPUESTO

habría pedido
habrías pedido
habría pedido
habríamos pedido
habríais pedido
habrían pedido

MODO SUBJUNTIVO

PRESENTE	PRETÉRITO IMPERFECTO		FUTURO IMPERFECTO (2)
pida	pidiera	or pidiese	pidiere
pidas	pidieras	or pidieses	pidieres
pida	pidiera	or pidiese	pidiere
pidamos	pidiéramos	or pidiésemos	pidiéremos
pidáis	pidierais	or pidieseis	pidiereis
pidan	pidieran	or pidiesen	pidieren

PRETÉRITO PERFECTO	PRETÉRITO PLUSCUAMPERFECTO		FUTURO PERFECTO (3)
haya pedido	hubiera or hubiese pedido		hubiere pedido
hayas pedido	hubieras or hubieses pedido		hubieres pedido
haya pedido	hubiera or hubiese pedido		hubiere pedido
hayamos pedido	hubiéramos or hubiésemos pedido		hubiéremos pedido
hayáis pedido	hubierais or hubieseis pedido		hubiereis pedido
hayan pedido	hubieran or hubiesen pedido		hubieren pedido

MODO IMPERATIVO

PRESENTE

pide	tú
pida	él/ella/usted
pidamos	nosotros/as
ped id	vosotros/as
pidan	ellos/ellas/ustedes

FORMAS NO PERSONALES

FORMAS SIMPLES

INFINITIVO	GERUNDIO	PARTICIPIO
pedir	pidiendo	ped ido

FORMAS COMPUESTAS

INFINITIVO	GERUNDIO
haber pedido	habiendo pedido

(1) or Perfecto simple. (2), (3) rarely used.

61. CORREGIR IRREGULAR (stem change e → i + spelling change g → j)   CORRECT

MODO INDICATIVO

PRESENTE	PRETÉRITO IMPERFECTO	PRETÉRITO INDEFINIDO (1)	FUTURO IMPERFECTO
corrijo	correg ía	correg í	corregir é
corriges	correg ías	correg iste	corregir ás
corrige	correg ía	corrigió	corregir á
correg imos	correg íamos	correg imos	corregir emos
correg ís	correg íais	correg isteis	corregir éis
corrigen	correg ían	corrigieron	corregir án

PRETÉRITO PERFECTO	PRETÉRITO PLUSCUAMPERFECTO	PRETÉRITO ANTERIOR	FUTURO PERFECTO
he corregido	había corregido	hube corregido	habré corregido
has corregido	habías corregido	hubiste corregido	habrás corregido
ha corregido	había corregido	hubo corregido	habrá corregido
hemos corregido	habíamos corregido	hubimos corregido	habremos corregido
habéis corregido	habíais corregido	hubisteis corregido	habréis corregido
han corregido	habían corregido	hubieron corregido	habrán corregido

CONDICIONAL SIMPLE

corregir ía
corregir ías
corregir ía
corregir íamos
corregir íais
corregir ían

CONDICIONAL COMPUESTO

habría corregido
habrías corregido
habría corregido
habríamos corregido
habríais corregido
habrían corregido

MODO SUBJUNTIVO

PRESENTE	PRETÉRITO IMPERFECTO		FUTURO IMPERFECTO (2)
corrija	corrigiera	or corrigiese	corrigiere
corrijas	corrigieras	or corrigieses	corrigieres
corrija	corrigiera	or corrigiese	corrigiere
corrijamos	corrigiéramos	or corrigiésemos	corrigiéremos
corrijáis	corrigierais	or corrigieseis	corrigiereis
corrijan	corrigieran	or corrigiesen	corrigieren

PRETÉRITO PERFECTO	PRETÉRITO PLUSCUAMPERFECTO		FUTURO PERFECTO (3)
haya corregido	hubiera or hubiese corregido		hubiere corregido
hayas corregido	hubieras or hubieses corregido		hubieres corregido
haya corregido	hubiera or hubiese corregido		hubiere corregido
hayamos corregido	hubiéramos or hubiésemos corregido		hubiéremos corregido
hayáis corregido	hubierais or hubieseis corregido		hubiereis corregido
hayan corregido	hubieran or hubiesen corregido		hubieren corregido

MODO IMPERATIVO

PRESENTE

corrige	tú
corrija	él/ella/usted
corrijamos	nosotros/as
correg id	vosotros/as
corrijan	ellos/ellas/ustedes

FORMAS NO PERSONALES

FORMAS SIMPLES

INFINITIVO	GERUNDIO	PARTICIPIO
corregir	corrigiendo	correg ido

FORMAS COMPUESTAS

INFINITIVO	GERUNDIO
haber corregido	habiendo corregido

(1) or Perfecto simple. (2), (3) rarely used.

model verb tables

62. SEGUIR IRREGULAR (stem change e → i + spelling change gu → g) *FOLLOW*

MODO INDICATIVO

PRESENTE	PRETÉRITO IMPERFECTO	PRETÉRITO INDEFINIDO (1)	FUTURO IMPERFECTO
sigo	segu ía	segu í	seguir é
sigues	segu ías	segu iste	seguir ás
sigue	segu ía	siguió	seguir á
segu imos	segu íamos	segu imos	seguir emos
segu ís	segu íais	segu isteis	seguir éis
siguen	segu ían	siguieron	seguir án

PRETÉRITO PERFECTO		PRETÉRITO PLUSCUAMPERFECTO		PRETÉRITO ANTERIOR		FUTURO PERFECTO	
he	seguido	había	seguido	hube	seguido	habré	seguido
has	seguido	habías	seguido	hubiste	seguido	habrás	seguido
ha	seguido	había	seguido	hubo	seguido	habrá	seguido
hemos	seguido	habíamos	seguido	hubimos	seguido	habremos	seguido
habéis	seguido	habíais	seguido	hubisteis	seguido	habréis	seguido
han	seguido	habían	seguido	hubieron	seguido	habrán	seguido

CONDICIONAL SIMPLE	CONDICIONAL COMPUESTO	
seguir ía	habría	seguido
seguir ías	habrías	seguido
seguir ía	habría	seguido
seguir íamos	habríamos	seguido
seguir íais	habríais	seguido
seguir ían	habrían	seguido

MODO SUBJUNTIVO

PRESENTE	PRETÉRITO IMPERFECTO		FUTURO IMPERFECTO (2)
siga	siguiera	or siguiese	siguiere
sigas	siguieras	or siguieses	siguieres
siga	siguiera	or siguiese	siguiere
sigamos	siguiéramos	or siguiésemos	siguiéremos
sigáis	siguierais	or siguieseis	siguiereis
sigan	siguieran	or siguiesen	siguieren

PRETÉRITO PERFECTO		PRETÉRITO PLUSCUAMPERFECTO			FUTURO PERFECTO (3)	
haya	seguido	hubiera	or hubiese	seguido	hubiere	seguido
hayas	seguido	hubieras	or hubieses	seguido	hubieres	seguido
haya	seguido	hubiera	or hubiese	seguido	hubiere	seguido
hayamos	seguido	hubiéramos	or hubiésemos	seguido	hubiéremos	seguido
hayáis	seguido	hubierais	or hubieseis	seguido	hubiereis	seguido
hayan	seguido	hubieran	or hubiesen	seguido	hubieren	seguido

MODO IMPERATIVO

PRESENTE

sigue	tú
siga	él/ella/usted
sigamos	nosotros/as
segu id	vosotros/as
sigan	ellos/ellas/ustedes

FORMAS NO PERSONALES

FORMAS SIMPLES

INFINITIVO	GERUNDIO	PARTICIPIO
seguir	siguiendo	segu ido

FORMAS COMPUESTAS

INFINITIVO	GERUNDIO
haber seguido	habiendo seguido

(1) or Perfecto simple. (2), (3) rarely used.

63. REÍR IRREGULAR (stem change e → i + spelling changes)   *LAUGH*

MODO INDICATIVO

PRESENTE	PRETÉRITO IMPERFECTO	PRETÉRITO INDEFINIDO (1)	FUTURO IMPERFECTO
río	re ía	re í	reir é
ríes	re ías	reíste	reir ás
ríe	re ía	rió	reir á
reímos	re íamos	reímos	reir emos
re ís	re íais	reísteis	reir éis
ríen	re ían	rieron	reir án

PRETÉRITO PERFECTO	PRETÉRITO PLUSCUAMPERFECTO	PRETÉRITO ANTERIOR	FUTURO PERFECTO
he reído	había reído	hube reído	habré reído
has reído	habías reído	hubiste reído	habrás reído
ha reído	había reído	hubo reído	habrá reído
hemos reído	habíamos reído	hubimos reído	habremos reído
habéis reído	habíais reído	hubisteis reído	habréis reído
han reído	habían reído	hubieron reído	habrán reído

CONDICIONAL SIMPLE	CONDICIONAL COMPUESTO
reir ía	habría reído
reir ías	habrías reído
reir ía	habría reído
reir íamos	habríamos reído
reir íais	habríais reído
reir ían	habrían reído

MODO SUBJUNTIVO

PRESENTE	PRETÉRITO IMPERFECTO		FUTURO IMPERFECTO (2)
ría	riera	or riese	riere
rías	rieras	or rieses	rieres
ría	riera	or riese	riere
riamos	riéramos	or riésemos	riéremos
riáis	rierais	or rieseis	riereis
rían	rieran	or riesen	rieren

PRETÉRITO PERFECTO	PRETÉRITO PLUSCUAMPERFECTO		FUTURO PERFECTO (3)
haya reído	hubiera	or hubiese reído	hubiere reído
hayas reído	hubieras	or hubieses reído	hubieres reído
haya reído	hubiera	or hubiese reído	hubiere reído
hayamos reído	hubiéramos	or hubiésemos reído	hubiéremos reído
hayáis reído	hubierais	or hubieseis reído	hubiereis reído
hayan reído	hubieran	or hubiesen reído	hubieren reído

MODO IMPERATIVO

PRESENTE

ríe	tú
ría	él/ella/usted
riamos	nosotros/as
reíd	vosotros/as
rían	ellos/ellas/ustedes

FORMAS NO PERSONALES

FORMAS SIMPLES

INFINITIVO	GERUNDIO	PARTICIPIO
reír	riendo	reído

FORMAS COMPUESTAS

INFINITIVO	GERUNDIO
haber reído	habiendo reído

(1) or Perfecto simple. (2), (3) rarely used.

model verb tables

64. TEÑIR IRREGULAR (stem change e → i + spelling change ñi → ñ) DYE

MODO INDICATIVO

PRESENTE	PRETÉRITO IMPERFECTO	PRETÉRITO INDEFINIDO (1)	FUTURO IMPERFECTO
tiño	teñ ía	teñ í	teñir é
tiñes	teñ ías	teñ iste	teñir ás
tiñe	teñ ía	tiñó	teñir á
teñ imos	teñ íamos	teñ imos	teñir emos
teñ ís	teñ íais	teñ isteis	teñir éis
tiñen	teñ ían	tiñeron	teñir án

PRETÉRITO PERFECTO	PRETÉRITO PLUSCUAMPERFECTO	PRETÉRITO ANTERIOR	FUTURO PERFECTO
he teñido	había teñido	hube teñido	habré teñido
has teñido	habías teñido	hubiste teñido	habrás teñido
ha teñido	había teñido	hubo teñido	habrá teñido
hemos teñido	habíamos teñido	hubimos teñido	habremos teñido
habéis teñido	habíais teñido	hubisteis teñido	habréis teñido
han teñido	habían teñido	hubieron teñido	habrán teñido

CONDICIONAL SIMPLE	CONDICIONAL COMPUESTO
teñir ía	habría teñido
teñir ías	habrías teñido
teñir ía	habría teñido
teñir íamos	habríamos teñido
teñir íais	habríais teñido
teñir ían	habrían teñido

MODO SUBJUNTIVO

PRESENTE	PRETÉRITO IMPERFECTO		FUTURO IMPERFECTO (2)
tiña	tiñera	or tiñese	tiñere
tiñas	tiñeras	or tiñeses	tiñeres
tiña	tiñera	or tiñese	tiñere
tiñamos	tiñéramos	or tiñésemos	tiñéremos
tiñáis	tiñerais	or tiñeseis	tiñereis
tiñan	tiñeran	or tiñesen	tiñeren

PRETÉRITO PERFECTO	PRETÉRITO PLUSCUAMPERFECTO		FUTURO PERFECTO (3)
haya teñido	hubiera or hubiese teñido		hubiere teñido
hayas teñido	hubieras or hubieses teñido		hubieres teñido
haya teñido	hubiera or hubiese teñido		hubiere teñido
hayamos teñido	hubiéramos or hubiésemos teñido		hubiéremos teñido
hayáis teñido	hubierais or hubieseis teñido		hubiereis teñido
hayan teñido	hubieran or hubiesen teñido		hubieren teñido

MODO IMPERATIVO

PRESENTE

tiñe	tú
tiña	él/ella/usted
tiñamos	nosotros/as
teñ id	vosotros/as
tiñan	ellos/ellas/ustedes

FORMAS NO PERSONALES

FORMAS SIMPLES

INFINITIVO	GERUNDIO	PARTICIPIO
teñir	tiñendo	teñ ido

FORMAS COMPUESTAS

INFINITIVO	GERUNDIO
haber teñido	habiendo teñido

(1) or Perfecto simple. (2), (3) rarely used.

Spanish Verb Manual

65. SENTIR IRREGULAR (stem change e → ie and i) *FEEL*

MODO INDICATIVO

PRESENTE	PRETÉRITO IMPERFECTO	PRETÉRITO INDEFINIDO (1)	FUTURO IMPERFECTO
siento	sent ía	sent í	sentir é
sientes	sent ías	sent iste	sentir ás
siente	sent ía	sintió	sentir á
sent imos	sent íamos	sent imos	sentir emos
sent ís	sent íais	sent isteis	sentir éis
sienten	sent ían	sintieron	sentir án

PRETÉRITO PERFECTO	PRETÉRITO PLUSCUAMPERFECTO	PRETÉRITO ANTERIOR	FUTURO PERFECTO
he sentido	había sentido	hube sentido	habré sentido
has sentido	habías sentido	hubiste sentido	habrás sentido
ha sentido	había sentido	hubo sentido	habrá sentido
hemos sentido	habíamos sentido	hubimos sentido	habremos sentido
habéis sentido	habíais sentido	hubisteis sentido	habréis sentido
han sentido	habían sentido	hubieron sentido	habrán sentido

CONDICIONAL SIMPLE	CONDICIONAL COMPUESTO
sentir ía	habría sentido
sentir ías	habrías sentido
sentir ía	habría sentido
sentir íamos	habríamos sentido
sentir íais	habríais sentido
sentir ían	habrían sentido

MODO SUBJUNTIVO

PRESENTE	PRETÉRITO IMPERFECTO	FUTURO IMPERFECTO (2)
sienta	sintiera or sintiese	sintiere
sientas	sintieras or sintieses	sintieres
sienta	sintiera or sintiese	sintiere
sintamos	sintiéramos or sintiésemos	sintiéremos
sintáis	sintierais or sintieseis	sintiereis
sientan	sintieran or sintiesen	sintieren

PRETÉRITO PERFECTO	PRETÉRITO PLUSCUAMPERFECTO	FUTURO PERFECTO (3)
haya sentido	hubiera or hubiese sentido	hubiere sentido
hayas sentido	hubieras or hubieses sentido	hubieres sentido
haya sentido	hubiera or hubiese sentido	hubiere sentido
hayamos sentido	hubiéramos or hubiésemos sentido	hubiéremos sentido
hayáis sentido	hubierais or hubieseis sentido	hubiereis sentido
hayan sentido	hubieran or hubiesen sentido	hubieren sentido

MODO IMPERATIVO

PRESENTE

siente	tú
sienta	él/ella/usted
sintamos	nosotros/as
sent id	vosotros/as
sientan	ellos/ellas/ustedes

FORMAS NO PERSONALES

FORMAS SIMPLES

INFINITIVO	GERUNDIO	PARTICIPIO
sentir	sintiendo	sent ido

FORMAS COMPUESTAS

INFINITIVO	GERUNDIO
haber sentido	habiendo sentido

(1) or Perfecto simple. (2), (3) rarely used.

model verb tables

66. DISCERNIR IRREGULAR (stem change e → ie) *DISTINGUISH*

MODO INDICATIVO

PRESENTE	PRETÉRITO IMPERFECTO	PRETÉRITO INDEFINIDO (1)	FUTURO IMPERFECTO
discierno	discern ía	discern í	discernir é
disciernes	discern ías	discern iste	discernir ás
discierne	discern ía	discern ió	discernir á
discern imos	discern íamos	discern imos	discernir emos
discern ís	discern íais	discern isteis	discernir éis
disciernen	discern ían	discern ieron	discernir án

PRETÉRITO PERFECTO		PRETÉRITO PLUSCUAMPERFECTO		PRETÉRITO ANTERIOR		FUTURO PERFECTO	
he	discernido	había	discernido	hube	discernido	habré	discernido
has	discernido	habías	discernido	hubiste	discernido	habrás	discernido
ha	discernido	había	discernido	hubo	discernido	habrá	discernido
hemos	discernido	habíamos	discernido	hubimos	discernido	habremos	discernido
habéis	discernido	habíais	discernido	hubisteis	discernido	habréis	discernido
han	discernido	habían	discernido	hubieron	discernido	habrán	discernido

CONDICIONAL SIMPLE	CONDICIONAL COMPUESTO	
discernir ía	habría	discernido
discernir ías	habrías	discernido
discernir ía	habría	discernido
discernir íamos	habríamos	discernido
discernir íais	habríais	discernido
discernir ían	habrían	discernido

MODO SUBJUNTIVO

PRESENTE	PRETÉRITO IMPERFECTO			FUTURO IMPERFECTO (2)
discierna	discern iera	or	discern iese	discern iere
disciernas	discern ieras	or	discern ieses	discern ieres
discierna	discern iera	or	discern iese	discern iere
discer namos	discern iéramos	or	discern iésemos	discern iéremos
discer náis	discern ierais	or	discern ieseis	discern iereis
disciernan	discern ieran	or	discern iesen	discern ieren

PRETÉRITO PERFECTO		PRETÉRITO PLUSCUAMPERFECTO				FUTURO PERFECTO (3)	
haya	discernido	hubiera	or hubiese	discernido		hubiere	discernido
hayas	discernido	hubieras	or hubieses	discernido		hubieres	discernido
haya	discernido	hubiera	or hubiese	discernido		hubiere	discernido
hayamos	discernido	hubiéramos	or hubiésemos	discernido		hubiéremos	discernido
hayáis	discernido	hubierais	or hubieseis	discernido		hubiereis	discernido
hayan	discernido	hubieran	or hubiesen	discernido		hubieren	discernido

MODO IMPERATIVO   FORMAS NO PERSONALES

PRESENTE

discierne	tú
discierna	él/ella/usted
discern amos	nosotros/as
discern id	vosotros/as
disciernan	ellos/ellas/ustedes

FORMAS SIMPLES

INFINITIVO	GERUNDIO	PARTICIPIO
discernir	discern iendo	discern ido

FORMAS COMPUESTAS

INFINITIVO	GERUNDIO
haber discernido	habiendo discernido

(1) or Perfecto simple. (2), (3) rarely used.

model verb tables

MODO INDICATIVO

PRESENTE	PRETÉRITO IMPERFECTO	PRETÉRITO INDEFINIDO (1)	FUTURO IMPERFECTO
adquiero	adquir ía	adquir í	adquirir é
adquieres	adquir ías	adquir iste	adquirir ás
adquiere	adquir ía	adquir ió	adquirir á
adquir imos	adquir íamos	adquir imos	adquirir emos
adquir ís	adquir íais	adquir isteis	adquirir éis
adquieren	adquir ían	adquir ieron	adquirir án

PRETÉRITO PERFECTO	PRETÉRITO PLUSCUAMPERFECTO	PRETÉRITO ANTERIOR	FUTURO PERFECTO
he adquirido	había adquirido	hube adquirido	habré adquirido
has adquirido	habías adquirido	hubiste adquirido	habrás adquirido
ha adquirido	había adquirido	hubo adquirido	habrá adquirido
hemos adquirido	habíamos adquirido	hubimos adquirido	habremos adquirido
habéis adquirido	habíais adquirido	hubisteis adquirido	habréis adquirido
han adquirido	habían adquirido	hubieron adquirido	habrán adquirido

CONDICIONAL SIMPLE

adquirir ía	
adquirir ías	
adquirir ía	
adquirir íamos	
adquirir íais	
adquirir ían	

CONDICIONAL COMPUESTO

habría	adquirido
habrías	adquirido
habría	adquirido
habríamos	adquirido
habríais	adquirido
habrían	adquirido

MODO SUBJUNTIVO

PRESENTE	PRETÉRITO IMPERFECTO	FUTURO IMPERFECTO (2)
adquiera	adquir iera *or* adquir iese	adquir iere
adquieras	adquir ieras *or* adquir ieses	adquir ieres
adquiera	adquir iera *or* adquir iese	adquir iere
adquir amos	adquir iéramos *or* adquir iésemos	adquir iéremos
adquir áis	adquir ierais *or* adquir ieseis	adquir iereis
adquieran	adquir ieran *or* adquir iesen	adquir ieren

PRETÉRITO PERFECTO	PRETÉRITO PLUSCUAMPERFECTO	FUTURO PERFECTO (3)
haya adquirido	hubiera *or* hubiese adquirido	hubiere adquirido
hayas adquirido	hubieras *or* hubieses adquirido	hubieres adquirido
haya adquirido	hubiera *or* hubiese adquirido	hubiere adquirido
hayamos adquirido	hubiéramos *or* hubiésemos adquirido	hubiéremos adquirido
hayáis adquirido	hubierais *or* hubieseis adquirido	hubiereis adquirido
hayan adquirido	hubieran *or* hubiesen adquirido	hubieren adquirido

MODO IMPERATIVO

PRESENTE

adquiere	tú
adquiera	él/ella/usted
adquir amos	nosotros/as
adquir id	vosotros/as
adquieran	ellos/ellas/ustedes

FORMAS NO PERSONALES

FORMAS SIMPLES

INFINITIVO	GERUNDIO	PARTICIPIO
adquirir	adquir iendo	adquir ido

FORMAS COMPUESTAS

INFINITIVO	GERUNDIO
haber adquirido	habiendo adquirido

(1) or Perfecto simple. (2), (3) rearly used.

model verb tables

68. DORMIR IRREGULAR (stem change o → ue and u)   *SLEEP*

MODO INDICATIVO

PRESENTE	PRETÉRITO IMPERFECTO	PRETÉRITO INDEFINIDO (1)	FUTURO IMPERFECTO
duermo	dorm ía	dorm í	dormir é
duermes	dorm ías	dorm iste	dormir ás
duerme	dorm ía	durmió	dormir á
dorm imos	dorm íamos	dorm imos	dormir emos
dorm ís	dorm íais	dorm isteis	dormir éis
duermen	dorm ían	durmieron	dormir án

PRETÉRITO PERFECTO	PRETÉRITO PLUSCUAMPERFECTO	PRETÉRITO ANTERIOR	FUTURO PERFECTO
he dormido	había dormido	hube dormido	habré dormido
has dormido	habías dormido	hubiste dormido	habrás dormido
ha dormido	había dormido	hubo dormido	habrá dormido
hemos dormido	habíamos dormido	hubimos dormido	habremos dormido
habéis dormido	habíais dormido	hubisteis dormido	habréis dormido
han dormido	habían dormido	hubieron dormido	habrán dormido

CONDICIONAL SIMPLE	CONDICIONAL COMPUESTO
dormir ía	habría dormido
dormir ías	habrías dormido
dormir ía	habría dormido
dormir íamos	habríamos dormido
dormir íais	habríais dormido
dormir ían	habrían dormido

MODO SUBJUNTIVO

PRESENTE	PRETÉRITO IMPERFECTO	FUTURO IMPERFECTO (2)
duerma	durmiera *or* durmiese	durmiere
duermas	durmieras *or* durmieses	durmieres
duerma	durmiera *or* durmiese	durmiere
durmamos	durmiéramos *or* durmiésemos	durmiéremos
durmáis	durmierais *or* durmieseis	durmiereis
duerman	durmieran *or* durmiesen	durmieren

PRETÉRITO PERFECTO	PRETÉRITO PLUSCUAMPERFECTO	FUTURO PERFECTO (3)
haya dormido	hubiera *or* hubiese dormido	hubiere dormido
hayas dormido	hubieras *or* hubieses dormido	hubieres dormido
haya dormido	hubiera *or* hubiese dormido	hubiere dormido
hayamos dormido	hubiéramos *or* hubiésemos dormido	hubiéremos dormido
hayáis dormido	hubierais *or* hubieseis dormido	hubiereis dormido
hayan dormido	hubieran *or* hubiesen dormido	hubieren dormido

---

MODO IMPERATIVO

PRESENTE

duerme	tú
duerma	él/ella/usted
durmamos	nosotros/as
dorm id	vosotros/as
duerman	ellos/ellas/ustedes

FORMAS NO PERSONALES

FORMAS SIMPLES

INFINITIVO	GERUNDIO	PARTICIPIO
dormir	durmiendo	dorm ido

FORMAS COMPUESTAS

INFINITIVO	GERUNDIO
haber dormido	habiendo dormido

(1) or Perfecto simple. (2), (3) rarely used.

Spanish Verb Manual

model verb tables

MODO INDICATIVO

PRESENTE	PRETÉRITO IMPERFECTO	PRETÉRITO INDEFINIDO (1)	FUTURO IMPERFECTO
traduzco	**traduc** ía	traduje	**traducir** é
traduc es	**traduc** ías	tradujiste	**traducir** ás
traduc e	**traduc** ía	tradujo	**traducir** á
traduc imos	**traduc** íamos	tradujimos	**traducir** emos
traduc ís	**traduc** íais	tradujisteis	**traducir** éis
traduc en	**traduc** ían	tradujeron	**traducir** án

PRETÉRITO PERFECTO		PRETÉRITO PLUSCUAMPERFECTO		PRETÉRITO ANTERIOR		FUTURO PERFECTO	
he	traducido	había	traducido	hube	traducido	habré	traducido
has	traducido	habías	traducido	hubiste	traducido	habrás	traducido
ha	traducido	había	traducido	hubo	traducido	habrá	traducido
hemos	traducido	habíamos	traducido	hubimos	traducido	habremos	traducido
habéis	traducido	habíais	traducido	hubisteis	traducido	habréis	traducido
han	traducido	habían	traducido	hubieron	traducido	habrán	traducido

CONDICIONAL SIMPLE	CONDICIONAL COMPUESTO	
traducir ía	habría	traducido
traducir ías	habrías	traducido
traducir ía	habría	traducido
traducir íamos	habríamos	traducido
traducir íais	habríais	traducido
traducir ían	habrían	traducido

MODO SUBJUNTIVO

PRESENTE	PRETÉRITO IMPERFECTO		FUTURO IMPERFECTO (2)
traduzca	tradujera	*or* tradujese	tradujere
traduzcas	tradujeras	*or* tradujeses	tradujeres
traduzca	tradujera	*or* tradujese	tradujere
traduzcamos	tradujéramos	*or* tradujésemos	tradujéremos
traduzcáis	tradujerais	*or* tradujeseis	tradujereis
traduzcan	tradujeran	*or* tradujesen	tradujeren

PRETÉRITO PERFECTO		PRETÉRITO PLUSCUAMPERFECTO			FUTURO PERFECTO (3)	
haya	traducido	hubiera	*or* hubiese	traducido	hubiere	traducido
hayas	traducido	hubieras	*or* hubieses	traducido	hubieres	traducido
haya	traducido	hubiera	*or* hubiese	traducido	hubiere	traducido
hayamos	traducido	hubiéramos	*or* hubiésemos	traducido	hubiéremos	traducido
hayáis	traducido	hubierais	*or* hubieseis	traducido	hubiereis	traducido
hayan	traducido	hubieran	*or* hubiesen	traducido	hubieren	traducido

MODO IMPERATIVO

PRESENTE

traduc e	tú
traduzca	él/ella/usted
traduzcamos	nosotros/as
traduc id	vosotros/as
traduzcan	ellos/ellas/ustedes

FORMAS NO PERSONALES

FORMAS SIMPLES

INFINITIVO	GERUNDIO	PARTICIPIO
traducir	**traduc** iendo	**traduc** ido

FORMAS COMPUESTAS

INFINITIVO	GERUNDIO
haber traducido	habiendo traducido

(1) or Perfecto simple. (2), (3) rarely used.

model verb tables

70. LUCIR IRREGULAR (stem change c → zc) *SHINE*

MODO INDICATIVO

PRESENTE	PRETÉRITO IMPERFECTO	PRETÉRITO INDEFINIDO (1)	FUTURO IMPERFECTO
luzco	luc ía	luc í	lucir é
luc es	luc ías	luc iste	lucir ás
luc e	luc ía	luc ió	lucir á
luc imos	luc íamos	luc imos	lucir emos
luc ís	luc íais	luc isteis	lucir éis
luc en	luc ían	luc ieron	lucir án

PRETÉRITO PERFECTO	PRETÉRITO PLUSCUAMPERFECTO	PRETÉRITO ANTERIOR	FUTURO PERFECTO
he lucido	había lucido	hube lucido	habré lucido
has lucido	habías lucido	hubiste lucido	habrás lucido
ha lucido	había lucido	hubo lucido	habrá lucido
hemos lucido	habíamos lucido	hubimos lucido	habremos lucido
habéis lucido	habíais lucido	hubisteis lucido	habréis lucido
han lucido	habían lucido	hubieron lucido	habrán lucido

CONDICIONAL SIMPLE	CONDICIONAL COMPUESTO
lucir ía	habría lucido
lucir ías	habrías lucido
lucir ía	habría lucido
lucir íamos	habríamos lucido
lucir íais	habríais lucido
lucir ían	habrían lucido

MODO SUBJUNTIVO

PRESENTE	PRETÉRITO IMPERFECTO		FUTURO IMPERFECTO (2)
luzca	luc iera	*or* luc iese	luc iere
luzcas	luc ieras	*or* luc ieses	luc ieres
luzca	luc iera	*or* luc iese	luc iere
luzcamos	luc iéramos	*or* luc iésemos	luc iéremos
luzcáis	luc ierais	*or* luc ieseis	luc iereis
luzcan	luc ieran	*or* luc iesen	luc ieren

PRETÉRITO PERFECTO	PRETÉRITO PLUSCUAMPERFECTO		FUTURO PERFECTO (3)
haya lucido	hubiera *or* hubiese lucido		hubiere lucido
hayas lucido	hubieras *or* hubieses lucido		hubieres lucido
haya lucido	hubiera *or* hubiese lucido		hubiere lucido
hayamos lucido	hubiéramos *or* hubiésemos lucido		hubiéremos lucido
hayáis lucido	hubierais *or* hubieseis lucido		hubiereis lucido
hayan lucido	hubieran *or* hubiesen lucido		hubieren lucido

MODO IMPERATIVO

PRESENTE

luc e	tú
luzca	él/ella/usted
luzcamos	nosotros/as
luc id	vosotros/as
luzcan	ellos/ellas/ustedes

FORMAS NO PERSONALES

FORMAS SIMPLES

INFINITIVO	GERUNDIO	PARTICIPIO
lucir	luc iendo	luc ido

FORMAS COMPUESTAS

INFINITIVO	GERUNDIO
haber lucido	habiendo lucido

(1) or Perfecto simple. (2), (3) rarely used.

Spanish Verb Manual

71. ABOLIR IRREGULAR (defective verb) *ABOLISH*

MODO INDICATIVO

PRESENTE	PRETÉRITO IMPERFECTO	PRETÉRITO INDEFINIDO (1)	FUTURO IMPERFECTO
—	abol ía	abol í	abolir é
—	abol ías	abol iste	abolir ás
—	abol ía	abol ió	abolir á
abol imos	abol íamos	abol imos	abolir emos
abol ís	abol íais	abol isteis	abolir éis
—	abol ían	abol ieron	abolir án

PRETÉRITO PERFECTO	PRETÉRITO PLUSCUAMPERFECTO	PRETÉRITO ANTERIOR	FUTURO PERFECTO
he abolido	había abolido	hube abolido	habré abolido
has abolido	habías abolido	hubiste abolido	habrás abolido
ha abolido	había abolido	hubo abolido	habrá abolido
hemos abolido	habíamos abolido	hubimos abolido	habremos abolido
habéis abolido	habíais abolido	hubisteis abolido	habréis abolido
han abolido	habían abolido	hubieron abolido	habrán abolido

CONDICIONAL SIMPLE	CONDICIONAL COMPUESTO
abolir ía	habría abolido
abolir ías	habrías abolido
abolir ía	habría abolido
abolir íamos	habríamos abolido
abolir íais	habríais abolido
abolir ían	habrían abolido

MODO SUBJUNTIVO

PRESENTE	PRETÉRITO IMPERFECTO	FUTURO IMPERFECTO (2)
—	abol iera *or* abol iese	abol iere
—	abol ieras *or* abol ieses	abol ieres
—	abol iera *or* abol iese	abol iere
—	abol iéramos *or* abol iésemos	abol iéremos
—	abol ierais *or* abol ieseis	abol iereis
—	abol ieran *or* abol iesen	abol ieren

PRETÉRITO PERFECTO	PRETÉRITO PLUSCUAMPERFECTO	FUTURO PERFECTO (3)
haya abolido	hubiera *or* hubiese abolido	hubiere abolido
hayas abolido	hubieras *or* hubieses abolido	hubieres abolido
haya abolido	hubiera *or* hubiese abolido	hubiere abolido
hayamos abolido	hubiéramos *or* hubiésemos abolido	hubiéremos abolido
hayáis abolido	hubierais *or* hubieseis abolido	hubiereis abolido
hayan abolido	hubieran *or* hubiesen abolido	hubieren abolido

MODO IMPERATIVO

FORMAS NO PERSONALES

PRESENTE	
—	tú
—	él/ella/usted
—	nosotros/as
abol id	vosotros/as
—	ellos/ellas/ustedes

FORMAS SIMPLES

INFINITIVO	GERUNDIO	PARTICIPIO
abolir	abol iendo	abol ido

FORMAS COMPUESTAS

INFINITIVO	GERUNDIO
haber abolido	habiendo abolido

(1) or Perfecto simple. (2), (3) rarely used.

model verb tables

72. ASIR IRREGULAR

GRASP

MODO INDICATIVO

PRESENTE	PRETÉRITO IMPERFECTO	PRETÉRITO INDEFINIDO (1)	FUTURO IMPERFECTO
asgo	as ía	as í	asir é
as es	as ías	as iste	asir ás
as e	as ía	as ió	asir á
as imos	as íamos	as imos	asir emos
as ís	as íais	as isteis	asir éis
as en	as ían	as ieron	asir án

PRETÉRITO PERFECTO	PRETÉRITO PLUSCUAMPERFECTO	PRETÉRITO ANTERIOR	FUTURO PERFECTO
he asido	había asido	hube asido	habré asido
has asido	habías asido	hubiste asido	habrás asido
ha asido	había asido	hubo asido	habrá asido
hemos asido	habíamos asido	hubimos asido	habremos asido
habéis asido	habíais asido	hubisteis asido	habréis asido
han asido	habían asido	hubieron asido	habrán asido

CONDICIONAL SIMPLE	CONDICIONAL COMPUESTO
asir ía	habría asido
asir ías	habrías asido
asir ía	habría asido
asir íamos	habríamos asido
asir íais	habríais asido
asir ían	habrían asido

MODO SUBJUNTIVO

PRESENTE	PRETÉRITO IMPERFECTO		FUTURO IMPERFECTO (2)
asga	as iera	or as iese	as iere
asgas	as ieras	or as ieses	as ieres
asga	as iera	or as iese	as iere
asgamos	as iéramos	or as iésemos	as iéremos
asgáis	as ierais	or as ieseis	as iereis
asgan	as ieran	or as iesen	as ieren

PRETÉRITO PERFECTO	PRETÉRITO PLUSCUAMPERFECTO		FUTURO PERFECTO (3)
haya asido	hubiera	or hubiese asido	hubiere asido
hayas asido	hubieras	or hubieses asido	hubieres asido
haya asido	hubiera	or hubiese asido	hubiere asido
hayamos asido	hubiéramos	or hubiésemos asido	hubiéremos asido
hayáis asido	hubierais	or hubieseis asido	hubiereis asido
hayan asido	hubieran	or hubiesen asido	hubieren asido

MODO IMPERATIVO | FORMAS NO PERSONALES

PRESENTE

as e	tú
asga	él/ella/usted
asgamos	nosotros/as
as id	vosotros/as
asgan	ellos/ellas/ustedes

FORMAS SIMPLES

INFINITIVO	GERUNDIO	PARTICIPIO
asir	as iendo	as ido

FORMAS COMPUESTAS

INFINITIVO	GERUNDIO
haber asido	habiendo asido

(1) or Perfecto simple. (2), (3) rarely used.

model verb tables

73. BENDECIR IRREGULAR (incl. stem change e → i) *BLESS*

MODO INDICATIVO

PRESENTE	PRETÉRITO IMPERFECTO	PRETÉRITO INDEFINIDO (1)	FUTURO IMPERFECTO
bendigo	bendec ía	bendije	bendecir é
bendices	bendec ías	bendijiste	bendecir ás
bendice	bendec ía	bendijo	bendecir á
bendec imos	bendec íamos	bendijimos	bendecir emos
bendec ís	bendec íais	bendijisteis	bendecir éis
bendicen	bendec ían	bendijeron	bendecir án

PRETÉRITO PERFECTO	PRETÉRITO PLUSCUAMPERFECTO	PRETÉRITO ANTERIOR	FUTURO PERFECTO
he bendecido	había bendecido	hube bendecido	habré bendecido
has bendecido	habías bendecido	hubiste bendecido	habrás bendecido
ha bendecido	había bendecido	hubo bendecido	habrá bendecido
hemos bendecido	habíamos bendecido	hubimos bendecido	habremos bendecido
habéis bendecido	habíais bendecido	hubisteis bendecido	habréis bendecido
han bendecido	habían bendecido	hubieron bendecido	habrán bendecido

CONDICIONAL SIMPLE

bendecir ía
bendecir ías
bendecir ía
bendecir íamos
bendecir íais
bendecir ían

CONDICIONAL COMPUESTO

habría bendecido
habrías bendecido
habría bendecido
habríamos bendecido
habríais bendecido
habrían bendecido

MODO SUBJUNTIVO

PRESENTE	PRETÉRITO IMPERFECTO		FUTURO IMPERFECTO (2)
bendiga	bendijera	or bendijese	bendijere
bendigas	bendijeras	or bendijeses	bendijeres
bendiga	bendijera	or bendijese	bendijere
bendigamos	bendijéramos	or bendijésemos	bendijéremos
bendigáis	bendijerais	or bendijeseis	bendijereis
bendigan	bendijeran	or bendijesen	bendijeren

PRETÉRITO PERFECTO	PRETÉRITO PLUSCUAMPERFECTO		FUTURO PERFECTO (3)
haya bendecido	hubiera	or hubiese bendecido	hubiere bendecido
hayas bendecido	hubieras	or hubieses bendecido	hubieres bendecido
haya bendecido	hubiera	or hubiese bendecido	hubiere bendecido
hayamos bendecido	hubiéramos	or hubiésemos bendecido	hubiéremos bendecido
hayáis bendecido	hubierais	or hubieseis bendecido	hubiereis bendecido
hayan bendecido	hubieran	or hubiesen bendecido	hubieren bendecido

MODO IMPERATIVO

PRESENTE

bendice	tú
bendiga	él/ella/usted
bendigamos	nosotros/as
bendec id	vosotros/as
bendigan	ellos/ellas/ustedes

FORMAS NO PERSONALES

FORMAS SIMPLES

INFINITIVO	GERUNDIO	PARTICIPIO
bendecir	bendiciendo	bendec ido

FORMAS COMPUESTAS

INFINITIVO	GERUNDIO
haber bendecido	habiendo bendecido

(1) or Perfecto simple. (2), (3) rarely used.

Spanish Verb Manual

model verb tables

74. DECIR   IRREGULAR (incl. stem change e → i)   *TELL, SAY*

MODO INDICATIVO

PRESENTE	PRETÉRITO IMPERFECTO	PRETÉRITO INDEFINIDO (1)	FUTURO IMPERFECTO
digo	**dec** ía	dije	diré
dices	**dec** ías	dijiste	dirás
dice	**dec** ía	dijo	dirá
dec imos	**dec** íamos	dijimos	diremos
dec ís	**dec** íais	dijisteis	diréis
dicen	**dec** ían	dijeron	dirán

PRETÉRITO PERFECTO	PRETÉRITO PLUSCUAMPERFECTO	PRETÉRITO ANTERIOR	FUTURO PERFECTO
he dicho	había dicho	hube dicho	habré dicho
has dicho	habías dicho	hubiste dicho	habrás dicho
ha dicho	había dicho	hubo dicho	habrá dicho
hemos dicho	habíamos dicho	hubimos dicho	habremos dicho
habéis dicho	habíais dicho	hubisteis dicho	habréis dicho
han dicho	habían dicho	hubieron dicho	habrán dicho

CONDICIONAL SIMPLE	CONDICIONAL COMPUESTO
diría	habría dicho
dirías	habrías dicho
diría	habría dicho
diríamos	habríamos dicho
diríais	habríais dicho
dirían	habrían dicho

MODO SUBJUNTIVO

PRESENTE	PRETÉRITO IMPERFECTO	FUTURO IMPERFECTO (2)
diga	dijera *or* dijese	dijere
digas	dijeras *or* dijeses	dijeres
diga	dijera *or* dijese	dijere
digamos	dijéramos *or* dijésemos	dijéremos
digáis	dijerais *or* dijeseis	dijereis
digan	dijeran *or* dijesen	dijeren

PRETÉRITO PERFECTO	PRETÉRITO PLUSCUAMPERFECTO	FUTURO PERFECTO (3)
haya dicho	hubiera *or* hubiese dicho	hubiere dicho
hayas dicho	hubieras *or* hubieses dicho	hubieres dicho
haya dicho	hubiera *or* hubiese dicho	hubiere dicho
hayamos dicho	hubiéramos *or* hubiésemos dicho	hubiéremos dicho
hayáis dicho	hubierais *or* hubieseis dicho	hubiereis dicho
hayan dicho	hubieran *or* hubiesen dicho	hubieren dicho

MODO IMPERATIVO	FORMAS NO PERSONALES

PRESENTE	
di	tú
diga	él/ella/usted
digamos	nosotros/as
dec id	vosotros/as
digan	ellos/ellas/ustedes

FORMAS SIMPLES

INFINITIVO	GERUNDIO	PARTICIPIO
decir	diciendo	dicho

FORMAS COMPUESTAS

INFINITIVO	GERUNDIO
haber dicho	habiendo dicho

(1) or Perfecto simple. (2), (3) rarely used.

75. DELINQUIR IRREGULAR (spelling change qu → c) *TRANSGRESS*

MODO INDICATIVO

PRESENTE	PRETÉRITO IMPERFECTO	PRETÉRITO INDEFINIDO (1)	FUTURO IMPERFECTO
delinco	delinq uía	delinq uí	delinquir é
delinq ues	delinq uías	delinq uiste	delinquir ás
delinq ue	delinq uía	delinq uió	delinquir á
delinq uimos	delinq uíamos	delinq uimos	delinquir emos
delinq uís	delinq uíais	delinq uisteis	delinquir éis
delinq uen	delinq uían	delinq uieron	delinquir án

PRETÉRITO PERFECTO		PRETÉRITO PLUSCUAMPERFECTO		PRETÉRITO ANTERIOR		FUTURO PERFECTO	
he	delinquido	había	delinquido	hube	delinquido	habré	delinquido
has	delinquido	habías	delinquido	hubiste	delinquido	habrás	delinquido
ha	delinquido	había	delinquido	hubo	delinquido	habrá	delinquido
hemos	delinquido	habíamos	delinquido	hubimos	delinquido	habremos	delinquido
habéis	delinquido	habíais	delinquido	hubisteis	delinquido	habréis	delinquido
han	delinquido	habían	delinquido	hubieron	delinquido	habrán	delinquido

CONDICIONAL SIMPLE	CONDICIONAL COMPUESTO	
delinquir ía	habría	delinquido
delinquir ías	habrías	delinquido
delinquir ía	habría	delinquido
delinquir íamos	habríamos	delinquido
delinquir íais	habríais	delinquido
delinquir ían	habrían	delinquido

MODO SUBJUNTIVO

PRESENTE	PRETÉRITO IMPERFECTO			FUTURO IMPERFECTO (2)
delinca	delinqu iera	or	delinqu iese	delinqu iere
delincas	delinqu ieras	or	delinqu ieses	delinqu ieres
delinca	delinqu iera	or	delinqu iese	delinqu iere
delincamos	delinqu iéramos	or	delinqu iésemos	delinqu iéremos
delincáis	delinqu ierais	or	delinqu ieseis	delinqu iereis
delincan	delinqu ieran	or	delinqu iesen	delinqu ieren

PRETÉRITO PERFECTO		PRETÉRITO PLUSCUAMPERFECTO			FUTURO PERFECTO (3)	
haya	delinquido	hubiera	or hubiese	delinquido	hubiere	delinquido
hayas	delinquido	hubieras	or hubieses	delinquido	hubieres	delinquido
haya	delinquido	hubiera	or hubiese	delinquido	hubiere	delinquido
hayamos	delinquido	hubiéramos	or hubiésemos	delinquido	hubiéremos	delinquido
hayáis	delinquido	hubierais	or hubieseis	delinquido	hubiereis	delinquido
hayan	delinquido	hubieran	or hubiesen	delinquido	hubieren	delinquido

---

MODO IMPERATIVO

FORMAS NO PERSONALES

PRESENTE

delinq ue	tú
delinca	él/ella/usted
delincamos	nosotros/as
delinqu id	vosotros/as
delincan	ellos/ellas/ustedes

FORMAS SIMPLES

INFINITIVO	GERUNDIO	PARTICIPIO
delinquir	delinqu iendo	delinqu ido

FORMAS COMPUESTAS

INFINITIVO	GERUNDIO
haber delinquido	habiendo delinquido

(1) or Perfecto simple. (2), (3) rarely used.

model verb tables

MODO INDICATIVO

PRESENTE	PRETÉRITO IMPERFECTO	PRETÉRITO INDEFINIDO (1)	FUTURO IMPERFECTO
irgo *or* yergo	ergu ía	ergu í	erguir é
irgues *or* yergues	ergu ías	ergu iste	erguir ás
irgue *or* yergue	ergu ía	irguió	erguir á
ergu imos	ergu íamos	ergu imos	erguir emos
ergu ís	ergu íais	ergu isteis	erguir éis
irguen *or* yerguen	ergu ían	irguieron	erguir án

PRETÉRITO PERFECTO	PRETÉRITO PLUSCUAMPERFECTO	PRETÉRITO ANTERIOR	FUTURO PERFECTO
he erguido	había erguido	hube erguido	habré erguido
has erguido	habías erguido	hubiste erguido	habrás erguido
ha erguido	había erguido	hubo erguido	habrá erguido
hemos erguido	habíamos erguido	hubimos erguido	habremos erguido
habéis erguido	habíais erguido	hubisteis erguido	habréis erguido
han erguido	habían erguido	hubieron erguido	habrán erguido

CONDICIONAL SIMPLE	CONDICIONAL COMPUESTO
erguir ía	habría erguido
erguir ías	habrías erguido
erguir ía	habría erguido
erguir íamos	habríamos erguido
erguir íais	habríais erguido
erguir ían	habrían erguido

MODO SUBJUNTIVO

PRESENTE	PRETÉRITO IMPERFECTO	FUTURO IMPERFECTO (2)
irga *or* yerga	irguiera *or* irguiese	irguiere
irgas *or* yergas	irguieras *or* irguieses	irguieres
irga *or* yerga	irguiera *or* irguiese	irguiere
irgamos *or* yergamos	irguiéramos *or* irguiésemos	irguiéremos
irgáis *or* yergáis	irguierais *or* irguieseis	irguiereis
irgan *or* yergan	irguieran *or* irguiesen	irguieren

PRETÉRITO PERFECTO	PRETÉRITO PLUSCUAMPERFECTO	FUTURO PERFECTO (3)
haya erguido	hubiera *or* hubiese erguido	hubiere erguido
hayas erguido	hubieras *or* hubieses erguido	hubieres erguido
haya erguido	hubiera *or* hubiese erguido	hubiere erguido
hayamos erguido	hubiéramos *or* hubiésemos erguido	hubiéremos erguido
hayáis erguido	hubierais *or* hubieseis erguido	hubiereis erguido
hayan erguido	hubieran *or* hubiesen erguido	hubieren erguido

MODO IMPERATIVO

PRESENTE

irgue *or* yergue	tú
irga *or* yerga	él/ella/usted
irgamos	nosotros/as
ergu id	vosotros/as
irgan *or* yergan	ellos/ellas/ustedes

FORMAS NO PERSONALES

FORMAS SIMPLES

INFINITIVO	GERUNDIO	PARTICIPIO
erguir	irguiendo	ergu ido

FORMAS COMPUESTAS

INFINITIVO	GERUNDIO
haber erguido	habiendo erguido

(1) or Perfecto simple. (2), (3) rarely used.

77. IR IRREGULAR   *GO*

MODO INDICATIVO

PRESENTE	PRETÉRITO IMPERFECTO	PRETÉRITO INDEFINIDO (1)	FUTURO IMPERFECTO
voy	iba	fui	ir é
vas	ibas	fuiste	ir ás
va	iba	fue	ir á
vamos	íbamos	fuimos	ir emos
vais	ibais	fuisteis	ir éis
van	iban	fueron	ir án

PRETÉRITO PERFECTO	PRETÉRITO PLUSCUAMPERFECTO	PRETÉRITO ANTERIOR	FUTURO PERFECTO
he ido	había ido	hube ido	habré ido
has ido	habías ido	hubiste ido	habrás ido
ha ido	había ido	hubo ido	habrá ido
hemos ido	habíamos ido	hubimos ido	habremos ido
habéis ido	habíais ido	hubisteis ido	habréis ido
han ido	habían ido	hubieron ido	habrán ido

CONDICIONAL SIMPLE	CONDICIONAL COMPUESTO
ir ía	habría ido
ir ías	habrías ido
ir ía	habría ido
ir íamos	habríamos ido
ir íais	habríais ido
ir ían	habrían ido

MODO SUBJUNTIVO

PRESENTE	PRETÉRITO IMPERFECTO	FUTURO IMPERFECTO (2)
vaya	fuera *or* fuese	fuere
vayas	fueras *or* fueses	fueres
vaya	fuera *or* fuese	fuere
vayamos	fuéramos *or* fuésemos	fuéremos
vayáis	fuerais *or* fueseis	fuereis
vayan	fueran *or* fuesen	fueren

PRETÉRITO PERFECTO	PRETÉRITO PLUSCUAMPERFECTO	FUTURO PERFECTO (3)
haya ido	hubiera *or* hubiese ido	hubiere ido
hayas ido	hubieras *or* hubieses ido	hubieres ido
haya ido	hubiera *or* hubiese ido	hubiere ido
hayamos ido	hubiéramos *or* hubiésemos ido	hubiéremos ido
hayáis ido	hubierais *or* hubieseis ido	hubiereis ido
hayan ido	hubieran *or* hubiesen ido	hubieren ido

MODO IMPERATIVO	FORMAS NO PERSONALES

PRESENTE

ve	tú
vaya	él/ella/usted
vayamos	nosotros/as
id	vosotros/as
vayan	ellos/ellas/ustedes

FORMAS SIMPLES

INFINITIVO	GERUNDIO	PARTICIPIO
ir	yendo	ido

FORMAS COMPUESTAS

INFINITIVO	GERUNDIO
haber ido	habiendo ido

(1) or Perfecto simple. (2), (3) rarely used.

model verb tables

MODO INDICATIVO

PRESENTE	PRETÉRITO IMPERFECTO	PRETÉRITO INDEFINIDO (1)	FUTURO IMPERFECTO
oigo	o ía	o í	oir é
oyes	o ías	o íste	oir ás
oye	o ía	oyó	oir á
o ímos	o íamos	o ímos	oir emos
o ís	o íais	o ísteis	oir éis
oyen	o ían	oyeron	oir án

PRETÉRITO PERFECTO		PRETÉRITO PLUSCUAMPERFECTO		PRETÉRITO ANTERIOR		FUTURO PERFECTO	
he	oído	había	oído	hube	oído	habré	oído
has	oído	habías	oído	hubiste	oído	habrás	oído
ha	oído	había	oído	hubo	oído	habrá	oído
hemos	oído	habíamos	oído	hubimos	oído	habremos	oído
habéis	oído	habíais	oído	hubisteis	oído	habréis	oído
han	oído	habían	oído	hubieron	oído	habrán	oído

CONDICIONAL SIMPLE   CONDICIONAL COMPUESTO

CONDICIONAL SIMPLE	CONDICIONAL COMPUESTO	
oir ía	habría	oído
oir ías	habrías	oído
oir ía	habría	oído
oir íamos	habríamos	oído
oir íais	habríais	oído
oir ían	habrían	oído

MODO SUBJUNTIVO

PRESENTE	PRETÉRITO IMPERFECTO		FUTURO IMPERFECTO (2)
oiga	oyera	*or* oyese	oyere
oigas	oyeras	*or* oyeses	oyeres
oiga	oyera	*or* oyese	oyere
oigamos	oyéramos	*or* oyésemos	oyéremos
oigáis	oyerais	*or* oyeseis	oyereis
oigan	oyeran	*or* oyesen	oyeren

PRETÉRITO PERFECTO		PRETÉRITO PLUSCUAMPERFECTO			FUTURO PERFECTO (3)	
haya	oído	hubiera	*or* hubiese	oído	hubiere	oído
hayas	oído	hubieras	*or* hubieses	oído	hubieres	oído
haya	oído	hubiera	*or* hubiese	oído	hubiere	oído
hayamos	oído	hubiéramos	*or* hubiésemos	oído	hubiéremos	oído
hayáis	oído	hubierais	*or* hubieseis	oído	hubiereis	oído
hayan	oído	hubieran	*or* hubiesen	oído	hubieren	oído

MODO IMPERATIVO   FORMAS NO PERSONALES

PRESENTE

oye	tú
oiga	él/ella/usted
oigamos	nosotros/as
o íd	vosotros/as
oigan	ellos/ellas/ustedes

FORMAS NO PERSONALES

FORMAS SIMPLES

INFINITIVO	GERUNDIO	PARTICIPIO
oír	oyendo	o ído

FORMAS COMPUESTAS

INFINITIVO	GERUNDIO
haber oído	habiendo oído

(1) or Perfecto simple. (2), (3) rarely used.

79. SALIR IRREGULAR

MODO INDICATIVO

PRESENTE	PRETÉRITO IMPERFECTO	PRETÉRITO INDEFINIDO (1)	FUTURO IMPERFECTO
salgo	sal ía	sal í	saldré
sal es	sal ías	sal iste	saldrás
sal e	sal ía	sal ió	saldrá
sal imos	sal íamos	sal imos	saldremos
sal ís	sal íais	sal isteis	saldréis
sal en	sal ían	sal ieron	saldrán

PRETÉRITO PERFECTO	PRETÉRITO PLUSCUAMPERFECTO	PRETÉRITO ANTERIOR	FUTURO PERFECTO
he salido	había salido	hube salido	habré salido
has salido	habías salido	hubiste salido	habrás salido
ha salido	había salido	hubo salido	habrá salido
hemos salido	habíamos salido	hubimos salido	habremos salido
habéis salido	habíais salido	hubisteis salido	habréis salido
han salido	habían salido	hubieron salido	habrán salido

CONDICIONAL SIMPLE	CONDICIONAL COMPUESTO
saldría	habría salido
saldrías	habrías salido
saldría	habría salido
saldríamos	habríamos salido
saldríais	habríais salido
saldrían	habrían salido

MODO SUBJUNTIVO

PRESENTE	PRETÉRITO IMPERFECTO	FUTURO IMPERFECTO (2)
salga	sal iera *or* sal iese	sal iere
salgas	sal ieras *or* sal ieses	sal ieres
salga	sal iera *or* sal iese	sal iere
salgamos	sal iéramos *or* sal iésemos	sal iéremos
salgáis	sal ierais *or* sal ieseis	sal iereis
salgan	sal ieran *or* sal iesen	sal ieren

PRETÉRITO PERFECTO	PRETÉRITO PLUSCUAMPERFECTO	FUTURO PERFECTO (3)
haya salido	hubiera *or* hubiese salido	hubiere salido
hayas salido	hubieras *or* hubieses salido	hubieres salido
haya salido	hubiera *or* hubiese salido	hubiere salido
hayamos salido	hubiéramos *or* hubiésemos salido	hubiéremos salido
hayáis salido	hubierais *or* hubieseis salido	hubiereis salido
hayan salido	hubieran *or* ubiesen salido	hubieren salido

MODO IMPERATIVO

FORMAS NO PERSONALES

PRESENTE	
sal	tú
salga	él/ella/usted
salgamos	nosotros/as
sal id	vosotros/as
salgan	ellos/ellas/ustedes

FORMAS SIMPLES

INFINITIVO	GERUNDIO	PARTICIPIO
salir	sal iendo	sal ido

FORMAS COMPUESTAS

INFINITIVO	GERUNDIO
haber salido	habiendo salido

(1) or Perfecto simple. (2), (3) rarely used.

model verb tables

MODO INDICATIVO

PRESENTE	PRETÉRITO IMPERFECTO	PRETÉRITO INDEFINIDO (1)	FUTURO IMPERFECTO
vengo	ven ía	vine	vendré
vienes	ven ías	viniste	vendrás
viene	ven ía	vino	vendrá
ven imos	ven íamos	vinimos	vendremos
ven ís	ven íais	vinisteis	vendréis
vienen	ven ían	vinieron	vendrán

PRETÉRITO PERFECTO		PRETÉRITO PLUSCUAMPERFECTO		PRETÉRITO ANTERIOR		FUTURO PERFECTO	
he	venido	había	venido	hube	venido	habré	venido
has	venido	habías	venido	hubiste	venido	habrás	venido
ha	venido	había	venido	hubo	venido	habrá	venido
hemos	venido	habíamos	venido	hubimos	venido	habremos	venido
habéis	venido	habíais	venido	hubisteis	venido	habréis	venido
han	venido	habían	venido	hubieron	venido	habrán	venido

CONDICIONAL SIMPLE	CONDICIONAL COMPUESTO	
vendría	habría	venido
vendrías	habrías	venido
vendría	habría	venido
vendríamos	habríamos	venido
vendríais	habríais	venido
vendrían	habrían	venido

MODO SUBJUNTIVO

PRESENTE	PRETÉRITO IMPERFECTO		FUTURO IMPERFECTO (2)
venga	viniera	or viniese	viniere
vengas	vinieras	or vinieses	vinieres
venga	viniera	or viniese	viniere
vengamos	viniéramos	or viniésemos	viniéremos
vengáis	vinierais	or vinieseis	viniereis
vengan	vinieran	or viniesen	vinieren

PRETÉRITO PERFECTO		PRETÉRITO PLUSCUAMPERFECTO			FUTURO PERFECTO (3)	
haya	venido	hubiera	or hubiese	venido	hubiere	venido
hayas	venido	hubieras	or hubieses	venido	hubieres	venido
haya	venido	hubiera	or hubiese	venido	hubiere	venido
hayamos	venido	hubiéramos	or hubiésemos	venido	hubiéremos	venido
hayáis	venido	hubierais	or hubieseis	venido	hubiereis	venido
hayan	venido	hubieran	or hubiesen	venido	hubieren	venido

MODO IMPERATIVO		FORMAS NO PERSONALES

PRESENTE

ven	tú
venga	él/ella/usted
vengamos	nosotros/as
ven id	vosotros/as
vengan	ellos/ellas/ustedes

FORMAS SIMPLES

INFINITIVO	GERUNDIO	PARTICIPIO
venir	viniendo	ven ido

FORMAS COMPUESTAS

INFINITIVO	GERUNDIO
haber venido	habiendo venido

(1) or Perfecto simple. (2), (3) rarely used.

Spanish Verb Manual

81. PASSIVE VOICE MODEL: AMAR REGULAR — LOVE

MODO INDICATIVO

PRESENTE		PRETÉRITO IMPERFECTO		PRETÉRITO INDEFINIDO (1)		FUTURO IMPERFECTO	
soy	amado	era	amado	fui	amado	seré	amado
eres	amado	eras	amado	fuiste	amado	serás	amado
es	amado	era	amado	fue	amado	será	amado
somos	amados	éramos	amados	fuimos	amados	seremos	amados
sois	amados	erais	amados	fuisteis	amados	seréis	amados
son	amados	eran	amados	fueron	amados	serán	amados

PRETÉRITO PERFECTO		PRETÉRITO PLUSCUAMPERFECTO		PRETÉRITO ANTERIOR		FUTURO PERFECTO	
he sido	amado	había sido	amado	hube sido	amado	habré sido	amado
has sido	amado	habías sido	amado	hubiste sido	amado	habrás sido	amado
ha sido	amado	había sido	amado	hubo sido	amado	habrá sido	amado
hemos sido	amados	habíamos sido	amados	hubimos sido	amados	habremos sido	amados
habéis sido	amados	habíais sido	amados	hubisteis sido	amados	habréis sido	amados
han sido	amados	habían sido	amados	hubieron sido	amados	habrán sido	amados

CONDICIONAL SIMPLE

sería	amado
serías	amado
sería	amado
seríamos	amados
seríais	amados
serían	amados

CONDICIONAL COMPUESTO

habría sido	amado
habrías sido	amado
habría sido	amado
habríamos sido	amados
habríais sido	amados
habrían sido	amados

MODO SUBJUNTIVO

PRESENTE		PRETÉRITO IMPERFECTO			FUTURO IMPERFECTO (2)	
sea	amado	fuera	or fuese	amado	fuere	amado
seas	amado	fueras	or fueses	amado	fueres	amado
sea	amado	fuera	or fuese	amado	fuere	amado
seamos	amados	fuéramos	or fuésemos	amados	fuéremos	amados
seáis	amados	fuerais	or fueseis	amados	fuereis	amados
sean	amados	fueran	or fuesen	amados	fueren	amados

PRETÉRITO PERFECTO		PRETÉRITO PLUSCUAMPERFECTO			FUTURO PERFECTO (3)	
haya sido	amado	hubiera	or hubiese sido	amado	hubiere sido	amado
hayas sido	amado	hubieras	or hubieses sido	amado	hubieres sido	amado
haya sido	amado	hubiera	or hubiese sido	amado	hubiere sido	amado
hayamos sido	amados	hubiéramos	or hubiésemos sido	amados	hubiéremos sido	amados
hayáis sido	amados	hubierais	or hubieseis sido	amados	hubiereis sido	amados
hayan sido	amados	hubieran	or hubiesen sido	amados	hubieren sido	amados

MODO IMPERATIVO

FORMAS NO PERSONALES

PRESENTE

sé amado	tú
sea amado	él/ella/usted
seamos amados	nosotros/as
sed amados	vosotros/as
sean amados	ellos/ellas/ustedes

FORMAS SIMPLES

INFINITIVO	GERUNDIO	PARTICIPIO
ser amado	siendo amado	sido amado

FORMAS COMPUESTAS

INFINITIVO	GERUNDIO
haber sido amado	habiendo sido amado

(1) or Perfecto simple. (2), (3) rarely used.

model verb tables

82. REFLEXIVE VERB MODEL: LAVARSE REGULAR   *WASH ONESELF*

MODO INDICATIVO

PRESENTE		PRETÉRITO IMPERFECTO		PRETÉRITO INDEFINIDO (1)		FUTURO IMPERFECTO	
me	lavo	me	lavaba	me	lavé	me	lavaré
te	lavas	te	lavabas	te	lavaste	te	lavarás
se	lava	se	lavaba	se	lavó	se	lavará
nos	lavamos	nos	lavábamos	nos	lavamos	nos	lavaremos
os	laváis	os	lavabais	os	lavasteis	os	lavaréis
se	lavan	se	lavaban	se	lavaron	se	lavarán

PRETÉRITO PERFECTO			PRETÉRITO PLUSCUAMPERFECTO			PRETÉRITO ANTERIOR			FUTURO PERFECTO		
me	he	lavado	me	había	lavado	me	hube	lavado	me	habré	lavado
te	has	lavado	te	habías	lavado	te	hubiste	lavado	te	habrás	lavado
se	ha	lavado	se	había	lavado	se	hubo	lavado	se	habrá	lavado
nos	hemos	lavado	nos	habíamos	lavado	nos	hubimos	lavado	nos	habremos	lavado
os	habéis	lavado	os	habíais	lavado	os	hubisteis	lavado	os	habréis	lavado
se	han	lavado	se	habían	lavado	se	hubieron	lavado	se	habrán	lavado

CONDICIONAL SIMPLE		CONDICIONAL COMPUESTO		
me	lavaría	me	habría	lavado
te	lavarías	te	habrías	lavado
se	lavaría	se	habría	lavado
nos	lavaríamos	nos	habríamos	lavado
os	lavaríais	os	habríais	lavado
se	lavarían	se	habrían	lavado

MODO SUBJUNTIVO

PRESENTE		PRETÉRITO IMPERFECTO					FUTURO IMPERFECTO (2)	
me	lave	me	lavara	or	me	lavase	me	lavare
te	laves	te	lavaras	or	te	lavases	te	lavares
se	lave	se	lavara	or	se	lavase	se	lavare
nos	lavemos	nos	laváramos	or	nos	lavásemos	nos	laváremos
os	lavéis	os	lavarais	or	os	lavaseis	os	lavareis
se	laven	se	lavaran	or	se	lavasen	se	lavaren

PRETÉRITO PERFECTO			PRETÉRITO PLUSCUAMPERFECTO						FUTURO PERFECTO (3)		
me	haya	lavado	me	hubiera	or	me	hubiese	lavado	me	hubiere	lavado
te	hayas	lavado	te	hubieras	or	te	hubieses	lavado	te	hubieres	lavado
se	haya	lavado	se	hubiera	or	se	hubiese	lavado	se	hubiere	lavado
nos	hayamos	lavado	nos	hubiéramos	or	nos	hubiésemos	lavado	nos	hubiéremos	lavado
os	hayáis	lavado	os	hubierais	or	os	hubieseis	lavado	os	hubiereis	lavado
se	hayan	lavado	se	hubieran	or	se	hubiesen	lavado	se	hubieren	lavado

MODO IMPERATIVO   FORMAS NO PERSONALES

PRESENTE

lávate	tú
lávese	él/ella/usted
lavémonos	nosotros/as
lavaos	vosotros/as
lávense	ellos/ellas/ustedes

FORMAS SIMPLES

INFINITIVO	GERUNDIO	PARTICIPIO
lavarse	lavándo*se*	—

FORMAS COMPUESTAS

INFINITIVO	GERUNDIO
haber*se* lavado	habiéndo*se* lavado

(1) or Perfecto simple. (2), (3) rarely used.

verb index

	Key
	*= irregular verb

verb		model/table
	a	
Abalanzarse	rush upon	cruzar 8
Abanderar	register	cantar 5
Abandonar	abandon	cantar 5
Abanicar	fan	atacar 7
Abaratar	cheapen	cantar 5
Abarcar	include, embrace	atacar 7
Abarquillar	warp, buckle	cantar 5
Abarrotar	overstock	cantar 5
* Abastecer	supply	obedecer 33
Abatir	knock down	vivir 51
Abdicar	abdicate	atacar 7
Abetunar	polish	cantar 5
Abigarrar	mottle	cantar 5
Abismar	humiliate	cantar 5
Abjurar	foreswear	cantar 5
Ablandar	soften	cantar 5
* Abnegar	renounce	negar 14
Abobar	stupefy	cantar 5
Abocar	arrive at, join	atacar 7
Abocetar	sketch	cantar 5
Abochornar	shame	cantar 5
Abocinar	widen	cantar 5
Abofetear	slap, insult	cantar 5
Abogar	plead	pagar 6
Abolir[1]	abolish	71
Abollar	dent, emboss	cantar 5
Abombar	stun	cantar 5
Abominar	abominate	cantar 5
Abonar	pay	cantar 5
Abordar	board, approach	cantar 5
* Aborrecer	hate	obedecer 33
Aborregarse	grow stupid	pagar 6
Abortar	have a miscarriage, abort	cantar 5
Abotargarse	swell	pagar 6
Abotonar	button	cantar 5
Abovedar	arch, vault	cantar 5
Abrasar	burn, shame	cantar 5

verb		model/table
Abrazar	embrace	cruzar 8
Abrevar	water	cantar 5
Abreviar	abbreviate	cantar 5
Abrigar	shelter, warm	pagar 6
Abrillantar	polish	cantar 5
* Abrir[2]	open	vivir 51
Abrochar	button	cantar 5
Abrogar	repeal	pagar 6
Abrumar	overwhelm	cantar 5
* Absolver[3]	absolve, acquit	mover 30
Absorber[4]	absorb	beber 24
* Abstenerse	abstain	tener 2
* Abstraer[5]	abstract	traer 47
Abuchear	boo	cantar 5
Abultar	enlarge	cantar 5
Abundar	abound	cantar 5
Aburguesarse	become bourgeois	cantar 5
Aburrir	bore	vivir 51
Abusar	abuse	cantar 5
Acabar	finish	cantar 5
* Acaecer[6]	occur	obedecer 33
Acallar	quiet	cantar 5
Acalorarse	become excited	cantar 5
Acampar	camp	cantar 5
Acanalar	groove	cantar 5
Acantonar	quarter	cantar 5
Acaparar	monopolize	cantar 5
Acaramelar	caramelize	cantar 5
Acariciar	caress	cantar 5
Acarrear	transport	cantar 5
Acartonarse	go stiff	cantar 5
Acatar	heed	cantar 5
Acatarrarse	catch cold	cantar 5
Acaudalar	amass	cantar 5
Acaudillar	lead	cantar 5
Acceder	consent	beber 24
Accidentarse	have an accident	cantar 5
Accionar	work	cantar 5
Acechar	watch, stalk	cantar 5
Acecinar	cure (meat)	cantar 5
Aceitar	oil	cantar 5
Acelerar	accelerate	cantar 5

verb	model/table	verb	model/table
Acendrar refine	cantar 5	Acorazar armor-plate	cruzar 8
Acentuar accent	actuar 10	Acorcharse go numb	cantar 5
Aceptar accept	cantar 5	* Acordar agree	contar 16
Acerar turn into steel	cantar 5	Acordonar lace up	cantar 5
Acercar bring near	atacar 7	Acorralar enclose	cantar 5
* Acertar guess right	pensar 13	Acortar shorten	cantar 5
Achabacanarse become vulgar	cantar 5	Acosar pursue	cantar 5
Achacar attribute	atacar 7	* Acostar put to bed	contar 16
Achantar frighten	cantar 5	Acostumbrar accustom	cantar 5
Achaparrarse get thick	cantar 5	Acotar restrict	cantar 5
Acharolar patent	cantar 5	* Acrecentar increase	pensar 13
Achatar flatten	cantar 5	Acreditar accredit	cantar 5
Achicar reduce	atacar 7	Acribillar riddle	cantar 5
Achicharrar burn	cantar 5	Acrisolar purify	cantar 5
Achinar scare	cantar 5	Acristalar glaze	cantar 5
Achispar make tipsy	cantar 5	Activar activate	cantar 5
Achuchar squash	cantar 5	Actualizar bring up to date	cruzar 8
Achularse become crude	cantar 5	Actuar act	10
Acicalarse groom	cantar 5	Acuartelar quarter	cantar 5
Acidificar acidify	atacar 7	Acuchillar stab	cantar 5
Acidular make sour	cantar 5	Acuciar urge on	cantar 5
Aclamar acclaim	cantar 5	Acuclillarse squat down	cantar 5
Aclarar clarify	cantar 5	Acudir come	vivir 51
Aclimatar acclimatize	cantar 5	Acumular accumulate	cantar 5
Acobardar intimidate	cantar 5	Acunar rock	cantar 5
Acodar elbow	cantar 5	Acuñar mint, coin	cantar 5
Acoger receive	coger 25	Acurrucarse curl up	atacar 7
Acogotar kill, knock down	cantar 5	Acusar accuse	cantar 5
Acojonar put the wind up	cantar 5	Adaptar adapt	cantar 5
Acolchar pad	cantar 5	Adecentar tidy up	cantar 5
Acometer attack, undertake	beber 24	Adecuar[7] make suitable	cantar 5
Acomodar arrange	cantar 5	Adelantar advance	cantar 5
Acompañar accompany	cantar 5	Adelgazar make thin	cruzar 8
Acompasar keep in time	cantar 5	Adentrarse enter deep	cantar 5
Acomplejar make to feel		Aderezar adorn	cruzar 8
inferior	cantar 5	Adeudar owe	cantar 5
Acondicionar fit out	cantar 5	* Adherir stick on	sentir 65
Acongojar distress	cantar 5	Adicionar add	cantar 5
Aconsejar advise	cantar 5	Adiestrar train	cantar 5
* Acontecer[6] occur	obedecer 33	Adinerarse get rich	cantar 5
Acoplar couple	cantar 5	Adivinar divine, guess	cantar 5
Acoquinar scare	cantar 5	Adjetivar use as an adjective	cantar 5

V

verb		model/table	verb		model/table
Adjudicar	award	atacar 7	Aflojar	loosen	cantar 5
Adjuntar	attach	cantar 5	Aflorar	outcrop	cantar 5
Adjurar	adjure	cantar 5	* Afluir	flow	concluir 59
Administrar	administer	cantar 5	Afofarse	turn soft	cantar 5
Admirar	admire	cantar 5	Afrancesarse	become French	cantar 5
Admitir	admit	vivir 51	Afrentar	insult	cantar 5
Adobar	marinate	cantar 5	Africanizar	Africanize	cruzar 8
Adocenar	divide into dozens	cantar 5	Afrontar	confront	cantar 5
Adoctrinar	indoctrinate	cantar 5	Agachar	bend	cantar 5
* Adolecer	fall ill	obedecer 33	Agarrar	grasp	cantar 5
Adoptar	adopt	cantar 5	Agarrotar	tie up	cantar 5
Adoquinar	pave	cantar 5	Agasajar	receive warmly	cantar 5
Adorar	adore	cantar 5	Agavillar	sheave	cantar 5
* Adormecer	make sleepy	obedecer 33	Agazaparse	crouch	cantar 5
Adormilarse	doze	cantar 5	Agenciar	find	cantar 5
Adornar	adorn	cantar 5	Agigantar	exaggerate	cantar 5
Adosar	lean	cantar 5	Agilizar	facilitate	cruzar 8
* Adquirir	acquire	67	Agitanar	make gypsy-like	cantar 5
* Adscribir[8]	ascribe	vivir 51	Agitar	shake	cantar 5
* Aducir	allege	traducir 69	Aglomerar	amass	cantar 5
Adueñarse	appropriate	cantar 5	Aglutinar	stick together	cantar 5
Adular	flatter	cantar 5	Agobiar	burden	cantar 5
Adulterar	adulterate	cantar 5	Agolparse	crowd, rush	cantar 5
Adverbializar	use as an adverb	cruzar 8	Agonizar	be dying	cruzar 8
* Advertir	warn	sentir 65	Agostarse	wither, hoe	cantar 5
Aerotransportar	make airborne	cantar 5	Agotar	empty	cantar 5
Afanarse	toil	cantar 5	Agraciar	grace, adorn	cantar 5
Afear	make ugly	cantar 5	Agradar	please	cantar 5
Afectar	affect	cantar 5	* Agradecer	thank	obedecer 33
Afeitar	shave	cantar 5	Agrandar	enlarge	cantar 5
Afelpar	make velvety	cantar 5	Agravar	worsen	cantar 5
Afeminar	make effeminate	cantar 5	Agraviar	offend	cantar 5
Aferrar	seize	cantar 5	Agredir[9]	attack	abolir 71
Afianzar	guarantee	cruzar 8	Agregar	add	pagar 6
Aficionar	make fond	cantar 5	Agremiar	form a guild	cantar 5
Afilar	sharpen	cantar 5	Agriar[10]	sour	desviar 9
Afiliar	affiliate	cantar 5	Agrietar	crack	cantar 5
Afinar	refine	cantar 5	Agrisar	gray	cantar 5
Afincar	come into property	atacar 7	Agrupar	group	cantar 5
Afirmar	affirm	cantar 5	Aguantar	put up with	cantar 5
Aflautar	make high-pitched	cantar 5	Aguar	water	averiguar 11
Afligir	afflict	dirigir 52	Aguardar	await	cantar 5

verb	model/table	verb	model/table
Agudizar worsen	cruzar 8	Aleccionar instruct	cantar 5
Aguijonear goad	cantar 5	Alegar allege	pagar 6
Agujerear make holes	cantar 5	Alegrar make happy	cantar 5
Agusanarse become wormy	cantar 5	Alejar move away	cantar 5
Aguzar sharpen	cruzar 8	Alelar bewilder	cantar 5
Aherrojar chain	cantar 5	* Alentar encourage	pensar 13
Ahogar drown	pagar 6	Alertar alert	cantar 5
Ahondar deepen	cantar 5	Aletargar make sleepy	pagar 6
Ahorcar hang	atacar 7	Aletear flap wings	cantar 5
Ahormar form, fit	cantar 5	Alfabetizar teach to read	cruzar 8
Ahorrar save	cantar 5	Alfombrar carpet	cantar 5
Ahuecar hollow	atacar 7	Algodonar pack with wool	cantar 5
Ahuevar stun	cantar 5	Alhajar deck with jewels	cantar 5
Ahumar smoke	maullar 12	Aliarse become allies	desviar 9
Ahuyentar scare	cantar 5	Alicatar tile	cantar 5
Aindiarse be like Indians	cantar 5	Alicortar clip wings	cantar 5
Airear air	cantar 5	Alienar alienate	cantar 5
Aislar[11] isolate	cantar 5	Aligerar lighten	cantar 5
Ajamonarse get plump	cantar 5	Alimentar feed	cantar 5
Ajar crumple	cantar 5	Alinear align	cantar 5
Ajardinar landscape	cantar 5	Aliñar season	cantar 5
Ajetrear exhaust	cantar 5	Alisar polish	cantar 5
Ajuntar make friends	cantar 5	Alistar prepare	cantar 5
Ajustar fit	cantar 5	Aliviar relieve	cantar 5
Ajusticiar execute	cantar 5	Allanar level	cantar 5
Alabar praise	cantar 5	Allegar collect	pagar 6
Alabear warp	cantar 5	Almacenar store	cantar 5
Alambicar distill	atacar 7	Almendrar almond-paste	cantar 5
Alambrar enclose with wire	cantar 5	Almibarar cover in syrup	cantar 5
Alardear boast	cantar 5	Almidonar starch	cantar 5
Alargar lengthen	pagar 6	Almohadillar pad	cantar 5
Alarmar alarm	cantar 5	Almohazar brush down	cruzar 8
Albardar saddle	cantar 5	* Almorzar eat lunch	forzar 19
Albergar house	pagar 6	Alocarse go mad	atacar 7
Alborear[12] dawn	cantar 5	Alojar lodge	cantar 5
Alborotar cause a riot	cantar 5	Alquilar rent	cantar 5
Alborozar make laugh	cruzar 8	Alterar alter	cantar 5
Alcahuetear procure	cantar 5	Alternar alternate	cantar 5
Alcalinizar alkalize	cruzar 8	Alucinar hallucinate	cantar 5
Alcantarillar lay sewers	cantar 5	Aludir allude to	vivir 51
Alcanzar reach	cruzar 8	Alumbrar light up	cantar 5
Alcoholizar alcoholize	cruzar 8	Alunizar land on the moon	cruzar 8

V

verb	model/table	verb	model/table
Alzar lift	cruzar 8	Amortiguar muffle	averiguar 11
Amadrinar yoke together	cantar 5	Amortizar amortize	cruzar 8
Amaestrar train	cantar 5	Amostazar make cross	cruzar 8
Amagar promise	pagar 6	Amotinar incite to riot	cantar 5
Amainar lower, calm	cantar 5	Amparar help	cantar 5
Amalgamar amalgamate	cantar 5	Ampliar enlarge	desviar 9
Amamantar breast-feed	cantar 5	Amplificar amplify	atacar 7
Amancebarse live together	cantar 5	Amputar amputate	cantar 5
* Amanecer[12] dawn	obedecer 33	Amueblar furnish	cantar 5
Amanerarse become affected	cantar 5	Amuermar bore	cantar 5
Amansar tame	cantar 5	Amurallar wall	cantar 5
Amañar arrange	cantar 5	Analizar analyze	cruzar 8
Amar love	cantar 5	Anarquizar make anarchy	cruzar 8
Amarar splash down	cantar 5	Anatematizar anathematize	cruzar 8
Amargar embitter	pagar 6	Anatomizar dissect	cruzar 8
Amarillear go yellow	cantar 5	Anclar anchor	cantar 5
Amarrar tie up	cantar 5	* Andar walk	22
Amartelar make jealous	cantar 5	Anegar flood	pagar 6
Amartillar hammer	cantar 5	Anestesiar anesthetize	cantar 5
Amasar knead	cantar 5	Anexionar annex	cantar 5
Ambicionar seek	cantar 5	Angostar narrow	cantar 5
Ambientar set	cantar 5	Angustiar anguish	cantar 5
Amedrentar scare	cantar 5	Anhelar long for	cantar 5
Amenazar threaten	cruzar 8	Anidar rest	cantar 5
Amenizar liven up	cruzar 8	Anillar put rings on	cantar 5
Americanizar Americanize	cruzar 8	Animalizar animalize	cruzar 8
Amerizar splash down	cruzar 8	Animar animate	cantar 5
Ametrallar machine-gun	cantar 5	Aniñarse become childish	cantar 5
Amigar make friends	pagar 6	Aniquilar annihilate	cantar 5
Amilanar frighten	cantar 5	Anisar flavor with aniseed	cantar 5
Aminorar reduce	cantar 5	* Anochecer[12] get dark	obedecer 33
Amnistiar amnesty	desviar 9	Anonadar overwhelm	cantar 5
Amodorrarse get sleepy	cantar 5	Anotar note down	cantar 5
Amojamar dry and salt	cantar 5	Anquilosar ankylose	cantar 5
Amoldar mold	cantar 5	Ansiar long for	desviar 9
Amonarse get drunk	cantar 5	Anteceder precede	beber 24
Amonestar warn	cantar 5	* Anteponer put in front	poner 41
Amontonar pile up	cantar 5	Anticipar advance	cantar 5
Amoratarse turn blue	cantar 5	Antojarse feel like	cantar 5
Amordazar gag	cruzar 8	Anudar knot	cantar 5
Amorriñarse weaken	cantar 5	Anular revoke	cantar 5
Amortajar shroud	cantar 5	Anunciar announce	cantar 5

verb	model/table	verb	model/table
Añadir add	*vivir* 51	Aplaudir applaud	*vivir* 51
Añorar miss	*cantar* 5	Aplazar postpone	*cruzar* 8
Apabullar squash	*cantar* 5	Aplicar apply	*atacar* 7
* Apacentar pasture	*pensar* 13	Apocar reduce	*atacar* 7
Apaciguar calm	*averiguar* 11	Apocopar apocopate	*cantar* 5
Apadrinar act as godfather	*cantar* 5	Apodar nickname	*cantar* 5
Apagar turn off	*pagar* 6	Apoderar empower	*cantar* 5
Apalabrar make an		Apolillarse get moth-eaten	*cantar* 5
agreement	*cantar* 5	Apologizar defend	*cruzar* 8
Apalancar lever up	*atacar* 7	Apoltronarse get lazy	*cantar* 5
Apalear thresh	*cantar* 5	Apoquinar fork out	*cantar* 5
Apañar patch up	*cantar* 5	Aporrear hit	*cantar* 5
Aparcar park	*atacar* 7	Aportar contribute	*cantar* 5
Aparear pair off	*cantar* 5	Aposentar lodge	*cantar* 5
* Aparecer appear	*obedecer* 33	* Apostar[13] bet	*contar* 16
Aparejar prepare	*cantar* 5	Apostatar apostatize	*cantar* 5
Aparentar feign	*cantar* 5	Apostillar add notes to	*cantar* 5
Apartar remove	*cantar* 5	Apostrofar apostrophize	*cantar* 5
Apasionar rouse	*cantar* 5	Apoyar support	*cantar* 5
Apear help down	*cantar* 5	Apreciar appraise	*cantar* 5
Apechar put up with	*cantar* 5	Aprehender apprehend	*beber* 24
Apechugar push with chest	*pagar* 6	Apremiar urge	*cantar* 5
Apedrear throw stones	*cantar* 5	Aprender learn	*beber* 24
Apegarse become attached to	*pagar* 6	Apresar seize	*cantar* 5
Apelar appeal	*cantar* 5	Aprestarse prepare	*cantar* 5
Apellidar call by surname	*cantar* 5	Apresurar quicken	*cantar* 5
Apelmazar make soggy	*cruzar* 8	* Apretar squeeze	*pensar* 13
Apelotonar roll into a ball	*cantar* 5	Apretujar squeeze hard	*cantar* 5
Apenar pain	*cantar* 5	Aprisionar imprison	*cantar* 5
Apercibir warn	*vivir* 51	* Aprobar approve	*contar* 16
Apergaminarse dry up	*cantar* 5	Apropiar make the	
Apesadumbrar upset	*cantar* 5	possession of, fit	*cantar* 5
Apestar stink	*cantar* 5	Aprovechar be useful to	*cantar* 5
* Apetecer crave for	*obedecer* 33	Aprovisionar supply	*cantar* 5
Apiadar move to pity	*cantar* 5	Aproximar bring nearer	*cantar* 5
Apilar pile up	*cantar* 5	Apuntalar prop up	*cantar* 5
Apiñar heap up	*cantar* 5	Apuntar point	*cantar* 5
Apisonar roll	*cantar* 5	Apuntillar kill with dagger	*cantar* 5
Aplacar placate	*atacar* 7	Apuñalar stab	*cantar* 5
Aplanar flatten	*cantar* 5	Apurar hurry	*cantar* 5
Aplastar squash	*cantar* 5	Aquejar trouble	*cantar* 5
Aplatanar make listless	*cantar* 5	Aquietar calm	*cantar* 5

V

Spanish Verb Manual

verb	model/table	verb	model/table
Aquilatar appraise	cantar 5	Arrogarse assume	pagar 6
Arañar scratch	cantar 5	Arrojar throw	cantar 5
Arar plow	cantar 5	Arrollar roll up	cantar 5
Arbitrar arbitrate	cantar 5	Arropar wrap up	cantar 5
Arbolar hoist	cantar 5	Arrostrar face up to	cantar 5
Archivar archive	cantar 5	Arrugar wrinkle	pagar 6
Arder burn	beber 24	Arruinar ruin	cantar 5
* Argüir[14] argue	concluir 59	Arrullar coo at	cantar 5
Argumentar dispute	cantar 5	Arrumbar discard	cantar 5
Armar arm	cantar 5	Articular articulate	cantar 5
Armonizar harmonize	cruzar 8	Asaetear shoot	cantar 5
Aromatizar perfume	cruzar 8	Asalariar fix a salary	cantar 5
Arponear harpoon	cantar 5	Asaltar attack	cantar 5
Arquear arch	cantar 5	Asar roast	cantar 5
Arracimarse bunch	cantar 5	* Ascender ascend	perder 29
Arraigar take root	pagar 6	Asear wash	cantar 5
Arramblar cover with sand	cantar 5	Asediar besiege	cantar 5
Arramplar make off with	cantar 5	Asegurar secure	cantar 5
Arrancar uproot	atacar 7	Asemejarse resemble	cantar 5
Arrasar level	cantar 5	* Asentar seat	pensar 13
Arrastrar haul	cantar 5	* Asentir agree	sentir 65
Arrear urge on	cantar 5	* Aserrar saw	pensar 13
Arrebatar snatch	cantar 5	Asesinar assassinate	cantar 5
Arrebolarse flush	cantar 5	Asesorar counsel	cantar 5
Arrebujar crumple	cantar 5	Asestar aim	pensar 13
Arreciar get worse	cantar 5	Aseverar assert	cantar 5
Arredrar move away	cantar 5	Asfaltar asphalt	cantar 5
Arregla fix	cantar 5	Asfixiar asphyxiate	cantar 5
Arrellanarse lounge	cantar 5	Asignar assign	cantar 5
Arremangar hitch up	pagar 6	Asilar put in a home	cantar 5
Arremeter attack	beber 24	Asimilar assimilate	cantar 5
Arremolinarse swirl	cantar 5	* Asir grasp	72
* Arrendar lease	pensar 13	Asistir attend	vivir 51
* Arrepentirse repent	sentir 65	Asociar associate	cantar 5
Arrestar arrest	cantar 5	Asolar[15] destroy	cantar 5
Arriar lower	desviar 9	Asomar show	cantar 5
Arribar arrive	cantar 5	Asombrar shade	cantar 5
Arriesgar risk	pagar 6	Aspar wind, annoy	cantar 5
Arrimar draw up	cantar 5	Asperjar sprinkle	cantar 5
Arrinconar corner	cantar 5	Aspirar aspire	cantar 5
Arrobar enrapture	cantar 5	Asquear sicken	cantar 5
Arrodillar kneel	cantar 5	Astillar splinter	cantar 5

verb	model/table	verb	model/table
Asumir assume	vivir 51	Atrancar bar	atacar 7
Asustar frighten	cantar 5	Atrapar trap	cantar 5
Atacar attack	7	Atrasar slow	cantar 5
Atajar take a shortcut	cantar 5	* Atravesar go through	pensar 13
Atañer[6] concern	tañer 27	Atreverse dare	beber 24
Atar tie up	cantar 5	* Atribuir attribute	concluir 59
* Atardecer[12] get late	obedecer 33	Atribular afflict	cantar 5
Atarugar pin	pagar 6	Atrincherar entrench	cantar 5
Atascar obstruct	atacar 7	Atrofiar atrophy	cantar 5
Ataviar adorn	desviar 9	* Atronar[12] deafen	contar 16
Atemorizar scare	cruzar 8	Atropellar knock down	cantar 5
Atemperar moderate	cantar 5	Atufar anger	cantar 5
Atenazar tear flesh	cruzar 8	Aturdir daze	vivir 51
* Atender[16] attend to	perder 29	Aturullar bewilder	cantar 5
* Atenerse adhere	tener 2	Atusar trim hair	cantar 5
Atentar attempt	cantar 5	Auditar audit	cantar 5
Atenuar lessen	actuar 10	Augurar predict	cantar 5
Aterrar scare	cantar 5	Aullar howl	maullar 12
Aterrizar land	cruzar 8	Aumentar increase	cantar 5
Aterrorizar terrify	cruzar 8	Aunar join	maullar 12
Atesorar hoard	cantar 5	Aupar lift up	maullar 12
Atestar stuff	cantar 5	Aureolar halo	cantar 5
Atestiguar attest	averiguar 11	Auscultar sound	cantar 5
Atiborrar cram	cantar 5	Ausentar absent	cantar 5
Atildar accent	cantar 5	Auspiciar patronize	cantar 5
Atinar find	cantar 5	Autenticar authenticate	atacar 7
Atiplar raise pitch	cantar 5	Autentificar legalize	atacar 7
Atirantar tighten	cantar 5	Autoasignarse self-assign	cantar 5
Atisbar watch	cantar 5	Autocalificarse self-assess	atacar 7
Atizar stir up	cruzar 8	Autocensurarse self-censor	cantar 5
Atocinar bump off	cantar 5	* Autocorregir self-correct	corregir 61
Atolondrar stun	cantar 5	* Autodestruirse self-destroy	concluir 59
Atomizar atomize	cruzar 8	Automatizar automate	cruzar 8
Atontar daze	cantar 5	Autopresentarse self-present	cantar 5
Atontolinar stupefy	cantar 5	Autorizar authorize	cruzar 8
Atorarse get clogged	cantar 5	Autorregularse regulate oneself	cantar 5
Atormentar torture	cantar 5	Autosugestionarse suggest to	
Atornillar screw on	cantar 5	oneself	cantar 5
Atosigar poison	pagar 6	Auxiliar assist	cantar 5
Atracar rob	atacar 7	Avalar guarantee	cantar 5
* Atraer attract	traer 47	Avanzar advance	cruzar 8
Atragantar choke	cantar 5	Avasallar enslave	cantar 5

verb	model/table	verb	model/table
Avecinarse get nearer	cantar 5	Balancear balance	cantar 5
Avecindar domicile	cantar 5	Balar bleat	cantar 5
Avejentar age	cantar 5	Balbucear stutter	cantar 5
* Avenir reconcile	venir 80	Balbucir[17] stammer	abolir 71
Aventajar come ahead of	cantar 5	Baldar cripple	cantar 5
* Aventar blow away	pensar 13	Baldear wash down	cantar 5
Aventurar risk	cantar 5	Bambolear sway	cantar 5
* Avergonzar shame	20	Bandear cross	cantar 5
Averiar damage	desviar 9	Banderillear stick	cantar 5
Averiguar investigate, find out	11	Bañar bathe	cantar 5
Avezar get used to	cruzar 8	Baquetear harden	cantar 5
Aviar prepare	desviar 9	Barajar mix up	cantar 5
Aviejar age	cantar 5	Barnizar varnish	cruzar 8
Avinagrar turn sour	cantar 5	Barrar smear	cantar 5
Avisar warn	cantar 5	Barrenar drill	cantar 5
Avisparse liven up	cantar 5	Barrer sweep	beber 24
Avistar glimpse	cantar 5	Barritar trumpet (elephant)	cantar 5
Avituallar provision	cantar 5	Barruntar have a feeling	cantar 5
Avivar revive	cantar 5	Basar base	cantar 5
Avizorar spy on	cantar 5	Bascular tilt	cantar 5
Ayudar help	cantar 5	Bastar suffice	cantar 5
Ayunar fast	cantar 5	Batallar battle	cantar 5
Azarar embarrass	cantar 5	Batear bat	cantar 5
Azogar silver	pagar 6	Batir beat	vivir 51
Azorar fluster	cantar 5	Bautizar baptize	cruzar 8
Azotar whip	cantar 5	Beatificar beatify	atacar 7
Azucarar sweeten	cantar 5	Beber drink	24
Azufrar sulphur	cantar 5	Becar grant a scholarship	atacar 7
Azulear look blue	cantar 5	* Bendecir[18] bless	73
Azuzar incite	cruzar 8	Beneficiar benefit	cantar 5
		Berrear low (calf)	cantar 5
		Besar kiss	cantar 5
		Bestializarse make bestial	cruzar 8
		Besuquear cover with kisses	cantar 5
		Bifurcar fork	atacar 7
		Biografiar write a biography	desviar 9
		Birlar bowl	cantar 5
Babear slobber	cantar 5	Bisar repeat, encore	cantar 5
Babosear dribble over	cantar 5	Bisbisear mumble	cantar 5
Bailar dance	cantar 5	Biselar bevel	cantar 5
Bailotear dance about	cantar 5	Bizquear be cross-eyed	cantar 5
Bajar descend	cantar 5	Blandir brandish	abolir 71

b

V

verb	model/table
Blanquear whiten	cantar 5
Blasfemar blaspheme	cantar 5
Blasonar emblazon	cantar 5
Blindar armor	cantar 5
Bloquear block	cantar 5
Bobear be silly	cantar 5
Bogar row	pagar 6
Boicotear boycott	cantar 5
Bombardear bomb	cantar 5
Bombear pump	cantar 5
Bonificar improve	atacar 7
Bordar embroider	cantar 5
Bordear border	cantar 5
Borrar erase	cantar 5
Bosquejar outline	cantar 5
Bostezar yawn	cruzar 8
Botar throw out	cantar 5
Boxear box	cantar 5
Bracear wave	cantar 5
Bramar bellow	cantar 5
Brasear braise	cantar 5
Brear thrash	cantar 5
Bregar struggle	pagar 6
Bribonear play the rascal	cantar 5
Bricolar do-it-yourself	cantar 5
Brillar shine	cantar 5
Brincar jump	atacar 7
Brindar toast	cantar 5
Bromear joke	cantar 5
Broncear tan	cantar 5
Brotar come up	cantar 5
Brujulear guess	cantar 5
Bruñir polish	58
Brutalizarse be brutalized	cruzar 8
Bucear skin-dive	cantar 5
Bufar snort	cantar 5
Bullir boil	mullir 57
Burbujear fizz	cantar 5
Burilar engrave	cantar 5
Burlar deceive	cantar 5
Buscar look for	atacar 7
Buzonear pass out flyers	cantar 5

C

verb	model/table
Cabalgar ride	pagar 6
Cabecear nod	cantar 5
* Caber fit	35
Cablear twist	cantar 5
Cablegrafiar cable	desviar 9
Cabrear get one's goat	cantar 5
Cabrillear shimmer	cantar 5
Cacarear cluck	cantar 5
Cachear search	cantar 5
Cachondearse treat as a joke, make fun of	cantar 5
Caducar expire	atacar 7
* Caer fall, be located	36
Cagar defecate	pagar 6
Calafetear caulk	cantar 5
Calar soak	cantar 5
Calcar trace	atacar 7
Calcetar knit	cantar 5
Calcificar calcify	atacar 7
Calcinar calcine	cantar 5
Calcografiar chalcograph	desviar 9
Calcular calculate	cantar 5
Caldear heat	cantar 5
* Calentar warm	pensar 13
Calibrar gauge	cantar 5
Calificar qualify	atacar 7
Caligrafiar write beautifully	desviar 9
Callar keep quiet	cantar 5
Callejear wander	cantar 5
Calmar calm	cantar 5
Calumniar slander	cantar 5
Calzar put on shoes	cruzar 8
Cambiar change	cantar 5
Camelar butter up	cantar 5
Caminar walk	cantar 5
Campar excel	cantar 5
Campear graze	cantar 5
Camuflar camouflage	cantar 5

verb	model/table	verb	model/table
Canalizar canalize	*cruzar* 8	Castigar punish	*pagar* 6
Cancelar cancel	*cantar* 5	Castrar castrate	*cantar* 5
Canjear exchange	*cantar* 5	Catalizar catalyze	*cruzar* 8
Canonizar canonize	*cruzar* 8	Catalogar catalogue	*pagar* 6
Cansar tire	*cantar* 5	Catapultar catapult	*cantar* 5
Cantar sing	5	Catar sample	*cantar* 5
Canturrear hum	*cantar* 5	Catear look for	*cantar* 5
Cañonear shell	*cantar* 5	Catequizar catechize	*cruzar* 8
Capacitar train	*cantar* 5	Causar cause	*cantar* 5
Capar castrate	*cantar* 5	Cauterizar cauterize	*cruzar* 8
Capear beguile, excite (bull)		Cautivar capture	*cantar* 5
with a cape	*cantar* 5	Cavar dig	*cantar* 5
Capitalizar capitalize	*cruzar* 8	Cavilar ponder	*cantar* 5
Capitanear command	*cantar* 5	Cazar hunt	*cruzar* 8
Capitular capitulate	*cantar* 5	Cebar bait	*cantar* 5
Capotar overturn	*cantar* 5	Cecear lisp	*cantar* 5
Capotear distract, dodge	*cantar* 5	Ceder yield	*beber* 24
Captar harness	*cantar* 5	* Cegar blind	*negar* 14
Capturar capture	*cantar* 5	Cejar back up	*cantar* 5
Caracolear prance	*cantar* 5	Celar supervise	*cantar* 5
Caracterizar characterize	*cruzar* 8	Celebrar celebrate	*cantar* 5
Caramelizar caramelize	*cruzar* 8	Cenar dine	*cantar* 5
Carbonatar carbonate	*cantar* 5	Censar take a census	*cantar* 5
Carbonizar carbonize	*cruzar* 8	Censurar censor	*cantar* 5
Carburar carburet	*cantar* 5	Centellear[12] sparkle	*cantar* 5
Carcajear roar with laughter	*cantar* 5	Centralizar centralize	*cruzar* 8
Carcomer eat away	*beber* 24	Centrar center	*cantar* 5
Cardar card (wool)	*cantar* 5	Centrifugar centrifuge	*pagar* 6
Carear confront	*cantar* 5	Centuplicar centuple	*atacar* 7
* Carecer lack	*obedecer* 33	* Ceñir gird	*teñir* 64
Cargar load	*pagar* 6	Cepillar brush	*cantar* 5
Cariarse decay	*cantar* 5	Cercar fence	*atacar* 7
Caricaturizar caricature	*cruzar* 8	Cercenar trim	*cantar* 5
Carraspear clear throat	*cantar* 5	Cerciorar assure	*cantar* 5
Cartearse correspond	*cantar* 5	* Cernir[6] sieve	*discernir* 66
Cartografiar draw a map	*desviar* 9	* Cerrar close	*pensar* 13
Casarse marry	*cantar* 5	Certificar certify	*atacar* 7
Cascabelear lure	*cantar* 5	Cesar cease	*cantar* 5
Cascar crack	*atacar* 7	Chafar flatten	*cantar* 5
Castañetear play castanets	*cantar* 5	Chalar drive crazy	*cantar* 5
Castellanizar give a Spanish		Chamullar speak	*cantar* 5
name to	*cruzar* 8	Chamuscar singe	*atacar* 7

verb	model/table	verb	model/table
Chancear joke	cantar 5	Cicatrizar scar	cruzar 8
Chancletear shuffle	cantar 5	Cifrar code	cantar 5
Chantajear blackmail	cantar 5	Cimbrear waggle	cantar 5
Chapar plate	cantar 5	Cimentar cement	cantar 5
Chapotear moisten	cantar 5	Cincelar chisel	cantar 5
Chapucear botch	cantar 5	Cinematografiar film	desviar 9
Chapurrear speak a little	cantar 5	Circuncidar[19] circumcise	cantar 5
Chapuzar duck	cruzar 8	Circunnavegar circumnavigate	pagar 6
Chaquetear be a turncoat	cantar 5	* Circunscribir[20] circumscribe	vivir 51
Charlar chat	cantar 5	Circunvalar surround	cantar 5
Charlatanear chatter	cantar 5	Ciscar dirty	atacar 7
Charlotear prattle	cantar 5	Citar make an appointment	cantar 5
Charolar varnish	cantar 5	Civilizar civilize	cruzar 8
Chascar click tongue	atacar 7	Cizañar sow discord	cantar 5
Chasquear play a trick	cantar 5	Clamar cry out	cantar 5
Chatear go for a few drinks	cantar 5	Clamorear appeal for	cantar 5
Chequear check	cantar 5	Clarear[12] light up	cantar 5
Chicolear compliment	cantar 5	Clarificar clarify	atacar 7
Chiflar make crazy	cantar 5	Clasificar classify	atacar 7
Chillar scream	cantar 5	Claudicar limp, shirk	atacar 7
Chinchar pester	cantar 5	Clausurar conclude	cantar 5
Chinchorrear gossip	cantar 5	Clavar nail	cantar 5
Chingar screw (vulgar)	pagar 6	Clavetear stud (with nails)	cantar 5
Chirigotear joke	cantar 5	Climatizar air-condition	cruzar 8
Chirriar creak	desviar 9	Clonar clone	cantar 5
Chismear gossip	cantar 5	Cloquear cluck	cantar 5
Chismorrear gossip	cantar 5	Cloroformizar chloroform	cruzar 8
Chispear[12] spark	cantar 5	Coaccionar coerce	cantar 5
Chisporrotear crackle	cantar 5	Coadyuvar help	cantar 5
Chistar answer	cantar 5	Coagular coagulate	cantar 5
Chivarse tell	cantar 5	Coaligarse associate	pagar 6
Chocar hit	atacar 7	Coartar hinder	cantar 5
Chochear dodder	cantar 5	Cobijar cover	cantar 5
Choricear make sausages	cantar 5	Cobrar earn	cantar 5
Chorrear flow	cantar 5	Cocear kick	cantar 5
Chotearse make fun	cantar 5	* Cocer cook, boil	34
Chulear get cocky	cantar 5	Cocinar cook	cantar 5
Chupar suck	cantar 5	Codear elbow	cantar 5
Chupetear suck at	cantar 5	Codiciar covet	cantar 5
Churruscar burn	atacar 7	Codificar codify	atacar 7
Chutar shoot ball	cantar 5	Coexistir coexist	vivir 51
Cicatear be stingy	cantar 5	Coger catch, seize	25

verb	model/table	verb	model/table
Cohabitar cohabit	cantar 5	Compatibilizar make compatble	cruzar 8
Coheredar inherit jointly	cantar 5	Compeler compel	beber 24
Cohibir inhibit	prohibir 55	Compendiar abridge	cantar 5
Coincidir coincide	vivir 51	Compenetrarse interpenetrate	cantar 5
Cojear limp	cantar 5	Compensar compensate	cantar 5
Colaborar collaborate	cantar 5	Competer[6] concern	beber 24
Colacionar collate	cantar 5	* Competir compete	pedir 60
Colapsar collapse	cantar 5	Compilar compile	cantar 5
* Colar strain	contar 16	* Complacer please	placer 39
Colear wag	cantar 5	Complementar complement	cantar 5
Coleccionar collect	cantar 5	Completar complete	cantar 5
Colectar collect	cantar 5	Complicar complicate	atacar 7
Colectivizar collectivize	cruzar 8	* Componer consist	poner 41
Colegiarse enroll in college	cantar 5	Comportar involve	cantar 5
* Colegir gather	corregir 61	Comprar buy	cantar 5
* Colgar hang	rogar 18	Comprender understand	beber 24
Colindar adjoin	cantar 5	Comprimir compress	vivir 51
Colisionar collide	cantar 5	* Comprobar prove	contar 16
Colmar fill up	cantar 5	Comprometer comprehend	beber 24
Colocar place	atacar 7	Compulsar compare	cantar 5
Colonizar colonize	cruzar 8	Computar compute	cantar 5
Colorear color	cantar 5	Computarizar computerize	cruzar 8
Columbrar glimpse	cantar 5	Comulgar receive communion	pagar 6
Columpiar swing	cantar 5	Comunicar communicate	atacar 7
Comadrear gossip	cantar 5	Concatenar link	cantar 5
Comandar command	cantar 5	* Concebir conceive	pedir 60
Combar bend	cantar 5	Conceder concede	beber 24
Combatir combat	vivir 51	Concelebrar concelebrate	cantar 5
Combinar combine	cantar 5	Concentrar concentrate	cantar 5
Comentar comment	cantar 5	Conceptuar consider	actuar 10
* Comenzar begin	empezar 15	* Concernir[6] concern	discernir 66
Comer eat	beber 24	* Concertar assemble, unite	pensar 13
Comercializar commercialize	cruzar 8	Conchabar gather together	cantar 5
Comerciar trade	cantar 5	Concienciar awaken	cantar 5
Cometer commit	beber 24	Conciliar reconcile	cantar 5
Comisionar commission	cantar 5	Concitar stir up	cantar 5
* Compadecer sympathize	obedecer 33	* Concluir conclude	59
Compaginar reconcile	cantar 5	* Concordar reconcile	contar 16
Comparar compare	cantar 5	Concretar state explicitly	cantar 5
* Comparecer appear	obedecer 33	Concretizar concretize	cruzar 8
Compartimentar partition	cantar 5	Conculcar infringe	atacar 7
Compartir share	vivir 51	Concurrir converge	vivir 51

verb	model/table	verb	model/table
Concursar compete	*cantar* 5	Conllevar bear with	*cantar* 5
Condecorar decorate	*cantar* 5	Conmemorar commemorate	*cantar* 5
Condenar condemn	*cantar* 5	Conmensurar commensurate	*cantar* 5
Condensar condense	*cantar* 5	Conminar menace	*cantar* 5
* Condescender yield	*perder* 29	Conmocionar shock	*cantar* 5
Condicionar fit	*cantar* 5	* Conmover move	*mover* 30
Condimentar season	*cantar* 5	Conmutar commute	*cantar* 5
* Condolerse feel pity	*mover* 30	Connotar connote	*cantar* 5
Condonar condone	*cantar* 5	* Conocer know, meet	32
* Conducir drive	*traducir* 69	Conquistar conquer	*cantar* 5
Conectar connect	*cantar* 5	Consagrar dedicate	*cantar* 5
Conexionarse make connections	*cantar* 5	* Conseguir obtain	*seguir* 62
Confabular converse	*cantar* 5	Consensuar be consensual	*actuar* 10
Confeccionar make up	*cantar* 5	* Consentir consent	*sentir* 65
Confederar confederate	*cantar* 5	Conservar preserve	*cantar* 5
Conferenciar converse	*cantar* 5	Considerar consider	*cantar* 5
* Conferir confer	*sentir* 65	Consignar earmark	*cantar* 5
* Confesar confess	*pensar* 13	Consistir consist	*vivir* 51
Confiar trust	*desviar* 9	* Consolar console	*contar* 16
Configurar shape	*cantar* 5	Consolidar consolidate	*cantar* 5
Confinar confine	*cantar* 5	Consonantizar change to a	
Confirmar confirm	*cantar* 5	consonant	*cruzar* 8
Confiscar confiscate	*atacar* 7	Conspirar conspire	*cantar* 5
Confitar candy	*cantar* 5	Constar consist	*cantar* 5
Conflagrar blaze	*cantar* 5	Constatar verify	*cantar* 5
* Confluir converge	*concluir* 59	Consternar dismay	*cantar* 5
Conformar conform	*cantar* 5	Constipar constrict	*cantar* 5
Confortar comfort	*cantar* 5	Constitucionalizar	
Confraternizar fraternize	*cruzar* 8	constitutionalize	*cruzar* 8
Confrontar confront	*cantar* 5	* Constituir constitute	*concluir* 59
Confundir[21] confuse	*vivir* 51	* Constreñir constrain	*teñir* 64
Congelar freeze	*cantar* 5	* Construir construct	*concluir* 59
Congeniar get along	*cantar* 5	Consultar consult	*cantar* 5
Congestionar congest	*cantar* 5	Consumar complete	*cantar* 5
Conglomerar conglomerate	*cantar* 5	Consumir consume	*vivir* 51
Congraciar win over	*cantar* 5	Contabilizar enter	*cruzar* 8
Congratular congratulate	*cantar* 5	Contactar contact	*cantar* 5
Congregar congregate	*pagar* 6	Contagiar contaminate	*cantar* 5
Conjeturar conjecture	*cantar* 5	Contaminar pollute	*cantar* 5
Conjugar conjugate	*pagar* 6	* Contar count, relate	16
Conjuntar coordinate	*cantar* 5	Contemplar contemplate	*cantar* 5
Conjurar plot	*cantar* 5	Contemporizar comply	*cruzar* 8

verb	model/table	verb	model/table
* Contender contend	perder 29	Copular link	cantar 5
* Contener contain	tener 2	Coquetear flirt	cantar 5
Contentar content	cantar 5	Corear sing in chorus	cantar 5
Contestar answer	cantar 5	Coreografiar choreograph	desviar 9
Contextualizar contextualize	cruzar 8	Cornear gore	cantar 5
Continuar continue	actuar 10	Coronar crown	cantar 5
Contonearse sway hips	cantar 5	* Corregir[22] correct	61
Contornear sketch	cantar 5	Correr run	beber 24
Contorsionarse contort	cantar 5	Corresponder return	beber 24
Contraatacar counterattack	atacar 7	Corretear loiter	cantar 5
* Contradecir contradict	decir 74	Corroborar corroborate	cantar 5
* Contraer contract	traer 47	* Corroer corrode	roer 43
Contraindicar contraindicate	atacar 7	Corromper[23] corrupt	beber 24
Contrapesar counterbalance	cantar 5	Cortar cut	cantar 5
* Contraponer oppose	poner 41	Cortejar woo	cantar 5
Contrariar annoy	desviar 9	Coscarse shrug shoulders	atacar 7
Contrarrestar counteract	cantar 5	Cosechar harvest	cantar 5
Contrastar resist	cantar 5	Coser sew	beber 24
Contratar contract	cantar 5	Cosquillear tickle	cantar 5
* Contravenir contravene	venir 80	* Costar cost	contar 16
* Contribuir contribute	concluir 59	Costear pay for	cantar 5
Contristar sadden	cantar 5	Cotejar compare	cantar 5
Controlar control	cantar 5	Cotillear gossip	cantar 5
Conturbar trouble	cantar 5	Cotizar quote a price	cruzar 8
Contusionar contuse	cantar 5	Cotorrear chatter	cantar 5
* Convalecer convalesce	obedecer 33	Crear create	cantar 5
Convalidar ratify	cantar 5	* Crecer grow	obedecer 33
Convencer convince	vencer 26	* Creer believe	leer 28
* Convenir agree	venir 80	Crepitar crackle	cantar 5
Converger converge	coger 25	Criar raise	desviar 9
Conversar converse	cantar 5	Cribar sift	cantar 5
* Convertir convert	sentir 65	Crispar tense	cantar 5
Convidar invite	cantar 5	Cristalizar crystallize	cruzar 8
Convivir cohabit	vivir 51	Cristianar christen	cantar 5
Convocar convoke	atacar 7	Cristianizar Christianize	cruzar 8
Convulsionar convulse	cantar 5	Criticar criticize	atacar 7
Coñearse take a piss	cantar 5	Croar croak	cantar 5
Cooperar cooperate	cantar 5	Cromar chrome	cantar 5
Coordinar coordinate	cantar 5	Cronometrar time	cantar 5
Copar win	cantar 5	Crucificar crucify	atacar 7
Copear booze	cantar 5	Crujir gnash	vivir 51
Copiar copy	cantar 5	Cruzar cross	8

verb	model/table	verb	model/table
Cuadrar square	cantar 5	Decantar decant	cantar 5
Cuadricular grid	cantar 5	Decapitar decapitate	cantar 5
Cuadruplicar quadruple	atacar 7	Decepcionar disappoint	cantar 5
Cuajar congeal	cantar 5	Decidir decide	vivir 51
Cualificar qualify	atacar 7	* Decir tell, say	74
Cuantificar quantify	atacar 7	Declamar declaim	cantar 5
Cuartear quarter	cantar 5	Declarar declare	cantar 5
* Cubrir[24] cover	vivir 51	Declinar decline	cantar 5
Cuchichear whisper	cantar 5	Decodificar decode	atacar 7
Cuestionar question	cantar 5	Decolorar discolor	cantar 5
Cuidar care for	cantar 5	Decomisar confiscate	cantar 5
Culminar culminate	cantar 5	Decorar decorate	cantar 5
Culpabilizar blame	cruzar 8	Decorticar decorticate	atacar 7
Culpar blame	cantar 5	* Decrecer decrease	obedecer 33
Cultivar cultivate	cantar 5	Decretar decree	cantar 5
Culturizar educate	cruzar 8	Dedicar dedicate	atacar 7
Cumplimentar compliment	cantar 5	* Deducir deduce	traducir 69
Cumplir carry out	vivir 51	Defecar defecate	atacar 7
Cundir spread	vivir 51	* Defender defend	perder 29
Curar heal	cantar 5	Defenestrar dismiss, remove	cantar 5
Curiosear pry	cantar 5	Definir define	vivir 51
Currar toil	cantar 5	Deforestar deforest	cantar 5
Cursar study	cantar 5	Deformar deform	cantar 5
Curtir tan	vivir 51	Defraudar defraud	cantar 5
Curvar curve	cantar 5	Degenerar degenerate	cantar 5
Custodiar guard	cantar 5	Deglutir swallow	vivir 51
		* Degollar cut the throat	contar 16
		Degradar degrade	cantar 5
		Degustar taste	cantar 5
d		Deificar deify	atacar 7
		Dejar leave	cantar 5
		Delatar denounce	cantar 5
Damnificar harm	atacar 7	Delegar delegate	pagar 6
Danzar dance	cruzar 8	Deleitar delight	cantar 5
Dañar harm	cantar 5	Deletrear spell	cantar 5
* Dar give	23	Deliberar deliberate	cantar 5
Datar date	cantar 5	Delimitar delimit	cantar 5
Deambular stroll	cantar 5	Delinear delineate	cantar 5
Debatir debate	vivir 51	* Delinquir transgress	75
Deber have to (must)	beber 24	Delirar be delirious	cantar 5
Debilitar debilitate	cantar 5	Demacrarse waste away	cantar 5
Debutar debut	cantar 5	Demandar sue	cantar 5
* Decaer decline	caer 36		

verb	model/table	verb	model/table
Demarcar demarcate	atacar 7	Desabrochar unfasten	cantar 5
Democratizar democratize	cruzar 8	Desacatar be disrespectful to	cantar 5
* Demoler demolish	mover 30	Desacelerar decelerate	cantar 5
Demorar delay	cantar 5	* Desacertar be mistaken	pensar 13
* Demostrar show	contar 16	Desacomodar inconvenience	cantar 5
Demudarse change	cantar 5	Desaconsejar dissuade	cantar 5
* Denegar refuse	negar 14	Desacoplar uncouple	cantar 5
Denigrar denigrate	cantar 5	Desacostumbrar break of	
Denominar name	cantar 5	the habit	cantar 5
* Denostar insult	contar 16	Desacreditar discredit	cantar 5
Denotar denote	cantar 5	Desactivar deactivate	cantar 5
Denunciar denounce	cantar 5	Desacuartelar remove from	
Deparar afford	cantar 5	barracks	cantar 5
Departir converse	vivir 51	Desafiar challenge	desviar 9
Depauperar impoverish	cantar 5	Desafinar go out of tune	cantar 5
Depender depend	beber 24	Desagradar displease	cantar 5
Depilar depilate	cantar 5	Desagraviar make amends to	cantar 5
Deplorar deplore	cantar 5	Desaguar drain	averiguar 11
* Deponer depose	poner 41	Desahogar vent	pagar 6
Deportar deport	cantar 5	Desahuciar[25] evict	cantar 5
Depositar deposit	cantar 5	Desairar[11] snub	cantar 5
Depravar deprave	cantar 5	Desajustar spoil	cantar 5
Depreciar depreciate	cantar 5	Desalar desalt	cantar 5
Depredar pillage	cantar 5	* Desalentar dishearten	pensar 13
Deprimir depress	vivir 51	Desalinear put out of line	cantar 5
Depurar purify	cantar 5	Desaliñar disarrange	cantar 5
Derivar derive	cantar 5	Desalojar dislodge	cantar 5
Derogar rescind	pagar 6	Desalquilar vacate	cantar 5
Derramar spill	cantar 5	Desamortizar disentail	cruzar 8
Derrapar skid	cantar 5	Desamparar abandon	cantar 5
Derrengar twist	pagar 6	Desamueblar remove furniture	cantar 5
* Derretir melt	pedir 60	Desanclar weigh anchor	cantar 5
Derribar demolish	cantar 5	* Desandar go back	andar 22
Derrocar knock down	atacar 7	Desangrar bleed	cantar 5
Derrochar squander	cantar 5	Desanimar depress	cantar 5
Derrotar defeat	cantar 5	Desanudar untie	cantar 5
* Derruir demolish	concluir 59	* Desaparecer disappear	obedecer 33
Derrumbar throw down	cantar 5	Desaparcar unpark	atacar 7
* Desabastecer deprive	obedecer 33	Desapasionarse lose interest	cantar 5
Desabollar smooth out	cantar 5	Desapegar separate	pagar 6
Desabotonar unbutton	cantar 5	* Desapretar loosen	pensar 13
Desabrigar uncover	pagar 6	* Desaprobar disapprove	contar 16

verb	model/table	verb	model/table
Desaprovechar waste	cantar 5	Descalcificar decalcify	atacar 7
Desarbolar dismast	cantar 5	Descalificar disqualify	atacar 7
Desarmar disarm	cantar 5	Descalzar take off shoes	cruzar 8
Desarraigar uproot	pagar 6	Descamar scale off	cantar 5
Desarreglar mess up	cantar 5	Descambiar change back	cantar 5
* Desarrendar stop renting	pensar 13	Descansar rest	cantar 5
Desarrimar move away	cantar 5	Descaperuzar unhood	cruzar 8
Desarrollar develop	cantar 5	Descapotar put the hood down	cantar 5
Desarropar undress	cantar 5	Descargar unload	pagar 6
Desarrugar smooth	pagar 6	Descarnar strip flesh	cantar 5
Desarticular disjoint	cantar 5	Descarriar lead astray	desviar 9
* Desasir release	asir 72	Descarrilar derail	cantar 5
Desasistir desert	vivir 51	Descartar discard	cantar 5
Desasnar polish up	cantar 5	Descasar annul	cantar 5
* Desasosegar disturb	negar 14	Descascarillar husk	cantar 5
Desatar untie	cantar 5	Descastar be cold	cantar 5
Desatascar unblock	atacar 7	* Descender descend	perder 29
* Desatender neglect	perder 29	Descentralizar decentralize	cruzar 8
Desatinar exasperate	cantar 5	Descentrar unbalance	cantar 5
Desatornillar unscrew	cantar 5	Descerebrar decerebrate	cantar 5
Desatrancar unbar	atacar 7	Descerrajar force	cantar 5
Desautorizar deny	cruzar 8	Descifrar decipher	cantar 5
Desayunar breakfast	cantar 5	Desclasificar declassify	atacar 7
Desazonar make insipid	cantar 5	Desclavar unnail	cantar 5
Desbancar supplant	atacar 7	Descocarse be brazen	atacar 7
Desbarajustar upset	cantar 5	Descodificar decode	atacar 7
Desbaratar spoil	cantar 5	* Descolgar take down	rogar 18
Desbarbar trim	cantar 5	* Descollar excel	contar 16
Desbarrar slip	cantar 5	Descolocar become unemployed	atacar 7
Desbastar polish	cantar 5	Descolonizar decolonize	cruzar 8
Desbloquear unblock	cantar 5	Descompensar decompensate	cantar 5
Desbocar break the rim	atacar 7	* Descomponer decompose	poner 41
Desbordar overflow	cantar 5	Descomprimir decompress	vivir 51
Desbravar tame	cantar 5	* Desconcertar disconcert	pensar 13
Desbrozar clear of weeds	cruzar 8	Desconchar flake	cantar 5
Descabalar spoil	cantar 5	Desconectar disconnect	cantar 5
Descabalgar dismount	pagar 6	Desconfiar distrust	desviar 9
Descabellar ruffle the hair	cantar 5	Descongelar defrost	cantar 5
Descabezar behead	cruzar 8	Descongestionar decongest	cantar 5
Descacharrar break	cantar 5	* Desconocer not know	conocer 32
Descafeinar decaffeinate	cantar 5	Desconsiderar be inconsiderate	cantar 5
Descalabrar injure the head	cantar 5	Descontaminar decontaminate	cantar 5

verb		model/table	verb		model/table
* Descontar	discount	contar 16	Desempatar	break the tie	cantar 5
Descontentar	displease	cantar 5	* Desempedrar	unpave	pensar 13
Descontrolar	lose control	cantar 5	Desempeñar	redeem	cantar 5
Desconvocar	call off	atacar 7	Desempolvar	dust	cantar 5
Descorazonar	dishearten	cantar 5	Desempotrar	take out	cantar 5
Descorchar	uncork	cantar 5	Desenamorar	lose the love (for)	cantar 5
Descorrer	draw back	beber 24	Desencadenar	unchain	cantar 5
Descoser	unstitch	beber 24	Desencajar	dislocate	cantar 5
Descoyuntar	dislocate	cantar 5	Desencajonar	uncrate	cantar 5
Descremar	skim	cantar 5	Desencallar	refloat	cantar 5
* Describir²⁶	describe	vivir 51	Desencaminar	mislead	cantar 5
Descuadrar	get off square	cantar 5	Desencantar	disenchant	cantar 5
Descuajar	liquefy	cantar 5	Desencapotar	clear	cantar 5
Descuajeringar	pull to pieces	pagar 6	Desencarcelar	free	cantar 5
Descuartizar	quarter	cruzar 8	Desenchufar	unplug	cantar 5
* Descubrir²⁷	discover	vivir 51	Desenclavar	unnail	cantar 5
Descuidar	neglect	cantar 5	Desencolar	unglue	cantar 5
* Desdecir	be unworthy	decir 74	Desencorvar	straighten	cantar 5
Desdeñar	scorn	cantar 5	Desencuadernar	unbind	cantar 5
Desdibujar	blur	cantar 5	Desenfadar	calm down	cantar 5
Desdoblar	straighten	cantar 5	Desenfocar	unfocus	atacar 7
Desdramatizar	defuse	cruzar 8	Desenfrenar	unbridle	cantar 5
Desear	desire	cantar 5	Desenfundar	draw a pistol	cantar 5
Desecar	dry up	atacar 7	Desenfurruñar	calm down	cantar 5
Desechar	discard	cantar 5	Desenganchar	unhook	cantar 5
Desembalar	unpack	cantar 5	Desengañar	enlighten	cantar 5
Desembarazar	clear	cruzar 8	Desengrasar	degrease	cantar 5
Desembarcar	disembark	atacar 7	Desenhebrar	unthread	cantar 5
Desembargar	clear	pagar 6	Desenjaular	uncage	cantar 5
Desembarrancar	refloat	atacar 7	Desenladrillar	remove	cantar 5
Desembarrar	clear of mud	cantar 5	Desenlatar	take out of can	cantar 5
Desembocar	flow	atacar 7	Desenlazar	unfasten	cruzar 8
Desembolsar	pay	cantar 5	Desenmarañar	untangle	cantar 5
Desembragar	disengage	pagar 6	Desenmascarar	unmask	cantar 5
Desembrollar	sort out	cantar 5	Desenraizar¹¹	uproot	cruzar 8
Desembrujar	remove a spell	cantar 5	Desenredar	unravel	cantar 5
Desembuchar	disgorge	cantar 5	Desenrollar	unroll	cantar 5
Desempacar	unpack	atacar 7	Desenroscar	unscrew	atacar 7
Desempañar	take diaper off	cantar 5	Desensillar	unsaddle	cantar 5
Desempapelar	unwrap	cantar 5	* Desentenderse	want no part of	perder 9
Desempaquetar	unpack	cantar 5	* Desenterrar	exhume	pensar 13
Desemparejar	separate	cantar 5	Desentoldar	remove awning	cantar 5

verb		model/table	verb		model/table
Desentonar	be out of tune	cantar 5	Deshilvanar	untack	cantar 5
Desentrañar	disembowel	cantar 5	Deshinchar	deflate	cantar 5
Desentrenar	get out of training	cantar 5	Deshojar	defoliate	cantar 5
* Desentumecer	revive the		Deshollinar	sweep	cantar 5
	feeling	obedecer 33	Deshonrar	dishonor	cantar 5
Desenvainar	unsheathe	cantar 5	Deshuesar	debone	cantar 5
* Desenvolver[28]	unwrap	mover 30	Deshumanizar	dehumanize	cruzar 8
Desequilibrar	put off balance	cantar 5	Designar	designate	cantar 5
Desertar	desert	cantar 5	Desigualar	make uneven	cantar 5
Desertizar	make desert	cruzar 8	Desilusionar	disappoint	cantar 5
Desescombrar	clear up	cantar 5	Desimantar	demagnetize	cantar 5
Desesperar	drive to despair	cantar 5	Desincrustar	descale	cantar 5
Desestabilizar	destablize	cruzar 8	Desinfectar	disinfect	cantar 5
Desestimar	underestimate	cantar 5	Desinflar	deflate	cantar 5
Desfalcar	embezzle	atacar 7	Desinformar	disinform	cantar 5
* Desfallecer	weaken	obedecer 33	Desinhibir	free of inhibitions	vivir 51
Desfasar	phase out	cantar 5	Desinsectar	clear of insects	cantar 5
* Desfavorecer	disadvantage	obedecer 33	Desintegrar	disintegrate	cantar 5
Desfigurar	disfigure	cantar 5	Desinteresarse	lose interest	cantar 5
Desfilar	parade	cantar 5	Desintoxicar	detoxicate	atacar 7
Desflecar	fray	atacar 7	Desistir	desist	vivir 51
Desflorar	deflower	cantar 5	Deslavazar	fade	cruzar 8
Desfogar	vent	pagar 6	Deslegalizar	make illegal	cruzar 8
Desfondar	go through	cantar 5	* Desleír	dissolve	reír 63
Desgajar	tear off	cantar 5	Desliar	unwrap	desviar 9
Desgañitarse	shout one's		Desligar	untie	pagar 6
	head off	cantar 5	Deslindar	demarcate	cantar 5
Desgarrar	rip	cantar 5	Deslizar	slide	cruzar 8
Desgastar	wear away	cantar 5	Deslomar	exhaust	cantar 5
Desglosar	detach	cantar 5	* Deslucir	spoil	lucir 70
Desgraciar	spoil	cantar 5	Deslumbrar	dazzle	cantar 5
Desgranar	shell	cantar 5	Desmadejarse	become weak	cantar 5
Desgravar	reduce the tax	cantar 5	Desmadrar	take from its mother	cantar 5
* Desguarnecer	strip of		Desmandar	revoke	cantar 5
	trimming	obedecer 33	Desmantelar	dismantle	cantar 5
Desguazar	rough hew	cruzar 8	Desmaquillar	remove makeup	cantar 5
Deshabitar	vacate	cantar 5	Desmarcarse	become unmarked	atacar 7
* Deshacer	undo	hacer 37	Desmayar	make faint	cantar 5
* Deshelar[12]	thaw	pensar 13	Desmejorar	spoil	cantar 5
Desheredar	disinherit	cantar 5	Desmelenar	dishevel	cantar 5
Deshidratar	dehydrate	cantar 5	* Desmembrar	dismember	pensar 13
Deshilachar	ravel	cantar 5	* Desmentir	deny	sentir 65

V

verb	model/table	verb	model/table
Desmenuzar chop up	*cruzar* 8	Despampanar prune	*cantar* 5
* Desmerecer be unworthy	*obedecer* 33	Despanzurrar disembowel	*cantar* 5
Desmigajar crumble	*cantar* 5	Desparejar separate	*cantar* 5
Desmigar crumble	*pagar* 6	Desparramar scatter	*cantar* 5
Desmilitarizar demilitarize	*cruzar* 8	Despatarrarse open one's	
Desmitificar demythologize	*atacar* 7	legs wide	*cantar* 5
Desmochar lop	*cantar* 5	Despechugar cut the breast off	*pagar* 6
Desmontar dismount	*cantar* 5	Despedazar tear to pieces	*cruzar* 8
Desmoralizar demoralize	*cruzar* 8	* Despedir see off	*pedir* 60
Desmoronar wear away	*cantar* 5	Despegar unstick	*pagar* 6
Desmotivar discourage	*cantar* 5	Despeinar dishevel hair	*cantar* 5
Desmovilizar demobilize	*cruzar* 8	Despejar clear	*cantar* 5
Desnacionalizar denationalize	*cruzar* 8	Despellejar skin	*cantar* 5
Desnatar skim	*cantar* 5	Despelotarse strip naked	*cantar* 5
Desnaturalizar denaturalize	*cruzar* 8	Despenalizar legalize	*cruzar* 8
Desnivelar make uneven	*cantar* 5	Despendolarse become	
Desnortarse lose sense of		uninhibited	*cantar* 5
direction	*cantar* 5	Despeñar hurl	*cantar* 5
Desnucar break neck	*atacar* 7	Despepitarse bawl	*cantar* 5
Desnuclearizar denuclearize	*cruzar* 8	Desperdiciar waste	*cantar* 5
Desnudar undress	*cantar* 5	Desperdigar scatter	*pagar* 6
Desnutrirse be undernourished	*vivir* 51	Desperezarse stretch	*cruzar* 8
* Desobedecer disobey	*obedecer* 33	Despersonalizar depersonalize	*cruzar* 8
* Desobstruir clear	*concluir* 59	* Despertar[30] wake up	*pensar* 13
Desocupar vacate	*cantar* 5	Despiezar carve up	*cruzar* 8
Desodorizar deodorize	*cruzar* 8	Despilfarrar squander	*cantar* 5
* Desoír ignore	*oír* 78	Despintar take paint off	*cantar* 5
Desojar break the eye of		Despiojar delouse	*cantar* 5
(needle)	*cantar* 5	Despistar mislead	*cantar* 5
* Desollar skin	*contar* 16	Desplanchar crease	*cantar* 5
Desorbitar exaggerate	*cantar* 5	Desplantar uproot	*cantar* 5
Desordenar disarrange	*cantar* 5	Desplazar displace	*cruzar* 8
Desorejar cut ears off	*cantar* 5	* Desplegar unfold	*negar* 14
Desorganizar disorganize	*cruzar* 8	Desplomar scold	*cantar* 5
Desorientar confuse	*cantar* 5	Desplumar pluck	*cantar* 5
* Desosar[29] bone	*contar* 16	* Despoblar depopulate	*contar* 16
Desovar lay eggs	*cantar* 5	Despojar deprive	*cantar* 5
Desovillar unwind	*cantar* 5	Despolitizar depoliticize	*cruzar* 8
Desoxidar deoxidize	*cantar* 5	Desportillar chip	*cantar* 5
Despabilar snuff	*cantar* 5	Desposar wed	*cantar* 5
Despachar dispatch	*cantar* 5	* Desposeer dispossess	*leer* 28
Despachurrar squash	*cantar* 5	Despotricar rant on	*atacar* 7

V

verb	model/table	verb	model/table
Despreciar despise	cantar 5	Desvendar unbandage	cantar 5
Desprender remove	beber 24	* Desvestir undress	pedir 60
Despreocuparse be neglectful	cantar 5	Desviar deviate	9
Desprestigiar discredit	cantar 5	Desvincular release	cantar 5
Despresurizar depressurize	cruzar 8	Desvirgar deflower	pagar 6
Desprivatizar deprivatize	cruzar 8	Desvirtuar spoil	actuar 10
* Desproveer[31] deprive	leer 28	Desvivirse long for	vivir 51
Despuntar blunt	cantar 5	Detallar detail	cantar 5
Desquiciar unhinge	cantar 5	Detectar detect	cantar 5
Desquitar compensate	cantar 5	* Detener stop	tener 2
Desratizar derat	cruzar 8	Detentar hold illegally	cantar 5
Desriñonar cripple	cantar 5	Deteriorar deteriorate	cantar 5
Desrizar take the curls out	cruzar 8	Determinar determine	cantar 5
Destacar emphasize	atacar 7	Detestar detest	cantar 5
Destapar uncork	cantar 5	Devaluar devalue	actuar 10
Destaponar unplug	cantar 5	Devanar reel	cantar 5
Destejer unweave	beber 24	Devastar devastate	cantar 5
Destellar flash	cantar 5	Devengar be owed	pagar 6
Destemplar untune	cantar 5	* Devenir occur	venir 80
Destensar loosen	cantar 5	* Devolver[32] return	mover 30
* Desteñir discolor	teñir 64	Devorar devour	cantar 5
Desternillarse die laughing	cantar 5	Diagnosticar diagnose	atacar 7
* Desterrar banish	pensar 13	Dializar dialyze	cruzar 8
Destetar wean	cantar 5	Dialogar dialogue	pagar 6
Destilar distill	cantar 5	Dibujar draw	cantar 5
Destinar destine	cantar 5	Dictaminar consider	cantar 5
* Destituir dismiss	concluir 59	Dictar dictate	cantar 5
Destornillar unscrew	cantar 5	Diezmar tithe, decimate	cantar 5
Destrenzar unbraid	cruzar 8	Difamar defame	cantar 5
Destripar gut	cantar 5	Diferenciar differentiate	cantar 5
Destronar dethrone	cantar 5	* Diferir defer	sentir 65
Destrozar ruin	cruzar 8	Dificultar hamper	cantar 5
* Destruir destroy	concluir 59	Difuminar stump	cantar 5
Desubicar disorient	atacar 7	Difundir[33] spread	vivir 51
Desunir disunite	vivir 51	* Digerir digest	sentir 65
Desusar make obsolete	cantar 5	Digitalizar digitize	cruzar 8
Desvalijar rob	cantar 5	Dignarse deign	cantar 5
Desvalorizar depreciate	cruzar 8	Dignificar dignify	atacar 7
* Desvanecer dispel	obedecer 33	Dilapidar waste	cantar 5
Desvariar rave	desviar 9	Dilatar delay	cantar 5
Desvelar keep awake	cantar 5	Diligenciar go through steps	
Desvencijar break	cantar 5	to obtain	cantar 5

V

verb	model/table	verb	model/table
Dilucidar explain	*cantar* 5	Disputar dispute	*cantar* 5
* Diluir dilute	*concluir* 59	Distanciarse drift away	*cantar* 5
Diluviar[12] pour down	*cantar* 5	Distar be distant	*cantar* 5
Dimanar flow	*cantar* 5	* Distender distend	*perder* 29
Dimitir resign	*vivir* 51	*Distinguir* distinguish	53
Dinamitar dynamite	*cantar* 5	Distorsionar distort	*cantar* 5
Dinamizar blast	*cruzar* 8	* Distraer distract	*traer* 47
Diplomar grant a diploma	*cantar* 5	* Distribuir distribute	*concluir* 59
Diptongar make into a		Disuadir dissuade	*vivir* 51
diphthong	*pagar* 6	Divagar digress	*pagar* 6
Dirigir direct, address	52	Divergir diverge	*dirigir* 52
Dirimir settle	*vivir* 51	Diversificar diversify	*atacar* 7
* *Discernir* discern	66	* Divertir amuse	*sentir* 65
Disciplinar discipline	*cantar* 5	Dividir divide	*vivir* 51
* Discordar disagree	*contar* 16	Divinizar deify	*cruzar* 8
Discrepar differ	*cantar* 5	Divisar discern	*cantar* 5
Discriminar discriminate	*cantar* 5	Divorciarse divorce	*cantar* 5
Disculpar excuse	*cantar* 5	Divulgar divulge	*pagar* 6
Discurrir reflect	*vivir* 51	Doblar fold	*cantar* 5
Discutir discuss	*vivir* 51	Doblegar bend	*pagar* 6
Disecar dissect	*atacar* 7	Doctorar confer a doctorate	*cantar* 5
Diseccionar dissect	*cantar* 5	Documentar document	*cantar* 5
Diseminar disseminate	*cantar* 5	Dogmatizar dogmatize	*cruzar* 8
* Disentir disagree	*sentir* 65	* Doler hurt	*mover* 30
Diseñar design	*cantar* 5	Domar tame	*cantar* 5
Disertar discourse	*cantar* 5	Domeñar subdue	*cantar* 5
Disfrazar disguise	*cruzar* 8	Domesticar domesticate	*atacar* 7
Disfrutar enjoy	*cantar* 5	Domiciliar domicile	*cantar* 5
Disgregar disintegrate	*pagar* 6	Dominar dominate	*cantar* 5
Disgustar displease	*cantar* 5	Donar donate	*cantar* 5
Disimilar dissimilate	*cantar* 5	Doparse drug	*cantar* 5
Disimular conceal	*cantar* 5	Dorar gild	*cantar* 5
Disipar dissipate	*cantar* 5	* *Dormir* sleep	68
Dislocar dislocate	*atacar* 7	Dormitar doze	*cantar* 5
* Disminuir lower	*concluir* 59	Dosificar proportion	*atacar* 7
Disociar dissociate	*cantar* 5	Dotar endow	*cantar* 5
* Disolver[34] dissolve	*mover* 30	Dragar dredge	*pagar* 6
Disparar fire	*cantar* 5	Dramatizar dramatize	*cruzar* 8
Disparatar talk nonsense	*cantar* 5	Drenar drain	*cantar* 5
Dispensar bestow	*cantar* 5	Driblar dribble	*cantar* 5
Dispersar disperse	*cantar* 5	Drogar drug	*pagar* 6
* Disponer arrange	*poner* 41	Duchar shower	*cantar* 5

V

verb	model/table	verb	model/table
Dudar doubt	cantar 5	Embalsar dam	cantar 5
Dulcificar sweeten	atacar 7	Embarazar embarrass	cruzar 8
Duplicar duplicate	atacar 7	Embarcar embark	atacar 7
Durar last	cantar 5	Embargar overcome	pagar 6
		Embarrancar run aground	atacar 7
		Embarrar sling mud	cantar 5
e		Embarullar muddle	cantar 5
		Embaucar deceive	atacar 7
		Embazarse be amazed	cruzar 8
Echar throw	cantar 5	Embeber absorb	beber 24
Eclipsar eclipse	cantar 5	Embelesar delight	cantar 5
Economizar economize	cruzar 8	* Embellecer embellish	obedecer 33
Edificar build	atacar 7	* Embestir attack	pedir 60
Editar edit	cantar 5	Embetunar polish	cantar 5
Educar educate	atacar 7	* Emblanquecer whiten	obedecer 33
Edulcorar sweeten	cantar 5	Embobar astound	cantar 5
Efectuar effect	actuar 10	Embolsar pocket	cantar 5
Ejecutar execute	cantar 5	Emborrachar get drunk	cantar 5
Ejemplarizar exemplify	cruzar 8	Emborrascarse become stormy	atacar 7
Ejemplificar illustrate	atacar 7	Emborronar scribble	cantar 5
Ejercer exercise	vencer 26	Emboscar ambush	atacar 7
Ejercitar exercise	cantar 5	Embotar blunt	cantar 5
Elaborar elaborate	cantar 5	Embotellar bottle	cantar 5
Electrificar electrify	atacar 7	Embotijar put in jugs	cantar 5
Electrizar electrify	cruzar 8	Embozar muzzle	cruzar 8
Electrocutar electrocute	cantar 5	Embragar engage	pagar 6
Electrolizar electrolyze	cruzar 8	* Embravecer enrage	obedecer 33
* Elegir[35] choose	corregir 61	Embrear tar	cantar 5
Elevar elevate	cantar 5	Embriagar intoxicate	pagar 6
Elidir weaken	vivir 51	Embridar bridle	cantar 5
Eliminar eliminate	cantar 5	Embrollar muddle	cantar 5
Elogiar praise	cantar 5	Embromar tease	cantar 5
Elucidar elucidate	cantar 5	Embrujar bewitch	cantar 5
Elucubrar work laboriously	cantar 5	* Embrutecer brutalize	obedecer 33
Eludir avoid	vivir 51	Embuchar cram	cantar 5
Emanar emanate	cantar 5	Embutir stuff	vivir 51
Emancipar emancipate	cantar 5	Emerger emerge	coger 25
Emascular emasculate	cantar 5	Emigrar emigrate	cantar 5
Embadurnar smear	cantar 5	Emitir emit	vivir 51
Embalar pack	cantar 5	Emocionar excite	cantar 5
Embaldosar title	cantar 5	Empacar pack	atacar 7
Embalsamar embalm	cantar 5	Empachar satiate	cantar 5

verb	model/table	verb	model/table
Empadronar take a census	cantar 5	Empujar push	cantar 5
Empalagar satiate	pagar 6	Empuñar seize	cantar 5
Empalar impale	cantar 5	Emular emulate	cantar 5
* Empalidecer turn pale	obedecer 33	Emulsionar emulsify	cantar 5
Empalmar join	cantar 5	Enajenar alienate	cantar 5
Empanar bread	cantar 5	* Enaltecer ennoble	obedecer 33
Empantanar swamp	cantar 5	Enamorar win the heart	cantar 5
Empañar diaper	cantar 5	Enamoriscarse take a fancy	atacar 7
Empapar soak	cantar 5	Enarbolar hoist	cantar 5
Empapelar wallpaper	cantar 5	Enarcar arch	atacar 7
Empapuzar stuff (with food)	cruzar 8	* Enardecer inflame	obedecer 33
Empaquetar package	cantar 5	Enarenar sand	cantar 5
Emparedar imprison	cantar 5	Encabalgar mount	pagar 6
Emparejar pair, match	cantar 5	Encabestrar halter	cantar 5
Emparentar become related	cantar 5	Encabezar head	cruzar 8
Empastar paste	cantar 5	Encabezonarse settle	cantar 5
Empatar draw, tie	cantar 5	Encabritarse rear up	cantar 5
Empavonar grease	cantar 5	Encabronar piss off	cantar 5
* Empecer prevent	obedecer 33	Encadenar chain	cantar 5
Empecinarse be stubborn	cantar 5	Encajar fit	cantar 5
* Empedrar pave	pensar 13	Encajonar box	cantar 5
Empeñar pawn	cantar 5	Encalar whitewash	cantar 5
Empeorar worsen	cantar 5	Encallar run aground	cantar 5
* Empequeñecer reduce	obedecer 33	Encallarse harden	cantar 5
Emperejilar dress up	cantar 5	* Encallecer become hard	obedecer 33
Emperifollar doll up	cantar 5	Encallejonar run down an alley	cantar 5
Emperrarse be dead set on	cantar 5	Encamar go to bed	cantar 5
* Empezar begin	15	Encaminar direct	cantar 5
Empinar stand up	cantar 5	Encanarse go gray	cantar 5
Empitonar gore	cantar 5	Encandilar dazzle	cantar 5
* Emplastecer plaster	obedecer 33	* Encanecer go gray	obedecer 33
Emplazar summon	cruzar 8	Encanijar weaken	cantar 5
Emplear employ	cantar 5	Encantar delight	cantar 5
Emplomar cover with lead	cantar 5	Encanutar lay pipes	cantar 5
Emplumar feather	cantar 5	Encañonar channel	cantar 5
* Empobrecer impoverish	obedecer 33	Encapotar cloak	cantar 5
Empollar brood	cantar 5	Encapricharse take a fancy	cantar 5
Empolvar cover with dust	cantar 5	Encapsular encapsulate	cantar 5
Emponzoñar poison	cantar 5	Encapuchar hood	cantar 5
* Emporcar soil	trocar 17	Encaramar elevate	cantar 5
Empotrar embed	cantar 5	Encarar climb	cantar 5
Emprender undertake	beber 24	Encarcelar imprison	cantar 5

verb		model/table	verb		model/table
* Encarecer	raise the price	obedecer 33	Encorvar	curve	cantar 5
Encargar	put in charge of	pagar 6	Encrespar	curl tightly	cantar 5
Encariñar	endear	cantar 5	Encuadernar	bind	cantar 5
Encarnar	become incarnate	cantar 5	Encuadrar	frame	cantar 5
Encarnizar	flesh	cruzar 8	* Encubrir[36]	hide	vivir 51
Encarpetar	pigeonhole	cantar 5	Encuestar	take a poll	cantar 5
Encarrilar	guide	cantar 5	Encumbrar	elevate	cantar 5
Encartar	implicate	cantar 5	Encurdarse	become drunk	cantar 5
Encartonar	cover with cardboard	cantar 5	Encurtir	pickle	vivir 51
Encasillar	tabulate	cantar 5	Endemoniar	bedevil	cantar 5
Encasquetar	put on a hat	cantar 5	Enderezar	straighten	cruzar 8
Encasquillar	shoe	cantar 5	Endeudarse	be in debt	cantar 5
Encastrar	embed	cantar 5	Endilgar	palm off	pagar 6
Encausar	prosecute	cantar 5	Endiñar	land a hit	cantar 5
Encauzar	canalize	cruzar 8	Endiosar	deify	cantar 5
Encebollar	cook with onions	cantar 5	Endomingarse	put on Sunday best	pagar 6
Encelar	make jealous	cantar 5	Endosar	endorse	cantar 5
Enceldar	imprison	cantar 5	Endulzar	sweeten	cruzar 8
Encenagarse	get stuck	pagar 6	* Endurecer	harden	obedecer 33
* Encender	light	perder 29	Enemistar	make enemies	cantar 5
Encerar	wax	cantar 5	Enervar	enervate	cantar 5
* Encerrar	enclose	pensar 13	Enfadar	annoy	cantar 5
Encestar	make a basket	cantar 5	Enfajar	bind	cantar 5
Encharcar	flood	atacar 7	Enfangar	cover with mud	pagar 6
Enchufar	plug in	cantar 5	Enfatizar	emphasize	cruzar 8
Encintar	beribbon	cantar 5	Enfermar	sicken	cantar 5
Encizañar	sow discord	cantar 5	Enfervorizar	encourage	cruzar 8
Enclaustrar	cloister	cantar 5	Enfilar	thread	cantar 5
Enclavar	nail	cantar 5	* Enflaquecer	make thin	obedecer 33
Encocorar	annoy	cantar 5	Enfocar	focus	atacar 7
Encofrar	timber	cantar 5	Enfoscar	fill with mortar	atacar 7
Encoger	shrink	coger 25	Enfrascarse	get engrossed	atacar 7
Encolar	glue	cantar 5	Enfrentar	confront	cantar 5
Encolerizar	infuriate	cruzar 8	Enfriar	cool	desviar 9
* Encomendar	commend	pensar 13	Enfundar	sheathe	cantar 5
Encomiar	praise	cantar 5	* Enfurecer	infuriate	obedecer 33
Enconar	inflame	cantar 5	Enfurruñarse	sulk	cantar 5
* Encontrar	find	contar 16	Engalanar	adorn	cantar 5
Encopetar	put on airs	cantar 5	Enganchar	hook	cantar 5
Encorajinar	provoke	cantar 5	Engañar	deceive	cantar 5
* Encordar	string	contar 16	Engarabitar	climb	cantar 5
Encorsetar	corset	cantar 5	Engarzar	thread	cruzar 8

verb	model/table	verb	model/table
Engastar set, mount	cantar 5	Enmarañar entangle	cantar 5
Engatusar wheedle	cantar 5	Enmarcar frame	atacar 7
Engendrar engender	cantar 5	Enmascarar mask	cantar 5
Englobar include	cantar 5	* Enmendar amend	pensar 13
Englutir gulp down	vivir 51	* Enmohecer rust	obedecer 33
Engolar become arrogant	cantar 5	Enmoquetar carpet	cantar 5
Engolfarse make for open sea	cantar 5	* Enmudecer silence	obedecer 33
Engolosinar entice	cantar 5	* Ennegrecer blacken	obedecer 33
Engomar glue	cantar 5	* Ennoblecer ennoble	obedecer 33
Engominarse use hair spray	cantar 5	Enojar anger	cantar 5
Engordar fatten	cantar 5	* Enorgullecer make proud	obedecer 33
Engranar engage, mesh	cantar 5	Enquistar encyst	cantar 5
* Engrandecer exalt	obedecer 33	Enrabietar enrage	cantar 5
Engrasar grease	cantar 5	Enraizar[11] take root	cruzar 8
* Engreírse become conceited	reír 63	* Enrarecerse rarefy	obedecer 33
Engrescar antagonize	atacar 7	Enredar entangle	cantar 5
Engrosar enlarge	cantar 5	Enrejar rail off	cantar 5
Enguachinar flood	cantar 5	* Enriquecer enrich	obedecer 33
Enguantar put gloves on	cantar 5	Enrocar castle	atacar 7
Engullir gulp down	mullir 57	* Enrojecer blush	obedecer 33
Engurruñar crease	cantar 5	Enrolar enroll	cantar 5
Enharinar flour	cantar 5	Enrollar roll up	cantar 5
Enhebrar thread	cantar 5	* Enronquecer become hoarse	obedecer 33
Enjabonar soap	cantar 5	Enroscar screw in	atacar 7
Enjaezar harness	cruzar 8	Ensalzar exalt	cruzar 8
Enjalbegar whitewash	pagar 6	Ensamblar assemble	cantar 5
Enjaretar reel off	cantar 5	Ensanchar enlarge	cantar 5
Enjaular cage	cantar 5	* Ensangrentar stain with blood	pensar 13
Enjoyar adorn with jewels	cantar 5	Ensañar enrage	cantar 5
Enjuagar rinse	pagar 6	Ensartar rattle off	cantar 5
Enjugar wipe up	pagar 6	Ensayar try out	cantar 5
Enjuiciar prosecute	cantar 5	Enseñar teach	cantar 5
Enladrillar pave with bricks	cantar 5	Enseñorearse lord over	cantar 5
Enlatar can (food)	cantar 5	Ensillar saddle	cantar 5
Enlazar link	cruzar 8	Ensimismarse be deep in thought	cantar 5
Enlodar muddy	cantar 5	* Ensoberbecer make proud	obedecer 33
* Enloquecer madden	obedecer 33	* Ensombrecer darken	obedecer 33
Enlosar tile	cantar 5	* Ensordecer deafen	obedecer 33
* Enlucir plaster	lucir 70	Ensortijar curl	cantar 5
Enlutar bereave	cantar 5	Ensuciar dirty	cantar 5
Enmadrarse be very attached to mother	cantar 5	Entablar start	cantar 5
		Entablillar splint	cantar 5

verb	model/table	verb	model/table
Entallar sculpture	cantar 5	Enunciar declare	cantar 5
Entarimar parquet	cantar 5	Envainar sheathe	cantar 5
Entelar cloud the view	cantar 5	Envalentonar make brave	cantar 5
* Entender understand	perder 29	* Envanecer make conceited	obedecer 33
* Entenebrecer darken	obedecer 33	Envarar hinder movement	cantar 5
Enterar inform	cantar 5	Envasar bottle, can	cantar 5
* Enternecer soften	obedecer 33	* Envejecer age	obedecer 33
* Enterrar bury	pensar 13	Envenenar poison	cantar 5
Entibiar make lukewarm	cantar 5	Enviar send	desviar 9
Entintar ink	cantar 5	Enviciar corrupt	cantar 5
Entoldar cover with an awning	cantar 5	Envidar bluff	cantar 5
Entonar intone	cantar 5	Envidiar envy	cantar 5
* Entontecer dumbfound	obedecer 33	* Envilecer degrade	obedecer 33
Entornar half-close	cantar 5	Enviudar become a widow	cantar 5
* Entorpecer numb	obedecer 33	* Envolver[38] wrap	mover 30
Entrampar trap	cantar 5	Enyesar plaster	cantar 5
Entrañar involve	cantar 5	Enzarzar cause trouble	cruzar 8
Entrar enter	cantar 5	Epatar astonish	cantar 5
* Entreabrir[37] half-open	vivir 51	Epilogar sum up	pagar 6
Entrechocar chatter (teeth)	atacar 7	Equidistar be equidistant	cantar 5
Entrecomillar put in quotes	cantar 5	Equilibrar balance	cantar 5
Entrecortar cut partially	cantar 5	Equipar equip	cantar 5
Entrecruzar interlace	cruzar 8	Equiparar compare	cantar 5
Entregar deliver	pagar 6	* Equivaler be equal	valer 48
Entrelazar interwine	cruzar 8	Equivocar mistake	atacar 7
Entremeter mix	beber 24	* Erguir raise	76
Entremezclar intermingle	cantar 5	Erigir erect	dirigir 52
Entrenar train	cantar 5	Erisipelar get erysipelas	cantar 5
Entresacar thin	atacar 7	Erizar bristle	cruzar 8
Entretejer interweave	beber 24	Erosionar erode	cantar 5
* Entretener entertain	tener 2	Erradicar eradicate	atacar 7
* Entrever glimpse	ver 49	* Errar[39] err	pensar 13
Entrevistar interview	cantar 5	Eructar belch	cantar 5
* Entristecer sadden	obedecer 33	Esbozar sketch	cruzar 8
Entrometer mix	beber 24	Escabechar marinate	cantar 5
Entroncar enthrone	atacar 7	Escabullir slip away	mullir 57
Entronizar worship	cruzar 8	Escacharrar break, bust	cantar 5
Entubar tube	cantar 5	Escachifollar humiliate	cantar 5
* Entumecer numb	obedecer 33	Escalar scale	cantar 5
Enturbiar cloud	cantar 5	Escaldar scald	cantar 5
Entusiasmar inspire	cantar 5	Escalfar poach (eggs)	cantar 5
Enumerar enumerate	cantar 5	Escalonar grade	cantar 5

V

verb	model/table	verb	model/table
Escamar scale (fish)	cantar 5	Esmaltar enamel	cantar 5
Escamotear make disappear	cantar 5	Esmerarse take pains	cantar 5
Escampar⁶ stop raining	cantar 5	Esmerilar grind	cantar 5
Escanciar pour	cantar 5	Esnifar sniff	cantar 5
Escandalizar scandalize	cruzar 8	Espabilar snuff	cantar 5
Escapar escape	cantar 5	Espachurrar squash	cantar 5
Escaquearse dodge	cantar 5	Espaciar spread out	cantar 5
Escarbar scratch	cantar 5	Espantar scare	cantar 5
Escardar weed	cantar 5	Españolear make Spanish	cantar 5
Escarchar¹² frost	cantar 5	Españolizar hispanicize	cruzar 8
Escarificar scarify	atacar 7	Esparcir scatter	54
* Escarmentar learn a lesson	pensar 13	Especializar specialize	cruzar 8
* Escarnecer scoff at	obedecer 33	Especificar specify	atacar 7
Escasear be scarce	cantar 5	Especular speculate	cantar 5
Escatimar spare	cantar 5	Espejear shine	cantar 5
Escayolar put in a cast	cantar 5	Espeluznar make hair stand	
Escenificar dramatize	atacar 7	on end	cantar 5
Escindir split	vivir 51	Esperanzar give hope	cruzar 8
* Esclarecer clarify	obedecer 33	Esperar wait, hope	cantar 5
Esclavizar enslave	cruzar 8	Espesar thicken	cantar 5
Esclerosar produce sclerosis	cantar 5	Espetar spit	cantar 5
Escobar sweep	cantar 5	Espiar spy	desviar 9
* Escocer sting	cocer 34	Espichar prick	cantar 5
Escoger choose	coger 25	Espigar glean	pagar 6
Escolarizar provide schooling	cruzar 8	Espirar exhale	cantar 5
Escoltar escort	cantar 5	Espiritualizar spiritualize	cruzar 8
Esconder hide	beber 24	Espolear spur	cantar 5
Escorar prop	cantar 5	Espoliar exfoliate	cantar 5
Escotar scoop out	cantar 5	Espolvorear sprinkle	cantar 5
* Escribir⁴⁰ write	vivir 51	Esponjar make spongy	cantar 5
Escriturar notarize	cantar 5	Esposar handcuff	cantar 5
Escrutar scrutinize	cantar 5	Espulgar delouse	pagar 6
Escuchar listen	cantar 5	Espumar skim	cantar 5
Escudarse shield	cantar 5	Espurrear spray	cantar 5
Escudriñar examine	cantar 5	Esputar spit	cantar 5
Esculpir sculpture	vivir 51	Esquejar cut	cantar 5
Escupir spit	vivir 51	Esquematizar schematize	cruzar 8
Escurrir drain	vivir 51	Esquiar ski	desviar 9
* Esforzarse make an effort	forzar 19	Esquilar shear	cantar 5
Esfumarse disappear	cantar 5	Esquilmar harvest	cantar 5
Esgrimir brandish	vivir 51	Esquinar put in a corner	cantar 5
Eslabonar link	cantar 5	Esquivar evade	cantar 5

V

verb	model/table	verb	model/table
Estabilizar stabilize	cruzar 8	Estresar cause stress	cantar 5
* Establecer establish	obedecer 33	Estriar groove	desviar 9
Estabular stable	cantar 5	Estribar rest	cantar 5
Estacionar park	cantar 5	Estropear damage	cantar 5
Estafar swindle	cantar 5	Estructurar structure	cantar 5
Estallar explode	cantar 5	Estrujar squeeze	cantar 5
Estampar stamp	cantar 5	Estucar stucco	atacar 7
Estampillar rubber-stamp	cantar 5	Estuchar wrap in paper	cantar 5
Estancar stop the flow	atacar 7	Estudiar study	cantar 5
Estandarizar standardize	cruzar 8	Estuprar rape	cantar 5
* Estar be	4	Eternizar eternalize	cruzar 8
Estatalizar nationalize	cruzar 8	Etimologizar etymologize	cruzar 8
* Estatuir enact	concluir 59	Etiquetar label	cantar 5
Estenografiar write shorthand	desviar 9	Europeizar[11] Europeanize	cruzar 8
Estercolar manure	cantar 5	Evacuar evacuate	cantar 5
Estereotipar stereotype	cantar 5	Evadir evade	vivir 51
Esterilizar sterilize	cruzar 8	Evaluar evaluate	actuar 10
Estibar pack tight	cantar 5	Evangelizar evangelize	cruzar 8
Estigmatizar stigmatize	cruzar 8	Evaporar evaporate	cantar 5
Estilarse be used	cantar 5	Evidenciar show	cantar 5
Estilizar stylize	cruzar 8	Evitar avoid	cantar 5
Estimar esteem	cantar 5	Evocar evoke	atacar 7
Estimular stimulate	cantar 5	Evolucionar evolve	cantar 5
Estipular stipulate	cantar 5	Exacerbar exasperate	cantar 5
Estirajar stretch	cantar 5	Exagerar exaggerate	cantar 5
Estirar stretch	cantar 5	Exaltar exalt	cantar 5
Estocar stab	atacar 7	Examinar examine	cantar 5
Estofar stew	cantar 5	Exasperar exasperate	cantar 5
Estomagar sicken	pagar 6	Excarcelar release	cantar 5
Estoquear stab	cantar 5	Excavar dig	cantar 5
Estorbar impede	cantar 5	Exceder exceed	beber 24
Estornudar sneeze	cantar 5	Exceptuar except	actuar 10
Estragar devastate	pagar 6	Excitar rouse	cantar 5
Estrangular strangle	cantar 5	Exclamar exclaim	cantar 5
Estraperlear deal on black		Exclaustrar secularize	cantar 5
market	cantar 5	* Excluir exclude	concluir 59
Estratificar stratify	atacar 7	Excomulgar excommunicate	pagar 6
Estrechar narrow	cantar 5	Excretar excrete	cantar 5
Estrellar smash	cantar 5	Exculpar exculpate	cantar 5
* Estremecer shake	obedecer 33	Excusar excuse	cantar 5
Estrenar use for first time	cantar 5	Execrar loathe	cantar 5
* Estreñir constipate	teñir 64	Exfoliar exfoliate	cantar 5

verb	model/table	verb	model/table
Exhalar exhale	cantar 5	Extinguir[44] extinguish	distinguir 53
Exhibir exhibit	vivir 51	Extirpar uproot	cantar 5
Exhortar exhort	cantar 5	Extorsionar extort	cantar 5
Exhumar exhume	cantar 5	Extractar summarize	cantar 5
Exigir demand	dirigir 52	Extraditar extradite	cantar 5
Exiliar exile	cantar 5	* Extraer extract	traer 47
Eximir[41] exempt	vivir 51	Extralimitarse overdo	cantar 5
Existir exist	vivir 51	Extranjerizar introduce foreign	
Exonerar exonerate	cantar 5	customs	cruzar 8
Exorcizar exorcize	cruzar 8	Extrañar surprise	cantar 5
Expandir expand	vivir 51	Extrapolar extrapolate	cantar 5
Expansionar expand	cantar 5	Extraviar get lost	desviar 9
Expatriar banish	desviar 9	Extremar overdo	cantar 5
Expectorar expectorate	cantar 5	Exudar exude	cantar 5
Expedientar investigate	cantar 5	Exultar exult	cantar 5
* Expedir dispatch	pedir 60	Eyacular ejaculate	cantar 5
Expeler expel	beber 24		
Expender retail	beber 24		
Experimentar experiment	cantar 5		
Expiar expiate	desviar 9	**f**	
Expirar expire	cantar 5		
Explayar spread out	cantar 5		
Explicar explain	atacar 7	Fabricar make	atacar 7
Explicitar make explicit	cantar 5	Fabular tell stories	cantar 5
Explicotearse explain	cantar 5	Facilitar facilitate	cantar 5
Explorar explore	cantar 5	Facturar invoice	cantar 5
Explosionar explode	cantar 5	Facultar empower	cantar 5
Explotar exploit	cantar 5	Faenar fish	cantar 5
Expoliar despoil	cantar 5	Fagocitar gobble up	cantar 5
* Exponer expound	poner 41	Fajar gird	cantar 5
Exportar export	cantar 5	Faldear skirt	cantar 5
Expresar[42] express	cantar 5	Fallar pronounce	cantar 5
Exprimir squeeze	vivir 51	* Fallecer die	obedecer 33
Expropiar expropriate	cantar 5	Falsear falsify	cantar 5
Expugnar take by storm	cantar 5	Falsificar counterfeit	atacar 7
Expulsar eject	cantar 5	Faltar be lacking	cantar 5
Expurgar expurgate	pagar 6	Familiarizar familiarize	cruzar 8
Extasiar enrapture	desviar 9	Fanatizar fanaticize	cruzar 8
* Extender[43] spread out	perder 29	Fanfarronear show off	cantar 5
Extenuar exhaust	actuar 10	Fantasear daydream	cantar 5
Exteriorizar show	cruzar 8	Fardar outfit	cantar 5
Exterminar exterminate	cantar 5	Farfullar jabber	cantar 5
		Farolear brag	cantar 5

V

verb	model/table	verb	model/table
Fascinar fascinate	cantar 5	* Florecer flower	obedecer 33
Fastidiar upset	cantar 5	Flotar float	cantar 5
Fatigar tire	pagar 6	Fluctuar fluctuate	actuar 10
* Favorecer favor	obedecer 33	Fluidificar fluidify	atacar 7
Fechar date	cantar 5	* Fluir flow	concluir 59
Fecundar fertilize	cantar 5	Foguear harden	cantar 5
Federar federate	cantar 5	Foliar foliate	cantar 5
Felicitar congratulate	cantar 5	Follar blow	cantar 5
* Fenecer die	obedecer 33	Fomentar promote	cantar 5
Feriar trade	cantar 5	Fondear anchor	cantar 5
Fermentar ferment	cantar 5	Forcejear struggle	cantar 5
Fertilizar fertilize	cruzar 8	Forestar plant trees	cantar 5
Festejar celebrate	cantar 5	Forjar forge	cantar 5
Festonear festoon	cantar 5	Formalizar formalize	cruzar 8
Fiar trust	desviar 9	Formar form	cantar 5
Fichar index	cantar 5	Formatear format	cantar 5
Figurar figure	cantar 5	Formular formulate	cantar 5
Fijar [45] fix	cantar 5	Fornicar fornicate	atacar 7
Filetear fillet	cantar 5	Forrajear forage	cantar 5
Filiar take the particulars	cantar 5	Forrar line	cantar 5
Filmar film	cantar 5	* Fortalecer strengthen	obedecer 33
Filosofar philosophize	cantar 5	Fortificar fortify	atacar 7
Filtrar filter	cantar 5	* Forzar force	19
Finalizar finalize	cruzar 8	* Fosforescer phosphoresce	obedecer 33
Financiar finance	cantar 5	Fosilizarse fossilize	cruzar 8
Fingir feign	dirigir 52	Fotocopiar photocopy	cantar 5
Finiquitar settle	cantar 5	Fotografiar photograph	desviar 9
Firmar sign	cantar 5	Fracasar fail	cantar 5
Fiscalizar supervise	cruzar 8	Fraccionar divide	cantar 5
Fisgar pry into	pagar 6	Fracturar fracture	cantar 5
Fisgonear spy on	cantar 5	Fragmentar fragment	cantar 5
Flagelar whip	cantar 5	Fraguar forge	averiguar 11
Flamear flame	cantar 5	Franquear clear	cantar 5
Flanquear flank	cantar 5	Frasear phrase	cantar 5
Flaquear weaken	cantar 5	Fraternizar fraternize	cruzar 8
Flechar draw	cantar 5	Frecuentar frequent	cantar 5
Fletar freight	cantar 5	* Fregar scrub, annoy	negar 14
Flexibilizar make supple	cruzar 8	Fregotear wipe quickly	cantar 5
Flexionar bend	cantar 5	* Freír [46] fry	reír 63
Flirtear flirt	cantar 5	Frenar brake	cantar 5
Flojear ease up	cantar 5	Fresar mill	cantar 5
Florear decorate with flowers	cantar 5	Friccionar rub	cantar 5

verb	model/table	verb	model/table
Frisar frizz (cloth)	cantar 5	Gasear gas	cantar 5
Frivolizar frivolize	cruzar 8	Gasificar gasify	atacar 7
Frotar rub	cantar 5	Gastar spend	cantar 5
Fructificar fructify	atacar 7	Gatear crawl	cantar 5
Fruncir gather (cloth)	esparcir 54	* Gemir groan	pedir 60
Frustrar frustrate	cantar 5	Generalizar generalize	cruzar 8
Fugarse escape	pagar 6	Generar generate	cantar 5
Fulgurar flash	cantar 5	Germanizar Germanize	cruzar 8
Fulminar fulminate	cantar 5	Germinar germinate	cantar 5
Fumar smoke	cantar 5	Gestar gestate	cantar 5
Fumigar fumigate	pagar 6	Gesticular gesticulate	cantar 5
Funcionar function	cantar 5	Gestionar procure	cantar 5
Fundamentar establish	cantar 5	Gibar curve	cantar 5
Fundar found	cantar 5	Gimotear whimper	cantar 5
Fundir cast	vivir 51	Girar revolve	cantar 5
Fusilar shoot	cantar 5	Gitanear cajole	cantar 5
Fusionar fuse	cantar 5	Glasear glaze	cantar 5
Fustigar whip	pagar 6	Globalizar globalize	cruzar 8
		Gloriar glory	desviar 9
		Glorificar glorify	atacar 7
		Glosar gloss	cantar 5
		* Gobernar govern	pensar 13
		Golear score	cantar 5
Gafar hook	cantar 5	Golfear behave like a scoundrel	cantar 5
Galantear flatter	cantar 5	Golosear nibble delicacies	cantar 5
Galardonar reward	cantar 5	Golpear hit	cantar 5
Gallardear strut	cantar 5	Golpetear beat	cantar 5
Galopar gallop	cantar 5	Gorgoritear warble	cantar 5
Galvanizar galvanize	cruzar 8	Gorgotear gurgle	cantar 5
Gallear tread	cantar 5	Gorjear chirp	cantar 5
Ganar win	cantar 5	Gorronear scrounge	cantar 5
Gandulear idle	cantar 5	Gotear drip	cantar 5
Gangrenarse gangrene	cantar 5	Gozar enjoy	cruzar 8
Gansear do something crazy	cantar 5	Grabar record	cantar 5
Gañir yelp	bruñir 58	Graduar graduate	actuar 10
Garabatear scribble	cantar 5	Granar seed	cantar 5
Garantizar guarantee	cruzar 8	Granizar[12] hail	cruzar 8
Gargajear spit	cantar 5	Granjearse earn	cantar 5
Gargarizar gargle	cruzar 8	Granular granulate	cantar 5
Garrapatear scrawl	cantar 5	Grapar staple	cantar 5
Garrapiñar freeze	cantar 5		

g

verb	model/table	verb	model/table
Gratificar gratify	atacar 7	Hastiar disgust	desviar 9
Gratinar cook au gratin	cantar 5	Hebraizar[11] Hebraize	cruzar 8
Gravar tax	cantar 5	Hechizar bewitch	cruzar 8
Gravitar gravitate	cantar 5	* Heder stink	perder 29
Graznar caw	cantar 5	* Helar[12] freeze	pensar 13
Grillarse sprout	cantar 5	Helenizar Hellenize	cruzar 8
Grisear make gray	cantar 5	* Henchir[48] cram	pedir 60
Gritar shout	cantar 5	* Hendir[49] split	discernir 66
Gruñir grunt	bruñir 58	* Heñir knead	teñir 64
Guardar guard	cantar 5	Heredar inherit	cantar 5
* Guarecer protect	obedecer 33	* Herir injure	sentir 65
* Guarnecer provide	obedecer 33	Hermanar combine	cantar 5
Guarnicionar garrison	cantar 5	Hermosear beautify	cantar 5
Guarrear dirty	cantar 5	Herniarse rupture	cantar 5
Guasearse joke	cantar 5	* Herrar shoe	pensar 13
Guerrear war	cantar 5	Herrumbrar rust	cantar 5
Guerrillear skirmish	cantar 5	* Hervir boil	sentir 65
Guiar guide	desviar 9	Hibernar hibernate	cantar 5
Guillotinar guillotine	cantar 5	Hidratar hydrate	cantar 5
Guiñar wink	cantar 5	Higienizar make hygienic	cruzar 8
Guipar see	cantar 5	Hilar spin	cantar 5
Guisar stew	cantar 5	Hilvanar baste	cantar 5
Guisotear cook	cantar 5	Himplar growl	cantar 5
Gulusmear taste	cantar 5	Hincar nail	atacar 7
Gustar please	cantar 5	Hinchar inflate	cantar 5
		Hipar hiccup	cantar 5
		Hipertrofiarse hypertrophy	cantar 5

h

		Hipnotizar hypnotize	cruzar 8
		Hipotecar mortgage	atacar 7
		Hispanizar Hispanize	cruzar 8
* Haber have	1	Historiar[50] depict	cantar 5
Habilitar enable	cantar 5	Hocicar come up against	atacar 7
Habitar inhabit	cantar 5	Hojaldrar make puff pastry	cantar 5
Habituar habituate	actuar 10	Hojear leaf through	cantar 5
Hablar speak	cantar 5	* Holgar rest	rogar 18
* Hacer do, make	37	Holgazanear loaf	cantar 5
Hacinar stack	cantar 5	* Hollar tread	contar 16
Halagar flatter	pagar 6	Homenajear honor	cantar 5
Hallar find	cantar 5	Homogeneizar[11] homogenize	cruzar 8
Haraganear loaf, idle	cantar 5	Homologar confirm	pagar 6
Hartar[47] satiate	cantar 5		

verb		model/table	verb		model/table
Hondear	sound	cantar 5	Ilustrar	illustrate	cantar 5
Honorificar	honor	atacar 7	Imaginar	imagine	cantar 5
Honrar	honor	cantar 5	Imantar	magnetize	cantar 5
Horadar	drill	cantar 5	Imbricar	overlap	atacar 7
Hormiguear	swarm	cantar 5	* Imbuir	imbue	concluir 59
Hornear	bake	cantar 5	Imitar	imitate	cantar 5
Horripilar	terrify	cantar 5	Impacientar	exasperate	cantar 5
Horrorizar	horrify	cruzar 8	Impactar	impact	cantar 5
Hospedar	lodge	cantar 5	Impartir	impart	vivir 51
Hospitalizar	hospitalize	cruzar 8	* Impedir	prevent	pedir 60
Hostigar	whip	pagar 6	Impeler	propel	beber 24
Hostilizar	antagonize	cruzar 8	Imperar	rule	cantar 5
Hozar	root up	cruzar 8	Impermeabilizar	waterproof	cruzar 8
* Huir	flee	concluir 59	Impersonalizar	use impersonally	cruzar 8
Humanizar	humanize	cruzar 8	Implantar	implant	cantar 5
Humar	smoke	cantar 5	Implementar	implement	cantar 5
Humear	smoke	cantar 5	Implicar	imply	atacar 7
* Humedecer	humidify	obedecer 33	Implorar	implore	cantar 5
Humidificar	humidify	atacar 7	* Imponer	impose	poner 41
Humillar	humiliate	cantar 5	Importar	be important	cantar 5
Hundir	sink	vivir 51	Importunar	importune	cantar 5
Hurgar	stir up	pagar 6	Imposibilitar	make impossible	cantar 5
Huronear	ferret	cantar 5	Impostar	sign out	cantar 5
Hurtar	steal	cantar 5	Imprecar	imprecate	atacar 7
Husmear	smell out	cantar 5	Impregnar	impregnate	cantar 5
			Impresionar	impress	cantar 5
			Imprimir[51]	print	vivir 51
			Improvisar	improvise	cantar 5
			Impugnar	challenge	cantar 5
			Impulsar	impel	cantar 5
			Imputar	impute	cantar 5
			Inaugurar	inaugurate	cantar 5
Idealizar	idealize	cruzar 8	Incapacitar	incapacitate	cantar 5
Idear	conceive	cantar 5	Incardinar	incardinate	cantar 5
Identificar	identify	atacar 7	Incautarse	confiscate	cantar 5
Idiotizar	idiotize	cruzar 8	Incendiar	set on fire	cantar 5
Idolatrar	worship	cantar 5	* Incensar	incense	pensar 13
Ignorar	ignore	cantar 5	Incentivar	incentivize	cantar 5
Igualar	equal	cantar 5	Incidir	fall into	vivir 51
Ilegitimar	illegitimate	cantar 5	Incinerar	incinerate	cantar 5
Iluminar	illuminate	cantar 5	Incitar	incite	cantar 5
Ilusionar	deceive	cantar 5	Inclinar	incline	cantar 5

V

verb	model/table	verb	model/table
* Incluir include	concluir 59	Infrautilizar underutilize	cruzar 8
Incoar[52] begin	cantar 5	Infravalorar undervalue	cantar 5
Incomodar inconvenience	cantar 5	Infringir infringe	dirigir 52
Incomunicar isolate	atacar 7	Infundir infuse	vivir 51
Incordiar pester	cantar 5	Ingeniar invent	cantar 5
Incorporar incorporate	cantar 5	* Ingerir ingest	sentir 65
Incrementar increase	cantar 5	Ingresar enter	cantar 5
Increpar scold	cantar 5	Inhabilitar disable	cantar 5
Incriminar incriminate	cantar 5	Inhalar inhale	cantar 5
Incrustar encrust	cantar 5	Inhibir inhibit	vivir 51
Incubar incubate	cantar 5	Inhumar bury	cantar 5
Inculcar inculcate	atacar 7	Iniciar initiate	cantar 5
Inculpar accuse	cantar 5	Inicializar initialize	cruzar 8
Incumbir[6] be the duty	vivir 51	* Injerir insert	sentir 5
Incumplir fail to fulfill	vivir 51	Injertar[54] graft	cantar 5
Incurrir[53] incur	vivir 51	Injuriar offend	cantar 5
Incursionar raid	cantar 5	Inmigrar immigrate	cantar 5
Indagar investigate	pagar 6	* Inmiscuir mix	concluir 59
Indemnizar indemnify	cruzar 8	Inmolar immolate	cantar 5
Independizar free	cruzar 8	Inmortalizar immortalize	cruzar 8
Indicar indicate	atacar 7	Inmovilizar immobilize	cruzar 8
Indigestarse cause indigestion	cantar 5	Inmunizar immunize	cruzar 8
Indignar infuriate	cantar 5	Inmutar alter	cantar 5
Indisciplinarse become unruly	cantar 5	Innovar innovate	cantar 5
* Indisponer indispose	poner 41	Inocular inoculate	cantar 5
Individualizar individualize	cruzar 8	Inquietar disturb	cantar 5
* Inducir induce	traducir 69	* Inquirir inquire	adquirir 67
Indultar pardon	cantar 5	Insalivar insalivate	cantar 5
Industrializar industrialize	cruzar 8	* Inscribir[55] inscribe	vivir 51
Infamar defame	cantar 5	Inseminar inseminate	cantar 5
Infartar cause infarct	cantar 5	Insensibilizar anesthetize	cruzar 8
Infectar infect	cantar 5	Insertar[56] insert	cantar 5
* Inferir infer	sentir 65	Insinuar insinuate	actuar 10
Infestar infest	cantar 5	Insistir insist	vivir 51
Infiltrar infiltrate	cantar 5	Insolentar make insolent	cantar 5
Inflamar inflame	cantar 5	Insonorizar soundproof	cruzar 8
Inflar inflate	cantar 5	Inspeccionar inspect	cantar 5
Infligir inflict	dirigir 52	Inspirar inspire	cantar 5
Influenciar influence	cantar 5	Instalar install	cantar 5
* Influir influence	concluir 59	Instar urge	cantar 5
Informar inform	cantar 5	Instaurar set up	cantar 5
Informatizar computerize	cruzar 8	Instigar instigate	pagar 6

verb	model/table	verb	model/table
Instilar **instill**	cantar 5	* Intuir **sense**	concluir 59
Institucionalizar **institutionalize**	cruzar 8	Inundar **flood**	cantar 5
* Instituir **institute**	concluir 59	Inutilizar **ruin**	cruzar 8
* Instruir **instruct**	concluir 59	Invadir **invade**	vivir 51
Instrumentar **orchestrate**	cantar 5	Invalidar **invalidate**	cantar 5
Instrumentalizar **instrumentalize**	cruzar 8	Inventar **invent**	cantar 5
Insubordinar **make rebellious**	cantar 5	Inventariar **inventory**	desviar 9
Insuflar **insulfate**	cantar 5	Invernar **winter**	cantar 5
Insultar **insult**	cantar 5	* Invertir **invest**	sentir 65
Insurreccionarse **rebel**	cantar 5	Investigar **investigate**	pagar 6
Integrar **integrate**	cantar 5	* Investir **invest**	pedir 60
Intelectualizar **intellectualize**	cruzar 8	Invitar **invite**	cantar 5
Intensificar **intensify**	atacar 7	Invocar **invoke**	atacar 7
Intentar **attempt**	cantar 5	Involucionar **react**	cantar 5
Interaccionar **interact**	cantar 5	Involucrar **involve**	cantar 5
Intercalar **interpolate**	cantar 5	Inyectar **inject**	cantar 5
Intercambiar **interchange**	cantar 5	Ionizar **ionize**	cruzar 8
Interceder **intercede**	beber 24	* **Ir** **go**	77
Interceptar **intercept**	cantar 5	Irisar **iridesce**	cantar 5
Interesar **interest**	cantar 5	Ironizar **ridicule**	cruzar 8
* Interferir **interfere**	sentir 65	Irradiar **irradiate**	cantar 5
Interiorizar **interiorize**	cruzar 8	Irrigar **irrigate**	pagar 6
Intermediar **mediate**	cantar 5	Irritar **irritate**	cantar 5
Internacionalizar **internationalize**	cruzar 8	Irrumpir **burst into**	vivir 51
Internar **intern**	cantar 5	Islamizar **Islamize**	cruzar 8
Interpelar **question officially**	cantar 5	Italianizar **Italianize**	cruzar 8
Interpolar **interpolate**	cantar 5	Iterar **iterate**	cantar 5
* Interponer **interpose**	poner 41	Izar **hoist**	cruzar 8
Interpretar **interpret**	cantar 5		
Interrogar **interrogate**	pagar 6		
Interrumpir **interrupt**	vivir 51		
* Intervenir **intervene**	venir 80		
Interviuvar **interview**	cantar 5		
Intimar **notify**	cantar 5	Jabonar **soap**	cantar 5
Intimidar **intimidate**	cantar 5	Jactarse **boast**	cantar 5
Intitular **entitle**	cantar 5	Jadear **pant**	cantar 5
Intoxicar **intoxicate**	atacar 7	Jalar **stuff**	cantar 5
Intranquilizar **worry**	cruzar 8	Jalear **urge on**	cantar 5
Intrigar **intrigue**	pagar 6	Jalonar **stake out**	cantar 5
Intrincar **confuse**	atacar 7	Jamar **stuff**	cantar 5
* Introducir **introduce**	traducir 69	Jaranear **go on a binge**	cantar 5
Intubar **intubate**	cantar 5	Jarrear **get water with a pitcher**	cantar 5

verb	model/table	verb	model/table
Jaspear marble	cantar 5	Largar release	pagar 6
Jerarquizar arrange		Lastimar hurt	cantar 5
hierarchically	cruzar 8	Lastrar ballast	cantar 5
Jeringar inject	pagar 6	Lateralizar lateralize	cruzar 8
Joder fuck, pester	beber 24	Latinizar Latinize	cruzar 8
Jorobar get on nerves	cantar 5	Latir beat	vivir 51
Jubilar retire	cantar 5	Laurear reward	cantar 5
Judaizar[11] Judaize	cruzar 8	Lavar wash	cantar 5
Juerguearse enjoy	cantar 5	Lavotear wash badly	cantar 5
* Jugar play	21	Laxar loosen	cantar 5
Juguetear toy	cantar 5	* Leer read	28
Juntar[57] unite	cantar 5	Legalizar legalize	cruzar 8
Juramentar swear in	cantar 5	Legar bequeath	pagar 6
Jurar swear	cantar 5	Legislar legislate	cantar 5
Justificar justify	atacar 7	Legitimar legitimate	cantar 5
Justipreciar appraise	cantar 5	Legrar scrape	cantar 5
Juzgar judge	pagar 6	Lesionar wound	cantar 5
		Levantar lift	cantar 5
		Levar weigh anchor	cantar 5
		Levitar levitate	cantar 5
		Lexicalizar convert to lexical	
		form	cruzar 8
Labializar labialize	cruzar 8	Liar bind	desviar 9
Laborar work	cantar 5	Libar suck	cantar 5
Labrar work for	cantar 5	Liberalizar liberalize	cruzar 8
Lacerar lacerate	cantar 5	Liberar liberate	cantar 5
Lacrar seal	cantar 5	Libertar free	cantar 5
Lactar nurse	cantar 5	Librar rescue	cantar 5
Ladear lean	cantar 5	Licenciar license	cantar 5
Ladrar bark	cantar 5	Licitar bid for	cantar 5
Ladrillar brick	cantar 5	Licuar[7] liquefy	cantar 5
Lagrimear weep	cantar 5	Liderar lead	cantar 5
Laicizar laicize	cruzar 8	Lidiar fight	cantar 5
Lamentar lament	cantar 5	Ligar bind	pagar 6
Lamer lick	beber 24	Lijar sand	cantar 5
Laminar laminate	cantar 5	Limar file	cantar 5
Lampar crave	cantar 5	Limitar limit	cantar 5
Lancear lance	cantar 5	Limosnear beg	cantar 5
* Languidecer languish	obedecer 33	Limpiar clean	cantar 5
Lanzar launch	cruzar 8	Linchar lynch	cantar 5
Lapidar stone	cantar 5	Lindar border	cantar 5
Laquear lacquer	cantar 5		

verb	model/table	verb	model/table
Liofilizar freeze-dry	cruzar 8	Magrear pet	cantar 5
Liquidar liquidate	cantar 5	Magullar bruise	cantar 5
Lisiar disable	cantar 5	Majar crush	cantar 5
Lisonjear flatter	cantar 5	Malcasar mismate	cantar 5
Listar list	cantar 5	Malcomer eat badly	beber 24
Litigar litigate	pagar 6	Malcriar spoil	desviar 9
Litografiar lithograph	desviar 9	* Maldecir[58] curse	bendecir 73
Lizar smooth	cruzar 8	Malear ruin	cantar 5
Llagar wound	pagar 6	Maleducar raise badly	atacar 7
Llamar call	cantar 5	Malgastar squander	cantar 5
Llamear blaze	cantar 5	* Malherir wound badly	sentir 65
Llanear ride on the flat	cantar 5	Malhumorar upset	cantar 5
Llegar arrive	pagar 6	Maliciar make bad	cantar 5
Llenar fill	cantar 5	Malmeter waste	beber 24
Llevar take	cantar 5	Malograr waste	cantar 5
Llorar cry	cantar 5	Maltear malt	cantar 5
Lloriquear whimper	cantar 5	* Maltraer ill-treat	traer 47
* Llover[12] rain	mover 30	Maltratar mistreat	cantar 5
Lloviznar[12] drizzle	cantar 5	Malvender sell at a loss	beber 24
Loar praise	cantar 5	Malversar embezzle	cantar 5
Localizar locate	cruzar 8	Malvivir live badly	vivir 51
Lograr achieve	cantar 5	Mamar suckle	cantar 5
Loquear play the fool	cantar 5	Manar flow	cantar 5
Lubricar lubricate	atacar 7	Manchar spot	cantar 5
Lubrificar lubricate	atacar 7	Mancillar stain	cantar 5
* Lucir shine	70	Mancipar enslave	cantar 5
Lucrar obtain	cantar 5	Mancomunar unite	cantar 5
Lucubrar work laboriously	cantar 5	Mandar send	cantar 5
Luchar struggle	cantar 5	Manducar eat	atacar 7
Lustrar polish	cantar 5	Manejar manage, drive	cantar 5
Luxar dislocate	cantar 5	Mangar steal, mooch	pagar 6
		Mangonear organize	cantar 5
		Maniatar handcuff	cantar 5
		* Manifestar[59] manifest	pensar 13
		Maniobrar operate	cantar 5
		Manipular manipulate	cantar 5
Macerar mortify	cantar 5	Manosear handle	cantar 5
Machacar pound	atacar 7	Manotear steal	cantar 5
Madrugar get up early	pagar 6	Mantear toss	cantar 5
Madurar mature	cantar 5	* Mantener maintain	tener 2
Magnetizar magnetize	cruzar 8	Manufacturar manufacture	cantar 5
Magnificar magnify	atacar 7	Manumitir emancipate	vivir 51

m

verb	model/table	verb	model/table
* Manuscribir[60] write by hand	vivir 51	Medicar medicate	atacar 7
Maquilar collect miller's toll	cantar 5	Medicinar treat	cantar 5
Maquillar make up	cantar 5	* Medir measure	pedir 60
Maquinar plot	cantar 5	Meditar meditate	cantar 5
Maquinizar mechanize	cruzar 8	Medrar thrive	cantar 5
Maravillar astonish	cantar 5	Mejorar improve	cantar 5
Marcar mark	atacar 7	Mellar notch	cantar 5
Marchar walk, march	cantar 5	Memorizar memorize	cruzar 8
Marchitar[61] wilt	cantar 5	Mencionar mention	cantar 5
Marear make sick	cantar 5	Mendigar beg	pagar 6
Marginar write margin notes	cantar 5	Menear shake	cantar 5
Maridar marry	cantar 5	Menguar decrease	averiguar 11
Marinar marinate	cantar 5	Menoscabar reduce	cantar 5
Mariposear flirt	cantar 5	Menospreciar despise	cantar 5
Marrar turn out badly	cantar 5	Menstruar menstruate	actuar 10
Marrullar cajole	cantar 5	Mentalizar indoctrinate	cruzar 8
Martillar hammer	cantar 5	* Mentar mention	pensar 13
Martillear pound on ears	cantar 5	* Mentir lie	sentir 65
Martirizar martyr	cruzar 8	Menudear retail	cantar 5
Masacrar massacre	cantar 5	Mercadear trade	cantar 5
Mascar chew	atacar 7	Mercantilizar commercialize	cruzar 8
Masculinizar masculinize	cruzar 8	Mercar buy	atacar 7
Mascullar mumble	cantar 5	* Merecer deserve	obedecer 33
Masificar mass-produce	atacar 7	* Merendar picnic	pensar 13
Masticar chew	atacar 7	Mermar reduce	cantar 5
Masturbar masturbate	cantar 5	Merodear prowl	cantar 5
Matar kill	cantar 5	Mesar tear	cantar 5
Matasellar postmark	cantar 5	Mestizar crossbreed	cruzar 8
Materializar materialize	cruzar 8	Mesurar restrain	cantar 5
Maternizar treat as a mother	cruzar 8	Metaforizar metaphorize	cruzar 8
Matizar match	cruzar 8	Metalizar metallize	cruzar 8
Matricular register	cantar 5	Metamorfosear metamorphose	cantar 5
Matrimoniar marry	cantar 5	Meteorizar produce bloat	cruzar 8
Maullar meow	12	Meter put	beber 24
Maximizar maximize	cruzar 8	Metodizar methodize	cruzar 8
Mear urinate	cantar 5	Mezclar mix	cantar 5
Mecanizar mechanize	cruzar 8	Microfilmar microfilm	cantar 5
Mecanografiar type	desviar 9	Migar crumble	pagar 6
Mecer rock	vencer 26	Militar soldier	cantar 5
Mechar lard	cantar 5	Militarizar militarize	cruzar 8
Mediar intervene	cantar 5	Mimar coddle	cantar 5
Mediatizar mediatize	cruzar 8	Minar mine	cantar 5

verb	model/table	verb	model/table
Mineralizar mineralize	cruzar 8	Motejar label	cantar 5
Minimizar minimize	cruzar 8	Motivar motivate	cantar 5
Ministrar minister	cantar 5	Motorizar motorize	cruzar 8
Minusvalorar underestimate	cantar 5	* Mover move	30
Mirar look at	cantar 5	Movilizar mobilize	cruzar 8
Mistificar falsify	atacar 7	Mudar change	cantar 5
Mitificar mythologize	atacar 7	Mugir moo	dirigir 52
Mitigar mitigate	pagar 6	Mullir soften, fluff	57
Mixtificar falsify	atacar 7	Multar fine	cantar 5
Mocar blow nose	atacar 7	Multicopiar duplicate	cantar 5
Modelar model	cantar 5	Multiplicar multiply	atacar 7
Moderar moderate	cantar 5	Municipalizar municipalize	cruzar 8
Modernizar modernize	cruzar 8	Murar wall	cantar 5
Modificar modify	atacar 7	Murmurar murmur	cantar 5
Modular modulate	cantar 5	Musitar whisper	cantar 5
Mofar mock	cantar 5	Mustiar wilt	cantar 5
Mojar wet	cantar 5	Mutar change	cantar 5
Moldar mold	cantar 5	Mutilar mutilate	cantar 5
Moldear mold	cantar 5		
* Moler grind	mover 30		
Molestar bother	cantar 5		
Momificar mummify	atacar 7		**n**
Mondar hull	cantar 5		
Monologar soliloquize	pagar 6	* Nacer be born	31
Monopolizar monopolize	cruzar 8	Nacionalizar nationalize	cruzar 8
Monoptongar reduce to		Nadar swim	cantar 5
monophthong	pagar 6	Narcotizar narcotize	cruzar 8
Montar ride	cantar 5	Narcofinanciar finance narcotics	cantar 5
Monumentalizar make		Narrar narrate	cantar 5
monumental	cruzar 8	Nasalizar nasalize	cruzar 8
Moquear run (nose)	cantar 5	Naturalizar naturalize	cruzar 8
Moralizar moralize	cruzar 8	Naufragar shipwreck	pagar 6
Morar reside	cantar 5	Navegar navigate	pagar 6
* Morder bite	mover 30	Necesitar need	cantar 5
Mordisquear nibble	cantar 5	* Negar deny, refuse	14
Morigerar moderate	cantar 5	Negociar negotiate	cantar 5
* Morir[62] die	dormir 68	Negrear blacken	cantar 5
Mortificar mortify	atacar 7	Neutralizar neutralize	cruzar 8
Mosconear annoy	cantar 5	* Nevar[12] snow	pensar 13
Mosquear swat	cantar 5	Ningunear ignore	cantar 5
* Mostrar show	contar 16	Niñear act childishly	cantar 5
Motear speckle	cantar 5	Niquelar nickel-plate	cantar 5

verb	model/table	verb	model/table
Nivelar level	cantar 5	Ofertar offer	cantar 5
Nombrar appoint	cantar 5	Oficializar officialize	cruzar 8
Nominar nominate	cantar 5	Oficiar officiate	cantar 5
Noquear knock out	cantar 5	* Ofrecer offer	obedecer 33
Normalizar normalize	cruzar 8	Ofrendar make an offering	cantar 5
Notar note	cantar 5	Ofuscar dazzle	atacar 7
Notificar notify	atacar 7	* Oír hear, listen to	78
Novelar novelize	cantar 5	Ojear stare at	cantar 5
Nublar cloud	cantar 5	* Oler smell	38
Numerar count	cantar 5	Olfatear sniff	cantar 5
Nutrir nourish	vivir 51	Olisquear pry into	cantar 5
		Olvidar forget	cantar 5
		Omitir omit	vivir 51
		Ondear undulate	cantar 5

verb	model/table	verb	model/table
		Ondular wave	cantar 5
		Operar operate	cantar 5
Obcecarse be blinded	atacar 7	Opinar give an opinion	cantar 5
* Obedecer obey	33	* Oponer oppose	poner 41
Objetar object	cantar 5	Opositar take an exam	cantar 5
Objetivar objectivize	cantar 5	Oprimir oppress	vivir 51
Obligar obligate	pagar 6	Optar opt	cantar 5
Obliterar obliterate	cantar 5	Optimar optimize	cantar 5
Obnubilar dazzle	cantar 5	Optimizar optimize	cruzar 8
Obrar do	cantar 5	Orar pray	cantar 5
Obsequiar bestow	cantar 5	Ordenar put in order	cantar 5
Observar observe	cantar 5	Ordeñar milk	cantar 5
Obsesionar obsess	cantar 5	Orear air	cantar 5
Obstaculizar hinder	cruzar 8	Organizar organize	cruzar 8
Obstar obstruct	cantar 5	Orientar orientate	cantar 5
Obstinarse become obstinate	cantar 5	Originar originate	cantar 5
* Obstruir block	concluir 59	Orillar trim	cantar 5
* Obtener obtain	tener 2	Orinar urinate	cantar 5
Obturar plug, stop up	cantar 5	Orlar border	cantar 5
Obviar remove, surmount	cantar 5	Ornamentar adorn	cantar 5
Ocasionar cause	cantar 5	Ornar embellish	cantar 5
Ociar idle	cantar 5	Orquestar orchestrate	cantar 5
* Ocluir close, hide	concluir 59	Osar dare	cantar 5
Ocultar conceal	cantar 5	Oscilar oscillate	cantar 5
Ocupar occupy	cantar 5	* Oscurecer[12] darken	obedecer 33
Ocurrir happen	vivir 51	Ostentar show off	cantar 5
Odiar hate	cantar 5	Otear scan	cantar 5
Ofender offend	beber 24	Otorgar grant	pagar 6

verb	model/table	verb	model/table
Ovacionar give an ovation	cantar 5	Parlotear chatter	cantar 5
Ovalar make oval	cantar 5	Parodiar parody	cantar 5
Ovar lay eggs	cantar 5	Parpadear blink	cantar 5
Ovillar roll in a ball	cantar 5	Parrandear go on a binge	cantar 5
Ovular ovulate	cantar 5	Participar participate	cantar 5
Oxidarse get rusty	cantar 5	Particularizar particularize	cruzar 8
Oxigenar oxygenate	cantar 5	Partir divide	vivir 51
		Pasar pass	cantar 5
		Pasear take a walk	cantar 5
		Pasmar astound	cantar 5
		Pastar pasture	cantar 5

verb	model/table	verb	model/table
		Pasteurizar pasteurize	cruzar 8
* Pacer graze	nacer 31	Pastorear shepherd	cantar 5
Pacificar pacify	atacar 7	Patalear kick	cantar 5
Pactar make a pact	cantar 5	Patear trample	cantar 5
* Padecer suffer	obedecer 33	Patentar patent	cantar 5
Pagar pay	6	Patentizar show	cruzar 8
Paginar paginate	cantar 5	Patinar skate	cantar 5
Paladear relish	cantar 5	Patrocinar sponsor	cantar 5
Palatalizar palatalize	cruzar 8	Patrullar patrol	cantar 5
Paliar extenuate	cantar 5	Pausar pause	cantar 5
* Palidecer turn pale	obedecer 33	Pautar rule	cantar 5
Palmar die	cantar 5	Pavimentar pave	cantar 5
Palmear applaud	cantar 5	Pavonear deceive	cantar 5
Palmotear clap	cantar 5	Peatonalizar pedestrianize	cruzar 8
Palpar touch	cantar 5	Pecar sin	atacar 7
Palpitar palpitate	cantar 5	Pechar push	cantar 5
Panificar make bread	atacar 7	Pedalear pedal	cantar 5
Papear eat	cantar 5	* Pedir ask for, order	60
Parabolizar parabolize	cruzar 8	Pedorrear pass wind	cantar 5
Parafrasear paraphrase	cantar 5	Pegar hit	pagar 6
Paralizar paralyze	cruzar 8	Pegotear patch, plaster	cantar 5
Parangonar compare	cantar 5	Peinar comb	cantar 5
Parapetarse barricade	cantar 5	Pelar peel	cantar 5
Parar stop	cantar 5	Pelear fight	cantar 5
Parcelar parcel out	cantar 5	Peligrar endanger	cantar 5
Parchear patch	cantar 5	Pellizcar pinch	atacar 7
Parcializar partialize	cruzar 8	Pelotear kick a ball	cantar 5
* Parecer seem	obedecer 33	Penalizar penalize	cruzar 8
Parir give birth	vivir 51	Penar punish	cantar 5
Parlamentar converse, parley	cantar 5	Pender hang	beber 24
Parlar chat	cantar 5	Pendonear gallivant	cantar 5

verb	model/table	verb	model/table
Penetrar penetrate	*cantar* 5	Pervivir survive	*vivir* 51
* *Pensar* think	13	Pesar weigh	*cantar* 5
Pensionar pension	*cantar* 5	Pescar fish	*atacar* 7
Peraltar tilt	*cantar* 5	Pespuntear backstitch	*cantar* 5
Percatarse perceive	*cantar* 5	Pestañear blink	*cantar* 5
Percibir notice	*vivir* 51	Petar gratify	*cantar* 5
Percutir strike	*vivir* 51	Petardear backfire (car)	*cantar* 5
* *Perder* lose, miss	29	Peticionar petition	*cantar* 5
Perdonar forgive	*cantar* 5	Petrificar petrify	*atacar* 7
Perdurar last	*cantar* 5	Piafar paw the ground	*cantar* 5
* *Perecer* perish	*obedecer* 33	Piar chirp	*desviar* 9
Peregrinar travel, roam	*cantar* 5	Picar bite, burn	*atacar* 7
Perennizar make perennial	*cruzar* 8	Picotear peck	*cantar* 5
Perfeccionar perfect	*cantar* 5	Pifiar miscue	*cantar* 5
Perfilar profile	*cantar* 5	Pigmentar pigment	*cantar* 5
Perforar perforate	*cantar* 5	Pillar plunder	*cantar* 5
Perfumar perfume	*cantar* 5	Pilotar pilot	*cantar* 5
Pergeñar sketch out	*cantar* 5	Pimplar booze	*cantar* 5
Periclitar be in danger	*cantar* 5	Pincelar draw	*cantar* 5
Peritar give expert appraisal	*cantar* 5	Pinchar tease	*cantar* 5
Perjudicar damage	*atacar* 7	Pintar paint	*cantar* 5
Perjurar perjure	*cantar* 5	Pintarrajear daub	*cantar* 5
Perlar pearl	*cantar* 5	Pinzar pinch	*cruzar* 8
* *Permanecer* remain	*obedecer* 33	Pirarse buzz off	*cantar* 5
Permitir allow	*vivir* 51	Piratear pirate	*cantar* 5
Permutar exchange	*cantar* 5	Piropear compliment	*cantar* 5
Pernoctar stay out all night	*cantar* 5	Pirrarse rave about	*cantar* 5
Perorar make a speech	*cantar* 5	Piruetear pirouette	*cantar* 5
Perpetrar perpetrate	*cantar* 5	Pisar tread on	*cantar* 5
Perpetuar perpetuate	*actuar* 10	Pisotear trample	*cantar* 5
* *Perseguir* persecute	*seguir* 62	Pitar whistle	*cantar* 5
Perseverar persevere	*cantar* 5	Pitorrearse make fun of	*cantar* 5
Persignar cross	*cantar* 5	Pivotar pivot	*cantar* 5
Persistir persist	*vivir* 51	* *Placer*[1] like	39
Personalizar personalize	*cruzar* 8	Plagar plague	*pagar* 6
Personarse appear in person	*cantar* 5	Plagiar plagiarize	*cantar* 5
Personificar personify	*atacar* 7	Planchar iron	*cantar* 5
Persuadir persuade	*vivir* 51	Planear plan	*cantar* 5
* *Pertenecer* belong	*obedecer* 33	Planificar plan	*atacar* 7
Pertrechar supply	*cantar* 5	Plantar plant	*cantar* 5
Perturbar disturb	*cantar* 5	Plantear expound	*cantar* 5
* *Pervertir* pervert	*sentir* 65	Plantificar institute	*atacar* 7

verb	model/table	verb	model/table
Plañir wail	*bruñir* 58	Precaver guard against	*beber* 24
Plasmar mold	*cantar* 5	Preceder precede	*beber* 24
Plastificar plasticize	*atacar* 7	Preciarse be vain	*cantar* 5
Platear silver-plate	*cantar* 5	Precintar seal	*cantar* 5
Platicar converse	*atacar* 7	Precipitar precipitate	*cantar* 5
* Plegar bend	*negar* 14	Precisar specify	*cantar* 5
Pleitear plead	*cantar* 5	* Preconcebir preconceive	*pedir* 60
Plisar pleat	*cantar* 5	Preconizar praise	*cruzar* 8
Pluralizar pluralize	*cruzar* 8	Predatar predate	*cantar* 5
* Poblar populate	*contar* 16	* Predecir[64] predict	*bendecir* 73
Podar prune	*cantar* 5	Predestinar predestine	*cantar* 5
* Poder be able	40	Predeterminar predetermine	*cantar* 5
Poetizar poetize	*cruzar* 8	Predicar preach	*atacar* 7
Polarizar polarize	*cruzar* 8	* Predisponer predispose	*poner* 41
Polemizar argue	*cruzar* 8	Predominar predominate	*cantar* 5
Policromar polychrome	*cantar* 5	Preexistir preexist	*vivir* 51
Polinizar pollinate	*cruzar* 8	* Preferir prefer	*sentir* 65
Politizar politicize	*cruzar* 8	Prefigurar prefigure	*cantar* 5
Ponderar ponder	*cantar* 5	Prefijar prefix	*cantar* 5
* Poner put, place	41	Pregonar proclaim	*cantar* 5
Pontificar pontificate	*atacar* 7	Preguntar ask	*cantar* 5
Popularizar popularize	*cruzar* 8	Prejuzgar prejudge	*pagar* 6
Pordiosear beg	*cantar* 5	Preludiar prelude	*cantar* 5
Porfiar persist	*desviar* 9	Premeditar premeditate	*cantar* 5
Pormenorizar detail	*cruzar* 8	Premiar reward	*cantar* 5
Portar carry	*cantar* 5	Prendar fall in love	*cantar* 5
Portear slam	*cantar* 5	Prender[65] seize	*beber* 24
Posar alight	*cantar* 5	Prensar press	*cantar* 5
* Poseer[63] possess	*leer* 28	Preñar get pregnant	*cantar* 5
Posesionar hand over	*cantar* 5	Preocupar worry	*cantar* 5
Posibilitar facilitate	*cantar* 5	Preparar prepare	*cantar* 5
Posicionar position	*cantar* 5	Preponderar preponderate	*cantar* 5
Positivar make a positive of	*cantar* 5	Presagiar presage	*cantar* 5
* Posponer postpone	*poner* 41	Prescindir disregard	*vivir* 51
Postergar put off	*pagar* 6	* Prescribir[66] prescribe	*vivir* 51
Postinear show off	*cantar* 5	Preseleccionar seed	*cantar* 5
Postrarse prostrate onself	*cantar* 5	Presenciar witness	*cantar* 5
Postular postulate	*cantar* 5	Presentar present	*cantar* 5
Potabilizar make drinkable	*cruzar* 8	* Presentir have a foreboding	*sentir* 65
Potar booze	*cantar* 5	Preservar preserve	*cantar* 5
Potenciar give power	*cantar* 5	Presidir preside over	*vivir* 51
Practicar practice	*atacar* 7	Presintonizar preprogram	*cruzar* 8

verb		model/table	verb		model/table
Presionar	press	cantar 5	Promulgar	promulgate	pagar 6
Prestar	lend	cantar 5	Pronosticar	forecast	atacar 7
Prestigiar	give prestige	cantar 5	Pronunciar	pronounce	cantar 5
Presumir	presume	vivir 51	Propagar	propagate	pagar 6
* Presuponer	presuppose	poner 41	Propalar	spread	cantar 5
Presupuestar	budget	cantar 5	Propasar	overstep	cantar 5
Presurizar	pressurize	cruzar 8	Propender[67]	tend	beber 24
Pretender	seek	beber 24	Propiciar	placate	cantar 5
Pretextar	use as a pretext	cantar 5	Propinar	give	cantar 5
* Prevalecer	prevail	obedecer 33	* Proponer	propose	poner 41
Prevaricar	betray trust	atacar 7	Proporcionar	proportion	cantar 5
* Prevenir	prepare	venir 80	Propugnar	defend	cantar 5
* Prever	foresee	ver 49	Propulsar	propel	cantar 5
Primar	take priority	cantar 5	Prorratear	share out	cantar 5
Pringar	get grease on	pagar 6	Prorrogar	prolong	pagar 6
Privar	deprive	cantar 5	Prorrumpir	burst out	vivir 51
Privatizar	privatize	cruzar 8	* Proscribir[68]	banish	vivir 51
Privilegiar	privilege	cantar 5	* Proseguir	pursue	seguir 62
* Probar	try	contar 16	Prosificar	put into prose	atacar 7
Proceder	proceed	beber 24	Prosperar	prosper	cantar 5
Procesar	process	cantar 5	Prosternarse	prostrate oneself	cantar 5
Proclamar	proclaim	cantar 5	* Prostituir	prostitute	concluir 59
Procrear	procreate	cantar 5	Protagonizar	star in	cruzar 8
Procurar	procure	cantar 5	Proteger	protect	coger 25
Prodigar	lavish	pagar 6	Protestar	protest	cantar 5
* Producir	produce	traducir 69	* Proveer[69]	provide	leer 28
Profanar	profane	cantar 5	* Provenir	issue from	venir 80
* Proferir	utter	sentir 65	Provocar	provoke	atacar 7
Profesar	profess	cantar 5	Proyectar	project	cantar 5
Profesionalizar	professionalize	cruzar 8	Psicoanalizar	psychoanalyze	cruzar 8
Profetizar	prophesy	cruzar 8	Publicar	publish	atacar 7
Profundizar	deepen	cruzar 8	Publicitar	advertise	cantar 5
Programar	program	cantar 5	* Pudrir[70]	rot	vivir 51
Progresar	progress	cantar 5	Puentear	bridge	cantar 5
Prohibir	prohibit	55	Pugnar	struggle	cantar 5
Proliferar	proliferate	cantar 5	Pujar	bid up	cantar 5
Prologar	prologue	pagar 6	Pulimentar	polish	cantar 5
Prolongar	prolong	pagar 6	Pulir	polish	abolir 71
Promediar	average out	cantar 5	Pulsar	press	cantar 5
Prometer	promise	beber 24	Pulular	swarm	cantar 5
Promocionar	promote	cantar 5	Pulverizar	pulverize	cruzar 8
* Promover	foster	mover 30	Puntear	dot	cantar 5

verb	model/table	verb	model/table
Puntualizar arrange	*cruzar* 8	Raptar abduct	*cantar* 5
Puntuar punctuate	*actuar* 10	Rarificar rarefy	*atacar* 7
Punzar prick	*cruzar* 8	Rasar graze	*cantar* 5
Purgar purge	*pagar* 6	Rascar scratch	*atacar* 7
Purificar purify	*atacar* 7	Rasgar rip	*pagar* 6
Putear go whoring	*cantar* 5	Rasguear strum	*cantar* 5
		Raspar scrape	*cantar* 5
		Rastrear track	*cantar* 5

		Rastrillar rake	*cantar* 5
		Rastrojar glean	*cantar* 5
		Rasurar shave	*cantar* 5
Quebrantar break	*cantar* 5	Ratificar ratify	*atacar* 7
* Quebrar break	*pensar* 13	Rayar line	*cantar* 5
Quedar remain	*cantar* 5	Razonar reason	*cantar* 5
Quejarse complain	*cantar* 5	* Reabrir[72] reopen	*vivir* 51
Quemar burn	*cantar* 5	Reabsorber reabsorb	*beber* 24
Querellarse lodge a complaint	*cantar* 5	Reaccionar react	*cantar* 5
* Querer want, love	42	Reactivar reactivate	*cantar* 5
Quintuplicar quintuple	*atacar* 7	Readaptar readapt	*cantar* 5
Quitar remove	*cantar* 5	Readmitir readmit	*vivir* 51
		Reafirmar reaffirm	*cantar* 5
		Reagrupar regroup	*cantar* 5
		Reajustar readjust	*cantar* 5
		Realistarse be realistic	*cantar* 5
		Realizar carry out	*cruzar* 8

		Realquilar sublet	*cantar* 5
		Realzar highlight	*cruzar* 8
		Reanimar revive	*cantar* 5
		Reanudar renew	*cantar* 5
Rabiar rage	*cantar* 5	* Reaparecer reappear	*obedecer* 33
Racanear not work	*cantar* 5	Rearmar rearm	*cantar* 5
Racionalizar rationalize	*cruzar* 8	Reavivar revive	*cantar* 5
Racionar ration	*cantar* 5	Rebajar reduce	*cantar* 5
Radiar radiate	*cantar* 5	Rebanar slice	*cantar* 5
Radicalizar radicalize	*cruzar* 8	Rebañar finish off	*cantar* 5
Radicar reside	*atacar* 7	Rebasar exceed	*cantar* 5
Radiodifundir broadcast	*vivir* 51	Rebatir refute	*vivir* 51
Radiografiar radiograph	*desviar* 9	Rebelarse rebel	*cantar* 5
Radiotelegrafiar radiotelegraph	*desviar* 9	* Reblandecer soften	*obedecer* 33
* Raer[71] scrape	*caer* 36	Rebobinar rewind	*cantar* 5
Rajar slice	*cantar* 5	Rebordear flange	*cantar* 5
Ralentizar slow down	*cruzar* 8	Rebosar overflow	*cantar* 5
Rallar grate	*cantar* 5		
Ramificar ramify	*atacar* 7		
Ramonear prune	*cantar* 5		
Rapar nick	*cantar* 5		

verb	model/table	verb	model/table
Rebotar rebound	cantar 5	Reconciliar reconcile	cantar 5
Rebozar bread	cruzar 8	Reconcomerse be consumed	beber 24
Rebrotar sprout	cantar 5	* Reconducir renew	traducir 69
Rebuscar search	atacar 7	Reconfirmar reconfirm	cantar 5
Rebuznar bray	cantar 5	Reconfortar comfort	cantar 5
Recabar obtain	cantar 5	* Reconocer recognize	conocer 32
* Recaer fall back	caer 36	Reconquistar reconquer	cantar 5
Recalar soak	cantar 5	Reconsiderar reconsider	cantar 5
Recalcar stress	atacar 7	* Reconstituir reconstitute	concluir 59
* Recalentar reheat	pensar 13	* Reconstruir rebuild	concluir 59
Recamar embroider	cantar 5	* Recontar recount	contar 16
Recambiar change	cantar 5	* Reconvenir reproach	venir 80
Recapacitar consider	cantar 5	* Reconvertir reconvert	sentir 65
Recapitular recapitulate	cantar 5	Recopilar compile	cantar 5
Recargar reload	pagar 6	* Recordar remember	contar 16
Recatarse take care	cantar 5	Recorrer tour	beber 24
Recauchutar retread	cantar 5	Recortar trim	cantar 5
Recaudar collect	cantar 5	Recoser darn	beber 24
Recelar suspect	cantar 5	* Recostar lean	contar 16
Recetar prescribe	cantar 5	Recrear amuse	cantar 5
Rechazar reject	cruzar 8	Recriminar recriminate	cantar 5
Rechinar squeak	cantar 5	* Recrudecer rise again	obedecer 33
Rechistar whisper	cantar 5	Rectificar rectify	atacar 7
Recibir receive	vivir 51	Recuadrar frame	cantar 5
Reciclar retrain	cantar 5	* Recubrir[74] cover	vivir 51
Recidivar relapse	cantar 5	Recular reverse	cantar 5
Recitar recite	cantar 5	Recuperar recuperate	cantar 5
Reclamar claim	cantar 5	Recurrir resort	vivir 51
Reclinar lean	cantar 5	Recusar reject	cantar 5
* Recluir[73] confine	concluir 59	Redactar write	cantar 5
Reclutar recruit	cantar 5	Redimir redeem	vivir 51
Recobrar recover	cantar 5	* Redistribuir redistribute	concluir 59
* Recocer recook	cocer 34	Redoblar redouble	cantar 5
Recochinearse mock	cantar 5	Redondear round off	cantar 5
Recoger collect	coger 25	* Reducir reduce	traducir 69
Recolectar gather	cantar 5	Redundar abound	cantar 5
* Recomendar commend	pensar 13	Reduplicar reduplicate	atacar 7
* Recomenzar begin again	empezar 15	Reedificar rebuild	atacar 7
Recomerse be consumed	beber 24	Reeditar reprint	cantar 5
Recompensar reward	cantar 5	Reeducar reeducate	atacar 7
* Recomponer repair	poner 41	* Reelegir reelect	corregir 61
Reconcentrar concentrate	cantar 5	Reembarcar reembark	atacar 7

verb		model/table	verb		model/table
Reembolsar	reimburse	cantar 5	* Regir[76]	rule	corregir 61
Reemplazar	replace	cruzar 8	Registrar	search	cantar 5
Reencarnar	reincarnate	cantar 5	Reglamentar	regulate	cantar 5
* Reencontrar	reunite	contar 16	Reglar	rule	cantar 5
Reencuadernar	rebind	cantar 5	Regocijar	delight	cantar 5
Reenganchar	reenlist	cantar 5	Regodearse	delight	cantar 5
Reensayar	retest	cantar 5	Regresar	return	cantar 5
Reenviar	return	desviar 9	Regular	regulate	cantar 5
Reestrenar	revive	cantar 5	Regularizar	regularize	cruzar 8
Reestructurar	reorganize	cantar 5	Regurgitar	vomit	cantar 5
Reexaminar	reexamine	cantar 5	Rehabilitar	rehabilitate	cantar 5
* Reexpedir	forward	pedir 60	* Rehacer	redo	hacer 37
Reexportar	reexport	cantar 5	Rehogar	brown	pagar 6
* Referir	refer	sentir 65	* Rehuir	avoid	concluir 59
Refinar	refine	cantar 5	* Rehumedecer	soak	obedecer 33
Reflejar	reflect	cantar 5	Rehundir	sink again	reunir 56
Reflexionar	think	cantar 5	Rehusar	refuse	maullar 12
* Reflorecer	blossom	obedecer 33	Reimplantar	reintroduce	cantar 5
Reflotar	refloat	cantar 5	Reimportar	reimport	cantar 5
* Refluir	flow back	concluir 59	Reimprimir[77]	reprint	vivir 51
Refocilarse	delight	cantar 5	Reinar	reign	cantar 5
Reforestar	reforest	cantar 5	Reinaugurar	reinaugurate	cantar 5
Reformar	reform	cantar 5	Reincidir	relapse	vivir 51
* Reforzar	reinforce	forzar 19	Reincorporar	reincorporate	cantar 5
Refractar	refract	cantar 5	Reingresar	return	cantar 5
* Refregar	rub	negar 14	* Reinscribir[78]	reinscribe	vivir 51
* Refreír[75]	refry	reír 63	Reinsertar	reinsert	cantar 5
Refrenar	check	cantar 5	Reinstalar	reinstall	cantar 5
Refrendar	visa	cantar 5	Reintegrar	reintegrate	cantar 5
Refrescar	refresh	atacar 7	* Reír	laugh	63
Refrigerar	refrigerate	cantar 5	Reiterar	reiterate	cantar 5
Refugiarse	take refuge	cantar 5	Reivindicar	vindicate	atacar 7
Refulgir	shine	dirigir 52	Rejonear	thrust a lance	
Refundir	recast	vivir 51		into (bull)	cantar 5
Refunfuñar	grumble	cantar 5	* Rejuvenecer	rejuvenate	obedecer 33
Refutar	refute	cantar 5	Relacionar	relate	cantar 5
Regalar	give	cantar 5	Relajarse	relax	cantar 5
Regañar	scold	cantar 5	Relamer	lick	beber 24
* Regar	water	negar 14	Relampaguear[12]	sparkle	cantar 5
Regatear	haggle over	cantar 5	Relanzar	repulse	cruzar 8
Regenerar	regenerate	cantar 5	Relatar	relate	cantar 5
Regentar	manage	cantar 5	Relativizar	treat as a relative	cruzar 8

verb	model/table	verb	model/table
* Releer reread	leer 28	Reorganizar reorganize	cruzar 8
Relegar relegate	pagar 6	Repanchingarse loll	pagar 6
Relevar exempt	cantar 5	Reparar repair	cantar 5
Religar retie	pagar 6	Repartir hand out	vivir 51
Relinchar neigh	cantar 5	Repasar review	cantar 5
Rellenar fill	cantar 5	Repatear annoy	cantar 5
* Relucir shine	lucir 70	Repatriar repatriate	desviar 9
Relumbrar sparkle	cantar 5	Repeinar recomb	cantar 5
Remachar rivet	cantar 5	Repeler repel	beber 24
Remangar roll up	pagar 6	* Repensar reconsider	pensar 13
Remansarse flow slowly	cantar 5	Repercutir affect	vivir 51
Remar row	cantar 5	Repescar give a second chance	atacar 7
Remarcar mark again	atacar 7	* Repetir repeat	pedir 60
Rematar sell cheap	cantar 5	Repicar ring	atacar 7
Rembolsar reimburse	cantar 5	Repintar repaint	cantar 5
Remedar copy	cantar 5	Repiquetear pitter-patter	cantar 5
Remediar remedy	cantar 5	Replantar replant	cantar 5
Rememorar recall	cantar 5	Replantear restate	cantar 5
* Remendar mend	pensar 13	* Replegar fold up	negar 14
Remeter tuck in	beber 24	Replicar answer	atacar 7
Remitir ship	vivir 51	* Repoblar repopulate	contar 16
Remodelar remodel	cantar 5	* Reponer replace	poner 41
Remojar soak	cantar 5	Reportar report	cantar 5
Remolcar tow	atacar 7	Reposar rest	cantar 5
Remolonear shirk	cantar 5	Repostar refuel	cantar 5
Remontar repair	cantar 5	Reprender reprimand	beber 24
* Remorder gnaw	mover 30	Representar represent	cantar 5
* Remover remove	mover 30	Reprimir repress	vivir 51
Remozar modernize	cruzar 8	* Reprobar condemn	contar 16
Remplazar replace	cruzar 8	Reprocesar reprosecute	cantar 5
Remunerar remunerate	cantar 5	Reprochar reproach	cantar 5
* Renacer be reborn	nacer 31	* Reproducir reproduce	traducir 69
Renacionalizar renationalize	cruzar 8	Reptar slither	cantar 5
* Rencontrar reunite	contar 16	Repudiar repudiate	cantar 5
* Rendir subdue	pedir 60	Repugnar loathe	cantar 5
* Renegar renounce	negar 14	Repujar emboss	cantar 5
Renegociar renegotiate	cantar 5	Repulir repolish	vivir 51
Renombrar rename	cantar 5	Reputar repute	cantar 5
* Renovar renovate	contar 16	* Requebrar flatter	pensar 13
Renquear limp	cantar 5	* Requerir urge	sentir 65
Renunciar resign	cantar 5	Requisar inspect	cantar 5
* Reñir quarrel	teñir 64	Resaltar stand out	cantar 5

verb	model/table	verb	model/table
Resarcir compensate	esparcir 54	* Retener hold	tener 2
Resbalar slide	cantar 5	* Retentar threaten a relapse	pensar 13
Rescatar recover	cantar 5	* Reteñir redye	teñir 64
Rescindir rescind	vivir 51	Retirar remove	cantar 5
* Rescribir[79] send a reply	vivir 51	Retocar retouch	atacar 7
Resecar dry up	atacar 7	Retomar take up again	cantar 5
* Resentirse resent	sentir 65	Retoñar sprout	cantar 5
Reseñar review	cantar 5	* Retorcer twist	cocer 34
Reservar reserve	cantar 5	Retornar return	cantar 5
Resfriar cool	desviar 9	Retozar romp	cruzar 8
Resguardar protect	cantar 5	Retractarse retract	cantar 5
Residir reside	vivir 51	* Retraer dissuade	traer 47
Resignar resign	cantar 5	Retransmitir pass on	vivir 51
Resinar tap for resin	cantar 5	Retrasar delay	cantar 5
Resistir resist	vivir 51	Retratar portray	cantar 5
* Resolver[80] solve	mover 30	Retreparse lean back	cantar 5
* Resonar resound	contar 16	* Retribuir reward	concluir 59
Resoplar puff and blow	cantar 5	Retroceder go back	beber 24
Respaldar support	cantar 5	* Retrotraer antedate	traer 47
Respetar respect	cantar 5	Retumbar echo	cantar 5
Respingar kick	pagar 6	Reunificar reunify	atacar 7
Respirar breathe	cantar 5	Reunir meet	56
* Resplandecer shine	obedecer 33	Revacunar revaccinate	cantar 5
Responder respond	beber 24	Revalidar revalidate	cantar 5
Responsabilizar make		Revalorizar revalue	cruzar 8
responsible	cruzar 8	Revaluar revalue	actuar 10
Resquebrajar crack	cantar 5	Revelar reveal	cantar 5
* Restablecer restore	obedecer 33	Revender resell	beber 24
Restallar crackle	cantar 5	* Reventar burst	pensar 13
Restañar stanch	cantar 5	Reverberar reverberate	cantar 5
Restar subtract	cantar 5	* Reverdecer revive	obedecer 33
Restaurar restore	cantar 5	Reverenciar venerate	cantar 5
* Restituir restitute	concluir 59	* Revertir revert	sentir 65
* Restregar scrub	negar 14	* Revestir clothe, take on	pedir 60
Restringir restrict	dirigir 52	Revindicar claim	atacar 7
Restructurar restructure	cantar 5	Revisar revise	cantar 5
Resucitar resuscitate	cantar 5	Revitalizar revitalize	cruzar 8
Resultar result	cantar 5	Revivir revive	vivir 51
Resumir summarize	vivir 51	Revocar revoke	atacar 7
Resurgir rise up again	dirigir 52	* Revolcar defeat	trocar 17
Retar challenge	cantar 5	Revolotear fly about	cantar 5
Retardar slow down	cantar 5	Revolucionar revolutionize	cantar 5

verb	model/table	verb	model/table
* Revolver[81] mix	mover 30		
Rezagarse fall behind	pagar 6		
Rezar pray	cruzar 8		
Rezongar grumble	pagar 6		
Rezumar ooze	cantar 5	* Saber know	44
Ribetear border	cantar 5	Sablear sponge	cantar 5
Ridiculizar ridicule	cruzar 8	Saborear taste	cantar 5
Rielar[6] glitter	cantar 5	Sabotear sabotage	cantar 5
Rifar raffle	cantar 5	Sacar take out	atacar 7
Rimar rhyme	cantar 5	Saciar satiate	cantar 5
Ripiar riprap	cantar 5	Sacralizar make sacred	cruzar 8
Rivalizar rival	cruzar 8	Sacramentar consecrate	cantar 5
Rizar curl	cruzar 8	Sacrificar sacrifice	atacar 7
Robar steal	cantar 5	Sacudir shake	vivir 51
* Robustecer strengthen	obedecer 33	Sajar lance	cantar 5
Rociar sprinkle	desviar 9	Salar salt	cantar 5
* Rodar roll	contar 16	Saldar liquidate	cantar 5
Rodear enclose	cantar 5	* Salir leave, go out	79
* Roer gnaw	43	Salivar salivate	cantar 5
* Rogar beg	18	Salmodiar sing psalms	cantar 5
Romanizar Romanize	cruzar 8	Salpicar sprinkle	atacar 7
* Romper[82] break	beber 24	* Salpimentar season	pensar 13
Roncar snore	atacar 7	Saltar jump	cantar 5
Rondar patrol	cantar 5	Saltear rob	cantar 5
Ronronear purr	cantar 5	Saludar greet	cantar 5
Ronzar crunch	cruzar 8	Salvaguardar safeguard	cantar 5
Roscar thread	atacar 7	Salvar[83] save	cantar 5
Rotar rotate	cantar 5	Sanar heal	cantar 5
Rotular label	cantar 5	Sancionar sanction	cantar 5
Roturar break up	cantar 5	Sanear drain	cantar 5
Rozar graze	cruzar 8	Sangrar bleed	cantar 5
Ruborizar make blush	cruzar 8	Santificar sanctify	atacar 7
Rubricar initial	atacar 7	Santiguar bless	averiguar 11
Rugir roar	dirigir 52	Saquear plunder	cantar 5
Rular roll	cantar 5	Satinar glaze, calender	cantar 5
Rumiar ruminate	cantar 5	Satirizar satirize	cruzar 8
Rumorear rumor	cantar 5	* Satisfacer satisfy	45
Runrunear rumor	cantar 5	Saturar saturate	cantar 5
Rutilar[1] shine	cantar 5	Sazonar flavor	cantar 5
		Secar dry	atacar 7
		Seccionar section	cantar 5
		Secretar secrete	cantar 5

S

verb	model/table	verb	model/table
Secretear whisper	*cantar* 5	Simpatizar get along well	*cruzar* 8
Secuenciar sequence	*cantar* 5	Simplificar simplify	*atacar* 7
Secuestrar kidnap	*cantar* 5	Simular simulate	*cantar* 5
Secularizar secularize	*cruzar* 8	Simultanear do at same time	*cantar* 5
Secundar second	*cantar* 5	Sincerarse exonerate	*cantar* 5
Sedar sedate	*cantar* 5	Sincopar syncopate	*cantar* 5
Sedimentar settle	*cantar* 5	Sincronizar synchronize	*cruzar* 8
* Seducir seduce	*traducir* 69	Sindicarse join a union	*atacar* 7
* Segar reap	*negar* 14	Singularizar single out	*cruzar* 8
Segmentar segment	*cantar* 5	Sintetizar synthesize	*cruzar* 8
Segregar segregate	*pagar* 6	Sintonizar tune	*cruzar* 8
* Seguir follow	62	Sisar pilfer	*cantar* 5
Seleccionar select	*cantar* 5	Sisear hiss	*cantar* 5
Sellar seal	*cantar* 5	Sistematizar systematize	*cruzar* 8
* Sembrar sow	*pensar* 13	Sitiar besiege	*cantar* 5
Semejar seem	*cantar* 5	Situar place	*actuar* 10
Sensibilizar sensitize	*cruzar* 8	Sobar knead	*cantar* 5
* Sentar seat	*pensar* 13	Sobornar bribe	*cantar* 5
Sentenciar sentence	*cantar* 5	Sobrar be left over	*cantar* 5
* Sentir feel	65	Sobrealimentar overfeed	*cantar* 5
Señalar mark	*cantar* 5	Sobreañadir put in as extra	*vivir* 51
Señalizar signpost	*cruzar* 8	Sobrecargar overload	*pagar* 6
Separar separate	*cantar* 5	Sobrecoger startle	*coger* 25
Sepultar bury	*cantar* 5	Sobreexcitar overexcite	*cantar* 5
* Ser be	3	Sobrehilar whipstitch	*cantar* 5
Serenar calm	*cantar* 5	Sobrellevar endure	*cantar* 5
Seriar mass-produce	*cantar* 5	* Sobrentender understand	*perder* 29
Sermonear sermonize	*cantar* 5	Sobremedicar overmedicate	*atacar* 7
Serpentear slither	*cantar* 5	Sobrepasar surpass	*atacar* 7
* Serrar saw	*pensar* 13	* Sobreponer superimpose	*poner* 41
* Servir serve	*pedir* 60	* Sobresalir stick out	*salir* 79
Sesear pronounce Spanish		Sobresaltar startle	*cantar* 5
c and *z* like *s*	*cantar* 5	* Sobreseer desist, stay	*leer* 28
Sesgar slant	*pagar* 6	Sobrestimar overestimate	*cantar* 5
Sestear take a siesta	*cantar* 5	* Sobrevenir occur	*venir* 80
Sextuplicar sextuple	*atacar* 7	Sobrevivir survive	*vivir* 51
Significar mean	*atacar* 7	* Sobrevolar overfly	*contar* 16
Silabear syllabify	*cantar* 5	Socarrar scorch	*cantar* 5
Silbar whistle	*cantar* 5	Socavar undermine	*cantar* 5
Silenciar silence	*cantar* 5	Socializar socialize	*cruzar* 8
Siluetear silhouette	*cantar* 5	Socorrer help	*beber* 24
Simbolizar symbolize	*cruzar* 8	Sofisticar adulterate	*atacar* 7

verb	model/table	verb	model/table
Soflamar singe	cantar 5	* Sostener support	tener 2
Sofocar suffocate	atacar 7	* Soterrar bury	pensar 13
* Sofreír[84] fry	reír 63	Sovietizar Sovietize	cruzar 8
Sojuzgar subdue	pagar 6	Suavizar soften	cruzar 8
Solapar overlap	cantar 5	Subalimentar undernourish	cantar 5
Solazar amuse	cruzar 8	Subalternar subordinate	cantar 5
* Soldar weld	contar 16	* Subarrendar sublet	pensar 13
Solear sun	cantar 5	Subastar auction	cantar 5
Solemnizar solemnize	cruzar 8	Subdelegar subdelegate	pagar 6
* Soler[1] be in the habit of	46	Subdividir subdivide	vivir 51
Solfear sing sol-fa	cantar 5	Subestimar underestimate	cantar 5
Solicitar request	cantar 5	Subir go up, increase	vivir 51
Solidarizarse make common		Subjetivar subjectivize	cantar 5
cause	cruzar 8	Sublevar incite	cantar 5
Solidificar solidify	atacar 7	Sublimar sublimate	cantar 5
Soliloquiar soliloquize	cantar 5	Subordinar subordinate	cantar 5
Soliviantar rouse	cantar 5	Subrayar underline	cantar 5
Sollozar sob	cruzar 8	Subrogar subrogate	pagar 6
* Soltar[85] release	contar 16	Subsanar overlook	cantar 5
Solucionar solve	cantar 5	Subsidiar subsidize	cantar 5
Solventar settle	cantar 5	Subsistir subsist	vivir 51
Sombrear cast a shadow	cantar 5	Subsumir subsume	vivir 51
Someter submit	beber 24	Subtitular subtitle	cantar 5
* Sonar sound	contar 16	Subvencionar subsidize	cantar 5
Sondar probe	cantar 5	* Subvenir assist	venir 80
Sondear sound	cantar 5	* Subyacer underlie	yacer 50
Sonorizar record soundtrack	cruzar 8	Subyugar subjugate	pagar 6
* Sonreír smile	reír 63	Succionar suck	cantar 5
Sonrojarse blush	cantar 5	Suceder happen	beber 24
Sonsacar cajole	atacar 7	Sucumbir succumb	vivir 51
* Soñar dream	contar 16	Sudar sweat	cantar 5
Sopapear slap	cantar 5	Sufragar defray	pagar 6
Sopar sop	cantar 5	Sufrir suffer	vivir 51
Sopesar weigh up	cantar 5	* Sugerir suggest	sentir 65
Soplar blow	cantar 5	Sugestionarse be influenced	cantar 5
Soportar endure	cantar 5	Suicidarse commit suicide	cantar 5
Sorber suck	beber 24	Sujetar[86] fasten	cantar 5
Sorprender surprise	beber 24	Sulfatar sulfate	cantar 5
Sortear cast lots	cantar 5	Sulfurar sulfurize, anger	cantar 5
* Sosegar calm	negar 14	Sumar add	cantar 5
Soslayar evade	cantar 5	Sumariar indict	cantar 5
Sospechar suspect	cantar 5	Sumergir submerge	dirigir 52

V

verb	model/table	verb	model/table
Suministrar supply	cantar 5	Tallar carve	cantar 5
Sumir sink	vivir 51	Tambalear stagger	cantar 5
Supeditar subdue	cantar 5	Tamborilear drum	cantar 5
Superabundar superabound	cantar 5	Tamizar sift	cruzar 8
Superar surpass	cantar 5	Tantear estimate	cantar 5
* Superponer superimpose	poner 41	Tañer play (instrument)	27
Supervalorar overvalue	cantar 5	Tapar cover	cantar 5
Supervisar supervise	cantar 5	Tapiar enclose	cantar 5
Suplantar supplant	cantar 5	Tapizar upholster	cruzar 8
Suplicar supplicate	atacar 7	Taponar plug	cantar 5
Suplir replace	vivir 51	Taquigrafiar take shorthand	desviar 9
* Suponer suppose	poner 41	Tarar tare	cantar 5
Suprimir suppress	vivir 51	Taracear inlay	cantar 5
Supurar fester	cantar 5	Tararear hum	cantar 5
Surcar plow	atacar 7	Tardar take (time)	cantar 5
Surgir appear	dirigir 52	Tarifar tariff	cantar 5
Surtir supply	vivir 51	Tarjetearse exchange cards	cantar 5
Suscitar provoke	cantar 5	Tartajear stutter	cantar 5
* Suscribir[87] sign	vivir 51	Tartamudear stammer	cantar 5
Suspender[88] suspend	beber 24	Tasar appraise	cantar 5
Suspirar sigh	cantar 5	Tatarear sing unintelligibly	cantar 5
Sustanciar condense	cantar 5	Tatuar tattoo	actuar 10
Sustantivar make substantive	cantar 5	Teatralizar make theatrical	cruzar 8
Sustentar sustain	cantar 5	Techar root	cantar 5
* Sustituir substitite	concluir 59	Teclear type	cantar 5
* Sustraer remove	traer 47	Tecnificar make more technical	atacar 7
Susurrar murmur	cantar 5	Teledirigir guide by remote	dirigir 52
Suturar suture	cantar 5	Tejer weave	beber 24
		Telefonear telephone	cantar 5
		Telegrafiar telegraph	desviar 9
		Televisar televise	cantar 5

t

verb	model/table	verb	model/table
		* Temblar tremble	pensar 13
		Temblequear quiver	cantar 5
Tabicar wall off	atacar 7	Temer fear	beber 24
Tablear saw into planks	cantar 5	Temperar temper	cantar 5
Tabular tabulate	cantar 5	Templar moderate	cantar 5
Tachar cross out	cantar 5	Temporizar temporize	cruzar 8
Tachonar stud	cantar 5	* Tender spread	perder 29
Taconear tap heels	cantar 5	* Tener hold, have	2
Tajar slice	cantar 5	Tensar tighten	cantar 5
Taladrar drill	cantar 5	* Tentar tempt	pensar 13
Talar fell	cantar 5	* Teñir dye	64

verb	model/table	verb	model/table
Teologizar theologize	cruzar 8	Torturar torture	cantar 5
Teorizar theorize	cruzar 8	Toser cough	beber 24
Terciar divide in thirds	cantar 5	* Tostar toast	contar 16
Tergiversar distort	cantar 5	Totalizar add up	cruzar 8
Terminar finish	cantar 5	Trabajar work	cantar 5
Terraplenar level off	cantar 5	Trabar lock	cantar 5
Tersar polish	cantar 5	* Traducir translate	69
Testar erase	cantar 5	* Traer bring, wear	47
Testificar testify	atacar 7	Traficar traffic, trade	atacar 7
Testimoniar bear witness	cantar 5	Tragar swallow	pagar 6
Tildar put a tilde on	cantar 5	Traicionar betray	cantar 5
Timar swindle	cantar 5	Trajearse wear	cantar 5
Timbrar stamp	cantar 5	Trajinar carry	cantar 5
Tintar tint	cantar 5	Tramar scheme	cantar 5
Tintinear clink	cantar 5	Tramitar negotiate	cantar 5
Tipificar typify	atacar 7	Trampear cheat	cantar 5
Tiranizar tyrannize	cruzar 8	Trancar bolt	atacar 7
Tirar throw	cantar 5	Tranquilizar tranquilize	cruzar 8
Tiritar shiver	cantar 5	Transbordar transfer	cantar 5
Tirotear fire at	cantar 5	* Transcribir[90] transcribe	vivir 51
Titilar[6] twinkle	cantar 5	Transcurrir pass (time)	vivir 51
Titubear stagger	cantar 5	* Transferir transfer	sentir 65
Titular entitle, name	cantar 5	Transfigurar transfigure	cantar 5
Titularizar confirm in a post	cruzar 8	Transformar transform	cantar 5
Tiznar blacken	cantar 5	Transfundir transfuse	vivir 51
Tocar touch	atacar 7	Transgredir[1] transgress	abolir 71
Toldar cover	cantar 5	Transigir compromise	dirigir 52
Tolerar tolerate	cantar 5	Transitar travel	cantar 5
Tomar take	cantar 5	Transliterar transliterate	cantar 5
Tonificar tone up	atacar 7	Transmigrar transmigrate	cantar 5
Tonsurar tonsure	cantar 5	Transmitir transmit	vivir 51
Tontear fool around	cantar 5	Transmutar transmute	cantar 5
Topar bump into	cantar 5	Transparentar reveal	cantar 5
Toquetear fondle	cantar 5	Transpirar transpire	cantar 5
* Torcer[89] twist	cocer 34	Transportar transport	cantar 5
Torear fight (a bull)	cantar 5	Trapacear cheat	cantar 5
Tornar return	cantar 5	Trapichear scheme	cantar 5
Tornasolar make iridescent	cantar 5	Traquetear agitate	cantar 5
Tornear turn	cantar 5	Trasbordar ferry across	cantar 5
Torpedear torpedo	cantar 5	* Trascender transcend	perder 29
Torrarse be toasted	cantar 5	* Trasegar upset	negar 14
Torrefactar parch, scorch	cantar 5	Trashumar move to pasture	cantar 5

verb	model/table	verb	model/table
Trasladar **move**	*cantar* 5	* Tropezar **trip**	*empezar* 15
* Traslucirse **make transparent**	*lucir* 70	Troquelar **coin**	*cantar* 5
Trasmutar **transmute**	*cantar* 5	Trotar **trot**	*cantar* 5
Trasnochar **stay up all night**	*cantar* 5	Trovar **write verse**	*cantar* 5
Traspapelarse **get lost**	*cantar* 5	Trucar **make a bet**	*atacar* 7
Traspasar **pass through**	*cantar* 5	Trufar **lie**	*cantar* 5
Trasplantar **transplant**	*cantar* 5	Truncar **truncate**	*atacar* 7
* Trasponer **disappear**	*poner* 41	Tullir **maim**	*mullir* 57
Trasquilar **cut down**	*cantar* 5	Tumbar **knock down**	*cantar* 5
Trastabillar **stagger**	*cantar* 5	Tundir **shear**	*vivir* 51
Trastear **rummage**	*cantar* 5	Tupir **thicken**	*vivir* 51
Trastocar **upset**	*atacar* 7	Turbar **disturb**	*cantar* 5
Trastornar **ruin**	*cantar* 5	Turnar **take turns**	*cantar* 5
Trasvasar **decant**	*cantar* 5	Tutear **address as *tú***	*cantar* 5
Tratar **try**	*cantar* 5	Tutelar **tutor**	*cantar* 5
Traumatizar **traumatize**	*cruzar* 8		
* Travestirse **be a transvestite**	*pedir* 60		
Trazar **draw**	*cruzar* 8		
Tremolar **flutter**	*cantar* 5		
Trenzar **braid**	*cruzar* 8		**u**
Trepanar **trephine**	*cantar* 5		
Trepar **climb**	*cantar* 5	Ubicar **be located**	*atacar* 7
Trepidar **shake**	*cantar* 5	Ufanarse **be proud**	*cantar* 5
Tributar **pay**	*cantar* 5	Ulcerar **ulcerate**	*cantar* 5
Tricotar **knit**	*cantar* 5	Ultimar **finalize**	*cantar* 5
Trillar **thresh**	*cantar* 5	Ultrajar **outrage**	*cantar* 5
Trinar **warble**	*cantar* 5	Ulular **howl**	*cantar* 5
Trincar **bind**	*atacar* 7	Uncir **yoke**	*esparcir* 54
Trinchar **carve**	*cantar* 5	Ungir **anoint**	*dirigir* 52
Triplicar **triplicate**	*atacar* 7	Unificar **unify**	*atacar* 7
Triptongar **make into a**		Uniformar **standardize**	*cantar* 5
triphthong	*pagar* 6	Unir **unite**	*vivir* 51
Tripular **man**	*cantar* 5	Universalizar **universalize**	*cruzar* 8
Triturar **grind**	*cantar* 5	Untar **grease**	*cantar* 5
Triunfar **triumph**	*cantar* 5	Urbanizar **urbanize**	*cruzar* 8
Trivializar **trivialize**	*cruzar* 8	Urdir **warp**	*vivir* 51
Trizar **tear up**	*cruzar* 8	Urgir **urge**	*dirigir* 52
* *Trocar* **exchange**	17	Usar **use, wear**	*cantar* 5
Trocear **cut up**	*cantar* 5	Usufructuar **usufruct**	*actuar* 10
Trompetear **play trumpet**	*cantar* 5	Usurar **practice usury**	*cantar* 5
* Tronar[12] **thunder**	*contar* 16	Usurpar **usurp**	*cantar* 5
Tronchar **fell**	*cantar* 5	Utilizar **utilize**	*cruzar* 8

verb	model/table	verb	model/table
		Verificar verify	atacar 7
		Versar deal with	cantar 5
V		Versificar versify	atacar 7
		Vertebrar support	cantar 5
Vacar fall vacant	atacar 7	* Verter pour	perder 29
Vaciar empty	desviar 9	* Vestir dress	pedir 60
Vacilar vacillate	cantar 5	Vetar veto	cantar 5
Vacunar vaccinate	cantar 5	Vetear streak	cantar 5
Vadear ford	cantar 5	Viabilizar make viable	cruzar 8
Vagabundear wander	cantar 5	Viajar travel	cantar 5
Vagar roam	pagar 6	Vibrar vibrate	cantar 5
Vaguear loaf	cantar 5	Viciar vitiate	cantar 5
* Valer be worth, cost	48	Victorear cheer	cantar 5
Validar validate	cantar 5	Vidriar glaze	cantar 5
Vallar fence	cantar 5	Vigilar watch	cantar 5
Valorar value	cantar 5	Vigorizar invigorate	cruzar 8
Valorizar value	cruzar 8	Vilipendiar vilify	cantar 5
Vanagloriarse boast	cantar 5	Vincular link	cantar 5
Vaporizar vaporize	cruzar 8	Vindicar vindicate	atacar 7
Vapulear spank	cantar 5	Violar violate	cantar 5
Varar beach	cantar 5	Violentar force	cantar 5
Variar vary	desviar 9	Virar tack	cantar 5
Vaticinar prophesy	cantar 5	Virilizarse be virile	cruzar 8
Vedar forbid	cantar 5	Visar visa	cantar 5
Vegetar vegetate	cantar 5	Visibilizar make visible	cruzar 8
Vejar vex	cantar 5	Visionar preview	cantar 5
Velar stay awake	cantar 5	Visitar visit	cantar 5
Vencer conquer	26	Vislumbrar glimpse	cantar 5
Vendar bandage	cantar 5	Visualizar visualize	cruzar 8
Vender sell	beber 24	Vitorear acclaim	cantar 5
Vendimiar harvest	cantar 5	Vitrificar vitrify	atacar 7
Venerar venerate	cantar 5	Vituperar berate	cantar 5
Vengar avenge	pagar 6	Vivaquear bivouac	cantar 5
* *Venir* come, go	80	Vivificar animate	atacar 7
Ventajear take advantage	cantar 5	*Vivir* live	51
Ventear[12] air out	cantar 5	Vocalizar vocalize	cruzar 8
Ventilar ventilate	cantar 5	Vocear cry out	cantar 5
Ventisquear[12] blow a blizzard	cantar 5	Vociferar vociferate	cantar 5
Ventosear break wind	cantar 5	* Volar fly	contar 16
* *Ver* see, look at	49	Volatilizar make volatile	cruzar 8
Veranear spend summer	cantar 5	* Volcar tip over	trocar 17
Verdear turn green	cantar 5	Volear volley	cantar 5

verb	model/table	verb	model/table
Voltear turn	cantar 5	Yuntar yoke	cantar 5
* Volver[91] return	mover 30	* Yuxtaponer juxtapose	poner 41
Vomitar vomit	cantar 5		
Vosear address as *vos*	cantar 5		
Votar vote	cantar 5		**Z**
Vulcanizar vulcanize	cruzar 8		
Vulgarizar vulgarize	cruzar 8		
Vulnerar injure	cantar 5	Zafarse escape	cantar 5
		* Zaherir reprimand	sentir 65
		Zamarrear shake	cantar 5
	X	Zambullir plunge	mullir 57
		Zampar wolf down	cantar 5
		Zanganear loaf	cantar 5
Xerocopiar photocopy	cantar 5	Zanjar settle	cantar 5
Xerografiar photocopy	desviar 9	Zapar excavate	cantar 5
Xilografiar xylograph	cantar 5	Zapatear tread on	cantar 5
		Zarandear sift	cantar 5
		Zarpar weigh anchor	cantar 5
	Y	Zascandilear snoop	cantar 5
		Zigzaguear zigzag	cantar 5
		Zonificar zone	atacar 7
* Yacer[1] be lying down	50	Zorrear use guile	cantar 5
Yantar eat	cantar 5	Zozobrar capsize	cantar 5
Yermar lay waste	cantar 5	Zumbar buzz	cantar 5
Yodurar iodize	cantar 5	Zurcir mend	esparcir 54
Yugular nip in the bud	cantar 5	Zurrar whip	cantar 5

NOTES

(1) Defective verb.

(2) Irregular participle: **Abierto**.

(3) Irregular participle: **Absuelto**.

(4) 2 participles: **Absorbido** and *absorto*.

(5) 2 participles: **Abstraído** and *abstracto*.

(6) Third-person defective verb.

(7) Accented like *averiguar* (*Table 11*, page 39); it is incorrect to accent *adecúa, adecúa*, etc. The same goes for *licuar*.

(8) Irregular participle: **Adscrito**.

(9) Like *abolir*, except for the wider use of other forms, e.g., *agrede, agreda, agredan*.

(10) The accentation of this verb varies: it matches *desviar*, but also encountered are *agrio, agrias*, etc.

(11) When the root takes an accent in the present tenses, the accent is written on the -i (present indicative: *aíslo, aíslas, aísla, aíslan*; present subjunctive: *aísle, aísles, aísle, aíslen*; imperative: *aísla, aísle, aíslen)*. The same applies for *desairar, desenraizar, enraizar, europeizar, hebraizar, homogeneizar, judaizar*.

(12) Atmospheric third-person defective verb.

(13) The verb *apostar*, in the sense of "to place someone on watch," is regular, like *cantar* (*Table 5*, page 33).

(14) The verb *argüir* loses the dieresis when a -y is inserted between the root and the ending; e.g., *arguyó*.

(15) Two verbs *asolar* exist: their meaning are different and one is regular and the other irregular (like *contar, Table 16*, page 44). Nowadays both are conjugated as regular verbs.

(16) 2 participles: **Atendido** and *atento*.

(17) Defective verb. Only those forms with -i in their ending are conjugated. The remaining are replaced by *balbucear*.

(18) 2 participles: **Bendecido** and *bendito*.

(19) 2 participles: **Circuncidado** and *circunciso*.

(20) Irregular participle: **Circunscrito**.

(21) 2 participles: **Confundido** and *confuso*.

(22) 2 participles: **Corregido** and *correcto*.

(23) 2 participles: **Corrompido** and *corrupto*.

(24) Irregular participle: **Cubierto**.

(25) The current trend is to pronounce -au as a diphthong: *desahucio*.

(26) Irregular participle: **Descrito**.

(27) Irregular participle: **Descubierto**.

(28) Irregular participle: **Desenvuelto**.

(29) An *h* is inserted before the diphthong -ue. However, the regular verb *deshuesar* is used much more frequently.

(30) 2 participles: **Despertado** and *despierto*.

(31) 2 participles: **Desproveído** and *desprovisto*.

(32) Irregular participle: **Devuelto**.

(33) 2 participles: **Difundido** and *difuso*.

(34) Irregular participle: **Disuelto**.

(35) 2 participles: **Elegido** and *electo*.

(36) Irregular participle: **Encubierto**.

(37) Irregular participle: **Entreabierto**.

verb index

(38) Irregular participle: **Envuelto**.

(39) Has a further spelling change: substitute the -*i* of the diphthong -*ie* with -*y* (*yerro, yerras,* etc.)

(40) Irregular participle: **Escrito**.

(41) 2 participles: **Eximido** and *exento*.

(42) 2 participles: **Expresado** and *expreso*.

(43) 2 participles: **Extendido** and *extenso*.

(44) 2 participles: **Extinguido** and *extinto*.

(45) 2 participles: **Fijado** and *fijo*.

(46) 2 participles: **Freído** and *frito*.

(47) 2 participles: **Hartado** and *harto*.

(48) The suppression of the -*i* in the third person of the pretérito indefinido sometimes occurs, and then it follows *teñir* (Table 64, page 94).

(49) Used less frequently than *hender*.

(50) There also exists, though it is less accepted, the accentuation *historío*, following *desviar* (*Table 9*, page 37).

(51) 2 participles: **Imprimido** and *impreso*.

(52) Defective verb. Conjugates like *abolir* (*Table 71*, page 101).

(53) 2 participles: **Incurrido** and *incurso*.

(54) 2 participles: **Injertado** and *injerto*.

(55) Irregular participle: **Inscrito**.

(56) 2 participles: **Insertado** and *inserto*.

(57) 2 participles: **Juntado** and *junto*.

(58) 2 participles: **Maldecido** and *maldito*.

(59) 2 participles: **Manifestado** and *manifiesto*.

(60) Irregular participle: **Manuscrito**.

(61) 2 participles: **Marchitado** and *marchito*.

(62) Irregular participle: **Muerto**.

(63) 2 participles: **Poseído** and *poseso*.

(64) 2 participles: **Predecido** and *predicho*.

(65) 2 participles: **Prendido** and *preso*.

(66) Irregular participle: **Prescrito**.

(67) 2 participles: **Propendido** and *propenso*.

(68) Irregular participle: **Proscrito**.

(69) 2 participles: **Proveído** and *provisto*.

(70) Irregular participle: **Podrido**.

(71) 2 participles: **Raído** and *raso*.

(72) Irregular participle: **Reabierto**.

(73) 2 participles: **Recluido** and *recluso*.

(74) Irregular participle: **Recubierto**.

(75) 2 participles: **Refreído** and *refrito*.

(76) 2 participles: **Regido** and *recto*.

(77) 2 participles: **Reimprimido** and *reimpreso*.

(78) Irregular participle: **Reinscrito**.

(79) Irregular participle: **Rescrito**.

(80) Irregular participle: **Resuelto**.

(81) Irregular participle: **Revuelto**.

(82) Irregular participle: **Roto**.

(83) 2 participles: **Salvado** and *salvo*.

(84) 2 participles: **Sofreído** and *sofrito*.

(85) 2 participles: **Soltado** and *suelto*.

(86) 2 participles: **Sujetado** and *sujeto*.

(87) Irregular participle: **Suscrito**.

(88) 2 participles: **Suspendido** and *suspenso*.

(89) 2 participles: **Torcido** and *tuerto*.

(90) Irregular participle: **Transcrito**.

(91) Irregular participle: **Vuelto**.

prepositions
used with verbs

Abalanzarse
contra *un árbol;* **hacia** *la salida;* **sobre** *alguien.*
Abandonarse
a *la mala vida;* **en manos de** *la doctora.*
Abastecer(se) con/de *alimentos.*
Abatirse con/por *las dificultades.*
Abdicar
de *los poderes;* **en** *la primogénita;* **en contra de** *su voluntad.*
Abismarse en *la lectura.*
Abjurar de *la religión.*
Abocar al *fracaso.*
Abochornarse de/por *algo.*
Abogar
a favor de/en favor de/por *su hermana;* **ante** *el juez.*
Abominar del *crimen.*
Abonarse a *la ópera.*
Aborrecer
con *todas las fuerzas;* **de muerte.**
Abrasarse
de *calor;* **en** *deseos.*
Abrazarse
a *un amigo;* **con** *la rival.*
Abrevar
con *agua;* **en** *la alberca.*
Abrigarse
bajo *techo;* **con** *una manta;* **contra** *la lluvia;* **del** *chaparrón;* **para** *dormir;* **por** *precaución.*
Abrir
al *público;* **de par en par;* **en** *canal;* **hacia** *dentro.*
Abrirse
a *la gente;* **de** *piernas;* **hacia** *dentro.*
Abrumar
con *halagos;* **de** *regalos.*
Absolver
al *culpable;* **del** *delito.*
Abstenerse de *fumar.*
Abstraerse
ante *la belleza del cuadro;* **con** *la música;* **del** *entorno.*
Abundar en *lo dicho.*

Aburrirse
con *los niños;* **de** *no hacer nada;* **en** *el fútbol;* **por** *todo;* ***sin*** *motivo.*
Abusar
de *la confianza;* **en** *el precio.*
Acabar
a *tiempo;* **con** *la paciencia;* **de** *llegar;* **en** *la miseria;* **entre** *rejas;* **por** *hacerlo.*
Acaecer
(algo) **a** *alguien;* **bajo** *Felipe II;* **en** *el siglo xvi.*
Acalorarse
con *la política;* **de** *hacer ejercicio;* **en** *público;* **por** *nada;* **sin** *razón.*
Acarrear
a *hombros;* **con** *grúas;* **desde** *el almacén;* **en** *carros;* **entre** *varios;* **hasta** *la oficina;* **sin** *descanso.*
Acceder a *los deseos.*
Acelerarse por *la prisa.*
Aceptar
(algo) **de** *alguien;* **por** *compañero;* **sin** *vacilar.*
Acercarse
a *un lugar;* **hacia** *la costa;* **hasta** *la frontera;* **por** *otro camino.*
Acertar
a *la lotería;* **con** *la decisión;* **en** *la elección.*
Achicarse ante *el hermano mayor.*
Achicharrarse
a/bajo *el sol;* **de/por** *el calor.*
Achuchar a *alguien*
Aclamar
al *jefe;* **con** *vítores.*
Aclimatarse
a *otra ciudad;* **entre** *extraños.*
Acobardarse
ante *la gente;* **con** *el frío;* **frente a** *los extraños;* **por** *las circunstancias.*
Acodarse
a *la verja;* **en** *la ventana;* **sobre** *la mesa.*
Acoger
bajo *techo;* **en** *el país;* **entre** *los suyos.*
Acogerse
al *texto;* **bajo** *techo;* **en** *el refugio.*
Acometer a/contra *alguien*
Acomodarse
a *los tiempos;* **en** *la butaca.*
Acompañar

al *cine*; con *ejemplos*; de *pruebas*; en *el sentimiento*; hasta *el aeropuerto*.
Acompañarse
al *pianos*; de *expertos*.
Acondicionar
con *buena calefacción*; en *cajas*; para *el traslado*; según *indicaciones*.
Aconsejar
en *un tema*; sobre *la decisión*.
Aconsejarse
de *personas serias*; en *el tema*.
Acontecer
a *cualquiera*; bajo *la tiranía*; según *lo previsto*.
Acoplar
al *televisor*; en *el cajón*; entre *los dos*.
Acorazarse
contra *el dolor*; de *indiferencia*; para *la batalla*.
Acordar entre *varios*.
Acordarse de *lo sucedido*.
Acortar con/por *el atajo*.
Acostarse
con *alguien*; de *noche*; en *la cama*; por *la noche*.
Acostumbrarse al *trabajo*.
Acreditarse
con *informes*; en *la profesión*.
Acribillar a *balazos*.
Actuar
bajo *presión*; con *prisas*; contra *lo dispuesto*; para *los espectadores*; por *lo legal*; según *las normas*.
Acudir
a *la cita*; ante *el jurado*; desde *otro pueblo*; en *su ayuda*; sin *dudarlo*.
Acumular (*datos*) sobre *datos*.
Acusar
ante *el profesor*; con *mala intención*; de *una falta*.
Acusarse de *una falta*.
Adaptarse a *la realidad*.
Adelantar
en *los estudios*; por *el centro*. (No adelantar nada) con *gritar*.
Adelantarse
a *la mayoría*; en *los estudios*; por *el lateral*.
Adentrarse en *el bosque*.
Adherirse a *una opinión*.

Adiestrarse
con *las armas*; en *los idiomas*; para *la competición*.
Admirarse
ante *lo ocurrido*; de *seguir vivo*; en *el espejo*; por *la gran acogida*.
Admitir en *el club*.
Adolecer de *una enfermedad*.
Adoptar
a *alguien*; por *hijo*.
Adorar
(*a alguien*) con *el alma*; de *todo corazón*.
Adornar
con *luces*; de *flores*.
Adueñarse de *la voluntad*.
Advertir
(*a alguien*) del *peligro*; en *secreto*.
Afanarse
en *las tareas*; por *el premio*.
Aferrarse
a *la vida*; con *esfuerzo*.
Afianzarse
ante *el director*; con *una recomendación*; en *las creencias*; para *el salto*; sobre *una mesa*.
Aficionarse a *un deporte*.
Afilar
con *una navaja*; en *la piedra*.
Afiliarse a *un partido*.
Afirmarse en *una postura*.
Afligirse por *una mala noticia*.
Aflojar en *los esfuerzos*.
Aflorar a *la superficie*.
Afrentar con *insultos*.
Afrontar con *valor*.
Agarrar
de *la mano*; por *la cintura*.
Agarrarse a/de *la barandilla*.
Agazaparse
bajo *una escalera*; tras *los arbustos*.
Agobiarse con/de/por *el trabajo*.
Agraciar con *una medalla*.
Agradar a *alguien*.
Agraviarse por *una broma pesada*.
Agregar (*algo*) a *algo*.
Agregarse al *grupo*.
Aguantarse con *el chaparrón*.
Aguardar
a *mejores tiempos*; en *el bar*.
Ahogarse
de *calor*; en *un vaso de agua*.

p

prepositions used with verbs

Ahondar
con *una pala*; en *la herida.*
Ahorcarse
con *una cuerda*; de/en *un árbol.*
Ahorrarse *(explicaciones)* con *alguien.*
Aislarse de *los demás.*
Ajetrearse de *un sitio* a/para *otro.*
Ajustar(se)
(los gastos) a *un presupuesto*; *(un encargo)* en *cinco mil pesetas*; *(cuentas)* con *alguien.*
Alabar
a *un amigo*; por *su habilidad.*
Alargarse
en *la charla*; hasta *la ciudad.*
Alcanzar
al *techo*; hasta *el verano.*
Aleccionar en *el comportamiento.*
Alegar
con *documentos*; de *prueba*; en *defensa.*
Alegrarse con/de/por *la buena noticia.*
Alejarse
de *la familia*; en *el mar*; por *el aire.*
Alentar con *palabras amables.*
Aliarse *(unos)* a/con/contra *otros.*
Alimentarse
a base de *proteínas*; de *frutas*; con *pan.*
Alinear(se)
bajo *la bandera*; con *las tablas*; de *portero*; en *el equipo.*
Alistarse en *la marina.*
Aliviar
de *la carga*; en *el trabajo.*
Alquilar en/por *cincuenta mil pesetas.*
Alternar
con *las amigas*; en *discotecas.*
Alternarse en *el trabajo.*
Alucinar(se)
con/por *lo visto*; en *el espectáculo.*
Aludir a *un tema.*
Alumbrarse
con *una vela*; en *la oscuridad.*
Alzar
(la vista) a *lo alto*; del *suelo.*
Alzarse
con *la victoria*; del *suelo*; en *armas.*
Amagar con *un gesto.*
Amanecer
con *frío*; en *Berlin*; entre *los arbustos*; por *las montañas.*

Amañarse
con *otros*; para *hacer algo.*
Amar de *verdad.*
Amargar con *hiel.*
Amarrar
a *un árbol*; con *cuerdas.*
Amenazar
a *la garganta*; con *un cuchillo*; de *muerte.*
Amparar del *peligro.*
Ampararse
bajo *un árbol*; con *una manta*; contra *el viento*; de *la lluvia*; en *el portal.*
Amueblar con *gusto.*
Andar
a *tientas*; con *cuidado*; de *puntillas*; detrás de *alguien*; en *pleitos*; entre *amigos*; por *lograr algo*; tras *un asunto*; sobre *la nieve.*
Andarse por *las ramas.*
Anegar en/de *agua.*
Anegar(se) en *llanto.*
Anhelar
a *más*; por *mayor fortuna.*
Animar
al *examen*; con *elogios.*
Anteponer *(algo)* a *algo.*
Anticipar *(dinero)* sobre *el sueldo.*
Anticiparse a *los acontecimientos.*
Anunciar(se)
en *el periódico*; por *la radio.*
Añadir a *lo dicho.*
Apañarse con *cualquier cosa.*
Aparecer
en *pantalla*; entre *las flores*; por *el horizonte.*
Aparecerse
a/ante *una persona*; en *casa*; entre *sueños.*
Apartar(se)
a *un lado*; de *la ocasión.*
Apasionarse con/de/por *la música.*
Apearse
a/para *comprar algo*; del *tren*; en *marcha*; por *la puerta trasera.*
Apechugar con *las consecuencias.*
Apegarse a *un cargo.*
Apelar
a/ante *la justicia*; contra *la sentencia.*
Apelotonarse a *la entrada.*

p

Apencar   con *las consecuencias.*
Apesadumbrarse   **con/por** *la noticia.*
Apestar   a *ajo.*
Apiadarse   de *los enfermos.*
Aplicar(se)
a *los estudios;* en *clase.*
Apoderarse   de *todo.*
Aportar
(algo) a *la comunidad;* en *dinero.*
Apostar
a/por *un caballo; (algo)* con *alguien.*
Apostatar   de *las creencias.*
Apoyar   con *documentos.*
Apoyarse
en *la pared;* **sobre** *la barandilla.*
Apreciar
en *mucho;* por *sus cualidades.*
Aprender
a *leer;* con *diccionario;* de *un hermano*
mayor; **por** *obligación.*
Aprestarse   a *la lucha.*
Apresurarse
a *hacer algo;* por *llegar a tiempo.*
Apretar
a *llover;* con *las piernas;* **contra** *uno*
mismo; **entre** *los brazos.*
Aprisionar
bajo *la escalera;* con *los brazos;* **en/entre**
la espada y la pared; **tras** *la puerta.*
Aprobar
en *griego;* por *unanimidad.*
Apropiarse   de *lo ajeno.*
Aprovechar
en *el estudio;* **para** *escribir.*
Aprovecharse   de *la situación.*
Aprovisionar
con *alimentos;* de *víveres.*
Aproximar *(algo)* a *algo.*
Aproximarse   a *la ciudad.*
Apuntar
al *enemigo;* con *el rifle;* en *la cuenta;*
hacia *la solución.*
Apurarse
con *algo;* en *las dificultades;* **por** *todo.*
Arder
con *llamas inmensas;* en *deseos.*
Argüir
a *favor* del *delincuente;* con *documentos;*
en contra/en favor del   *acusado;* en
apoyo de *su postura.*

Armar
con *cuchillos;* **hasta** *los dientes.*
Armarse   de *paciencia.*
Armonizar   *(algo)* con *algo.*
Arraigar   en *el suelo.*
Arraigarse   en *la costa.*
Arrancar(se)
a *bailar;* con *cien pesetas;* de *raíz;* **por**
peteneras.
Arrasarse   *(los ojos)* **de/en**   *lágrimas.*
Arrastrar
en *la caída;* por *tierra.*
Arrastrarse
a *los pies;* por *el suelo.*
Arrebatar   **de/de entre**   *las manos.*
Arreglarse
al *común acuerdo;* con *su ex-cónyuge.*
Arrellanarse   en *el sofá.*
Arremeter   **al/con/contra**   *el asaltante.*
Arremolinarse
a *la sombra* del *árbol;* **alrededor** del
escaparate; en *el vestíbulo.*
Arrepentirse   de *su reacción.*
Arribar   a *la costa.*
Arriesgarse
a *entrar;* en *público.*
Arrimarse   a *la chimenea.*
Arrinconarse   en *una esquina.*
Arrojar
al/en   *el patio;* de *la mesa;* **desde** *la ven-*
tana; **por** *la alcantarilla.*
Arrojarse
a *los brazos de alguien;* **contra** *el agresor;*
de *cabeza;* **desde** *una ventana;* en *la lagu-*
na; **por** *un puente;* **sobre** *el tren.*
Arroparse   **con/en**   *una manta.*
Asaetear   **a/con**   *preguntas.*
Asar
a *baja temperatura;* en *el horno.*
Asarse   de *calor.*
Ascender
a *directora;* de *rango;* en *su profesión;*
por *una colina.*
Asegurar(se)
de *algo;* **contra** *todo riesgo.*
Asemejarse
a *alguien;* **en/por**   *algo.*
Asentarse
a *medio camino;* en *un sitio.*
Asentir   a *una propuesta.*

prepositions used with verbs

Asesorarse
con *buenos especialistas*; en *derecho laboral*.
Asimilar a *una desagradable experiencia*.
Asir
a *la perrita*; con *ambas manos*; por *el pescuezo*.
Asirse
a *su espalda*; con *dificultad*; de *la barra*.
Asistir
a *la función*; de *incógnito*; en *su domicilio*.
Asociarse
a *la compañía*; con *alguien*.
Asomarse a/por *la ventana*.
Asombrarse
de/por *algo*; con *su tenacidad*.
Aspirar a *algo mejor*.
Asquearse de *la hipocresía*.
Asustarse de/por *algo*.
Atacar a *alguien*.
Atar
a/de *la barandilla*; con *una cuerda*; por *un extremo*.
Atarse a *alguien*.
Atascarse en *un punto*.
Ataviarse con *esmero*.
Atemorizarse por *una tormenta*.
Atender a *la llamada*.
Atenerse a *lo acordado*.
Atentar a/contra *la verdad*.
Aterrorizarse por *algo*.
Atestiguar
con *su declaración*; sobre *su inocencia*.
Atinar
al *balón*; con *una piedra*; desde *la ventana*.
Atormentarse con/por *algo*.
Atraer
a *alguien*; con *mentiras*.
Atragantarse con *un caramelo*.
Atrancarse en *la redacción*.
Atreverse a/con *algo*.
Atravesar
con *una aguja*; en *barca*; por *el centro de la carretera*.
Atravesarse en *su vida*.
Atreverse a/con *todo*.
Atribuir a *los astros*.
Atribularse en/con/por *una situación*.

Atrincherarse con *los soldados*; en/tras *las barricadas*.
Atropellar
con *el coche*; por *una imprudencia*.
Atropellarse en *su declaración*.
Atufar(se) con/por *la basura*.
Aumentar de/en *tamaño*.
Aunarse con *las protestas*.
Ausentarse de *un sitio*.
Autorizar
a *alguien*; para *hacer algo*; por *escrito*.
Avanzar
a/hacia/hasta *la playa*; por *la arena*; sobre *las conchas*.
Avenirse
a *hacer algo*; entre *los dos*.
Aventajar en *sabiduría*.
Aventurarse a *explorar la isla*.
Avergonzar
a *alguien*; con/por *su conducta*.
Avergonzarse
de *uno mismo*; por *su pereza*.
Aviarse
con *esmero*; para *ir a la ópera*.
Avisar
a *alguien*; de *algo*.
Ayudar
a *hacer los deberes*; con *gusto*; en *la adversidad*.
Ayudarse con/de *las muletas*.
Azotar
con *el cinturón*; en *la espalda*.

Bailar
al *son que tocan*; ante *un público entendido*; con *alguien*; por *bulerías*.
Bajar
al *sótano*; del *avión*; en *ascensor*; hacia *el pueblo*; por *las escaleras*.
Balancear
a *la niña*; en *la mecedora*.
Balar de *hambre*.
Bambolearse en *el trapecio*.
Bañar(se)
con/en *agua caliente*; por *higiene*.

Basarse
en *sólidos argumentos*; **sobre** *lo aprendido*.
Bastar
a/para *su ambición*; **con** *lo dicho*.
Batallar
con/contra *la opinión generalizada*; **por** *sus derechos*.
Beber
a/por *la memoria de alguien*; **con** *ganas*; **de** *la botella*; **en** *el arroyo*.
Beneficiarse con/de *algo*.
Besar en *la mano*.
Blasfemar contra/de/por *algo*.
Bordar
a *mano*; **con** *máquina*; **en** *tapiz*.
Borrar
con *una goma*; **de** *la agenda*.
Bostezar de *sueño*.
Botar de *entusiasmo*.
Bramar de *cólera*.
Bregar
con *los problemas*; **contra** *los adversarios*; **en** *el trabajo*; **por** *su reconocimiento*.
Brillar
a *la luz*; **con** *luz propia*; **por** *su inteligencia*.
Brindar
a *los presentes*; **con** *vino*; **por** *los novios*.
Brindarse a *revisar el manuscrito*.
Brotar de/en *una flor*.
Bucear en *el mar*.
Bufar de *indignación*.
Bullir en/por *su estómago*.
Burilar en *estaño*.
Burlar a *los vigilantes*.
Burlarse de *alguien*.
Buscar
a *alguien*; **por** *todas partes*.

Cabalgar
a *pelo*; **en/sobre** *una yegua*; **por** *la sierra*; **sin** *montura*.
Caber

de *cuerpo entero*; **en** *el armario*; **entre** *las perchas*; **hasta** *dos personas más*.
Caer(se)
al *agua*; **con** *las piernas dobladas*; **de/desde** *lo alto*; **en** *un pozo*; **hacia/hasta** *el fondo*; **por** *el terraplén*; **sobre** *las rocas*.
Calar(se) de *agua*.
Calentar(se)
a *fuego lento*; **con** *su calor*; **junto a** *la chimenea*; **en** *la cama*.
Calificar
con *sobresaliente*; **de** *incompetente*.
Callar por *temor*.
Cambiar
(*una cosa*) **con/por** *otra*; **de** *idea*; **en** *el fondo*.
Cambiarse
a *otro colegio*; **de** *ropa*; **en** *los camerinos*.
Caminar
a *paso ligero*; **con** *elegancia*; **de** *lado*; **hacia/para** *la fuente*; **por** *lo más llano*.
Campar por *sus respetos*.
Canjear (*una cosa*) **por** *otra*.
Cansarse con/de *tanto ruido*.
Cantar
a *pleno pulmón*; **con** *toda su alma*; **de** *alegría*; **en** *un conjunto*; **por** *dinero*.
Capitular
con *los invasores*; **de** *puro agotamiento*.
Caracterizarse
de *bufón*; **por** *su gran talento*.
Carcajearse de *la pregunta*.
Carecer de *riquezas*.
Cargar
a *cuestas*; **con** *las maletas*; **sobre** *la espalda*.
Cargarse con/de *obligaciones*.
Casar a *los novios*.
Casarse
con *alguien*; **en** *una iglesia*; **por** *el juzgado*.
Castigar
a *alguien*; **con** *quedarse en casa*; **de** *modo irrevocable*; **por** *su conducta*; **sin** *salir*.
Catalogar (*a alguien*) **de** *inmaduro*.
Catequizar para *conseguir fieles*.
Cautivar con/por *su belleza*.
Cavar en *el huerto*.
Cavilar
para *obtener beneficios*; **sobre** *lo ocurrido*.
Cazar
al *vuelo*; **con** *tirachinas*.

prepositions used with verbs

Cebarse **con/en** *su enemigo.*
Ceder
a/ante *su petición;* **de** *sus derechos;* **en**
su favor.
Cegarse
con *sus sentimientos;* **de** *dolor;* **por** *los*
celos.
Cejar
ante *la adversidad;* **en** *el empeño.*
Censurar
a *alguien;* **por** *su conducta.*
Centrarse **en** *algo.*
Ceñir
a *la cintura;* **con** *un cinturón;* **de** *un*
extremo a otro.
Ceñirse
a *un plan;* **en** *sus respuestas.*
Cerciorarse **de** *algo.*
Cernerse **sobre** *alguien.*
Cerrar
a *cal y canto;* **con** *llave;* **contra** *la volun-*
tad; **hacia** *media mañana;* **por** *vacacio-*
nes; **tras** *de sí.*
Cerrarse
a *cualquier sugerencia;* **de** *golpe;* **en** *banda.*
Cesar
de *llover;* **en** *sus funciones.*
Chancearse
con *alguien;* **de/por** *algo/alguien.*
Chapar **con/de/en** *oro.*
Chapotear **en** *el agua.*
Chiflarse **por** *algo.*
Chivarse **al** *profesor.*
Chocar **con/contra** *algo.*
Cifrar (*su vida*) **en** *la poesía.*
Cifrarse **en** *dos millones.*
Cimentarse **en** *la conducta práctica.*
Circunscribirse **a** *los países de habla*
castellana.
Clamar **al** *cielo;* **por** *su liberación.*
Clamorear
a *voz en grito;* **por** *su animosidad.*
Clasificar
de *la a a la zeta;* **en** *un fichero;*
por/según *temas.*
Clavar **en** *la pared.*
Coadyuvar **a/en** *el trabajo.*
Cobijarse
bajo *techo;* **con** *una manta;* **de** *la lluvia;*
en *un portal.*

Cobrar
con *regularidad;* **del** *banco;* **en** *metálico;*
por *transferencia.*
Cocer
a *fuego lento;* **con** *sal;* **en** *agua salada.*
Codearse **con** *los intelectuales.*
Coexistir **con** *algo.*
Coger
a *manos llenas;* **con** *las manos en la*
masa; **de** *buen humor;* **en** *su salsa;* **entre**
la espada y la pared; **por** *casualidad.*
Cohibirse
ante *alguien;* **con** *los elogios;* **de** *volver a*
llamar.
Coincidir
con *alguien;* **en** *algo.*
Cojear **de/por** *un dolor.*
Colaborar
con *alguien;* **en** *algo.*
Colarse
en *una fiesta;* **por** *un agujero.*
Colegir **de/por** *el aspecto de su casa.*
Colgar
de *la cuerda;* **en** *la pared.*
Coligarse **con** *todas las mujeres.*
Colindar **con** *la oficina de correos.*
Colmar **de** *bienes.*
Colocar
al *revés;* **con** *cuidado;* **en** *un cajón;*
entre *los libros;* **por** *la base.*
Colocarse **de** *secretario.*
Colorear **de** *azul.*
Combatir
con *medicinas;* **contra** *la enfermedad;*
por *la justicia .*
Combinar (*una cosa*) **con** *otra.*
Comenzar
a *estudiar;* **por** *el principio.*
Comer
a *dos carrillos;* **con** *un amigo;* **hasta**
reventar.
Comerciar
con *un cliente;* **en** *especias.*
Compadecerse
de *alguien;* **por** *algo.*
Compaginar **con** *otros intereses.*
Comparar **con** *alguien.*
Compartir **con/entre** *todos.*
Compeler **a** *decir la verdad.*
Compensar

con *unas buenas vacaciones;* de/por *su dedicación.*
Competir
con *alguien;* por *algo.*
Complacer
a *todo el mundo;* con *su amabilidad.*
Complacerse con/de/en *su fortuna.*
Completar con *citas.*
Complicar con *demasiadas notas.*
Componer
a *marchas forzadas;* con *diferentes materiales.*
Componerse
de *varios elementos.*
Comprar
a *plazos;* por *piezas.*
Comprender
con *dificultad;* de *súbito.*
Comprimirse en *un caja.*
Comprobar
con *datos;* en *el laboratorio.*
Comprometer
a *alguien;* en *algo.*
Comprometerse
a *algo;* con *alguien;* en/para *un proyecto.*
Computar en *horas.*
Comulgar
con *alguien;* en *una idea.*
Comunicar
a *los asistentes;* con *la centralita;* por *escrito.*
Comunicarse
con *alguien;* por *teléfono.*
Concebir *(un sentimiento)* hacia/contra/por *una persona.*
Concentrar en *un sitio.*
Concentrarse en *algo.*
Conceptuar de *bueno.*
Concernir *(algo)* a *alguien.*
Concertar
con *alguien;* en *la reunión;* entre *los representantes;* por *teléfono.*
Conciliar con *sus ideales.*
Concluir
con *un discurso;* en medio de *un general regocijo;* por *cese de contrato.*
Concordar *(el verbo)* con *el sujeto.*
Concretarse con/en *hechos.*
Concurrir a/en *el encuentro.*
Condenar a *tres años de cárcel.*

Condensar en *una síntesis.*
Condescender
a *hacer algo;* con *su actitud.*
Condicionar *(algo)* a *algo.*
Condolerse de *la desgracia.*
Conducir
a/hacia *algún sitio;* en *moto;* por *el centro.*
Conectar con *alguien.*
Confabular(se)
con/contra *alguien;* para *un fin.*
Confederarse con *otros.*
Conferir con *notables ganancias.*
Confesar
(algo) a *alguien;* en *privado;* entre *bastidores.*
Confesarse
a *sí mismo;* con *el corazón en la mano.*
Confiar en *la gente.*
Confiarse a *alguien.*
Confinar a/en *el campo.*
Confirmar en *dos horas.*
Confirmarse en *su deseo.*
Confluir a/en *la convocatoria.*
Conformarse
con *lo que haya;* por *necesidad.*
Confrontar
con *otras opiniones;* entre *todos.*
Confundir *(una cosa)* con *otra.*
Confundirse
con/en *la talla;* de *puerta.*
Congeniar con *los compañeros.*
Congraciarse con *los demás.*
Congratularse
con *los agraciados;* del/por *el premio obtenido.*
Conjugar *(el trabajo)* con *el placer.*
Conjurar(se)
con *los rebeldes;* contra *el régimen imperante.*
Conminar
(a alguien) a *hacer algo;* con *amenazas.*
Conmutar
(una pena) con/por *trabajos forzados.*
Conocer
de *oídas;* en *profundidad.*
Consagrarse a *la poesía.*
Conseguir *(algo)* de *alguien.*
Consentir en *hacerlo.*
Conservarse

prepositions used with verbs

con/en *buena forma física;* **hasta** *dos meses.*

Considerar
a *sus semejantes;* **de/en** *forma solidaria;* **por** *sí mismos.*

Consignar **a nombre de** *alguien.*

Consistir **en** *un resumen.*

Consolar
de/por *los malos resultados;* **en** *su tristeza.*

Consolarse
con *la bebida;* **de** *un disgusto;* **en** *soledad.*

Conspirar
con *otros;* **contra** *la dictadura;* **para** *dar un golpe.*

Constar
de *varios elementos;* **en** *la memoria;* **por medio de** *un contrato.*

Constituirse **en** *asociación.*

Constreñir **a** *hacer algo.*

Constreñirse **al** *presupuesto.*

Construir
con *paciencia;* **en** *el ático;* **entre** *varios.*

Consultar
a/con *alguien;* **en** *privado;* **para** *solicitar su conformidad;* **por/respecto a/sobre** *un tema.*

Consumirse
a causa de/por *algo;* **con/en** *la espera;* **de** *ansiedad.*

Contagiarse **con/de/por** *el virus.*

Contaminarse
con *el agua estancada;* **de** *un virus;* **en** *el hospital.*

Contar
(algo) **a** *alguien;* **con** *los dedos;* **de cabo a rabo;* **desde** *la letra g;* **entre** *los asistentes;* **hasta** *mil.*

Contemplar
al *niño;* **en** *silencio.*

Contemporizar **con** *alguien.*

Contender
con/contra *los detractores;* **en** *una discusión;* **por/sobre** *algo.*

Contenerse
en *su actitud;* **por** *educación.*

Contentarse **con** *un beso.*

Contestar
a *sus requerimientos;* **con** *una negativa;* **de modo** *tajante;* **por** *escrito.*

Continuar
con *la conversación;* **desde** *el punto anterior;* **en** *compañía;* **hacia** *el río;* **hasta** *el final;* **por** *inercia.*

Contradecirse **con** *el testimonio ajeno.*

Contraer *(un compromiso)* **con** *alguien.*

Contrapesar **con** *los nuevos gastos.*

Contraponer *(una cosa)* **a/con** *otra.*

Contrastar *(una cosa)* **a/con** *otra.*

Contratar
de/en *prueba;* **para** *un proyecto;* **por** *un año.*

Contravenir **a** *las órdenes.*

Contribuir **a/con/en/para** *algo.*

Convalecer **de** *una enfermedad.*

Convencer
a *alguien;* **de** *algo.*

Convencerse **de** *su valía.*

Convenir
(algo) **a** *alguien;* *(algo)* **con** *alguien;* **en** *hacer algo.*

Convenirse **a/con** *los planes.*

Converger
al *debate;* **en** *las últimas sesiones.*

Conversar
con *un amigo;* **en** *el parque;* **sobre** *los sucesos.*

Convertir
(a alguien) **a** *la fe;* *(algo)* **en** *ganancia.*

Convertirse
a *una religión;* **en** *una figura pública.*

Convidar
a/con *una buena comida;* **para** *la fiesta.*

Convivir
con *la pareja;* **en** *un piso pequeño.*

Convocar
a *una reunión;* **por** *una circular.*

Cooperar
con *los demás;* **en** *una misma tarea.*

Copiar
a *alguien;* **de** *una foto;* **en** *un papel.*

Coquetear **con** *alguien.*

Coronar
con *una corona de oro;* **de** *gloria;* **en** *la catedral.*

Corregir
con/en *rojo;* **de/por** *a iniciativa propia.*

Corregirse **de** *su error.*

Correr

a *gran velocidad*; con/sin *deportivas*;
de *un lado* para *otro*; en busca de
ayuda; entre *los árboles*; por *la arena*;
sobre *la alfombra*; tras *el ladrón*.
Correrse de *bochorno*.
Corresponder
a *una invitación*; con *generosidad*; de/en
la manera adecuada.
Cortar
con *las tijeras*; de/desde *(la) raíz*;
por *la mitad*.
Coser
a *mano*; con *bastidor*; por *encargo*; para
alguien.
Cotejar
con *la versión oficial*; por *partes*.
Crecer
a *ojos vistas*; en *consideración*.
Creer
a *alguien*; en *algo*.
Criar
a *sus pechos*; con *cariño*.
Criarse
en *buenas manos*; para *el arte*.
Cristalizar(se) en *una obra de perfec-
to acabado*.
Cruzar
de *una orilla* a *otra*; por *lo menos pro-
fundo*.
Cruzarse
con *alguien*; en *el ascensor*; por *la calle*.
Cuadrar con *su temperamento*.
Cubrir(se) de/con *una buena manta*.
Cuidar
con *esmero*; de *su jardín*.
Cuidarse de *los enemigos*.
Culminar
con *una obra maestra*; en *el momento
justo*.
Culpar
de *un delito*; por *su desinterés*.
Cumplir con *sus responsabilidades*.
Curar
con *medicinas*; de *sus heridas*.
Curarse
con *un buen tratamiento*; de *la gripe*.
Curiosear
con *interés*; en/por *los cajones*.
Curtirse
a/con *el aire*; del *sol*; en *la montaña*.

Dañar
a *alguien*; con *la actitud*; de *palabra*; en
su orgullo.
Dar
con *la fórmula apropiada*; contra *la
pared*; de *bruces*; por *bueno*.
Darse
a *las habladurías*; de *listo*; por *vencido*.
Datar de *un siglo antes*.
Deambular por *la ciudad*.
Deberse a *sus obligaciones*.
Decantarse por *la mejor propuesta*.
Decidir
de *forma conjunta*; en/sobre *el asunto*.
Decidirse
a *cambiar*; por *un cambio de vida*.
Decir
(algo) a/de *alguien*; en *secreto*; por
carta.
Declarar
a/ante *el juez*; en *el juzgado*; sobre *el
particular*.
Declararse a/a favor/en contra de
alguien.
Declinar
a/hacia *poniente*; de *una actitud*.
Dedicar(se) a *descansar*.
Deducir de *su salario*.
Defender
con *una ley*; contra *los ataques*; de *la
especulación*.
Defraudar
al *electorado*; con *trampas*; en *sus expec-
tativas*.
Degenerar en *sus costumbres*.
Dejar
a *la espera*; de *trabajar*; en *depósito*; por
imposible; sin *terminar*.
Dejarse de *cuentos*.
Delatarse
a/ante *los presentes*; con *sus acciones*.
Delegar
de *sus funciones*; en *un representante*.
Deleitarse
con/en *el recital*; de *la brisa marina*.

p

prepositions used with verbs

Deliberar
en *asamblea*; **entre** *sí*; **sobre** *la decisión.*
Delirar
en *sueños*; **por** efecto del *agotamiento.*
Demandar
a *alguien*; **ante** *las autoridades*; **de/por**
fraude; **en** *un recurso judicial.*
Demorarse **en** *salir.*
Demostrar **con** *hechos contundentes.*
Departir
con *la gente*; **sobre** *la gestión.*
Depender **de** *una beca.*
Deponer **ante** *la concurrencia*; **de** *su actitud.*
Deportar
al *extranjero*; **de** *su país.*
Depositar
bajo *llave*; **en** *el banco*; **sobre** *la repisa.*
Derivar
de *tono*; **hacia** *otros temas.*
Derramar
a/en/encima de/por *el mantel*; **sobre** *su cabeza.*
Derretirse **de** *amor.*
Derribar
al *adversario*; **del** *pedestal*; **en/por** *el césped.*
Derrocar
al *dictador*; **del** *poder*; **por** *decisión popular.*
Desacostumbrarse
a *la ciudad*; **de** *comer demasiado.*
Desacreditar
a *los editores*; **ante/entre** *los demás*; **con** *rumores falsos*; **en** *su prestigio.*
Desafiar
a *una carrera*; **de** *palabra*; **con** *su actitud*; **en** *el juego.*
Desaguar
en *el pantano*; **por** *la tubería.*
Desahogarse
con *sus amigas*; **de** *su congoja*; **en** *sollozos.*
Desairar **con/en** *sus contestaciones.*
Desalojar **de** *la casa ocupada.*
Desaparecer
ante *sus ojos*; **de** *la vista.*
Desarraigar(se) **de** *su ciudad natal.*
Desasirse **de** *una atadura.*
Desatarse
de *una silla*; **en** *insultos.*

Desayunar(se) **con** *café y tostadas.*
Desbancar
a *alguien*; **de** *su puesto.*
Desbordarse
de *su cauce*; **por** *la lluvia torrencial.*
Descabalarse
en *sus cuentas*; **con/por** *el desorden.*
Descabalgar **del** *caballo.*
Descalabrar(se) **con** *una piedra.*
Descansar
del *viaje*; **en** *la paz del hogar*; **sobre** *el sofá.*
Descargar
contra *los empleados*; **de** *la furgoneta*; **en/sobre** *la acera.*
Descargarse **con/contra/en** *los responsables.*
Descarriarse **de** *la senda elegida.*
Descender
a/hacia *el piso de abajo*; **de/desde** *la terraza*; **en** *su estima*; **por** *una escalera.*
Desclavar **de** *la pared.*
Descolgarse
de/desde *el tejado*; **hasta** *el suelo*; **por** *las rocas.*
Descollar
en *el grupo*; **entre/sobre** *todos.*
Descomponerse
en *cuatro apartados*; **por** *el calor.*
Desconfiar
de *su cariño*; **hasta** *de su sombra.*
Descontar **del** *sueldo.*
Descubrir **al** *espía.*
Descubrirse
a/con *sus padres*; **ante** *su empeño.*
Descuidarse **de/en** *el trabajo.*
Desdecir **de** *su educación.*
Desdecirse **de** *lo afirmado.*
Desdoblarse **en** *dos personalidades.*
Desechar **de** *la cabeza (una idea).*
Desembarazarse **de** *alguien.*
Desembarcar
del *transatlántico*; **en** *el puerto.*
Desembocar **en** *el mar.*
Desempeñar **de** *forma eficaz.*
Desenfrenarse **en** *el beber.*
Desengañarse **de** *las falsas promesas.*
Desenredarse **de** *la cuerda.*
Desentenderse **de** *sus obligaciones.*

Desenterrar de *la orilla del mar.*
Desentonar con *el resto.*
Desertar
al *otro bando;* del *ejército.*
Desesperar de *descubrirlo.*
Desfallecer de *sed.*
Desfogarse
con *su familia;* en *privado.*
Desgajar(se) del *tallo.*
Deshacerse
a/en *explicaciones;* de *los curiosos;* por
su familia.
Designar
con *un mote;* para *la dirección de la
revista;* por *méritos.*
Desinteresarse de/por *lo sucedido.*
Desistir de *la intención.*
Desleír en *un vaso de leche.*
Desligarse de *un grupo.*
Deslizarse
al *agua;* en/entre/por/sobre *la
nieve.*
Deslucirse
al *aire;* por *el sol.*
Desmentir
a *alguien; (algo)* de *algo.*
Desmerecer de *su persona.*
Desmontar del *columpio.*
Desnudarse
de *los pies* a *la cabeza;* desde/hasta *la
cintura;* por *completo.*
Desorientarse en *una ciudad desconocida.*
Despacharse con/contra *los empleados.*
Desparramarse
en/por *el suelo;* entre *los cubiertos.*
Despedirse de *las amigas.*
Despegarse
de *la familia;* por *una esquina.*
Despeñarse
al *barranco;* por *un precipicio.*
Despepitarse por *salir.*
Desperdigarse
entre *los árboles;* por *la playa.*
Despertar
a *sus hermanos;* de *súbito.*
Despertarse con *apetito.*
Despoblarse de *jóvenes.*
Despojar(se) del *jersey.*
Desposarse

ante *testigos;* con *el ser amado;* por
amor.
Desposeer de *su parte de herencia.*
Despotricar contra *el tráfico.*
Desprenderse de *sus riquezas.*
Despreocuparse de *todo.*
Despuntar
en *ingenio;* entre *la media;* por *su originalidad.*
Desquitarse de *los malos ratos.*
Destacar
de/entre *los demás;* en *el conjunto;*
por *su belleza.*
Desternillarse de *risa.*
Desterrar
a *una isla lejana;* de *su hogar;* por *traicionar a su pueblo.*
Destinar
a/en *Madrid;* para *el consumo.*
Destituir
de *su cargo;* por *malversación.*
Desvelarse por *los demás.*
Desvestirse de *la cintura* para *arriba.*
Desviarse
de *la carretera;* hacia *otro lado.*
Desvivirse por *ella.*
Detenerse
a *repostar gasolina;* en *la estación.*
Determinarse
a *concursar;* a favor de/por *un lugar
tranquilo.*
Detraer de *su sueldo.*
Devolver a *su propietaria.*
Dictaminar sobre *la reclamación.*
Diferenciarse
de *sus hermanos;* en/por *el aspecto.*
Diferir
a/hasta; para *el próximo verano;* de *la
opinión;* en *algún punto;* entre *sí.*
Difundir
en/por *la calle;* entre *la gente.*
Dignarse a *considerarlo.*
Dilatar *(la decisión)* hasta/para *más
tarde.*
Dilatarse en *responder.*
Diluir en *agua fría.*
Dimanar de *una antigua creencia.*
Dimitir de *un alto cargo.*
Diptongar *(la o)* en *ue.*

p

prepositions used with verbs

Dirigir
a/hacia *el albergue;* en *el proyecto;* por
el camino más corto.
Dirigirse a/hacia *los presentes.*
Discernir
con *agudeza;* entre *las propuestas.*
Discordar de/en/sobre *el parecer del
grupo.*
Discrepar de/en/con *el parecer del
grupo.*
Disculpar
a *los responsables;* con *una buena defensa.*
Disculparse
ante *la reunión;* con *los componentes;*
de/por *no asistir.*
Discurrir
de *acuerdo* con/según *el sentido
común;* en *voz alta; (un río)* entre/por
el pinar; sobre *los problemas.*
Discutir
(algo) a *alguien;* con *su padre;* de/sobre
filosofía; por *todo.*
Diseminar en/entre/por/por entre *la
espesura.*
Disentir del *acuerdo tomado.*
Disertar
con *sencillez;* sobre *ciencia.*
Disfrazar con *buenas palabras.*
Disfrazarse
bajo *un traje de pirata;* de *pirata.*
Disfrutar
con/de *su compañía;* en *su casa del
campo.*
Disgregarse en *partes.*
Disgustarse con/de/por *su brusca
contestación.*
Disimular
ante *los otros;* con *un pretexto.*
Disolver
con *aguarrás;* en *aceite.*
Disonar
de *manera estrepitosa;* en medio de *la
actuación.*
Disparar contra *el techo;* hacia *ellos.*
Dispensar de *realizar su tarea.*
Dispersarse
en *muchas actividades;* entre/por *el
viento.*
Disponer

a *su antojo;* de *un pequeño capital;* en
montones distintos; por *colores.*
Disponerse a/para *venir.*
Disputar
con *los compañeros;* de *política;* por
todo; sobre *la enseñanza.*
Distanciarse de *sus amigos.*
Distar del *mar dos kilómetros.*
Distinguir
con *su afecto;* entre *la multitud.*
Distinguirse
de/entre *los otros niños;* en/por *su acti-
tud.*
Distraerse
con *el vuelo de una mosca;* de *sus preo-
cupaciones;* en *clase.*
Distribuir a/en/entre/por *todas las
librerías.*
Disuadir
a *alguien;* de *algo.*
Divagar de/sobre *algo.*
Divertirse
con *sus bromas;* en *hacerle una caricatu-
ra.*
Dividir
con/entre *sus seres queridos;* de *mutuo
acuerdo;* por *cuatro.*
Dividirse en *distintos proyectos.*
Divorciarse de *su marido.*
Divulgar entre *sus conocidos.*
Doblar a/hacia *la izquierda.*
Doblarse
de/por *el dolor;* por *la mitad;* hacia
atrás; hasta *romperse.*
Dolerse con/de *su rechazo.*
Domiciliarse en *Palma de Mallorca.*
Dominar en *todo.*
Dormir
al *raso;* bajo *las estrellas;* con *su madre;*
en *el campo;* hasta *tarde;* sobre *la tierra.*
Dotar
con/de *una ayuda económica;* en *herencia.*
Dudar
acerca de/de/sobre *sus intenciones;* en
la elección; entre *dos productos;* hasta
de *ella misma.*
Durar
en *su decisión;* por *mucho tiempo;* para
toda la vida.

Echar
a *la calle;* del *colegio;* en *falta;* **hacia/para** *adelante;* por *el suelo;* **sobre** *sí.*

Echarse
a *la calle;* en *la cama;* **entre** *sus brazos;* **hacia/para** *otro lado;* por *el suelo.*

Educar
en *una escuela;* **para** *abogado.*

Ejercer de *médico.*

Ejercitarse en *la danza.*

Elegir
de/entre *los primeros;* por *esposa.*

Elevarse
a/hasta *el techo;* del *suelo;* por *las nubes;* **sobre** *los otros.*

Eliminar
a un jugador; del *equipo.*

Emanar de *su autoridad.*

Emanciparse de *los padres.*

Embadurnar **con/de** *barro.*

Embarazarse
con *paquetes;* de *un niño.*

Embarcarse
con *un socio;* de *polizón;* en *un negocio;* **hacia/para** *América.*

Embeberse
con *la música;* de *sus palabras;* en *una novela.*

Embelesarse con *los bailarines.*

Embestir
a *traición;* con *el arma;* **contra** *el grupo;* por *la espalda.*

Embobarse
ante *el cuadro;* con *el niño;* **de/por** *cualquier cosa.*

Emborracharse **con/de** *vino.*

Emboscarse
en *la espesura;* **entre** *las matas.*

Embozarse
con *el manto;* en *el abrigo;* **hasta** *los ojos.*

Embravecerse
con/contra *los inferiores.*

Embriagarse
con *la bebida;* de *felicidad.*

Embutir
de *carne;* en *madera.*

Embutirse de *dulces.*

Emerger del *fondo.*

Emigrar
a *Uruguay;* de *Alemania;* **desde** *su patria.*

Emocionarse
con *la ópera;* en *el nacimiento* del *niño;* por *el suceso.*

Empacharse
con *la comida;* de *dulces.*

Empalagarse con *la tarta;* de *caramelos.*

Empalmar con *las vacaciones.*

Empapar
con *la toalla;* de *agua;* en *vino.*

Empaparse
bajo *la lluvia;* de *arte;* en *el lago.*

Empapuzarse de *pan.*

Emparejar(se) con *un extranjero.*

Emparentar con *otra familia.*

Empatar
a *un gol;* con *el otro equipo.*

Empedrar **con/de** *adoquines.*

Empeñarse
con *una tarea;* en *deudas;* **para/por** *conseguirlo.*

Emperrarse
con *una película;* en *ir al cine.*

Empezar
a *estudiar;* con *buen pie;* **desde** *el primer día;* en *buenas condiciones;* por *el final.*

Emplear *(el tiempo)* en *(hacer) algo útil.*

Emplearse
de *asistente;* en *un bar.*

Empotrar en *la pared.*

Emprender(la)
a *bofetadas;* con *alguien.*

Empujar
al *vacío;* con *las manos;* **contra** *el mueble;* **hacia** *el precipicio;* **hasta** *un barranco.*

Emular a *alguien.*

Emulsionar
con *plata;* en *oro.*

Enajenarse por *la locura.*

Enamorarse de *una actriz.*

Enamoriscarse del *profesor.*

Encajar
con *los gustos;* en *el marco.*

p

prepositions used with verbs

Encallar en *la arena.*
Encaminarse **a/hacia** *el museo.*
Encanecer
de *miedo;* **por** *el susto.*
Encapricharse **con/de** *una persona.*
Encaramarse
a *la lámpara;* **en** *un pino;* **sobre** *la tapia.*
Encararse **a/con** *su padre.*
Encargar
a *alguien;* **de** *contestar al teléfono.*
Encargarse **de** *la contabilidad.*
Encariñarse **con** *el gato.*
Encarnizarse **con/en** *los derrotados.*
Encasillarse **en** *un papel.*
Encastillarse **en** *su mundo.*
Encauzar **por** *la vía legal.*
Encauzarse **en** *la vida profesional.*
Encenegarse **en** *la corrupción.*
Encenderse **de** *rabia.*
Encerrar
en *el sótano;* **entre** *rejas.*
Encerrarse
en *uno mismo;* **entre** *cuatro paredes.*
Encharcarse
de *agua;* **en** *el fango.*
Encoger(se)
con *el agua caliente;* **de** *hombros.*
Encomendar **a** *su secretario.*
Encomendarse
al *diablo;* **en manos del** *doctor.*
Enconarse
con *el compañero;* **en** *la batalla.*
Encontrar
bajo *la cama;* **en** *el suelo;* **sobre** *la mesa;* **tras** *el mueble.*
Encontrarse
con *una dificultad;* **en** *un buen momento;* **entre** *amigos.*
Encuadernar
a *mano;* **en** *piel.*
Encuadrar **en** *un marco.*
Encuadrarse **en** *un equipo.*
Encumbrarse
a/en *la cima;* **hasta** *lo alto;* **sobre** *los otros.*
Endurecerse
con/por *el dolor;* **en** *la lucha.*
Enemistar **a** *uno* **con** *otro.*
Enemistarse **con** *un compañero.*
Enfadarse
con *el hermano;* **por** *nada.*

Enfermar
con/por *el esfuerzo;* **del** *corazón.*
Enfilar **hacia** *la cumbre.*
Enfocar
con *la linterna;* **desde** *otra perspectiva.*
Enfrascarse **en** *la lectura.*
Enfrentarse **a/con** *un adversario.*
Enfurecerse
al *recordarlo;* **con** *los alumnos;* **contra** *el vendedor;* **por** *cualquier cosa.*
Engalanar(se)
con *cintas;* **de** *flores.*
Enganchar(se) **con/en** *un clavo.*
Engañar
a *alguien;* **con** *falsas promesas.*
Engañarse
a *sí mismo;* **con** *falsas esperanzas;* **en** *el planteamiento;* **por** *las apariencias.*
Engarzar
con *perlas;* **en** *platino.*
Engastar
con *piedras preciosas;* **en** *oro.*
Engendrar
con/por *amor;* **(un hijo) de** *alguien.*
Englobar **en** *una sola idea.*
Engolfarse
con *malas compañías;* **en** *vicios.*
Engolosinarse **con** *las promesas.*
Engreírse **con/por** *su belleza.*
Enjuagarse **con** *agua.*
Enjugar **con** *el pañuelo.*
Enlazar *(una cosa)* **con** *otra.*
Enloquecer **de** *pena.*
Enmendarse
con *el castigo;* **de** *la falta;* **por** *la reprimenda.*
Enojarse
con/contra *él;* **por** *el olvido.*
Enorgullecerse **de** *sus logros.*
Enraizar
con *fuerza;* **en** *un país.*
Enredarse **con/en/entre** *las ramas.*
Enriquecer(se)
con *comisiones;* **en** *sabiduría.*
Enrolarse **en** *la marina.*
Ensangrentarse **con** *la operación.*
Ensañarse **con/en** *los débiles.*
Ensayar
con/en *el piano;* **para** *actuar en público.*

prepositions used with verbs

Enseñar
a *hablar;* con *cintas de vídeo.*
Enseñorearse de *un lugar.*
Ensimismarse en *los pensamientos.*
Ensoberbecerse
con *su belleza;* de *su dinero.*
Ensuciarse
con *barro;* de *comida;* en *la fábrica.*
Entender
de *arte;* en *pintura.*
Entenderse
con *todo el mundo;* en *alemán;* por *gestos.*
Enterarse
de *las noticias;* de boca/por boca de *un vecino;* en *el trabajo;* por *la televisión.*
Enternecerse con *un bebé.*
Enterrar en *el cementerio.*
Enterrarse en *vida.*
Entonar (*un color*) con *otro.*
Entrar
a *comprar;* con *buen pie;* de *cartero;* en *la tienda;* hacia *las diez;* hasta *el almacén;* por *la puerta grande.*
Entregar (*algo*) a *alguien.*
Entregarse
a *la familia;* en *manos del destino;* sin *condiciones.*
Entremezclar(se)
con *agua;* en *el asunto.*
Entrenarse
con *el monitor;* en *el equipo.*
Entresacar (*datos*) de *una revista.*
Entretenerse
con *un juego;* en *mirar tiendas.*
Entrevistarse
con *la directora;* en *el despacho.*
Entristecerse con/de/por *la desgracia.*
Entrometerse
en *todo;* entre *una pareja.*
Entroncar con *algo.*
Entronizar en *el corazón.*
Entusiasmarse
con *un viaje;* por *una persona.*
Envanecerse con/de/por *el éxito.*
Envejecer
con *buen ánimo;* de *golpe;* por *la vida dura.*
Envenenar
a *la víctima;* con *cianuro.*

Envenenarse de/por *tomar setas.*
Enviar
a *casa;* (a) por *comida;* con *franqueo de urgencia;* por *correo.*
Enviciarse
con *el tabaco;* en *el casino;* por *las malas compañías.*
Envolver(se)
con *una bufanda;* en *un papel;* entre *las sábanas.*
Enzarzarse en *una pelea.*
Equidistar de *Segovia y Ávila.*
Equipar(se) con/de *ropa de verano.*
Equiparar a/con *un modelo.*
Equivaler a *diez marcos.*
Equivocar (*unas cosas*) con *otras.*
Equivocarse
al *escribir;* de *persona;* en *un número.*
Erigir(se) en *juez.*
Errar
en *todo;* por *el mundo.*
Escabullirse
de *los compromisos;* de/de entre/por entre *la gente;* por *la puerta;*
Escamarse de/por *algo.*
Escandalizarse de/por *lo ocurrido.*
Escapar(se)
a *la carrera;* al *extranjero;* con *vida;* de *las manos;* en *una avioneta;* sobre *un caballo.*
Escarbar en *el pasado.*
Escarmentar
con/de/por *lo ocurrido;* en *la propia carne.*
Escindirse en *partes.*
Escoger
del *grupo;* entre *varios;* para *el papel principal;* por *compañero.*
Esconderse
bajo/debajo de *la mesa;* de *la policía;* en *el sótano;* entre *la multitud.*
Escribir
a *mano;* de/sobre *cine;* desde *Alicante;* en *papel de avión;* para *una revista;* por *encargo.*
Escuchar
con *atención;* en *silencio.*
Escudarse en *los padres.*
Escudriñar
entre *los papeles;* en *busca de algo.*

p

prepositions used with verbs

Esculpir
a cincel; en la piedra.

Escupir
a la cara; en la calle.

Escurrirse
al suelo; de/de entre/entre las manos; en el hielo.

Esforzarse
a/en estudiar; para no suspender; por aprobar.

Esfumarse
ante sus ojos; de la vista; en la distancia; por el aire.

Esmaltar
al fuego; con/de color.

Esmerarse
en el trabajo; por ser simpático.

Espantarse
al saber la verdad; ante lo ocurrido; con/de/por el ruido.

Esparcir por toda la casa.

Especializarse en Literatura.

Especular
con lo ajeno; en filosofía; sobre un suceso.

Esperar
a tener más suerte; de los amigos; en casa; para salir.

Espolvorear con canela.

Establecerse
de farmacéutico; en Barcelona.

Estafar
con billetes falsos; en un negocio.

Estampar
a mano; con un sello; contra la pared; en madera; sobre la tela.

Estancarse en la profesión.

Estar
a la disposición de alguien; bajo las órdenes de un superior; con fiebre; contra el régimen; de vuelta; en el fútbol; entre extraños; para salir; por un chico; sin sosiego; sobre un asunto; tras una mujer; tras de un empleo.

Estimar
a alguien; en pesetas.

Estimular
al estudio; con dinero.

Estirar de la cuerda.

Estragarse

con la bebida; de comer; por el exceso de grasa.

Estrechar
entre los brazos; (una relación) con alguien.

Estrellarse
con el coche; contra un árbol; en la piscina; sobre el pavimento.

Estremecerse de horror.

Estrenarse
con una novela; en un negocio.

Estribar en algo.

Estudiar
con un compañero; en casa; para ingeniero; por libre; sin ayuda.

Evadirse de los problemas.

Evaluar (los gastos) en un millón de pesetas.

Exagerar
con los regalos; en la cantidad.

Examinar(se)
a fin de mes; de latín; en el instituto; para nota; por parciales.

Exceder a la imaginación.

Excederse
de lo previsto; en los gastos.

Exceptuar de la regla.

Excitar a la violencia.

Excluir de la fiesta.

Exculpar de una falta.

Excusarse
con el amigo; de ir a la fiesta; por el retraso.

Exhortar
a dejar un vicio; con argumentos.

Exhumar del olvido.

Eximir del entrenamiento.

Exonerar de impuestos.

Expansionarse con la familia.

Expeler
del cuerpo; por la boca.

Explayarse
con las amigas; en discursos.

Exponerse
al peligro; ante el adversario.

Expresarse
con gestos; de palabra; en italiano; por escrito.

Expulsar de la escuela.

Expurgar de lo malo.

Extender   sobre la arena.
Extenderse
a/hacia/hasta   la costa; **de** lado **a** lado; **desde** Cáceres; **en** paralelo; **por** la frontera.
Extraer
con máquinas; **de** la mina.
Extralimitarse   **en** sus derechos.
Extrañarse   **de** lo sucedido.
Extraviarse
del camino; **en** sus reflexiones; **por** el camino.
Extremarse   **en** atenciones.

Fallar
a favor de/contra /en contra de/en favor de   el acusado; **por** su base.
Fallecer
a manos del asesino; **de** muerte natural; **en brazos de** la esposa; **en** un accidente aéreo.
Faltar
a la palabra; **de** casa; **en** algo; **por** hacer.
Familiarizarse   **con/en**   el uso del ordenador.
Fatigarse
de andar; **por** cualquier cosa.
Favorecer
a un pariente; **con** una beca.
Favorecerse   **de** la amistad.
Felicitarse   **de** los logros de los hijos.
Fiar   (algo) **a** un conocido.
Fiarse   **de** la palabra.
Fichar   **por** un club.
Figurar
de director; **en** cartelera.
Fijar
a/en   la pared; **con** chinchetas.
Fijarse   **en** todo.
Firmar
con la inicial; **de** propia mano; **en** blanco; **por** orden.
Fisgar   **en** los cajones.
Flamear
al viento; **en** el aire.
Flanquear   **por** todas partes.

Flaquear
en la voluntad; **por** la base.
Flojear
de las piernas; **en** el trabajo.
Florecer   **en** sabiduría.
Fluctuar   **en/entre**   varios puntos.
Fluir
de la fuente; **por** el grifo.
Forjar   **con/de/en**   acero.
Formar
con buenos principios; **en** fila; **entre** los soldados; **por** departamentos.
Forrar   **con /de/en**   tela.
Forrarse   **de** millones.
Fortificarse
con barricadas; **contra** el adversario; **en** el castillo.
Forzar
a ir; **con** amenazas.
Fracasar   **en** el examen.
Franquearse
a un hermano; **con** el compañero.
Freír
a fuego lento; **con/en**   aceite.
Frisar   **en/en torno a** los treinta.
Frotar
con las manos; **contra** la pared.
Fugarse   **de** casa.
Fumar
con/sin   boquilla; **en** pipa.
Fundarse   **en** argumentos.
Fundirse
a/con   el sol; **por** el cortacircuito.

Ganar
a las cartas; **con** el cambio; **en** el juego; **para** vivir; **por** la mano.
Gastar
con alegría; **en** juergas.
Girar
a/hacia   el extremo; **a cargo de** un banco; **alrededor del** poste; **en torno al** mismo punto; **sobre** su eje.
Gloriarse
de algo;   **en** el Señor.

prepositions used with verbs

Gobernarse **por** *extraños.*
Golpear **con** *un palo.*
Gotear **de** *la cañería.*
Gozar **de** *una buena situación.*
Grabar
al *aguafuerte;* **con** *micrófono;* **en** *cinta;*
sobre *madera.*
Graduarse
de *licenciado;* **en** *físicas.*
Gravar
con *impuestos;* **en** *un 15%.*
Gravitar **sobre** *la tierra.*
Guardar
bajo *llave;* **con** *candado;* **del** *calor;* **en** *la*
memoria; **entre** *la ropa;* **para** *otro*
momento.
Guardarse **de** *las malas compañías.*
Guarecerse
bajo *techo;* **del** *frío;* **en** *un portal.*
Guarnecer
con *ensalada;* **de** *patatas.*
Guasearse **de** *otro.*
Guerrear **con/contra** *los extranjeros.*
Guiar
a/hacia/hasta *la salida;* **a través**
de/por *el campo;* **con** *una linterna;* **en**
la oscuridad.
Guiarse **con/por** *una brújula.*
Gustar **de** *la buena comida.*

Haber
de *venir;* (*dinero*) **en** *el banco;* (*suficien-*
te) **para** *uno;* (*dos*) **por** *persona.*
Habilitar
con *muebles antiguos;* **de** *almacén;* **para**
el cargo.
Habitar **en** *León*
bajo *techo;* **con** *sus hijos;* **entre** *niños.*
Habituarse **a** *las costumbres.*
Hablar
acerca de/de/sobre *el tiempo;* **con** *los*
padres; **en** *nombre de todos;* **entre** *ellos;*
por *los otros;* **sin** *sentido.*
Hacer
(*algo*) **con** *mucho esfuerzo;* **de** *padre y*

madre; (*algo*) **en** *poco tiempo;* (*algo*)
para *el compañero;* (*todo*) **por** *los hijos;*
(*algo*) **sin** *ganas.*
Hacerse
al *trabajo;* **con/de** *los materiales adecua-*
dos; **en** *la forma correcta.*
Hallar
en *el suelo;* **por** *la calle.*
Hallarse
a *un paso de algún sitio;* **de** *paso;* **en** *el cine.*
Hartarse
a *correr;* **con** *pasteles;* **de** *vino.*
Hastiarse
con *los exámenes;* **de** *las fiestas.*
Helarse **de** *frío.*
Henchir
con *lana;* **de** *satisfacción.*
Heredar
a/de *un tío;* **por** *vía materna.*
Herir
de *gravedad;* **en** *el amor propio.*
Hermanar(se)
(*unos*) **con** *otros;* **entre** *sí.*
Herrar
a *fuego;* **en** *caliente.*
Hervir
a *fuego rápido;* **con** *poca agua;* (*un local*)
de *gente;* **en** *una olla;* **sobre** *el fogón.*
Hilar **con** *lana.*
Hincar **en** *la tierra.*
Hincarse
a *los pies;* **de** *rodillas.*
Hincharse
a *comer;* **con** *la comida;* **de** *bollos.*
Holgarse
con *su trato;* **de** *todo.*
Honrarse
con *la visita;* **en** *tener su amistad.*
Horrorizarse **con/de/por** *lo sucedido.*
Huir
a *otro país;* **ante** *los problemas;* **de** *casa.*
Humedecer
con *la lengua;* **de/en** *agua.*
Humillarse
a/ante *un superior;* **a** *hacer algo;* **con** *los*
inferiores.
Hundirse **en** *la miseria.*
Hurgar **en** *la herida.*
Hurtar
(*algo*) **al** *vendedor;* **de** *los almacenes.*

Hurtarse
a *la vista;* de *la mayoría.*

Identificar a *un delincuente.*
Identificar(se) con *los profesionales.*
Igualar(se)
a/con *los compañeros;* en *conocimientos.*
Imbuir de *ideas.*
Imitar
a *un actor;* con/en *los gestos.*
Impacientarse
con/por *el retraso;* de *esperar;* por *llegar.*
Impeler
a *hacer algo.*
Impermeabilizar
con *plástico;* contra *el agua.*
Implicar
a *la familia;* en *el asunto.*
Implicarse
con *alguien;* en *un tema.*
Imponer *(algo)* a/sobre *los demás;*
Importar
(algo) a *alguien; (algo)* de/desde *otro país.*
Importunar con *preguntas.*
Imposibilitar para *hacer algo.*
Impregnar(se) con/de/en *grasa.*
Imprimir
con *la impresora nueva;* en *el corazón;* sobre *papel satinado.*
Impulsar a *hacer cosas nuevas.*
Imputar *(algo)* al *rival.*
Incapacitar para *el deporte.*
Incautarse de *cosas.*
Incidir en *el tema.*
Incitar
a *la violencia;* contra *el enemigo.*
Inclinar
a *la benevolencia;* en favor de *los débiles.*
Inclinarse
a/hacia *un lado;* ante *las circunstancias;* hasta *el suelo;* por *un color;* sobre *la mesa.*

Incluir
en *los gastos;* entre *los invitados.*
Incorporar a/en *un archivo.*
Incorporarse al *trabajo.*
Incrementar(se) en *miles de pesetas.*
Incrustarse en *la piel.*
Inculcar
(una idea) a *los hijos;* en *la mente.*
Inculpar de *una infracción.*
Incumbir a *alguien.*
Incurrir en *delito.*
Indemnizar
con *dinero;* del *accidente;* por *el daño.*
Independizarse
de *la familia;* en *las cuestiones económicas.*
Indigestarse
con *pescado;* de *comer fruta;* por *beber leche.*
Indignarse
con *el novio;* contra *el vecino;* de/por *su conducta.*
Indisponer
con *mentiras;* contra *un amigo.*
Inducir a *cometer un crimen.*
Indultar
de *la pena;* por *buena conducta.*
Inferir
del *suceso;* por *lo visto.*
Infestar con/de *virus.*
Infiltrarse
en *el ejército enemigo;* entre *los otros.*
Inflamar(se) de/en *ira.*
Inflar(se) de *aire.*
Influir
ante *el jurado;* con *el compañero;* en *la decisión;* para *el perdón;* sobre *las conclusiones.*
Informar
del *viaje;* en *el congreso;* sobre *el tema.*
Infundir *(ánimos)* a/en *alguien.*
Ingeniarse
con *cualquier recurso;* para *sobrevivir.*
Ingerir
con *una paja;* de *un golpe;* por *la boca.*
Ingerirse en *asuntos ajenos.*
Ingresar en *la academia.*
Inhabilitar para *la carrera.*
Inhibirse
de *hacer algo;* en *el asunto.*

195

prepositions used with verbs

Iniciar(se) en *un idioma.*
Injertar en *una maceta.*
Inmiscuirse en *la vida de otro.*
Inmolar
a *los dioses;* en aras de *un ideal;* por *la patria.*
Inquietarse con/de/por *las notas.*
Inscribir(se) en *el club.*
Insertar en *un archivo.*
Insinuarse
a *alguien;* con *halagos.*
Insistir en *pagar*
Insolentarse con/contra *el oficial.*
Inspirar a *alguien.*
Inspirarse de *Cervantes;* en *El Quijote.*
Instalar en *la habitación.*
Instalarse en *otra ciudad.*
Instar
a *hacerlo;* sobre *el asunto.*
Instigar a *hacer una fechoría.*
Instruir
en *las ciencias;* sobre *química.*
Insubordinarse contra *el director.*
Insurreccionarse contra *el gobierno.*
Integrar(se) en *un equipo.*
Intercalar en *las actividades.*
Interceder
ante *el jefe;* en *favor* de *un compañero;* por *un amigo.*
Interesarse en/por *algo.*
Interferir(se) en *un asunto.*
Internar en *un colegio.*
Internarse
en *el bosque;* por *la jungla.*
Interponerse
en *la discusión;* entre *los hijos.*
Interpretar
del *alemán* al *español;* en *francés.*
Intervenir
con *el padre;* en *todo;* para *el reparto;* por *la acusada.*
Intimar con *María.*
Introducir(se)
en/por *todas partes;* entre *la gente.*
Inundar
de *agua;* en *lágrimas.*
Invernar en *el sur.*
Invertir en *un negocio.*
Investir
con *un título;* de *doctor honoris causa.*

Invitar
al *teatro;* con *una carta.*
Involucrar
a *un extraño;* en *el tema.*
Inyectar en *vena.*
Ir
a *comer;* con *la compañía;* contra *el equipo;* de *paseo;* de *un sitio* para *otro;* desde *Gijón;* en *tren;* entre *árboles;* hacia/hasta *Gerona;* por *el camino más corto;* tras *el delincuente.*
Irritarse
con/contra *el árbitro;* por *todo.*
Irrumpir en *la habitación.*

Jactarse de *los propios logros.*
Jaspear de *colores.*
Jubilar(se) del *trabajo.*
Jugar
al *tenis;* con *un amigo;* contra *una pareja;* por *otro.*
Juntar *(una cosa)* a/con *otra.*
Juntarse
con *los amigos;* en *una casa.*
Jurar
en *falso;* por *el honor;* sobre *la Biblia.*
Justificar(se)
ante *los padres;* con *el amigo;* de *lo ocurrido.*
Juzgar
a *un inocente;* de *imprudente;* entre *varios;* por *un crimen;* según *la costumbre.*

Labrar a *cincel*
Ladear(se) a/hacia *un lado.*
Ladrar a *un transeúnte.*
Lamentar(se) de/por *la desgracia.*
Languidecer de *tristeza.*
Lanzar

al *tejado;* con *un tirachinas;* contra *la gente;* de/desde *un escondite.*

Lanzarse
al *vacío;* con *salvavidas;* contra *el oponente;* en *paracaídas;* hacia *la izquierda;* sobre *la red.*

Largarse de *la oficina.*

Lastimarse
con *una zarza;* contra *el muro;* en *un pie.*

Lavar
con *agua;* en *la pila.*

Leer
a *Cortázar;* con *luz eléctrica;* de *corrido;* en *la biblioteca;* entre *líneas;* por *encima.*

Legar a *los hijos.*

Levantar
al *bebé;* de *la cuna;* en *brazos;* por *el aire;* sobre *los hombros.*

Levantarse
con *dolor de cabeza;* contra *la dictadura;* de *la cama;* en *armas.*

Liar con *bellas palabras.*

Liarse
a *golpes;* con *alguien.*

Liberar
al *rehén;* de *un deber.*

Liberarse de *una carga.*

Librar a cargo de/contra *una entidad.*

Licenciarse
del *ejército;* en *Periodismo.*

Lidiar con/contra *la gente;* por *algo.*

Ligar
a *Carlos;* con *Laura;* en *un bar.*

Ligarse con *una institución.*

Limitar
con *Galicia;* por *el Oeste.*

Limitarse a *escuchar.*

Limpiar
con *un trapo;* de *barro;* en *seco.*

Limpiarse
con *la esponja;* de *manchas;* en *la toalla.*

Lindar con *un prado.*

Lisonjear con *palabras amables.*

Litigar
con/contra *un compañero;* de/por *una medalla;* sobre *un aspecto.*

Llamar
a *la puerta;* con *los nudillos;* de *tú;* por *teléfono.*

Llamarse a *error.*

Llegar
al *cine;* con *un amigo;* de/desde *París;* en *tren;* hasta *la frontera;* por *los pelos.*

Llenar
con *agua;* de *leche;* hasta *el borde.*

Llevar
al *trabajo;* con *calma;* en *coche;* por *piezas;* sobre *los hombros.*

Llevarse
(bien) con *todos;* de *las pasiones; (algo)* por *delante.*

Llorar
con/de *emoción;* por *pena.*

Llover
a *cántaros;* sobre *el asfalto.*

Loar por *su paciencia.*

Localizar
a *un amigo;* en *la guía.*

Lograr *(algo)* de *alguien.*

Lucir
ante *todos;* **bajo** *los focos;* sobre *el vestido;* tras *las cortinas.*

Lucirse en *una representación.*

Lucrarse
a base de *robar;* con *los beneficios.*

Luchar
con/contra *el forastero;* contra *viento y marea;* por *un premio.*

Maldecir
al *culpable;* con *juramentos;* de/por *todo.*

Malearse con/por *las compañías.*

Malgastar en *caprichos.*

Malmeter con/contra *un compañero.*

Maltratar
a *los niños;* de *palabra;* hasta *hacer daño;* sin *piedad.*

Mamar
con *ansia;* de *la madre.*

Manar de *la fuente.*

Manchar
con *aceite;* de *tinta.*

Mandar

prepositions used with verbs

a *comprar algo;* **de** *recadero;* **en** *la pandilla;* **entre** *los amigos;* **por** *agua.*

Manifestarse
a favor/en contra de *una idea;* **en** *política;* **por** *la calle principal.*

Manipular
a *la gente;* **con** *cuidado;* **en** *la máquina.*

Mantener
(relaciones) **con** *alguien;* **en** *buen estado.*

Mantenerse
en *forma;* **del** *aire;* **con** *buen ánimo.*

Maquinar
con *un compañero;* **contra** *el jefe.*

Maravillarse con/de/por *el espectáculo.*

Marcar
a *mano;* **con** *rotulador;* **por** *todas partes.*

Marchar(se)
a *León;* **de** *Burgos;* **desde** *Salamanca;* **hacia** *Pamplona;* **hasta** *Valladolid;* **por** *tren.*

Matar
a *golpes;* **con** *una bala;* **de** *un disgusto;* **en** *la silla eléctrica;* **por** *accidente.*

Matizar con/de *numerosas precisiones.*

Matricularse
de *segundo curso;* **en** *el bachillerato;* **por** *libre.*

Mecer
a *la niña;* **con** *cuidado;* **en** *una cuna.*

Mediar
con/entre/por *los enfrentados;* **en** *la discusión.*

Medir
a *mano;* **con** *un metro;* **por** *palmos.*

Medirse
con *un metro;* **en** *la farmacia.*

Meditar en/sobre *los problemas sociales.*

Medrar en *el trabajo.*

Mejorar de/en *el nivel de vida.*

Merecer
con *creces;* **de/para** *su cargo;* **por** *su esfuerzo.*

Mermar en *volumen.*

Merodear por *la urbanización.*

Mesurarse en *las formas.*

Meter
(a alguien) **a** *trabajar;* **de** *jardinero;* **en/por** *vereda;* **entre** *el equipaje.*

Meterse
con *alguien;* **en** *un lío;* **entre** *el gentío.*

Mezclar
(algo) **a/con** *algo;* **en** *una sartén.*

Mezclarse
a/con/entre *los manifestantes;* **en** *jaleos.*

Militar en *un partido feminista.*

Mirar
a/hacia *el techo;* **con** *simpatía;* **de** *través;* **por** *sus derechos;* **sobre** *la mesa.*

Mirarse a/en *el espejo.*

Moderarse en *las críticas.*

Mofarse de *alguien.*

Mojar(se) con/en *agua fría.*

Moler(se)
a *trabajar;* **con** *tanto trabajo.*

Molestar con *demasiadas preguntas.*

Molestarse en *responder.*

Mondarse de *la risa.*

Montar
a *horcajadas;* **en** *barca;* **sobre** *sus espaldas.*

Morar en *una lujosa villa.*

Morir(se)
a causa de *una enfermedad;* **de** *pena;* **en** *su casa;* **entre** *sus seres queridos;* **para** *dar la vida a alguien.*

Mortificarse con *sentimientos de culpa.*

Motejar de *entrometido.*

Motivar
con *una recompensa;* **en** *el trabajo.*

Mover(se)
a *actuar;* **con** *decisión;* **de** *aquí para allá;* **por** *una causa justa.*

Mudar(se)
a *una casa más grande;* **de** *traje;* **en** *los propósitos.*

Multiplicar por *diez.*

Murmurar de *alguien.*

N

Nacer
al *mediodía;* **con** *pocos recursos;* **de** *padres campesinos;* **en** *un pueblo;* **para** *un alto destino.*

Nacionalizarse en *otro país.*
Nadar
a *braza;* **contra** *corriente;* **de** *espaldas;*
en *el río;* **hacia** *la orilla.*
Navegar
a/hacia/para *alta mar;* **con/en** *un barco pesquero;* **contra** *el viento;* **entre** *el oleaje.*
Necesitar
(alguien) **de** *algo;* **para** *comer.*
Negarse **a** *confesar los hechos.*
Negociar
con *una empresa;* **en** *un traspaso.*
Nivelarse **al/con** *el resto de los trabajadores.*
Nombrar **para** *ministro de defensa.*
Notar *(un cambio)* **en** *casa.*
Notificar **de** *un cambio de destino.*
Nutrir(se)
con/de *alimentos naturales;* **en** *abundancia.*

Obcecarse **con/en/por** *una idea fija.*
Obedecer
a *la profesora;* **con** *rapidez;* **sin** *dudarlo.*
Obligar
a *reparar su falta;* **con** *su autoridad;* **por** *la fuerza.*
Obrar
a *conciencia;* **con** *responsabilidad;* **en** *provecho propio;* **por** *el bien ajeno.*
Obsequiar **con** *dulces.*
Obsesionarse **con/por** *alguien.*
Obstar *(algo)* **a/para** *un fin.*
Obstinarse
(en ir) **contra** *todo;* **en** *llevar la contraria.*
Obtener(se)
(algo) **con** *esfuerzo;* **de** *buenas maneras de alguien.*
Ocultar
a/de *la vista;* **con** *unas cortinas;* **detrás de/tras** *la puerta;* **entre** *las páginas de un libro.*
Ocuparse **con/de/en** *el cuidado de sus animales.*

Ocurrir **con** *celeridad.*
Odiar **a/de** *muerte.*
Ofenderse **con/de/por** *un agravio.*
Oficiar **de** *testigo.*
Ofrecerse
a/para *trabajar;* **de** *camarero;* **en calidad de** *ayudante.*
Oír
bajo/en *secreto;* **con** *interés;* **de** *boca de alguien;* **por** *las paredes.*
Oler **a** *flores.*
Olvidarse **de** *guardar las apariencias.*
Operarse **de** *una rodilla.*
Opinar
acerca de/de/en/sobre *literatura;* **con** *juicio.*
Oponer *(algo)* **a/contra** *algo.*
Oponerse
al *sistema judicial;* **con** *firmeza.*
Opositar **a** *notarías.*
Oprimir
a *los ciudadanos;* **con** *violencia.*
Optar
a/por *una carrera;* **entre** *dos posibilidades.*
Orar **en favor de/por** *los muertos.*
Ordenar(se)
de *sacerdote;* **en/por** *colores.*
Organizar *(algo)* **en/por** *partes.*
Orientar(se)
a/hacia *el sur;* **por** *una brújula.*
Oscilar **entre** *dos deseos.*

Pactar
con/entre *los adversarios;* **por** *necesidad.*
Padecer **con/de/por** *unas fiebres.*
Pagar
a *un banco;* **de** *la fianza;* **en/con** *dinero en efectivo;* **por/para** *el alquiler del local.*
Paladearse **con** *un postre casero.*
Paliar *(algo)* **con** *algo.*
Palidecer
ante/bajo/con *las adversidades;* **de** *terror.*

prepositions used with verbs

Palpar
con *cuidado*; (*algo*) entre *algo*; por *encima*.
Parar(se)
a/ante/en *la entrada*; con *un frenazo*; de *golpe*; entre *los coches*.
Parecerse
a *alguien*; de/en *el perfil*.
Participar
de *los beneficios*; en *el sorteo*.
Particularizarse
(*algo*) con *precisión*; (*alguien*) en *el trato con alguien*.
Partir
a/hacia/para *América*; con *tristeza*; de *su tierra*; en busca de *fortuna*; por *necesidad*.
Pasar
al *salón*; ante *la audiencia*; bajo *la puerta*; de *fecha*; en *tropel*; entre *el público*; por/sobre *el puente*.
Pasarse
de *gracioso*; sin *trabajar*.
Pasear
a/con *los niños*; en/por *el campo*; sobre *la hierba*.
Pasearse a *caballo*.
Pasmarse con/de *la noticia*.
Pavonearse con/de *la victoria*.
Pecar
con/en *el pensamiento*; contra *la decencia*; de/por *franqueza*.
Pedir
a *los magistrados*; en *préstamo*; para el *autobús*; por *los necesitados*.
Pegar
(*algo*) a/en *algo*; con *pegamento*; contra *el reverso*.
Pegarse (*alguien*) a/con *alguien*.
Pelear(se)
con/contra *alguien*; en *defensa propia*; por *tonterías*.
Peligrar de *muerte*.
Penar
de *deseo*; en *el exilio*; por *su vida*.
Pender
ante/de/sobre *su cabeza*; en *el vacío*.
Penetrar
en *la casa*; entre/por *la espesura*; hacia/hasta *el interior*.

Pensar
(*algo*) de *alguien*; en/sobre *sus problemas*; entre/para *sí*.
Percatarse de *algo*.
Percibir (*algo*) por *algo*.
Perder a/en *el parchís*.
Perderse
en *la feria*; por *holgazán*.
Perecer
a *las doce de la noche*; de *pulmonía*; en *el hospital*.
Peregrinar a/por *tierras lejanas*.
Perfumar con *agua de rosas*.
Permanecer
con *salud*; en *silencio*; hasta *mañana*; sin *cambios*; tras *su objetivo*.
Permutar con/por *dos días de permiso*.
Perpetuar(se) en *sus obras*.
Perseguir
al *ladrón*; en *coche*; entre *la gente*.
Perseverar en *el empeño*.
Persistir en *la decisión tomada*.
Personarse
ante *la juez*; en *las urnas*.
Persuadir
con *ardor*; de *su valía*.
Pertenecer a *un partido*.
Pertrecharse
con/de *víveres*; para *el asedio*.
Pesar sobre *la conciencia*.
Picar
de *la nevera*; en *todo momento*.
Picarse
con *sus compañeros*; en *la reunión*; por *sus críticas*.
Pinchar(se)
con *una espina*; en *un dedo*.
Pintar
a *la acuarela*; con *pinceles*; de *rojo*; en *la pared*.
Pirrarse por *los dulces*.
Pisar
con *los pies descalzos*; en/por/sobre *las piedras*.
Pitorrearse de *alguien*.
Plagarse de *deudas*.
Planear sobre *las colinas*.
Plantar en *el jardín*.
Plantarse en medio de *una celebración*.

p

Plañir **de** dolor.
Plasmar (una idea) **en** un dibujo.
Pleitear
con/contra la empresa; **por** conseguir derechos.
Poblar
con/de pinos; **en** profundidad.
Poblarse **de** edificios.
Poder (subir) **con** dificultad.
Ponderar **de** grandioso.
Poner(se)
a/ante la vista; **bajo** resguardo; **como** condición; **contra** alguien; **de** manifiesto; **en** cuestión; **entre** interrogaciones; **sobre** el tablero.
Porfiar
con/contra los adversarios; **en** la lucha; **sobre** algo.
Portarse **con** dignidad.
Portear
con/en un camión; **por** tierra.
Posar
ante/para el fotógrafo; **en** una foto; **sobre** un caballo.
Posarse (un insecto) **en/sobre** algo.
Posesionarse **de** una propiedad.
Posponer **a/hasta** la primavera.
Postrarse
en/por el suelo; **ante** la concurrencia; **del** susto.
Practicar **en** un gimnasio.
Precaverse **contra/de** el frío.
Preceder **en** edad.
Preciarse **de** experto.
Precipitarse
a su encuentro; **de/desde** lo alto; **en** sus brazos; **por** la ladera.
Predestinar **a/para** la magia.
Predisponer (a una persona) **a/contra/para** algo.
Predominar (algo) **en/sobre** algo.
Preferir (algo) **a/entre** algo.
Preguntar
a los presentes; **con** curiosidad; **por** lo ocurrido.
Prendarse **de** sus ojos.
Prender
(un broche) **a/de/en** un vestido; **con** alfileres.
Preocuparse **con/de/por** alguien.

Prepararse
a oír de todo; **contra/para** el frío.
Prescindir **de** ayuda.
Presentar **para** concurso.
Presentarse
al auditorio; **bajo** candidatura; **con** retraso; **de** improviso; **en** su ciudad; **por** Sevilla.
Preservar(se) **contra/de** la gripe.
Presidir
en un certamen; **por** la antigüedad.
Prestar
(algo) **a** alguien; (algo) **para** una temporada; **sobre** garantía.
Prestarse **a** ayudar.
Presumir **de** riqueza.
Presupuestar **en** cinco millones de pesetas.
Prevalecer (algo) **entre/sobre** algo.
Prevenir (a alguien) **contra/de/sobre** algo.
Prevenirse
a tiempo; **con** unos ahorros; **contra/de/en/para** la escasez.
Principiar (algo) **con/en/por** algo.
Pringarse
con/de chocolate; **en** un delito.
Privar(se) **de** algo.
Probar
a hacer un injerto; **de** todo.
Proceder
a/en la investidura; **con/sin** orden; **contra** los acusados.
Procesar (a alguien) **por** algo.
Procurar (algo) **para/por** algo.
Prodigarse **en** palabras.
Producir(se)
(algo) **ante** alguien; **en** cadena.
Progresar **en** matemáticas.
Prohibir
bajo cualquier concepto; **de** forma terminante.
Prolongar(se) (la sesión) **en** horas.
Prometer
(algo) **a** alguien; **en** privado; (algo) **por** algo.
Promover (a alguien) **a/para** algo.
Pronunciarse **en** favor de/por alguien.
Propagar (un rumor) **en/por** todo el pueblo; **entre** la gente.

p

---

prepositions used with verbs

Propagarse *(un fuego)* **al** *piso de arriba;* **por** *todas partes.*

Propasarse
(alguien) **a costa de/con** *alguien; (alguien)* **en** *algo.*

Propender *(alguien)* **a** *algo.*

Proponer
(algo) **a** *alguien;* **en** *público; (a alguien)* **para/por** *algo.*

Proporcionar
(algo) **a** *alguien; (algo)* **para** *algo.*

Prorrogar **por** *un año.*

Prorrumpir **en** *sollozos.*

Proseguir *(alguien)* **con/en** *algo.*

Prosternarse
a/para *rezar;* **ante** *el icono;* **en** *la iglesia.*

Prostituir
a *alguien;* **en** *provecho propio;* **por** *interés.*

Proteger(se)
a *alguien;* **contra/de** *la lluvia.*

Protestar
contra/por *el desempleo;* **de** *forma organizada.*

Proveer
a *los agricultores;* **con/de** *suficiente maquinaria.*

Provenir **de** *un ambiente urbano.*

Provocar
a *alguien;* **con** *una actitud.*

Proyectar *(algo)* **a/en/sobre** *algo.*

Pudrirse **de** *aburrimiento.*

Pugnar
con/contra *la sociedad;* **en** *un debate;* **para/por** *la victoria.*

Pujar
con/contra *el vendedor;* **en/sobre** *un precio;* **por** *una rebaja.*

Purgar(se)
con *una dieta; (algo)* **de** *algo.*

Purificarse *(de algo)* **con** *algo.*

Quebrantar *(una norma)* **por** *necesidad.*

Quebrar(se)

con *estrépito;* **en** *cuatro trozos;* **por** *la mitad.*

Quedar(se)
a *comer;* **con** *la mejor parte;* **sin** *fuerzas.*

Quejarse
a/de *sus vecinos;* **por** *todo.*

Quemarse
con *una cerilla;* **de** *deseo;* **por** *su amor.*

Querellarse
ante *el juez;* **contra** *la empresa;* **por** *los impuestos.*

Querer **con** *pasión.*

Quitar(se) **de** *en medio.*

Rabiar
de *indignación;* **por** *el ultraje.*

Radiar **en/por** *onda larga.*

Radicar *(algo)* **en** *algo.*

Raer **con** *el uso.*

Ramificarse **en** *muchas direcciones.*

Ratificarse **en** *la oferta.*

Rayar
con *un lápiz;* **en** *lo imposible.*

Razonar
con *corrección;* **sobre** *filosofía.*

Rebajar
(una salsa) **con** *agua;* **del** *precio de venta.*

Rebajarse
a *reconocer su error;* **ante** *los asistentes;* **de** *su orgullo.*

Rebasar *(los límites)* **de** *algo.*

Rebatir
a *su interlocutor;* **con** *buenos argumentos;* **de** *su postura.*

Rebelarse **contra** *sus padres.*

Rebosar
de *salud; (algo)* **en** *algo;* **hasta** *el borde.*

Rebozar **en** *harina y huevo.*

Recabar
con *esfuerzo; (algo)* **de** *alguien.*

Recaer *(la responsabilidad)* **en/sobre** *alguien.*

Recapacitar **sobre** *su actitud.*

Recargar *(un vestido)* **con/de** *adornos.*

prepositions used with verbs

Recatarse de las miradas.
Recelar(se) de sus compañeros.
Recetar
al paciente; contra el dolor.
Recibir
a los invitados; de su madre; en préstamo; (una carta) por avión.
Reclamar
a/ante/de la justicia; contra/por un fraude; en el juzgado.
Reclinar (la cabeza) contra la pared; en/sobre sus rodillas.
Reclinarse en; sobre el sofá.
Recobrarse de un disgusto.
Recoger
a sus abuelos; con el coche; de/en la estación.
Recogerse a/en la cama temprano.
Recomendar
a su amiga; para el puesto.
Reconcentrarse en sus problemas.
Reconciliar(se) con su familia.
Reconocer
a/ante sus hijos; en el acto; entre la gente; por el rostro.
Reconquistar del olvido.
Reconvenir
con reproches; por su mala educación.
Reconvertir en una industria pesquera.
Recorrer de/desde un extremo al otro.
Recostarse en/sobre la cama.
Recrearse con/en la pintura.
Recubrir con una manta.
Recurrir
a la medicina natural; contra la sentencia.
Redimir de sus pecados.
Redondear en números exactos.
Reducir
a la mitad; de tamaño.
Reducirse
a lo esencial; en los gastos.
Redundar en un perjuicio.
Reemplazar
con/por otra empleada; en el puesto.
Reencarnarse en otro ser.
Referirse a sus negocios.
Reflejar
en el espejo; sobre la superficie.
Reflexionar
en solitario; sobre el problema.

Reformarse en el reformatorio.
Refregarse
con una esponja; contra la hierba.
Refrescarse
con una ducha; en la piscina.
Refugiarse
bajo un techo; contra la tormenta; en el interior.
Refundir
en bronce; para hacer una estatua.
Refutar con conocimiento de causa.
Regalar (algo) a alguien.
Regalarse
con una buena comida; en la conversación.
Regar
con poca agua; por la noche.
Reglarse a/por las normas.
Regocijarse de/con/por la noticia.
Regodearse con/en el éxito.
Regresar a su ciudad natal; del extranjero.
Rehabilitar al empleado; en su anterior cargo.
Rehacerse de una separación.
Rehogar
a fuego lento; con aceite.
Reinar
en Francia; sobre muchos países.
Reincidir en una mala conducta.
Reincorporar al equipo.
Reintegrar(se) a/en su puesto.
Reírse
con/de alguien; por todo; sin parar.
Relacionarse con/entre los demás estudiantes.
Relajar(se)
con un masaje; de sus obligaciones; en la playa.
Relamerse de gusto.
Relevar de la dirección.
Rellenar (un bizcocho) de crema.
Rematar
al moribundo; con crueldad.
Remitirse a los hechos.
Remontarse
a/hasta el pasado; en el vuelo; sobre las montañas.
Remover con una cuchara.
Renacer a la vida.

prepositions used with verbs

Rendirse
a *la evidencia;* con *resignación;* de *cansancio.*
Renegar   de *sus orígenes.*
Renunciar
a *un nombramiento;* en favor de *alguien.*
Reñir
a *sus hijos;* por *sus travesuras.*
Reparar
con *trabajo;* en *alguien.*
Repartir
a/entre   *las niñas;* en *el recreo.*
Repasar   por *las faltas.*
Repercutir   en *el ánimo.*
Reponerse   de *una discusión.*
Reposar   de *la carrera.*
Reprender   de *malas maneras.*
Representar
a *su país;* con *dignidad;* en/para   *las olimpiadas.*
Reprimirse   de *comer en exceso.*
Reputar
de/por   *bondadoso;* en *mucho.*
Requerir   de *amores.*
Resaltar   (un color) de *otro.*
Resarcirse
con *su desprecio;* de *la ofensa.*
Resbalar   con/en/sobre   *el hielo.*
Resbalarse   de/entre   *las manos.*
Rescatar
al *prisionero;* de *la cárcel;* por *el mar.*
Resentirse
con/contra   *alguien;* de/por   *un agravio.*
Reservar   (algo) a/para   *alguien.*
Reservarse
(alguien) a/para   *algo;* en *las confidencias.*
Resguardarse   del *frío.*
Residir
en *la capital;* entre *dos ciudades.*
Resignarse   a/con/en   *su tipo de vida.*
Resistir(se)   a *la tentación.*
Resolverse   a *actuar.*
Resonar
con *estrépito;* en *todo el edificio.*
Respaldarse
con *una buena abogada;* contra *la pared.*
Resplandecer
a/con/por   *la luz;* contra/en   *el horizonte;* de *belleza.*

Responder
a *las preguntas;* con *decisión;* de *su hijo.*
Responsabilizarse   de *un cargo.*
Restablecerse   de *una gripe.*
Restar   (algo) a/de   *algo.*
Restituir   a *su propietaria.*
Restregar   (algo) con/contra   *algo.*
Restringirse   al *presupuesto.*
Resucitar   de *la muerte.*
Resumir(se)   en *pocas palabras.*
Resurgir   de *sus cenizas.*
Retar
a *un desempate;* con *furia.*
Retener   en *la memoria.*
Retirarse
a *un convento;* del *mundo.*
Retorcerse   de/por   *un dolor.*
Retornar
a/de   *Italia;* en *un año.*
Retractarse   de *lo afirmado.*
Retraerse
a *su dolor;* de *las miradas.*
Retrasar   en *el pago.*
Retroceder
a/hacia   *el pasado;* en *el tiempo.*
Reunir   a *todos los vecinos.*
Reunirse   con *todos los vecinos.*
Reventar   de/por   *tanto comer.*
Revertir
a *largo plazo;* en *dinero.*
Revestir(se)   (algo) con/de   *algo.*
Revolcarse   en/por/sobre   *la arena.*
Revolver
con *prisas;* en/entre   *los cajones.*
Revolverse   contra/sobre   *el amo.*
Rezar
a/por   *sus muertos;* en *una ermita.*
Rimar   con *el verso anterior.*
Rivalizar
con *los oponentes;* en/por   *el poder.*
Rodar
al/por *el suelo;* bajo/de   *la mesa.*
Rodearse   de *buenas compañías.*
Roer   con *los dientes.*
Rogar
a *su madre;* por *los ausentes.*
Romper
a *llover;* con *la Iglesia;* en *carcajadas;* por *un extremo.*

Rozar(se)
con/contra *el techo;* **en** *el trato.*

S

Saber
a *gloria;* **de/por** *cierto.*
Saborear **con** *calma.*
Sacar
al *exterior;* **de** *la casa;* **en** *volandas;* **por** *conclusión.*
Saciar(se) **con/de** *fruta.*
Sacrificarse
a *trabajar duro;* **por** *sus padres.*
Sacudir(se) **de** *polvo.*
Salir
a *la calle;* **con** *frecuencia;* **en** *los periódicos;* **para** *senadora.*
Salpicar **con/de** *agua.*
Saltar
al *vacío;* **de** *rama en rama;* **en/por** *el aire.*
Salvar
a *su hijo;* **con/por** *sus atenciones;* **de** *caer enfermo.*
Sanar
a *los enfermos;* **con/por** *remedios tradicionales.*
Satisfacer
a *los trabajadores;* **con** *buenos sueldos.*
Saturarse **de** *trabajar.*
Secar(se)
al *aire;* **con** *el sol;* **sobre** *la hierba.*
Secundar **en** *la propuesta.*
Sedimentar **en** *la exposición* **al** *sol.*
Segar
a *mano;* **con** *tractor.*
Segregar *(algo)* **de** *algo.*
Seguir **con/en** *un proyecto.*
Seguirse *(algo)* **de** *lo hablado.*
Sembrar
con/de *grano;* **en** *la huerta;* **por** *mayo.*
Sentarse
a *la sombra;* **bajo** *un árbol;* **entre** *las flores;* **junto a** *la anfitriona;* **sobre** *un cojín;* **tras** *el arbusto.*
Sentenciar
a *la cárcel;* **en** *juicio público.*

Sentir
con *intensidad;* **en** *el alma; (algo)* **por** *alguien.*
Sentirse
con/sin *fuerzas;* **de** *buen humor.*
Señalar **con** *un cartel.*
Señalarse
en *la capacidad política;* **por** *su honestidad.*
Separar(se) **de** *su marido.*
Sepultar **bajo/en** *el olvido.*
Ser
a *gusto de todos;* **de** *buena calidad;* **por** *su bien.*
Servir
a *los ciudadanos;* **con** *lealtad;* **de** *ayuda.*
Servirse **de** *una oportunidad.*
Significar *(algo)* **a/para** *alguien.*
Significarse **por** *su rectitud.*
Simpatizar **con** *sus ideas.*
Simultanear **con** *otra ocupación.*
Sincerarse
ante/con *los amigos;* **de** *los hechos.*
Sincronizarse **con** *el ritmo de la empresa.*
Singularizarse
con/en/por *su trato;* **entre** *los demás.*
Sisar **de/en** *unos grandes almacenes.*
Sitiar **por** *todos los frentes.*
Situar(se) **en** *primera fila.*
Sobrepasar
a *los demás conductores;* **en** *inteligencia.*
Sobreponerse **a** *su nerviosismo.*
Sobresalir
en *ciencias;* **por** *sus aptitudes.*
Sobresaltarse **con/por** *un ruido.*
Sobrevivir **al** *accidente.*
Socorrer
con *casa y comida;* **de** *su grave situación.*
Solazarse
con *un concierto;* **en** *su casa del campo.*
Solicitar
(algo) **a/de** *alguien; (algo)* **para** *algo.*
Solidarizarse **con** *los oprimidos.*
Soltar(se)
a *hablar;* **de** *la cuerda.*
Someterse **a/bajo** *su custodia.*
Sonar
a *falso;* **en** *el piso de arriba.*
Sonreír **con** *tristeza.*
Soñar **con** *un viaje;* **en** *voz alta.*

---

prepositions used with verbs

Sorprender a *alguien.*
Sospechar de *sus intenciones.*
Sostener
al *bebé;* en *los brazos.*
Subdividir en *tres partes.*
Subir
al *avión;* en *el ascensor;* por *las escaleras.*
Subordinar (*algo*) a *algo.*
Subrogar (*algo*) con/por *algo.*
Subscribirse a *una revista.*
Subsistir
con *poco;* de *la asistencia social.*
Subvenir a *las necesidades.*
Suceder (*algo*) a *alguien.*
Sucumbir a/ante/bajo *la tentación.*
Sufrir
de *dolor de cabeza;* por *los demás.*
Sujetar(se)
a *la ley;* con *una cuerda;* por *la cintura.*
Sumarse a *las protestas.*
Sumergir(se) bajo/en *el agua.*
Sumirse en *la incertidumbre.*
Supeditar a *una votación.*
Superponer(se) a *la tristeza.*
Suplicar (*algo*) a *alguien.*
Suplir
(*alguien*) a *alguien;* en *un cargo.*
Surgir
en *el cielo;* entre *las nubes.*
Surtir a *alguien;* de *alimento.*
Suspender
en *una asignatura;* por *faltas de ortografía.*
Suspirar de *amor;* por *una casa.*
Sustentarse con/de *poco.*
Sustituir
(*alguien*) a *alguien;* en *la dirección.*
Sustraerse a/de *las miradas ajenas.*

Tachar
(*a alguien*) de *inútil;* por *incapaz.*
Tachonar
con *adornos;* (*el cielo*) de *estrellas.*
Tallar
a *mano;* en *mármol.*

Tañer con *entusiasmo.*
Tapar con *una sábana.*
Tardar en *hacer la comida.*
Tarifar con *su jefe.*
Tejer con *hilo.*
Televisar en *directo.*
Temblar
con *la noticia;* de *miedo;* por *la emoción.*
Temer
a/de *alguien;* por *su vida.*
Tender a *mejorar.*
Tenderse en/por *el suelo.*
Tener
a *mano;* ante *la vista;* de/por *amigo;*
entre *manos;* para *sí;* sobre *el regazo.*
Tenerse
a *lo dispuesto;* de/en *pie;* por *importante.*
Tentar
(*a alguien*) a *hacer algo;* con *una proposición.*
Teñir con/de/en *verde.*
Terciar
con *su rival;* en *la discusión;* entre *los enemigos.*
Terminar
de *hacer su trabajo;* en *punta;* por *convencerse.*
Testimoniar
con *su palabra;* sobre *el asunto.*
Tirar
a *matar;* con *fuerza;* contra *la muralla;*
de *la manta;* sobre *el objetivo.*
Tirarse
al/por *el suelo;* entre *la hierba.*
Tiritar de *frío.*
Titubear ante/en *la decisión.*
Tocar
a *rebato* (*las campanas*); con *la mano;*
de *oído;* en *la puerta.*
Tomar
a *broma;* bajo *su mando;* con/entre *sus manos;* de *la estantería;* para *sí;* por *tonto.*
Topar con/contra *la pared.*
Torcer a/hacia *un lado.*
Tostarse
al/bajo *el sol;* con *un bronceador.*
Trabajar
a *destajo;* de *profesor;* en *un oficio;* para *vivir;* por *hacerse valer.*

Trabar *(algo)* **con** *algo.*
Trabarse
al *hablar;* **con** *las palabras.*
Traducir **al/del/en** *latín.*
Traer
a *casa;* **ante** *sus padres;* **consigo;** **de** *Francia;* **en/entre** *manos.*
Traficar
con *armas;* **en** *drogas.*
Transferir
(algo) **a/en** *alguien;* **de** *un banco a otro.*
Transfigurarse
con/por *la noticia;* **en** *otra persona.*
Transformar(se) *(algo)* **en** *otra cosa.*
Transitar **por** *la carretera.*
Transmutar *(algo)* **en** *algo.*
Transpirar
con *el calor;* **por** *la piel.*
Transportar
a *hombros;* **de** *un lado a otro;* **en** *avión;* **sobre** *una plataforma.*
Trasbordar
a *otro tren;* **de** *un barco a otro.*
Trasegar *(el vino)* **de** *un recipiente a otro.*
Trasladar
a *otro despacho;* **de** *un sitio a otro.*
Traspasar *(algo)* **a** *alguien.*
Trasplantar **de** *un lado a otro.*
Tratar
a *los amigos;* **acerca de/sobre** *un problema;* **con** *los demás.*
Trepar
a *un árbol;* **por** *un cuerda.*
Triunfar
en *el encuentro;* **sobre** *los rivales.*
Trocar *(algo)* **en/por** *algo.*
Tropezar **con/contra/en** *una piedra.*
Turbarse **por** *la emoción.*

Ufanarse **con/de/por** *el triunfo.*
Ultrajar
con *insultos;* **de** *palabra y obra;* **en** *su honor.*

Uncir
al *carro;* *(un animal)* **con** *otro.*
Ungir(se)
con *aceite;* **por** *todo el cuerpo.*
Uniformar
a *todos;* **de** *rojo.*
Unir *(una cosa)* **a/con** *otra.*
Unirse
a/con *los demás;* **en** *la petición;* **entre** *todos.*
Untar
a *alguien;* **con/de** *aceite.*
Usar **de** *malas artes.*
Utilizar
a *una amiga;* **de** *prueba;* **en** *los viajes.*

Vaciar
de *contenido;* **en** *un molde.*
Vaciarse
de *líquido;* **por** *un agujero.*
Vacilar
en *la decisión;* **entre** *una cosa y otra.*
Vagabundear **de** *un lado* **a/para** *otro.*
Vagar **por** *el campo.*
Valer
para *médico;* **por** *dos.*
Valerse
de *alguien o de algo.*
Vanagloriarse **de/por** *sus hechos.*
Varar **en** *la arena.*
Variar **de** *opinión.*
Velar
a *un enfermo;* **en** *defensa* **de** *sus intereses;* **por** *su vida.*
Vencer
a *los enemigos;* **a/con/por** *traición;* **en** *el combate;* **por** *puntos.*
Vender
a/en/por *un precio muy alto;* **al/por** *mayor;* **con** *pérdidas;* **de** *contrabando.*
Venderse
a *alguien;* **por** *dinero.*
Vengarse
con *crueldad;* **de/por** *un crimen.*

prepositions used with verbs

Venir(se)
a *casa*; **con/en** *coche*; **de/desde** *allí*; **hacia/hasta** *aquí*; **para** *el verano*; **por** *buen camino*.

Ver
con *sus propios ojos*; **por** *la ventana*.

Veranear en *la montaña*.

Verse
con *los amigos*; **en** *el espejo*; **entre** *los suyos*; **sin** *recursos*.

Verter
al *suelo*; **de** *un tonel*; **hacia** *el mar*.

Vestir a *la moda*.

Vestirse de *gala*.

Viajar
a *pie*; **de** *noche*; **en/por** *avión*; **hacia/hasta** *la frontera*.

Viciarse
con/de/por *el trato de alguien*.

Vigilar
al *niño*; **en defensa de/por** *el bien común*.

Violentarse al/en *responder*.

Virar
a/hacia *mar adentro*; **de** *costado*; **en** *redondo*; **sobre** *el ancla*.

Vivir
a *gusto*; **con** *nada*; **de** *las rentas*; **en** *paz*; **hasta** *los cien años*; **para** *ver*; **sin** *pena ni gloria*.

Volar
a/por *el cielo*; **con** *sus propias alas*; **de** *rama* **en** *rama*; **en** *avión*; **sobre** *el mar*.

Volver
a/hacia/para *casa*; **de** *noche*; **en/sobre** *sí*; **por** *el mismo lugar*.

Votar
a *los candidatos*; **con** *la mayoría*; **en** *las elecciones*; **por** *su partido*.

Yacer
con *su amante*; **en** *un sepulcro*; **sin** *vida*; **sobre** *la cama*.

Zafarse de *la realidad*.

Zaherir con *insultos*.

Zambullir(se) bajo/en *el agua*.

Zarpar del *puerto*.

Zozobrar con/en/por *la tormenta*.

Zurcir con *hilo*.

idiomatic and figurative expressions

idiomatic expressions

1. ACORDARSE

1. Acordarse de la familia de alguien.
Insult someone at length (ironic expression).

2. "¡Te vas a acordar de mí!"
= "¡Ése se va a acordar de mí!"
"You'll be hearing from me!" (threat).

2. ACOSTARSE

Acostarse con las gallinas.
C. Go to bed very early.

3. AGARRARSE

Agarrarse a un clavo ardiendo.
Clutch at straws (*a burning nail*).

4. AGUANTAR

Aguantar carros y carretas.
= Tragar/pasar carros y carretas.
Put up with murder (*Bear cars and carts*).

5. AGUAR

Aguar la fiesta.
Throw cold water on the party.

6. AJUSTAR

Ajustarle las cuentas (a alguien).
A. Settle accounts with someone.
B. Tell someone off.

7. ANDAR

1. Andar de boca en boca.
Be in everyone's mouth.
2. Andar de cabeza.
Burn the candle at both ends.

⚠ *C* = very colloquial

8. ANUNCIAR
Anunciar a bombo y platillo.
Announce with a lot of ballyhoo.

9. APAGAR
"Entonces, apaga y vámonos."
C. "OK, let's just drop it"
(because there's no solution).

10. APEARSE
1. Apearse del burro.
= Bajarse del burro.
= Caer(se) del burro.
C. Admit a fault
(*Get off the donkey*).
2. Apearse del carro.
= Bajarse del carro.
C. Give up on an idea.

11. APRETAR
**1. Apretar las clavijas
(a alguien).**
Be hard on someone
(*Tighten the screws*).
APRETARSE
**2. Apretarse el
cinturón.**
Tighten one's belt.

12. ARMAR(SE)
1. Armar(se) un cristo.
**= Armar(se) la de Dios
es Cristo.**
C. Organize a riot (*a Christ*).
ARMARSE
2. Armarse la gorda.
C. Start a scandal or riot
(*the big one*).

13. ARRIMAR
1. Arrimar (alguien) el ascua a su sardina.
C. Do something in one's own interests.
2. Arrimar el hombro.
C. Put a shoulder to it.

14. ATAR
1. Atar cabos.
Put two and two together (*Tie ends*).
2. Atar corto a alguien.
Keep a tight rein on someone.

⚠ C = very colloquial

idiomatic expressions

15. BAILAR

1. **Bailarle el agua a alguien.**
= Hacerle la rosca/
la pelota a alguien.
Suck up to someone
(to obtain an advantage).
2. **"Otro/a que tal baila."**
C. "They are two of a kind"
(negative comment).
3. **"Que me quiten lo baila(d)o."**
"Nothing can take away the
good times I've had."

16. BAJAR

1. **Bajarle los humos a alguien.**
Take someone down a peg.
BAJAR(SE)
2. **Bajarse del burro.**
(See Apearse, 10, 1.)
3. **Bajarse del carro.**
(See Apearse, 10, 2.)

17. BARRER

**Barrer para/
hacia dentro.**
Look after number one.

18. BRILLAR

Brillar por su ausencia. (P.ej.: la simpatía.)
Be conspicuous by its (his/her) absence
(e.g., sympathy).

19. BUSCAR

1. **Buscarle (a alguien) las cosquillas.**
= Buscarle a alguien las pulgas.
C. Rub someone the wrong way, tease.
BUSCARSE
2. **Buscarse la vida.**
Try to scratch out a living.

20. (NO) CABER

1. **No caber(le) en la
cabeza (a alguien).**
= No entrarle algo en la cabeza
a alguien.
Be beyond someone.
2. **No caber un alfiler.** ——
Be crammed full (not have
room for a pin).

⚠ C = very colloquial

Spanish Verb Manual

21. CAER

1. Caer como una bomba.
Go down like a lead balloon.

2. Caer(se) del burro. (See Apearse, 10, 1.)

3. Caer en gracia.
Be in favor, please.

4. Caer en la cuenta.
Realize, understand.

5. Caer gordo.
Get on someone's nerves (Fall fat).

AERSE

Caerse de espaldas. ⟶
e very surprised by something
all on one's back).

7. Caérsele (a alguien) la baba (con/por alguien).
C. Pop one's buttons with pride.

8. Caérsele (a alguien) la cara de vergüenza.
Bow one's head in shame.

9. Caérsele (a alguien) la casa encima.
Have cabin fever.

10. Caérsele (a alguien) los anillos.
Not want to dirty one's fingernails with a job.

11. Caerse redondo.
Fall in a heap.

22. CALENTARSE

Calentarse la cabeza.
C. Think much about something.

23. CANTAR

Cantar las cuarenta.
C. Talk straight to someone
(Sing the forty).

24. CEPILLARSE

Cepillarse a alguien.
C. A. Get rid of someone (e.g., who is
an obstacle at work).
C. B. Throw a student out of a class.
C. C. Have sexual relations with someone.

⚠ C = very colloquial

idiomatic expressions

25. CERRAR
1. Cerrar con broche de oro.
End with a grand finale.
CERRARSE
2. Cerrarse en banda.
Stick to one's guns, refusing
to say anything more.

26. CLAVAR
1. Clavar (a alguien).
C. Stick it to someone (overcharge).
CLAVARSE
2. Clavarse/tener clavada una cosa en el alma.
Pierce one's heart.

27. COGER
1. Coger a alguien por banda.
Bug someone to get his/her attention.
2. "Dios nos coja confesados."
"Someone better be prayed up!" ("May God catch us confessed!").

28. COMER
1. Comer a dos carrillos.
= Ponerse morado.
C. Eat like a horse (with both cheeks).
2. Comerle el coco (a alguien).
C. Convince someone using pressure,
brainwash.
COMERSE
3. Comerse el coco/el tarro.
C. Worry a lot about something.

29. CORTAR
1. Cortar el bacalao.
= Partir el bacalao.
C. Be the boss (Cut the codfish).
2. Cortarle las alas (a alguien).
Clip someone's wings.
3. Cortar por lo sano.
Put an end to a bad situation (for the healthy one).
CORTARSE
4. Cortarse la coleta.
Abandon one's profession or activity
(bullfighting expression).

⚠ C = very colloquial

idiomatic expressions

30. CRUZAR

1. Cruzar el charco.
= Pasar el charco.
Go to America,
crossing the Atlantic (puddle).
2. Cruzarle la cara (a alguien).
= Romperle la cara (a alguien).
= Partirle la boca/la cara (a alguien).
C. Smash someone's face
(in a brutal manner).

31. CUBRIR

1. Cubrir el expediente.
Do as little work as possible.
2. Cubrir las apariencias.
= Guardar las apariencias.
Show a happy face.

32. CHUPAR

1. Chupar del bote.
C. Take advantage of.
CHUPARSE
2. (No) chuparse el dedo.
= (No) meterse el dedo en la boca.
C. Not be naive.
3. Estar (algo) (como) para chuparse los dedos.
C. Be finger-licking good.

33. DAR

1. Dar caña.
= Meter caña.
C. Make something be done very quickly.
2. Dar el golpe.
A. Shock by the way one dresses or acts.
B. Commit a holdup.
3. Dar en el blanco.
= Dar en el clavo.
Hit the bull's-eye.
4. Dar la cara.
= Plantarle cara a algo.
Face up to a dangerous situation.
5. Dar la lata.
= Dar la tabarra.
= Dar guerra.
C. Pester (especially of children).
6. Dar largas.
Give excuses to postpone or stop doing something.
7. Dar leña.
C. Hit someone.

⚠ C = very colloquial

idiomatic expressions

8. "Dale que dale."
="Dale que te pego."
"He/She/It goes on and on"
(tiresome repetition).
9. "Para dar y tomar."
"More than enough."
NO DAR
10. No dar abasto.
Not be able to keep up with the work.
11. No dar (ni) golpe.
Be a lazybones.
(NO) DAR
12. (No) darle (a alguien) la (real) gana.
= (No) salirle (a alguien) de las narices.
C. (Not) feel like doing something
(the negative form is more common).
13. No dar pie con bola.
Not be able to do a thing right.
DARSE
14. Darse aires de algo (generalmente de grandeza).
Put on airs.
15. Darse bombo.
Presume, act important.
16. Darse con un canto en los dientes.
Be satisfied with something that was difficult to obtain
17. Darse una leche.
C. Have an accident.

34. DECIR
(No/sin) decir "esta boca es mía."
= No decir ni mu.
C. Not say a word.

35. DEFENDER
Defender (algo o a alguien)
a capa y espada.
Defend (someone or something)
vigorously (with cape
and sword).

⚠ C = very colloquial

36. DEJAR
1. Dejar bien sentado.
Make everything clear.
2. Dejar caer.
Say something indirectly.
NO DEJAR
3. No dejar títere con cabeza.
Give destructive criticism of everything and everyone presented.
DEJARSE
4. Dejarse caer.
C. Drop in.

37. DIRIGIR
Dirigir el cotarro.
C. Be the boss.

38. DIVERTIRSE
Divertirse como un enano.
= Gozar como un enano.
C. Have a lot of fun.

39. ECHAR
1. Echar en cara.
Throw in someone's face (reproach).
2. Echar en falta.
= Echar de menos.
Miss someone.
3. Echar en saco roto.
Go in one ear and out the other.
4. Echar humo. ⎯⎯⎯⎯⎯⎯⎯⎯⎯⎯→
Burn with anger (smoke).
5. Echar la casa por la ventana.
= Tirar la casa por la ventana.
Spend all one's money
(usually on a party).
ECHARSE
6. Echarse un farol.
= Tirarse un farol.
C. Show off by spinning a yarn.

40. EMPINAR
Empinar el codo.
C. Drink a lot.

41. ENCOGERSE
1. Encogerse de hombros.
Shrug one's shoulders.
2. Encogérsele (a alguien) el corazón.
= Helársele (a alguien) la sangre en el pecho/corazón.
Make someone's heart sink.

⚠ C = very colloquial

idiomatic expressions

42. ENCONTRAR
1. Encontrar (alguien) la horma de su zapato.
Find (someone) just what the doctor ordered
(Find a shoe tree for one's shoe).
2. Encontrar (alguien) su media naranja.
Find Mr. or Miss Right.

43. ENGAÑAR
Engañar como a un chino.
C. Deceive someone easily and
completely (antiquated, racist
expression).

45. ENTREGARSE
Entregarse en cuerpo y alma.
Dedicate oneself body and soul.

44. ENSEÑAR
Enseñar los colmillos.
Show one's teeth,
threaten.

47. ESPERAR
Esperar a que caiga la breva.
C. Wait for a stroke of luck
(a fig to drop).

46. ESCURRIR
Escurrir el bulto.
C. Get out of something
(by avoiding the problem).

48. ESTAR
1. Estar a las duras y a las maduras.
Take the good with the bad.
2. Estar a sus anchas.
Be comfortable.
3. Estar al loro.
C. Be all ears (very attentive).
4. Estar cerrado a cal y canto.
Be totally closed.
5. Estar como Pedro por su casa.
C. Behave as if in one's own home.
6. Estar (alguien) como un tren.
C. Be very attractive (physically).
7. Estar cortado.
Act stilted and unnatural.

⚠ C = very colloquial

8. **Estar de capa caída.**
= **Ir de capa caída.**
Be in a bad way (*fallen cape*).

9. **Estar de mala leche.**
C. Be in a bad mood (*bad milk*).

10. **Estar en Babia.**
= **Estar en Belén (con los pastores).**
= **Estar en la inopia.**
Be daydreaming.

11. **Estar en el ajo.**
C. Be mixed up or involved in something (*in the garlic*).

12. **Estar en la cresta de la ola.** ——→
Be on the crest of the wave.

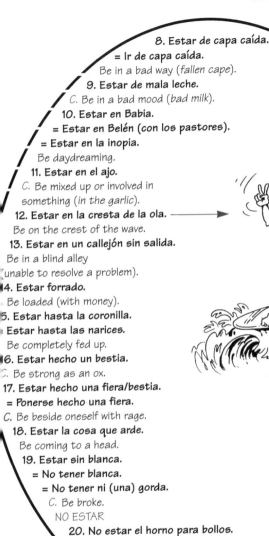

13. **Estar en un callejón sin salida.**
Be in a blind alley (unable to resolve a problem).

14. **Estar forrado.**
Be loaded (with money).

15. **Estar hasta la coronilla.**
= **Estar hasta las narices.**
Be completely fed up.

16. **Estar hecho un bestia.**
C. Be strong as an ox.

17. **Estar hecho una fiera/bestia.**
= **Ponerse hecho una fiera.**
C. Be beside oneself with rage.

18. **Estar la cosa que arde.**
Be coming to a head.

19. **Estar sin blanca.**
= **No tener blanca.**
= **No tener ni (una) gorda.**
C. Be broke.

NO ESTAR

20. **No estar el horno para bollos.**
C. Be a bad time to ask.

21. **No estar en sus cabales.**
Not be in one's right mind.

⚠ *C = very colloquial*

idiomatic expressions

49. GOZAR
Gozar como un enano.
(See *Divertirse*, 38.)

50. HABER
1. "No hay/había un alma."
"There is/was not a living soul there."
NO HABER
2. "No hay/había por donde coger (algo o a alguien)."
"There is/was no way around it" (a difficult or risky situation).

51. HABLAR
1. Hablar en cristiano.
C. Speak clearly.
2. Hablar por los codos.
C. Talk too much.

52. HACER
1. Hacer (algo) a trancas y barrancas.
Do (something) with great difficulty.
2. Hacer boca.
Whet one's appetite
(with food or drink).
3. Hacer bulto.
Take up space (without having
quality or importance).
4. Hacer de su capa un sayo.
Do as one pleases
(*make one's cape a tunic*).
5. Hacer el indio.
C. Play the fool
(slightly racist expression).
6. Hacer (alguien) su agosto.
C. Feather one's nest;
make hay while the
sun shines.

53. IMPORTAR
Importarle a alguien un bledo/un comino/un cuerno.
C. Not care less.

⚠️ C = very colloquial

54. IR

1. Ir a por todas.
Go for it all.

2. Ir al grano.
C. Get to the point.

3. Ir con el cuento a alguien.
Go with bad intentions to tell something.

4. Ir de cráneo.
C. Handle a matter very poorly.

5. Ir de punta en blanco.
Be all dressed up.

6. Ir hecho un adán.
Be terribly shabby.

7. Ir tirando.
Get along (a common reply to "¿Qué tal?").

8. "¡Vamos, anda!"
C. Beat it!

IRSE

9. Irse al garete (algo).
C. Be adrift, fall through.

10. Irse al otro barrio.
C. Die (Go to the other neighborhood).

11. Irse de la lengua.
C. Let the cat out of the bag.

12. Irse por los cerros de Úbeda.
C. Wander from the point (digress).

55. JODER

"¡No jodas!"
="¡No jorobes!"
C. "Don't tell me!"
(very vulgar expression
of surprise or incredulity).

56. JUGAR

1. Jugar con dos barajas.
Play both sides against the middle
(Play with two packs of cards).

2. Jugar con fuego.
Play with fire.

JUGARSE

3. Jugárselo todo a una carta.
= **Jugarse el todo por el todo.**
Risk everything on the
turn of a card.

⚠ C = very colloquial

idiomatic expressions

57. JUNTARSE
Juntarse el hambre con las ganas de comer.
C. Join together two people or things with identical needs or defects.

58. LEER
Leerle (a alguien) la cartilla.
Read someone the riot act.

59. (NO) LEVANTAR
No levantar cabeza.
Not be able to get out of a bad situation.

60. LLAMAR
"Llámalo hache".
C. "It doesn't make a bit of difference"
(*Call it "h" = no sound in Spanish*).

61. LLEVAR
1. Llevar (a alguien) al huerto.
C. Lead someone down the primrose path.
2. Llevar de cabeza (algo a alguien).
= Traer de cabeza (algo a alguien).
(Something) cause (someone) problems.
3. Llevar de cabeza (alguien a alguien).
= Traer de cabeza (alguien a alguien).
Drive someone crazy
(inspire with passion).
4. Llevar la batuta/la voz cantante.
C. Rule the roost (Take the baton/lead voice).
5. Llevar la contraria (a alguien).
Oppose someone.
6. Llevar (a alguien) por la calle de la amargura.
C. Give someone a bad time.

63. METER
1. Meter baza.
C. Butt in (Put in a trick).
2. Meter (a alguien) en cintura.
Make someone behave themselves.
3. Meter la pata.
C. Put one's foot in it.
4. Meter una bola/bolas.
C. Tell lies.

62. LUCHAR
Luchar a brazo partido.
Struggle with all one's strength.

⚠ *C = very colloquial*

METERSE

5. Meterse en camisa de once varas.
C. Poke one's nose in other people's business.

6. Meterse (a alguien) en el bolsillo.
Have someone in one's pocket.

7. Meterse en la boca del lobo.
Put one's head in the lion's mouth.

8. Meterse en un berenjenal.
Get into a fine mess
(a field of eggplants).

64. MORDER
Morder el anzuelo.
= Picar el anzuelo.
Take the bait.

65. PARAR
"¡Para el carro!"
C. "You can stop there!" (expression to shut someone up).

66. PARIR
"¡Éramos pocos y parió la abuela!"
C. "That's all we needed!"
(Grandmother gave birth).

67. PARTIR
Partirle la boca/la cara (a alguien). (See Cruzar, 30, 2.)

68. PASAR
1. Pasar carros y carretas.
(See Aguantar, 4.)
2. Pasar el charco. (See Cruzar, 30, 1.)
3. Pasar las de Caín.
C. Go through problems (like Cain).
4. Pasar por alto.
Pass over, ignore.
PASARSE
5. Pasárselo bomba/pipa.
C. Have a blast (youthful expression).
NO PASAR
6. No pasar los años para/por alguien.
Not seem to get any older.

 C = very colloquial

idiomatic expressions

69. PEDIR
1. Pedir cuentas (a alguien).
Call someone to account.
2. "¡Pide por esa boca!"
C. "Ask whatever you will!"
(Ask for this mouth).

70. PICAR
Picar el anzuelo.
(*See Morder, 64.*)

71. PLANTAR
Plantarle cara a algo.
(*See Dar, 33, 4.*)

72. NO PODER
No poder (alguien) con su alma.
Be very tired.

73. PONER
1. Poner a caldo.
C. Give someone a dressing-down.
2. Poner(le) el cascabel al gato.
Do something very difficult (*Bell the cat*).
3. Poner en bandeja.
= Servir en bandeja.
Serve something on a silver platter.
4. Poner (a alguien) hecho un cristo.
= Poner (a alguien) hecho un cromo.
C. Leave someone bruised and bleeding.
PONERSE
5. Ponerse ciego.
= Ponerse las botas.
= Ponerse morado.
C. Gorge oneself on food.
6. Ponerse hecho un cristo.
C. Get dirty, messed up.

74. NO PROBAR
No probar bocado.
Not eat.

⚠ *C* = very colloquial

75. QUEDAR

1. Quedar un cabo suelto.
Be at loose ends.

QUEDARSE

2. No saber a qué carta quedarse.
Not know which card to play.

3. Quedarse bizco/patidifuso/turulato.
= Quedarse con la boca abierta.
C. Be astonished, open-mouthed.

4. Quedarse con la copla.
Have an idea in mind and
repeat it over and over.

Quedarse corto.
. Not have said or done
everything one should have.
. Not have provided enough
of something.

6. Quedarse de brazos cruzados.
Sit with arms crossed (doing nothing).

7. Quedarse en blanco.
= Írse(le) el santo al cielo (a alguien).
Have one's mind go blank.

8. Quedarse frito.
C. Be zonked (deep sleep).

9. Quedarse tan ancho.
Take the broad view
(very calmly).

76. RASCARSE

**Rascarse alguien la barriga/
el ombligo. = Tocarse la barriga.**
C. Be shiftless, do nothing.

77. REMOVER

Remover cielo y tierra.
= Remover Roma con Santiago.
Move heaven and earth
(to achieve something).

78. ROMPER

1. Romperle la cara (a alguien).
(See Cruzar, 30, 2.)
ROMPERSE

2. Romperse los cuernos.
C. Work very hard
(Break horns).

79. SACAR

1. Sacar (a alguien) de sus casillas.
Make someone very angry.

2. Sacarle (a alguien) los colores.
Shame someone; make
someone blush.

⚠ C = very colloquial

idiomatic expressions

80. SALIR
1. Salir bordado (algo).
Be very well done.
2. Salir echando leches.
C. Leave at full speed.
NO SALIR
(See *No dar*, 33, 12.)

81. SENTAR
Sentar la cabeza.
Become level-headed.

82. SER
1. Ser ciento y la madre.
C. Be packed in like sardines
(*one hundred and the mother*).
2. Ser cuatro gatos.
C. Be almost no one there (*four cats*).
3. Ser de armas tomar (alguien).
Be someone of real character.
4. Ser de cajón (algo).
C. Be obvious, evident, easy to see.
5. Ser de la otra acera.
C. Be gay (*from the other sidewalk*).
6. Ser duro de cascos.
= Ser duro de mollera.
Be not very intelligent, be dense.
7. Ser el colmo.
= Ser la repera.
C. Be way too much.
8. Ser (algo) el cuento de nunca acabar.
Be an endless business.
9. Ser habas contadas.
Go without saying (*counted beans*).
10. Ser (algo) harina de otro costal.
Be a horse of another color
(*flour of another sack*).
11. Ser la flor y nata.
Be the best of the best (*flower and cream*).
12. Ser un agarra(d)o.
C. Be stingy, close-fisted.
13. Ser un aguafiestas.
Be a party pooper.
14. Ser (alguien) un cacho/trozo de pan.
C. Be a very good person (*crumb/bit of bread*).
15. "¡Estos son lentejas"
C. "That's absolutely true!"
NO SER
16. "No ser ni chicha ni limoná."
C. "Neither fish nor fowl."

⚠ C = very colloquial

idiomatic expressions

83. SUDAR

Sudar la gota gorda.
A. Be very hot, sweat profusely.
B. Strive unsuccessfully to get something (figurative).

84. TAPAR

Taparle la boca (a alguien).
Shut someone's mouth
(with arguments, bribery, etc.).

85. TENER

1. Tener agallas (alguien).
Have courage (guts).

2. Tener enchufe (alguien).
C. Have the right contacts to get something.

3. Tener (a alguien) entre ceja y ceja.
Be unable to stand someone (Have them *between* eyebrows).

4. Tener (alguien) las espaldas cubiertas.
Have one's back covered (protected from risks).

5. Tener mala leche.
Be in a bad mood (as a general disposition).

6. Tener mucho cuento.
Be a storyteller, liar, deceiver.

NO TENER

7. No tener arte ni parte.
Have nothing whatsoever to do with a thing.

8. No tener blanca.
= No tener ni (una) gorda.
(See Estar, 48, 19.)

9. No tener desperdicio (algo o alguien).
Be very good (with nothing bad).

86. TIRAR(SE)

Tirarse un farol.
(See Echarse, 39, 6.)

87. TOCAR

1. Tocarle a uno la china.
Have bad luck.
TOCARSE

2. Tocarse la barriga.
(See Rascarse, 76.)

 C = very colloquial

Spanish Verb Manual

idiomatic expressions

88. TOMAR
Tomar cartas en el asunto.
Get involved in the situation, taking over.

89. TORCER
Torcer el gesto.
Make an angry face
(*Twist the expression*).

90. TRAER
1. Traer cola.
Have consequences.
2. Traer de cabeza.
(*See Llevar, 61, 2, 3.*)
**3. Traer sin cuidado
(algo a alguien).**
Not to be concerned.

91. TRAGAR
1. Tragar bilis.
C. Swallow one's anger (*bile*).
2. Tragar carros y carretas.
(*See Aguantar, 4.*)
3. Tragar(se) un sapo. ⟶
C. Put up with a distasteful situation
(*Swallow a frog*).
TRAGARSE
4. Tragarse una/la bola.
C. Allow oneself to be deceived,
believe a lie.

92. VENIR
**1. Venir como agua de mayo
(alguien o algo).**
Be as welcome as the rains in May.
NO VENIR
2. No venir a cuento (algo).
= No venir al caso.
Have nothing to do with what
is being discussed.

93. VOLVER
Volver la cabeza a alguien.
A. Not want to greet someone.
B. Not help someone in need
(figurative).

⚠ *C* = very colloquial

regional use
of Spanish verbs

COUNTRIES AND REGIONS OF CENTRAL AND SOUTH AMERICA WHERE SPANISH IS SPOKEN

REGIONS

Mexico

Central Am.

Caribbean

South Am.

ABBREVIATIONS USED

Ant.	Antilles	Lat. Am.	Latin America
Argent.	Argentina	Mex.	Mexico
Bol.	Bolivia	Nicar.	Nicaragua
Cent. Am.	Central America	P. Rico	Puerto Rico
C. Rica	Costa Rica	Pan.	Panama
Col.	Colombia	Par.	Paraguay
Dom. Rep.	Dominican Republic	R. Plate	River Plate
Ecuad.	Ecuador	refl.	reflexive
El Salv.	El Salvador	S. Am.	South America
fam.	familiar	Urug.	Uruguay
fig.	figurative	Venez.	Venezuela
Guat.	Guatemala	vulg.	vulgar
Hond.	Honduras	[subject of the verb in brackets]	
impers.	impersonal verb		

Footnote references following some verbs refer to the Notes in the Verb index, pages 173–174.
Asterisks indicate irregular verbs.

EXPLANATION OF THE REGIONS

Latin America. Verbs used in almost all the countries or in several regions of Latin America.

Central America. Verbs used in one or several of the following countries: *Costa Rica, Guatemala, El Salvador, Honduras, Nicaragua, Panama.*

South America. Verbs used in one or several of the following countries: *Argentina, Bolivia, Chile, Colombia, Ecuador, Paraguay, Peru, Uruguay, Venezuela.*

Caribbean. Verbs used in one or several of the following countries: *Lesser Antilles (Antigua, Dominica, San Vicente, Santa Lucia), Cuba, Puerto Rico, Dominican Republic.*

Mexico. Verbs used in Mexico.

Spanish Verb Manual

regional use

VERB	REGION	MEANING	MODEL	TABLE
		A		
Ababillarse	S. Am.	*Chile.* Become sick in the knee joint [an animal].	*cantar*	5
Abacorar	Lat. Am.	**1.** *Ant., Venez.* Harass, persecute. **2.** *Lat. Am.* Hoard commercial goods.	*cantar*	5
Abalanzar(se)	S. Am.	*Argent., Urug.* Rear up [a horse].	*cruzar*	8
Abalear	Lat. Am.	Shoot someone, wound or kill by shooting.	*cantar*	5
Abanderar(se)	S. Am.	*Chile.* Form factions or gangs.	*cantar*	5
Abarajar	S. Am.	*Argent., Urug.* Grab or stop something in the air, especially a punch.	*cantar*	5
Abarcar	Lat. Am., S. Am.	**1.** *Lat. Am.* Hoard commercial goods (see *abacorar*, 2). **2.** *Ecuad.* Sit on eggs [a hen].	*atacar*	7
Abarrajarse	S. Am.	*Chile.* Corrupt, degrade or make someone evil.	*cantar*	5
Abarrotar	Lat. Am.	Saturate the market with products to decrease the selling price.	*cantar*	5
Abatanarse	S. Am., Mexico	*Bol., Mex.* Wear out through repeated use or washing [cloth].	*cantar*	5
Abatatar(se)	S. Am.	*Argent., Par., Urug.* Disturb, belittle, confuse.	*cantar*	5
Abejonear	Caribbean	*Dom. Rep.* Buzz like a bumblebee, irritate.	*cantar*	5
Abicharse	S. Am.	**1.** *Argent., Urug.* Become wormy [fruit]. **2.** *Argent., Urug.* Fester with worms [a wound].	*cantar*	5
Abismar	Lat. Am.	Be surprised, amazed, astonished.	*cantar*	5
Abofarse	Caribbean	*Cuba, Dom. Rep.* Become soft, swell up.	*cantar*	5
Abombar	S. Am.	*Argent., Chile, Ecuad.* Get tipsy, get drunk on wine.	*cantar*	5
Abonar	S. Am.	*Bol.* Reconcile, renew broken friendships or contracts without legal proceedings.	*cantar*	5

VERB	REGION	MEANING	MODEL	TABLE
Abotonar	Cent. Am.	*Nicar.* fig. Flatter to get something.	*cantar*	5
Abracar(se)	Lat. Am.	1. Embrace, encircle with one's arms. 2. Surround.	*atacar*	7
Abreviarse	Cent. Am.	*C. Rica, Nicar.* Hurry up.	*cantar*	5
*Abrir²	Lat. Am., S. Am.	1. *Lat. Am.* Turn from the direction it is walking [a horse]. 2. *Lat. Am.* Stop doing something, go back, separate oneself from a company or business. 3. *Argent., Venez.* Get back, detour, go to one side.	*vivir*	51
Abulonar	S. Am.	*Argent.* Fasten something with large screws.	*cantar*	5
Abusarse	Cent. Am.	*Guat.* Concentrate, wake up, be very attentive.	*cantar*	5
Acalambrarse	Lat. Am.	Contract one's muscles because of a cramp.	*cantar*	5
Acaserarse	S. Am.	*Chile.* Become a regular customer of a store.	*cantar*	5
Achajuanarse	S. Am., Mexico	*Bol., Col., Mex.* Suffocate by working hard when hot or very fat [an animal]; become fatigued.	*cantar*	5
Achaplinarse	S. Am.	*Chile.* Assume a halting attitude as portrayed by Charlie Chaplin.	*cantar*	5
Achiguarse	S. Am.	1. *Chile.* Bend or twist something. 2. *Chile.* Get a big belly.	*averiguar*	11
Achiquitar(se)	Lat. Am.	*Col., Guat., Mex., Dom. Rep.* Make something small, reduce.	*cantar*	5
Acholar	S. Am.	*Chile, Ecuad.* Run, shame, frighten someone. In *Peru,* refl. form only.	*cantar*	5
Achucharrar(se)	Lat. Am.	1. *Col., Chile, Hond.* Squash, flatten, squeeze. 2. *Mex.* Wrinkle, shrink, frighten.	*cantar*	5
Achucharse	S. Am.	*Argent., Urug.* Shake, shiver, tremble from cold or fever.	*cantar*	5
Achucuyar(se)	Cent. Am.	Except for *Nicar.* Intimidate, discourage. In *C. Rica,* refl. form only.	*cantar*	5

regional use

VERB	REGION	MEANING	MODEL	TABLE
Achunchar	S. Am.	*Bol., Chile.* Shame, disturb. In *Peru,* refl. form only.	*cantar*	5
Achuntar	S. Am.	*Bol., Chile.* fam., vulg. Be right, hit the bull's-eye.	*cantar*	5
Achurar	S. Am.	*Argent., Urug.* fig., fam. Slash someone or something.	*cantar*	5
Aciguatarse	Cent. Am.	*C. Rica.* fig., fam. Become sad.	*cantar*	5
Acolchonar	Lat. Am.	Place cotton, silk, wool, horsehair or other materials between two fabrics and baste them together; quilt.	*cantar*	5
Acolitar	Lat. Am.	Carry out the functions of an acolyte (in charge of the altar in the Roman Catholic Church).	*cantar*	5
Acollarar	S. Am.	**1**. *Argent.* Join two animals by the neck. **2**. *Argent.* vulg. Cohabit, have sexual relations [two people], especially when one is already engaged to someone else. **3**. *Argent., Chile.* fig. Join together two things or two people.	*cantar*	5
*Acomedirse	Lat. Am.	Offer oneself spontaneously and graciously to perform a service.	*pedir*	60
Acomodar	S. Am.	*Argent.* Plug in, place someone in a position or destination using personal influence.	*cantar*	5
Aconcharse	S. Am.	**1**. *Chile.* Become clear by separating the dregs [a liquid]. **2**. *Chile.* fig., fam. Become normalized, become peaceful or calm [turbulent situations].	*cantar*	5
Acoplar	S. Am.	**1**. *Argent., Chile, Par., Peru, Urug.* Join one or more vehicles to another for towing. **2**. *Argent., Peru, Urug.* Join and accompany one or more persons.	*cantar*	5
*Acordar	S. Am.	*Argent.* Become aware.	*contar*	16
Acortejarse	Caribbean	*P. Rico.* Cohabit (see *acollarar*, 2).	*cantar*	5
Acosijar	Mexico	Burden, harass.	*cantar*	5

VERB	REGION	MEANING	MODEL	TABLE
Acotejar	S. Am., Caribbean	1. *Col., Cuba, Ecuad., Dom. Rep.* Arrange, place objects in an orderly way. 2. *Col.* Stimulate, incite, favor. 3. *Cuba, Ecuad.* refl. Be accommodating; come to terms with someone; reach an agreement with someone. 4. *Cuba, Ecuad.* Live with someone with whom one has a sexual relationship. 5. *Cuba, Ecuad.* Obtain employment. 6. *Cuba, Ecuad., Dom. Rep.* Settle oneself, get comfortable.	*cantar*	5
Acriollarse	Lat. Am.	Adopt the local customs in a Spanish-speaking country [a foreigner].	*cantar*	5
Acullicar	S. Am.	*Bol.* Extract (in the mouth) the juice of coca leaves.	*atacar*	7
Acunar	Cent. Am.	*C. Rica.* Place a child in a crib.	*cantar*	5
Acundangarse	Caribbean	*Cuba.* Become effeminate.	*pagar*	6
Afiebrarse	Lat. Am.	Start to have a fever.	*cantar*	5
Afilar	S. Am.	1. *Bol., Urug.* Prepare oneself, make oneself ready for any task. 2. *Par., Urug.* Flirt with someone for whom one feels a sexual attraction. 3. *Chile.* vulg. Have sex with someone.	*cantar*	5
Afilorar(se)	Caribbean	*P. Rico.* Dress, adorn, put on something carefully.	*cantar*	5
Afirolar	Caribbean	*P. Rico.* See *afilorar(se)*.	*cantar*	5
Aflatarse	Cent. Am.	*Hond., Nicar.* Be grieved or troubled.	*cantar*	5
Aflojar	Caribbean	1. *Dom. Rep.* fig., fam. Give someone a punch; launch or shoot a projectile. 2. *Dom. Rep.* refl. Lose one's nerve.	*cantar*	5
Aforar	S. Am.	1. *Col.* Make out bills. 2. *Col.* Include (in the bills) every item and package. 3. *Col.* Deliver equipment or merchandise to a rail station, airport, etc. for sending on to its desination.	*cantar*	5

regional use

VERB	REGION	MEANING	MODEL	TABLE
Afrecharse	S. Am.	*Chile.* Become sick because of eating too much bran or husk [an animal].	*cantar*	5
Afrontilar	Mexico	Tie cattle by the horns to a post for training or slaughter.	*cantar*	5
Agachar	S. Am., Mexico	*Argent., Mex., Urug.* Prepare oneself or become available to do something.	*cantar*	5
Agarrar	Lat. Am.	**1.** fig. Surprise someone, catch someone unprepared. **2.** fig., fam. Obtain, procure, take control of something. **3.** fam. Leave, take the road toward, direct oneself toward.	*cantar*	5
Agauchar(se)	S. Am.	*Argent., Chile, Urug.* Cause a person to take on the look, the manners, and the customs of a *gaucho*.	*cantar*	5
Agringarse	Lat. Am.	Take on the look and customs of a *gringo*.	*pagar*	6
Aguachar	S. Am.	**1.** *Argent.* Become fat because of being pastured without exercise [a horse]. **2.** *Chile.* Domesticate an animal. **3.** *Chile.* refl. Tame; become attached to a place [an animal].	*cantar*	5
Aguadar	Cent. Am.	**1.** *Guat.* Water down, mix a liquid with water. **2.** *Guat.* Weaken, cause to flag.	*cantar*	5
Aguaitar	Lat. Am.	Await, wait for.	*cantar*	5
Aguantar	Caribbean	*Dom. Rep.* Substitute temporarily for someone in his/her work post.	*cantar*	5
Aguaraparse	Lat. Am.	Acquire the taste of *guarapo* (sugar cane).	*cantar*	5
Aguasarse	S. Am.	*Chile.* Take on the manners and customs of a *guaso* (Chilean peasant).	*cantar*	5
Ahuesarse	Lat. Am.	**1.** Remain useless or not prestigious [a person or thing]. **2.** Remain unsold [merchandise].	*cantar*	5
Ahuevar(se)	Cent. Am., S. Am.	**1.** *C. Rica.* Bore, annoy. **2.** *Col., Nicar., Pan.* Stun, fluster, frighten. In *Peru,* refl. form only.	*cantar*	5

regional use

VERB	REGION	MEANING	MODEL	TABLE
Ajear	S. Am.	*Bol.* Hurl curses and swear words at someone.	*cantar*	5
Ajorar	Caribbean	*P. Rico.* Bother, harass.	*cantar*	5
Ajotar	Cent. Am., Caribbean	*Cent. Am., P. Rico.* Cause trouble, incite.	*cantar*	5
Ajustar(se)	Lat. Am.	**1.** *Col., C. Rica, Mex., Nicar.* Fulfill, complete. **2.** *Col., C. Rica, Cuba, Nicar., Dom. Rep.* Contract by the piece.	*cantar*	5
Alagar(se)	S. Am.	*Argent., Bol.* Take on water with the risk of sinking [a boat or ship].	*pagar*	6
Alagartarse	Mexico, Cent. Am.	**1.** *Mex.* Spread out its legs to lower itself, allowing the rider an easy mount [a horse]. **2.** *C. Rica, Guat., Nicar.* Become greedy, commit usury, be stingy.	*cantar*	5
Albardear	Cent. Am.	Tame or break wild horses.	*cantar*	5
Alburear	Mexico	Say play-on-word phrases with double meanings, make puns.	*cantar*	5
Alebrestarse	Lat. Am.	Get upset, become agitated.	*cantar*	5
Alegar	Lat. Am.	Dispute, argue.	*pagar*	6
*Alentarse	Lat. Am.	Get better, recover, get over a disease.	*pensar*	13
Aleonar(se)	S. Am.	*Chile.* Make a racket or riot.	*cantar*	5
Alfalfar	S. Am.	*Chile, Peru.* Plant alfalfa in a plot of land.	*cantar*	5
Alinderar	Lat. Am.	Indicate or mark the borders of a plot of land.	*cantar*	5
Aliñar	S. Am.	*Chile.* Fix or set dislocated bones.	*cantar*	5
Alipegarse	Lat. Am.	Come together with others inopportunely, turn up uninvited.	*pagar*	6
Alistar	Cent. Am.	*C. Rica, Nicar.* Prepare and sew pieces of footwear.	*cantar*	5
Allanar	Lat. Am.	Search a house with a warrant, flatten.	*cantar*	5

Spanish Verb Manual

regional use

VERB	REGION	MEANING	MODEL	TABLE
Altear	S. Am.	**1.** *Ecuad.* Elevate, give more height to something, such as a wall, etc. **2.** *Par.* Raise the voice. **3.** *Par.* Order someone to halt in a march.	*cantar*	5
Alumbrar	S. Am.	*Venez.* fig., fam. Mistreat a person, hitting him/her.	*cantar*	5
Alunarse	Cent. Am., S. Am.	*Cent. Am., Venez.* Become infected [harness sores on a horse].	*cantar*	5
Aluzar	Lat. Am.	**1.** *Mex., P. Rico, Dom. Rep.* Brighten, fill with light and clarity. **2.** *P. Rico, Dom. Rep.* Examine with diffused light, especially eggs.	*cruzar*	8
Alzar	Lat. Am.	Run away and become wild [a domesticated animal].	*cruzar*	8
Amacharse	Lat. Am.	**1.** *Cuba, P. Rico, Dom. Rep.* Become sterile [a plant or female animal]. **2.** *Chile, Mex.* Resist, become obstinate, refuse to do something.	*cantar*	5
Amachinarse	Lat. Am., Cent. Am.	**1.** *Lat. Am.* Cohabit (see *acollarar*, 2). **2.** *Pan.* Become depressed, lose energy, become frightened.	*cantar*	5
Amachorrarse	Mexico	Become sterile [a female animal or a plant].	*cantar*	5
Amadrinar	S. Am.	Accustom horses to go in a herd behind the lead mare.	*cantar*	5
Amalayar	S. Am., Cent. Am.	**1.** *Argent., Hond.* Exclaim "*Amalaya!*" to express displeasure, compassion or desire. **2.** *Cent. Am., Venez.* Desire something fervently.	*cantar*	5
Amallarse	S. Am.	*Chile.* Withdraw from a game [the one who is winning].	*cantar*	5
*Amanecer(se)[12]	S. Am., Mexico	*Argent., Bol., Col., Chile, Ecuad., Mex., Peru.* Pass the night in a vigil, without sleep.	*obedecer*	33
Amangualar(se)	S. Am.	*Col.* Pay someone a salary, contract someone for low-level work, generally as a maid.	*cantar*	5

VERB	REGION	MEANING	MODEL	TABLE
Amañar	S. Am.	*Argent., Bol., Col., Ecuad.* Live together as unmarried sexual partners.	*cantar*	5
Amarcar	S. Am.	**1**. *Ecuad.* Take in one's arms. **2**. *Ecuad.* Be a godparent or stand up for a young child.	*atacar*	7
Amarrar	Lat. Am.	**1**. *Cent. Am., Col., Chile, Mex., Venez.* Bandage or wrap tightly. **2**. *Chile, Nicar., Peru, P. Rico.* Come to an agreement, make a pact.. **3**. *Col., Cuba, El Salv., Guat., Mex., Nicar., Pan., P. Rico.* refl. Get married, marry.	*cantar*	5
Amelcochar(se)	Lat. Am.	**1**. *Lat. Am.* Give to a candy the density of taffy. **2**. *Bol., C. Rica, Ecuad., Hond., Mex., Peru.* refl. fig. Become soft again. **3**. *Cuba, Guat., Mex., Peru.* fig. Be sugar sweet, fall madly in love, show oneself to be extremely sweet.	*cantar*	5
Ameritar	Lat. Am.	Deserve.	*cantar*	5
Amohosarse	Lat. Am.	Become full of mold.	*cantar*	5
Amorocharse	S. Am.	*Venez.* Come or meet together.	*cantar*	5
Amorriñar(se)	Cent. Am.	Become sick with dropsy [an animal].	*cantar*	5
Amostazarse	Lat. Am.	*Bol., Col., Ecuad., Hond., P. Rico.* Be ashamed.	*cruzar*	8
Amotetarse	Cent. Am.	*Nicar.* Group or pile together.	*cantar*	5
Amparar	S. Am.	*Chile.* Fulfill the conditions allowing one to work or benefit from a mine.	*cantar*	5
Amuchar(se)	S. Am.	*Argent., Bol., Chile, R. Plate.* Increase the number or quantity.	*cantar*	5
Amuñuñar	S. Am.	*Venez.* Squeeze hard.	*cantar*	5
Amurriñarse	Cent. Am.	*Hond.* Contract dropsy [horses or sheep] (see *amorriñar(se)*).	*cantar*	5
Anoticiar(se)	S. Am.	*Argent.* Make an announcement, make something known publicly.	*cantar*	5

regional use

VERB	REGION	MEANING	MODEL	TABLE
Antarquear(se)	S. Am.	**1.** *Argent.* Turn one's back. **2.** *Argent.* refl., fig., fam. Become vain, have an attitude of superiority and arrogance.	*cantar*	5
Antelar	S. Am.	*Chile.* Anticipate.	*cantar*	5
Antellevar	Mexico	Knock down.	*cantar*	5
Antipatizar	Lat. Am.	Feel antipathy against someone or something.	*cruzar*	8
Añangotarse	Caribbean	*Dom. Rep.* Become weak, crouch.	*cantar*	5
Apachar	Cent. Am.	*El Salv.* Flatten, crush.	*cantar*	5
Apañar	S. Am., Cent. Am.	*Argent., Bol., Nicar., Peru, Urug.* Cover up, hide or protect someone.	*cantar*	5
Apapachar	Mexico	Caress, cuddle.	*cantar*	5
Aparatarse	S. Am.	Be prepared, get ready. In *Col.,* often refers to a sky promising rain, snow or hail.	*cantar*	5
Aparejarse	Lat. Am.	Mate, come together [animals].	*cantar*	5
Aparragarse	S. Am., Cent. Am.	*Chile, Hond.* Develop to be short and bulky [person, animal or plant].	*pagar*	6
Apartar	Mexico	**1.** Separate cattle for classification. **2.** Extract the gold contained in bars of silver.	*cantar*	5
Apealar	Lat. Am.	Place hobbles on the legs of horses or bulls to control them.	*cantar*	5
Apear	Caribbean	*Cuba.* Eat with one's hands, without utensils.	*cantar*	5
Apegualar	S. Am.	*Chile.* Use a cinch to hold a saddle tightly in position.	*cantar*	5
Apelmazar	Cent. Am.	*El Salv., Nicar.* Flatten or smooth out earth, gravel, etc., using a steamroller.	*cruzar*	8
Apenarse	Lat. Am.	Feel embarrassed, ashamed.	*cantar*	5
Apendejarse	Lat. Am.	**1.** *Col., Pan., Dom. Rep.* Become a fool, stupid. **2.** *Cuba, Nicar., Dom. Rep.* Become cowardly.	*cantar*	5
Apensionar	S. Am.	*Col., Chile.* Become sad or grieved.	*cantar*	5

VERB	REGION	MEANING	MODEL	TABLE
Aperar	Lat. Am., S. Am.	**1**. *Lat. Am.* Provide instruments, tools or provisions. **2**. *Urug.* Saddle, harness (horses).	*cantar*	5
Apercollar	S. Am.	*Ecuad.* Demand something insistently and violently, especially relating to finances.	*cantar*	5
Aperrear	Cent. Am.	*Pan.* Mistreat someone verbally, deeply insulting them.	*cantar*	5
Apersogar(se)	S. Am.	**1**. *Venez.* Tie things together. **2**. *Venez.* refl. Come together to cohabit (see *amañar*).	*pagar*	6
Apestillar	S. Am.	*Chile.* Tie someone down so that they are unable to escape.	*cantar*	5
Apirgüinarse	S. Am.	*Chile.* Suffer from leeches [cattle].	*cantar*	5
Apirularse	S. Am.	*Chile.* Get dressed up, put on one's Sunday best.	*cantar*	5
Aplastar(se)	S. Am.	*Argent., Urug.* Make a horse run or work until it dies.	*cantar*	5
Aplatanar	Caribbean	*Ant.* Adopt the customs of the country in which a foreigner lives.	*cantar*	5
Aplazar	Lat. Am., Caribbean	**1**. *Lat. Am.* Fail an examination candidate. **2**. *Dom. Rep.* refl. Cohabit (as sexual partners) (see *acollarar* and *amañar*).	*cruzar*	8
Apochongarse	S. Am.	*Urug.* Be afraid, become cowardly.	*pagar*	6
Apolismar	Lat. Am.	**1**. *Cuba, Pan., P. Rico.* Damage, bruise. **2**. *C. Rica.* refl. Loaf, be lazy. **3**. *C. Rica, P. Rico, Venez.* Be cowardly, be foolish. **4**. *P. Rico.* Remain small, rachitic; not grow.	*cantar*	5
Apolvillarse	S. Am.	*Chile.* Come down with fungus [wheat and other cereal grains].	*cantar*	5
Apozarse	S. Am.	*Col., Chile.* Collect water or another liquid to form a pool.	*cruzar*	8
Aprensar	S. Am.	*Chile.* Tighten with force.	*cantar*	5

regional use

VERB	REGION	MEANING	MODEL	TABLE
Aprestigiar	S. Am.	*Col.* Give prestige, authority or importance.	*cantar*	5
*Aprevenir	S. Am., Cent. Am.	*Col., Guat.* Prevent, prepare.	*venir*	80
Apunarse	S. Am.	Suffer from mountain sickness or fear of heights.	*cantar*	5
Apuntalar(se)	Cent. Am.	*C. Rica.* Eat a snack between meals.	*cantar*	5
Apuntar	Mexico	Sprout [wheat and other cereal grains].	*cantar*	5
Apuñar	S. Am.	Knead dough with the fist, especially for bread.	*cantar*	5
Apurar(se)	Lat. Am.	Hurry up, be in a rush.	*cantar*	5
Aquintralarse	S. Am.	**1.** *Chile.* Become covered with *quintral* [trees and bushes]. **2.** *Chile.* Contract the disease *quintral* [melons and other plants].	*cantar*	5
Archivar	Mexico	Place in jail.	*cantar*	5
Arcionar	S. Am., Mexico	**1.** *Col., Mex.* Tie down cattle by placing a rope around the saddle-tree. **2.** *Mex.* Raise the leg of a steer above its tail (with saddle-tree or stirrup), tying it to the saddle to make the animal fall over.	*cantar*	5
Arisquear	S. Am.	*Argent., Urug.* Show oneself to be headstrong, surly.	*cantar*	5
Armar	Cent. Am., Mexico	**1.** *Guat., Mex.* Refuse to walk any further [an animal]. **2.** *Mex.* Become rich unexpectedly and without planning.	*cantar*	5
Arrabiatar	Cent. Am.	**1.** Tie one animal to the tail of another. **2.** refl. Submit oneself slavishly to the will of another.	*cantar*	5
Arraigar	Lat. Am.	Notify someone that he/she is not to leave the area, under penalty of law.	*pagar*	6
Arrancar	Caribbean, Mexico	Die.	*atacar*	7

VERB	REGION	MEANING	MODEL	TABLE
Arranchar	S. Am.	*Chile, Ecuad., Peru.* Take away something from someone, using violence.	*cantar*	5
Arrancharse	Lat. Am.	**1**. *Pan.* Take up residency in a friend's house, at the owner's displeasure, and show no signs of moving out. **2**. *Col., Chile.* Refuse obstinately to do something. **3**. *Mex., Venez.* Adapt to the idea of living in a place temporarily. **4**. *Cuba.* Remain in a place too long.	*cantar*	5
Arrechar	Cent. Am., Mexico	**1**. Have too much vivaciousness and energy. **2**. Become arrogant or worked up.	*cantar*	5
*****Arrendar**	Caribbean	*Cuba.* Cover the base of trees, especially vine trunks, with earth.	*pensar*	13
Arrequintar	Lat. Am.	Squeeze tightly using cords or bandages.	*cantar*	5
Arrodajarse	Cent. Am.	*C. Rica.* Sit cross-legged.	*cantar*	5
Asemillar	S. Am.	*Chile.* Fall [pollen from olive vines, wheat, and other plants].	*cantar*	5
Aserruchar	S. Am., Cent. Am.	*Col., Chile, Hond., Peru.* Cut or divide wood or other objects with a saw.	*cantar*	5
Asistir	S. Am.	*Col.* Live, inhabit.	*vivir*	51
Asorocharse	S. Am.	**1**. *S. Am.* Suffer from mountain sickness. **2**. *Chile.* Blush, feel ashamed.	*cantar*	5
Asuntar	Caribbean	*Ant.* Pay attention, listen well, understand something well.	*cantar*	5
Atarragar(se)	S. Am., Mexico	*Col., Mex., Venez.* Gorge, stuff with food.	*pagar*	6
Atembar(se)	S. Am.	*Col.* Daze, stun.	*cantar*	5
Atingir(se)	Lat. Am.	**1**. Concern, be the duty of, be the job of. **2**. Afflict, oppress, tyrannize.	*dirigir*	52
Atojar	Cent. Am., Caribbean	*C. Rica, Cuba, Pan.* Set a dog on someone.	*cantar*	5

regional use

VERB	REGION	MEANING	MODEL	TABLE
Atracar	S. Am.	*Chile.* Hit, beat up.	*atacar*	7
Atrincar	Lat. Am.	**1.** *Col., C. Rica, Cuba, Chile, Ecuad., Mex., Nicar., Peru, Dom. Rep., Venez.* Tie securely, hold down, secure with cords and ropes. **2.** *Cuba, Mex., Nicar., Peru.* Squeeze.	*atacar*	7
Atrojar	Mexico	Place fruit and grain in a backpack.	*cantar*	5
Atufar	S. Am.	*Bol., Ecuad.* Lose one's head.	*cantar*	5
*Aventar	Caribbean, S. Am.	**1.** *Cuba.* Expose sugar to the air and sunshine (in sugar mills). **2.** *Col.* Throw oneself at someone, jump someone.	*pensar*	13
Aviar	Lat. Am., S. Am.	**1.** *Lat. Am.* Loan money or other items to a laborer, cattleman or miner. **2.** *Chile.* Pay for work in a mine to make up for the cost of loans made to its owner.	*desviar*	9
Avispar(se)	S. Am.	*Chile.* Scare, frighten.	*cantar*	5
Azararse	S. Am., Cent. Am.	**1.** *Chile, Guat., Nicar.* Be disturbed, be ashamed. **2.** *Chile.* Become irritated, angry.	*cantar*	5
Azocar	Caribbean	*Cuba.* Tighten something too much.	*atacar*	7
Azucarar	Lat. Am.	Crystallize [syrup in preserves].	*cantar*	5
B				
Bachatear	Caribbean	*Cuba, P. Rico.* Have fun, joke.	*cantar*	5
Bajear	S. Am.	*Bol.* Accompany a song or melody with the low notes.	*cantar*	5
Balear	Lat. Am.	Fire, shoot bullets at someone or something.	*cantar*	5
Bandear	Lat. Am.	**1.** Go through, move from place to place; drill. **2.** Cross a river from one bank to the other.	*cantar*	5
Baquetear	Lat. Am.	fig., fam. Rule someone with an iron hand, treat someone harshly.	*cantar*	5

VERB	REGION	MEANING	MODEL	TABLE
Barajar	S. Am.	**1.** *Argent., Par., Urug.* Catch in midair (an object that is thrown). **2.** *Argent., Chile, Urug.* Stop the punches of an adversary.	*cantar*	5
Barbear	Mexico, Cent. Am.	**1.** *Mex.* fig. Fawn on, adulate, give a gift to someone with ulterior motives. **2.** *Mex.* fig. Tie down a small steer by the snout and nape or the horn, and twist its neck until the animal falls to the ground. **3.** *C. Rica.* fig. Flatter, adulate.	*cantar*	5
Bartulear	S. Am.	*Chile.* Ponder, rack one's brain, think deeply about something.	*cantar*	5
Basurear	S. Am.	*Argent., Peru, Urug.* fam. Treat a person badly or disrespectfully.	*cantar*	5
Batir	S. Am.	*Argent., Urug.* vulg. Denounce, accuse.	*vivir*	51
Bejuquear	Lat. Am.	**1.** *Ecuad., Guat., Mex., Nicar., P. Rico.* Beat down, thrash. **2.** *Mex.* Weave rattan.	*cantar*	5
Beneficiar	Caribbean, S. Am.	*Cuba, Chile, P. Rico.* Cut up a steer and sell it retail.	*cantar*	5
Bilmar	S. Am.	*Chile.* Use natural remedies to alleviate pain.	*cantar*	5
Bochar	Caribbean, S. Am.	*Dom. Rep., Urug., Venez.* fig., fam. Reject, snub, reprove.	*cantar*	5
Bogar	S. Am.	*Chile.* Skim, remove dross from metal.	*pagar*	6
Bolear(se)	S. Am., Mexico	**1.** *Argent.* Confuse, bewilder. **2.** *Urug.* fig. Wrap, entangle; play a dirty trick on someone. **3.** *Argent., Urug.* Throw *bolas* to immobilize an animal. **4.** *Argent.* Rear up on hind legs and fall on its back [a colt]. **5.** *Mex.* Polish a shoe, clean it, and shine it.	*cantar*	5
Bolichear	S. Am.	*Argent.* Frequent bars and dives.	*cantar*	5
Bolsear	Cent. Am., Mexico	*C. Rica, Guat., Hond., Mex.* Take away from people slyly what they have of value.	*cantar*	5

regional use

VERB	REGION	MEANING	MODEL	TABLE
Bolsiquear	S. Am.	Pick someone's pocket.	*cantar*	5
Bombear	S. Am.	*Argent.* fig. Harm someone deliberately.	*cantar*	5
Bostear	S. Am.	*Chile, Urug.* Vomit what was eaten [cattle and horses].	*cantar*	5
Botear	Caribbean	*Cuba.* Pick up travelers on a fixed route with different destinations.	*cantar*	5
Brocearse	S. Am.	Sterilize a mine.	*cantar*	5
Bruñir	Cent. Am.	*C. Rica, Nicar.* fig. Bother, irritate.		58
Buitrear	S. Am.	1. *Chile.* Hunt vultures. 2. *Chile, Peru.* Vomit.	*cantar*	5

		C		
Cabecear	S. Am., Caribbean	1. *Chile.* Form the tips of cigars. 2. *Cuba.* Bunch up tobacco leaves, tying them together by the stems.	*cantar*	5
Cabrear	S. Am.	1. *Peru.* Back out deceptively, especially in sports events or children's games. 2. *Chile.* Go jumping and skipping.	*cantar*	5
Cachar	Cent. Am., S. Am.	1. *Cent. Am., Col., Chile.* Gore, butt. 2. *Argent., Nicar., Urug.* vulg. Grab, seize, grasp. 3. *Cent. Am.* Rob. 4. *Argent., Chile.* fig., fam. Surprise or unmask someone. 5. *Chile.* Suspect someone. 6. *Argent., C. Rica, Ecuad., Par., Urug.* fig., fam. Mock people, making them the target of a joke, pull their leg. 7. *Cent. Am., Col., Venez.* Intercept the ball that one player is trying to throw to another (in certain games). 8. *Cent. Am., Col., Venez.* Grab any small object one person throws to another.	*cantar*	5
Cachetear	Lat. Am., S. Am.	1. *Lat. Am.* Slap someone in the face with an open hand. 2. *Chile.* refl. fam. Eat an abundance of food with pleasure.	*cantar*	5

Spanish Verb Manual

VERB	REGION	MEANING	MODEL	TABLE
Cachiporrearse	S. Am.	*Chile.* refl. Brag about oneself, praise oneself for something.	*cantar*	5
Caculear	Caribbean	*P. Rico.* fig. Change affections and feelings frequently, especially men in matters of love.	*cantar*	5
Calar	S. Am., Mexico	**1**. *Col.* Smash, ruin, exhibit one's power in order to humiliate someone. **2**. *Mex.* Remove a sample with a probe.	*cantar*	5
Caletear	S. Am.	*Chile.* Land a boat at every port on the coast, not just the larger ones (by extension, also applies to airplanes and trains).	*cantar*	5
Calimbar	Caribbean	*Cuba.* Brand, mark.	*cantar*	5
Calzar	S. Am., Cent. Am.	**1**. *Col., Ecuad.* Fill a tooth or molar. **2**. *Guat.* Cover with earth certain plants, such as celery, thistle, and endive, to tenderize and whiten them.	*cruzar*	8
Camandulear	Lat. Am.	Scheme, conduct oneself with hypocrisy.	*cantar*	5
Camaronear	S. Am., Mexico	**1**. *Peru.* Change one's opinion or loyalties because of favors or interests. **2**. *Mex.* Fish for shrimp.	*cantar*	5
Cambar	S. Am.	*Venez.* Bend, curve.	*cantar*	5
Camochar	Cent. Am.	*Hond.* Lop, prune trees and other plants.	*cantar*	5
Camorrear	S. Am.	*Argent., Urug.* Quarrel, kick up a row.	*cantar*	5
Campear	S. Am.	*Chile, R. Plate.* Leave to search for some person, animal or thing.	*cantar*	5
Cancanear	Lat. Am.	**1**. *Col., C. Rica, Nicar.* Stutter. **2**. *Cuba.* Shake with a particular noise when about to choke [a motor].	*cantar*	5
Canchear	S. Am.	Look for entertainment because of not working seriously.	*cantar*	5
Cangallar	S. Am.	*Bol., Chile.* Steal metals or metal-bearing rocks in the mines.	*cantar*	5
Cantaletear	Lat. Am., Mexico	**1**. *Lat. Am.* Repeat things until one becomes a nuisance.	*cantar*	5

regional use

VERB	REGION	MEANING	MODEL	TABLE
		2. *Mex.* Repeat a comical chorus, making fun of someone.		
Cantinflear	Mexico	**1.** Speak in a crazy, nonsensical manner like the comic actor Cantinflas. **2.** Act in the same way.	*cantar*	5
Capear	Cent. Am.	*Guat.* Miss classes with no justifiable excuse, behind the back of parents and tutors.	*cantar*	5
Caramelear	S. Am.	*Col.* fig., fam. Delay deceptively the resolution of a problematic situation.	*cantar*	5
Caratular	S. Am.	**1.** *Argent.* Insert a title page in a book. **2.** *Argent.* Cover one's face with a mask. **3.** *Argent.* Categorize, describe, entitle.	*cantar*	5
Cargosear	S. Am.	*Argent., Chile, Peru, Urug.* Pester, bother.	*cantar*	5
Carnear	Lat. Am., Mexico	**1.** *Lat. Am.* Kill and cut up cattle to eat the meat. **2.** *Mex.* vulg. Deceive someone.	*cantar*	5
Carpir	Lat. Am.	Clean or weed a lot, removing useless or harmful vegetation.	*vivir*	51
Carretear	Caribbean	*Cuba.* Squawk [parrots, especially young ones].	*cantar*	5
Castañear	Mexico	Chatter, make a sound with one's teeth.	*cantar*	5
Catatar	Lat. Am.	Enchant, fascinate.	*cantar*	5
Catear	Lat. Am., S. Am.	**1.** *Lat. Am.* Search a house with a warrant, fail. **2.** *Col., Chile, Ecuad., Peru.* Explore land in search of a mining vein.	*cantar*	5
Causear	S. Am.	**1.** *Chile.* Picnic, go on a picnic. **2.** *Chile.* Eat snacks between meals. **3.** *Chile.* Eat, in general. **4.** *Chile.* fig. Conquer someone easily.	*cantar*	5
Cayapear	S. Am.	*Venez.* Bring a large group together to attack one person without risk.	*cantar*	5
Cebar	S. Am.	*R. Plate.* Prepare *mate* (a medicinal herbal drink).	*cantar*	5

VERB	REGION	MEANING	MODEL	TABLE
Cecinar	S. Am.	*Ecuad.* Cut meat into cured strips.	*cantar*	5
Cedular	S. Am., Cent. Am.	*Col., Ecuad., Nicar.* Issue an identification or citizenship card.	*cantar*	5
Cepillar	Lat. Am.	Adulate, flatter.	*cantar*	5
Cerotear	S. Am.	*Chile.* Drip [the wax of lighted candles].	*cantar*	5
Chacanear	S. Am.	*Chile.* Force a horse to run faster.	*cantar*	5
Chacharear	Mexico	Trade in things that have little value.	*cantar*	5
Chacualear	Mexico	Splash, play in water.	*cantar*	5
Chalanear	Lat. Am.	Train horses.	*cantar*	5
Challar	S. Am.	**1.** *Bol.* Sprinkle the soil with liquor in homage to Mother Earth (*Pachamama*). **2.** *Bol.* Celebrate the purchase of a possession with food and drink.	*cantar*	5
Chambonear	Lat. Am.	Act like an awkward, clumsy bungler.	*cantar*	5
Champear	S. Am.	*Chile, Ecuad., Peru.* Place grass or sod in a lot or gate area.	*cantar*	5
Chancar	Cent. Am., S. Am.	**1.** *Cent. Am., Argent., Chile, Peru.* Grind, crush, mill, especially minerals. **2.** *Chile, Peru.* Hit, strike, mistreat. **3.** *Chile, Peru.* fig. Put down, defeat, surpass. **4.** *Chile, Ecuad.* fig. Do something poorly or halfway. **5.** *Peru.* fig. Study hard, bone up.	*atacar*	7
Chanflear	S. Am.	*Argent.* Round out a corner.	*cantar*	5
Chantar	Lat. Am., S. Am.	**1.** *Lat. Am.* Dress or put something on. **2.** *Argent., Ecuad., Peru.* Express in a direct manner what one thinks of someone. **3.** *Chile.* Strike or hit someone. **4.** *Chile.* Throw or put someone in a place against his/her will.	*cantar*	5
Chapear	Lat. Am.	*C. Rica, Cuba, Dom. Rep.* Clear the ground of weeds and grass with a machete.	*cantar*	5
Chapecar	S. Am.	*Chile.* Braid.	*atacar*	7

regional use

VERB	REGION	MEANING	MODEL	TABLE
Chapinizarse	Cent. Am.	Acquire the customs and manners of *chapines* (Guatemalans).	*cruzar*	8
Charquear	Lat. Am.	Make salted meat.	*cantar*	5
Chasconear	S. Am.	1. *Chile.* Entangle, muddle. 2. *Chile.* Pull or pull out hair. Have someone give a horse a short run. Cut the tips of plants.	*cantar*	5
Chequear	Cent. Am., Lat. Am.	1. *Cent. Am.* Write a check. 2. *Lat. Am.* Examine, check, inspect.	*cantar*	5
Chiclear	Mexico	Market chewing gum.	*cantar*	5
Chicotear	Lat. Am.	Whip someone.	*cantar*	5
Chinear	Cent. Am.	1. *Cent. Am.* Carry in one's arms or on one's back. 2. *C. Rica.* Pamper, care for with affection and great effort. 3. *C. Rica, Guat.* Take care of children as a nanny. 4. *Guat.* fig. Be very concerned about a person, situation or thing.	*cantar*	5
Chingar	Cent. Am., S. Am.	1. *Cent. Am.* Cut the tail off an animal. 2. *Argent., Urug.* Hang a suit or dress in a lopsided way. 3. *Argent., Chile, Peru.* Not be right, fail, become frustrated, miss.	*pagar*	6
Chinguear	Cent. Am.	1. *Hond.* Joke. 2. *C. Rica.* Domineer over others by inspiring fear.	*cantar*	5
Chiquear	Caribbean, Mexico	*Cuba, Mex.* Pamper, cuddle excessively, spoil.	*cantar*	5
Chivar	Lat. Am.	*Argent., Cuba, Guat., Urug., Venez.* Become angry, irritated.	*cantar*	5
Chivatear	S. Am., Caribbean	1. *Col., Cuba, P. Rico.* Accuse, denounce, squeal. 2. *Argent., Chile.* Shout like the war cry of the Chilean Arauca Indians. 3. *Argent.* Romp boisterously, talking gibberish [children].	*cantar*	5

Spanish Verb Manual

VERB	REGION	MEANING	MODEL	TABLE
Chopear	S. Am.	*Chile.* Work with a shovel.	*cantar*	5
Churrasquear	S. Am.	*Argent., Par., Urug.* Make and eat *churrascos* (grilled meat).	*cantar*	5
Chuzar	S. Am.	*Col.* Prick, puncture, wound.	*cruzar*	8
Cinchacear	Cent. Am.	*Guat.* fam. Whip someone with a belt.	*cantar*	5
Cinchar	S. Am.	**1.** *Argent., Urug.* fig., fam. Do all one can to make something happen. **2.** *Argent., Urug.* fig., fam. Work very hard.	*cantar*	5
Codear	S. Am.	Ask for something insistently; get something through cunning.	*cantar*	5
Coger	Lat. Am.	vulg. Have sexual intercourse.		25
Coimear	S. Am.	*Argent., Chile, Peru, Urug.* Give or receive a gift, in return for favors or to thank someone.	*cantar*	5
Colear	Mexico, S. Am.	**1.** *Mex.* Grab the tail of a running bull and trip it, using the stronger pulling power of one's horse. **2.** *Mex., Venez.* Pull on the tail of a steer, on horseback or on foot, causing the animal to fall.	*cantar*	5
Combalacharse	S. Am.	*Venez.* Band or work together, generally for bad purposes.	*cantar*	5
*Comedir	Lat. Am.	Offer oneself, be available for something.	*pedir*	60
Compadrear	S. Am.	*Argent., Par., Urug.* Brag, be conceited, provoke with contempt.	*cantar*	5
Complotar(se)	Lat. Am.	Conspire, plot, scheme, usually for political gain.	*cantar*	5
*Componer	Lat. Am.	*Argent., Chile, Guat., Mex., Peru, Urug.* Restore dislocated bones to their correct position.	*poner*	41
Conchabar(se)	S. Am.	Pay a salary, contract someone for menial services (generally domestic help).	*cantar*	5
Consubstanciarse	S. Am.	*Argent.* Identify oneself intimately with someone or with a particular view of reality.	*cantar*	5

regional use

VERB	REGION	MEANING	MODEL	TABLE
Contlapachear	Mexico	fam. Harbor someone, be someone's accomplice.	*cantar*	5
Contrapuntear(se)	S. Am., Caribbean	**1**. *Argent., Bol., Col., Chile, Venez.* Sing improvised verses [two or more singers]. **2**. *Bol., Col., Chile, Ecuad.* fig. Be in an argument [two or more people]. **3**. *Argent., Bol., Peru, P. Rico.* fig. Rival, compete against.	*cantar*	5
Coquear	S. Am.	*Bol.* Extract the juice of coca leaves into one's mouth.	*cantar*	5
Corar	Lat. Am.	Build indigenous farms.	*cantar*	5
Corbatear	S. Am.	*Col.* Grab someone by the tie.	*cantar*	5
Cortar	S. Am.	*Chile.* Begin to walk in a certain direction.	*cantar*	5
Coscachear	S. Am.	*Chile.* Punch someone lightly.	*cantar*	5
Costear	S. Am.	*Argent., Urug.* Be transplanted to a distant or hard-to-reach place.	*cantar*	5
Cotizar	Lat. Am.	Impose a limit on the amount of money to be used for a certain purpose.	*cruzar*	8
Coyotear	Mexico	fam. Act like a coyote (transporter of "wetbacks"), as an unofficial negotiator.	*cantar*	5
Coyundear	Cent. Am.	*Nicar.* Beat or punish with a strap or whip.	*cantar*	5
Cuadrar	S. Am.	*Chile.* Give or subscribe a large quantity of money.	*cantar*	5
Cuartear	S. Am., Mexico	**1**. *Argent.* Hitch a vehicle in trouble in order to tow it. **2**. *Mex.* Flog with a horsewhip.	*cantar*	5
Cuerear	S. Am., Cent. Am.	**1**. *S. Am.* Work in the preparation of leather. **2**. *Ecuad., Nicar.* Whip.	*cantar*	5
Cuerpear	S. Am.	**1**. *R. Plate.* Steal a body. **2**. *Argent.* fig. Avoid a difficulty or problem through astuteness.	*cantar*	5
Cuitear(se)	Cent. Am.	Defecate [birds].	*cantar*	5

VERB	REGION	MEANING	MODEL	TABLE
Cumbearse	Cent. Am.	*Hond.* Express praise to one another.	*cantar*	5
Cuotear	S. Am.	*Chile.* Prorate, distribute something equally among various people.	*cantar*	5
Cuquear	Caribbean	*Cuba.* Incite a dog to attack someone.	*cantar*	5
Curarse	S. Am.	*Chile.* fam. Get drunk, become intoxicated.	*cantar*	5
Curtir	S. Am.	*Argent., Urug.* fig. Punish by whipping.	*vivir*	51
D				
Debocar	S. Am.	*Argent.* vulg. Vomit.	*atacar*	7
Demeritar	Lat. Am.	Cast a slur on someone, take away merit.	*cantar*	5
Denguear	Lat. Am.	Move affectedly with the shoulders and hips when walking.	*cantar*	5
*Deponer	Cent. Am., Mexico	*Hond., Guat., Mex., Nicar.* Vomit.	*poner*	41
Derriscar(se)	Caribbean	*Cuba, P. Rico.* Hurl someone down.	*atacar*	7
Desastillar	Lat. Am.	Remove splinters from wood.	*cantar*	5
Desaterrar	Lat. Am.	Clear, clean up debris or dirt to level a place.	*cantar*	5
Desbabar	Lat. Am.	*Mex., Peru, P. Rico, Venez.* Remove the froth from coffee or hot chocolate.	*cantar*	5
Desbalagar	Mexico	Disperse, scatter.	*pagar*	6
Desbotonar	Lat. Am.	Remove the buds and main stem of plants (especially tobacco) to stunt their growth and increase the size of the remaining leaves.	*cantar*	5
Descabezar	S. Am., Caribbean	**1.** *Col.* Deprive, remove from office or job. **2.** *Bol., P. Rico.* Diminish the proof of liquor by adding water.	*cruzar*	8
Descachazar	Lat. Am.	Remove impurities from the *guarapo* drink.	*cruzar*	8
Descambiar	Lat. Am.	Change bills or coins for smaller or larger bills or coins.	*cantar*	5
Descarozar	Lat. Am.	Remove the pit from fruit.	*cruzar*	8

253

regional use

VERB	REGION	MEANING	MODEL	TABLE
Deschapar	S. Am.	*Argent., Bol., Chile, Ecuad., Peru.* Force a lock.	*cantar*	5
Descharchar	Cent. Am.	Dismiss, fire someone from a job.	*cantar*	5
Deschavetarse	S. Am.	*Col., Peru, Urug.* fam. Lose one's reason.	*cantar*	5
*Descomponer(se)	Mexico	Damage, ruin, spoil.	*poner*	41
Desconchabar(se)	Lat. Am.	*Cent. Am., Mex.* Break, dislocate.	*cantar*	5
Descrestar	S. Am.	*Col.* Deceive someone.	*cantar*	5
Descuadrilarse	Lat. Am.	Injure the hip [an animal].	*cantar*	5
Descuajeringar	Lat. Am.	**1**. Break, disunite, disconcert. **2**. Relax parts of the body because of tiredness.	*pagar*	6
Descuerar	Lat. Am.	Flay, skin.	*cantar*	5
Descunchar	S. Am.	*Col.* fam. Lose one's last cent in a game.	*cantar*	5
Desempeñar(se)	Lat. Am.	Act, work, dedicate oneself to an activity in a satisfactory way.	*cantar*	5
Desempercudir	Caribbean	*Cuba.* Launder clothes, cleansing them of all dirtiness.	*vivir*	51
Desengavetar	Cent. Am.	*Guat.* Take out something that was stored in a drawer for a long time.	*cantar*	5
Desentechar	Cent. Am., S. Am.	*Cent. Am., Col., Ecuad.* Take the roof off of a building.	*cantar*	5
Desentejar	Cent. Am., S. Am.	**1**. *Cent. Am., Col., Ecuad., Venez.* Remove tiles from the roofs of buildings or brambles from the walls. **2**. *Cent. Am., Col., Ecuad., Venez.* fig. Leave something with no hope of repair or defense.	*cantar*	5
Desgarrar	Lat. Am.	Get rid of phlegm or mucus.	*cantar*	5
Desguañangar	Lat. Am.	Break, pull to pieces.	*pagar*	6
Deshijar	Lat. Am., S. Am.	**1**. *Lat. Am.* Remove suckers from plants. **2**. *Argent.* Cease being a godparent, separate litters.	*cantar*	5

r

regional use

VERB	REGION	MEANING	MODEL	TABLE
Desmadrar	S. Am.	*Col.* Suffer the pathological descent of the uterus.	*cantar*	5
Desmalezar	Lat. Am.	Weed, clear, remove weeds.	*cruzar*	8
Desmanchar	Lat. Am.	1. Leave the flock or herd [an animal]. 2. Get lost, become disorientated. 3. Disband, flee, run away. 4. Abandon the group or company to which one belongs.	*cantar*	5
Desmechar	Mexico	fam. Pull out hair or beard with hands.	*cantar*	5
Desmonetizar(se)	S. Am., Caribbean	*Argent., Chile, Par., P. Rico.* Depreciate, discredit.	*cruzar*	8
Desocupar	S. Am., Cent. Am.	*Argent., Hond., Urug., Venez.* Give birth.	*cantar*	5
Despabilar	Lat. Am.	Slip away, leave.	*cantar*	5
Despancar	Lat. Am.	Remove the husk that covers the corn cob.	*atacar*	7
Desparpajar(se)	Cent. Am., Caribbean	*Hond., P. Rico.* Shake off sleepiness, wake up.	*cantar*	5
Desparramar	Lat. Am.	*Argent., Mex., Par., P. Rico.* Disseminate an announcement or notice.	*cantar*	5
Despelucar(se)	Lat. Am.	*Col., Chile, Mex., Pan.* Ruffle or mess up someone's hair.	*atacar*	7
Despeluzar	Caribbean, Cent. Am.	*Cuba, Nicar.* Pluck feathers; skin someone, leaving them with no money.	*cruzar*	8
Despenar	Lat. Am.	Put out of misery, help a dying person to die.	*cantar*	5
Despercudir(se)	Lat. Am.	1. Clean or wash something that is stained. 2. fig. Awaken, wake someone up. 3. refl. Whiten, lighten the skin.	*vivir*	51
Despernancarse	Lat. Am.	Spread one's legs, open one's legs wide.	*atacar*	7
Despezuñarse	Lat. Am.	1. *Col., Chile, Hond., P. Rico.* fig. Walk very fast. 2. *Col., Chile, Hond., P. Rico.* fig. Kill oneself to do something, put great effort into doing something.	*cantar*	5

Spanish Verb Manual

regional use

VERB	REGION	MEANING	MODEL	TABLE
Despicar(se)	S. Am.	*Col., Venez.* Cause a fighting rooster to lose the sharpest part of its beak.	*atacar*	7
Despichar	S. Am.	*Col., Chile, Venez.* Flatten, squash.	*cantar*	5
Despilarar	Lat. Am.	Tear down the supports in a mine.	*cantar*	5
Despintar	S. Am., Caribbean	*Col., Chile, P. Rico.* fig., fam. Look away from, lose sight of.	*cantar*	5
Despostar	S. Am.	*Argent., Bol., Chile, Ecuad., Urug.* Cut up a steer or bird in pieces.	*cantar*	5
Despotizar	S. Am.	*Chile, Ecuad.* Govern or treat someone despotically, tyrannize.	*cruzar*	8
Desprender(se)	S. Am., Caribbean	*Argent., Par., P. Rico, Urug.* Unlatch, unbutton.	*beber*	24
Despresar	S. Am.	Cut up an animal in pieces.	*cantar*	5
Desrielar(se)	Lat. Am.	Jump the tracks [a train, tram, etc.].	*cantar*	5
Desriscar(se)	S. Am., Caribbean	*Chile, P. Rico.* Hurl something from a cliff.	*atacar*	7
Destapar	Lat. Am.	Reveal the name of a person hiding his/her identity.	*cantar*	5
Destemplar	Lat. Am.	*Chile, Ecuad., Guat., Mex., Peru.* Feel pain in one's teeth and gums (also fig.).	*cantar*	5
Desternerar	S. Am., Caribbean	*Chile, P. Rico, Urug.* Wean calves or separate them from their mothers.	*cantar*	5
Destupir	Caribbean	*Cuba.* Remove obstructions.	*vivir*	51
Destusar	Cent. Am.	Remove the husk from corn.	*cantar*	5
Desubicar(se)	Lat. Am.	Place a person or thing out of its usual position.	*atacar*	7
***Devolverse**[32]	Lat. Am.	Turn around.	*mover*	30
Dictar	Lat. Am.	Give, deliver or lead classes, conferences, etc.	*cantar*	5

Spanish Verb Manual

VERB	REGION	MEANING	MODEL	TABLE
Difuntear	Lat. Am.	fam. Kill.	*cantar*	5
Discar	S. Am.	*Argent.* Dial a number on the telephone.	*atacar*	7
Dispararse	Lat. Am.	Leave or run headlong.	*cantar*	5
Doblar	Mexico	Shoot, discharge a gun at someone or something; wound or kill with bullets.	*cantar*	5
Dragonear	Lat. Am.	1. Act in a position without having a title for it. 2. Show off, presume.	*cantar*	5
E				
Echar	S. Am., Caribbean	*Argent., P. Rico.* Propose or present a person or animal as superior to its adversaries.	*cantar*	5
Emballestarse	Mexico	Contract deformed, curved hands.	*cantar*	5
Embancarse	Mexico, S. Am.	1. *Mex.* Stick debris to the walls of a foundry oven, ruining its operation. 2. *Chile, Ecuad.* Muddy a river, lake, etc. by flooding.	*atacar*	7
Embanquetar	Mexico	Place sidewalks or curbs in streets.	*cantar*	5
Embarrar(se)	Lat. Am.	1. *Cent. Am., Mex.* Get involved in something dirty. 2. *Lat. Am.* fig. Slander or discredit someone. 3. *Lat. Am.* Cause harm, annoy. 4. *Lat. Am.* Commit a crime.	*cantar*	5
Embarrialarse	Cent. Am., S. Am.	1. *Cent. Am., Venez.* See *embarrar(se)*. 2. *Cent. Am.* Get stuck.	*cantar*	5
Embejucar	Caribbean, S. Am.	1. *Ant., Col., P. Rico, Venez.* Cover or wrap with rattan (see *bejuquear*, 2). 2. *Col.* Disorient. 3. *Col., Venez.* refl. Get entangled. 4. *Col.* Get angry, annoyed.	*atacar*	7
Embicar(se)	Mexico	Bend the elbow, drink.	*atacar*	7
Embicharse	S. Am.	*Argent.* Fill with fly larvae [the wounds of animals].	*cantar*	5
Embijar	Mexico, Cent. Am.	*Mex., Nicar.* Stain, dirty, cover with mud.	*cantar*	5

VERB	REGION	MEANING	MODEL	TABLE
Embochinchar(se)	Lat. Am.	Cause an uproar or a disorder.	*cantar*	5
Embolatar	S. Am.	**1**. *Col.* Deceive with lies or false promises. **2**. *Col.* Delay, put off. **3**. *Col.* Entangle, confuse, muddle. **4**. *Col.* refl. Be absorbed by a matter, become engrossed. **5**. *Col.* Get lost, go astray. **6**. *Col.* Agitate.	*cantar*	5
Embolismar	S. Am.	*Chile.* Make a din, riot.	*cantar*	5
Embonar	Lat. Am.	*Cuba, Ecuad., Mex.* Connect, join, bind one thing to another.	*cantar*	5
Emborrascar	Cent. Am., Mexico	*Hond., Mex.* Weaken or lose the vein in a mine.	*atacar*	7
Emborucarse	Mexico	Be perplexed.	*atacar*	7
Embostar	S. Am.	**1**. *Venez.* Plaster walls with a mixture of horse manure and dirt. **2**. *Venez.* Leave soapy clothes for some time.	*cantar*	5
Embrocar	Cent. Am., Mexico	*Hond., Mex.* Turn a vase or plate upside down, and by extension, any other thing. Used also with refl.	*atacar*	7
Embrollar	S. Am.	*Chile, Urug.* Take something through deception.	*cantar*	5
Embromar(se)	Lat. Am.	**1**. *Chile, Mex., Peru.* Detain, cause to lose time. **2**. *Argent., Col., Cuba, Chile, Mex., Peru, P. Rico, Dom. Rep., Urug.* Annoy, bother. **3**. *Argent., Chile, P. Rico, Dom. Rep., Urug.* Hurt, cause moral or material harm.	*cantar*	5
Embroncarse	S. Am.	*Argent.* fam. Get mad, become angry, get annoyed.	*atacar*	7
Embullar	S. Am., Cent. Am.	*Col., C. Rica.* Make a racket, cause a disorder.	*cantar*	5
Emburujarse	Lat. Am.	*Mex., P. Rico, Venez.* Wrap oneself up, cover one's body well.	*cantar*	5
Empacar	Lat. Am.	Pack luggage.	*atacar*	7

VERB	REGION	MEANING	MODEL	TABLE
Empacarse	Lat. Am.	Refuse to walk [an animal] (see *armar, 1*).	*atacar*	7
Empajar	Lat. Am.	**1.** *Col., Chile, Ecuad., Nicar.* Put on a straw roof. **2.** *Chile.* Mix with straw, especially to make adobe bricks. **3.** *Chile.* refl. Produce a great deal of straw and little fruit [cereal grains]. **4.** *P. Rico, Venez.* Stuff oneself, fill up with food that has no substance.	*cantar*	5
Empalarse	S. Am.	**1.** *Chile.* Become obstinate or infatuated. **2.** *Chile.* Go numb, be frozen stiff.	*cantar*	5
Empamparse	S. Am.	Get lost in the *pampas* (the Argentine plains).	*cantar*	5
Empañetar	Lat. Am.	**1.** *Cent. Am., Ecuad., P. Rico.* Cover with mud, cover a wall with a mixture of mud, straw, and cow dung. **2.** *Col., P. Rico.* Apply plaster or mortar to the walls, roof or front of buildings. Clean or make shiny (silver, weapons, etc.).	*cantar*	5
Emparamar(se)	S. Am.	**1.** *Col., Venez.* Freeze. **2.** *Col., Venez.* Wet [rain, humidity or dew].	*cantar*	5
Empardar	S. Am.	*Argent.* Tie, come out equal, especially in card games.	*cantar*	5
Empastar(se)	Lat. Am.	**1.** *Chile, Mex., Nicar.* Turn into pasture. **2.** *Argent., Chile.* Suffer from bloating by eating grasses that produce gas [animals]. Used more with refl. **3.** *Chile.* refl. Fill up with weeds [a sown field].	*cantar*	5
Empatar	Lat. Am.	**1.** *Col., C. Rica, Mex., P. Rico, Venez.* Join, bind one thing to another. **2.** *Col.* Spend time doing tiresome things.	*cantar*	5
Empavonar	S. Am., Caribbean	*Col., P. Rico.* Grease, spread on.	*cantar*	5
Empelotarse	Lat. Am.	*Col., Cuba, Chile, Mex.* Get undressed, be naked.	*cantar*	5
Empertigar	S. Am.	*Chile.* Tie the shaft of a cart to the yoke.	*pagar*	6

regional use

VERB	REGION	MEANING	MODEL	TABLE
Empetatar	Mexico	Cover with mats, use palm matting to cover a floor or wrap a package.	*cantar*	5
Empilchar(se)	S. Am.	*Argent., Urug.* fam. Dress, especially with care.	*cantar*	5
Empilonar	Caribbean	*Cuba.* Make large piles of dry tobacco, placing the opened leaves on top of each other.	*cantar*	5
Empiparse	S. Am., Caribbean	*Chile, Ecuad., Peru, P. Rico.* Guzzle, gorge on food or drink.	*cantar*	5
Emplantillar	S. Am.	*Chile.* Make solid, fill (the foundations being laid) with rubble.	*cantar*	5
Emplomar	S. Am.	*Argent.* Put a filling in a tooth or molar (see *calzar, 1*).	*cantar*	5
Emplumar	S. Am., Caribbean	**1.** *Ecuad., Venez.* Send someone to a place of punishment. **2.** *Col., Ecuad., P. Rico.* Run away, flee, take off.	*cantar*	5
Emponcharse	S. Am.	*Argent., Ecuad., Peru, Urug.* Put on a *poncho.*	*cantar*	5
Empotrerar	Lat. Am.	Put out to pasture, put (cattle) in a field to graze.	*cantar*	5
Empozar	Lat. Am.	Remain on the ground, forming puddles [water].	*cruzar*	8
Empuntar	S. Am.	**1.** *Col., Ecuad.* Direct, guide, lead. **2.** *Col., Ecuad.* Go away, leave. **3.** *Venez.* refl. Be obstinate about a point.	*cantar*	5
Empuñar	S. Am.	*Chile.* Close the hand to form a fist.	*cantar*	5
Empurrarse	Cent. Am.	*C. Rica, Guat., Hond., Nicar.* Sulk or fly into a tantrum.	*cantar*	5
Enancarse	Lat. Am.	**1.** Mount over the rump of an animal. **2.** fig. Go into a place uninvited.	*atacar*	7
Enarcar	Mexico	Rear up [a horse].	*atacar*	7

VERB	REGION	MEANING	MODEL	TABLE
Encabuyar	Caribbean, S. Am.	*Cuba, P. Rico, Venez.* Bind, tie something up with hemp cord.	*cantar*	5
Encachar(se)	S. Am.	**1**. *Chile.* Lower the head to charge [cattle]. **2**. *Chile, Venez.* refl. Be obstinate, dead set. **3**. *Chile.* refl. Lower the head.	*cantar*	5
Encalambrarse	S. Am., Caribbean	*Col., Chile, P. Rico.* Get numb, be frozen.	*cantar*	5
Encalamocar(se)	S. Am.	*Venez.* Stupefy, be silly for love.	*atacar*	7
Encalillarse	S. Am.	*Chile.* Become indebted.	*cantar*	5
Encamotarse	S. Am., Cent. Am.	*Argent., C. Rica, Chile, Ecuad., Peru.* fam. Fall in love, fall madly in love.	*cantar*	5
Encampanar(se)	Lat. Am.	**1**. *Col., P. Rico, Dom. Rep., Venez.* Raise, elevate. **2**. *Mex.* Leave someone in the lurch. **3**. *Col.* refl. Fall in love. **4**. *Venez.* Go inside, move into.	*cantar*	5
Encanarse	S. Am.	*Col.* Go to jail (underworld slang).	*cantar*	5
Encandelillar	S. Am., Cent. Am.	**1**. *Argent., Col., Chile, Ecuad., Peru.* Whipstitch the bottom of a cloth. **2**. *Col., Chile, Ecuad., Hond., Peru, Venez.* Make starry-eyed, dazzle.	*cantar*	5
Encandilarse	Caribbean	*P. Rico.* Become angry.	*cantar*	5
Encapotar	Caribbean	*Cuba, P. Rico.* Be sad, with drooping wings [a bird].	*cantar*	5
Encarpetar	S. Am., Cent. Am.	*Argent., Chile, Ecuad., Nicar., Peru.* Shelve, leave pending.	*cantar*	5
Encartuchar(se)	S. Am., Caribbean	*Col., Chile, Ecuad., P. Rico.* Wrap in the form of a roll.	*cantar*	5
Encasquillar	Lat. Am., Caribbean	**1**. *Lat. Am.* Shoe or brand horses or oxen. **2**. *Cuba.* fig., fam. Become frightened, lose courage.	*cantar*	5
Enchamicar	S. Am.	*Ecuad.* Give thorn apple juice to someone (as a potion or poison).	*atacar*	7

regional use

VERB	REGION	MEANING	MODEL	TABLE
Enchicharse	S. Am.	*Col.* Get drunk.	*cantar*	5
Enchilar(se)	Cent. Am., Mexico	**1**. *C. Rica, Hond., Mex., Nicar.* Spread or prepare with chilies. **2**. *Mex., Nicar.* fig. Tease, bother, irritate.	*cantar*	5
Enchinar	Mexico	Curl one's hair.	*cantar*	5
Enchinchar	Cent. Am., Mexico	**1**. *Guat.* Pester, annoy. **2**. *Mex.* Cause someone to lose time.	*cantar*	5
Enchipar	S. Am.	*Col.* Coil, roll up.	*cantar*	5
Enchivarse	S. Am., Caribbean	*Col., Ecuad., P. Rico.* Fly into a tantrum, lose one's temper.	*cantar*	5
Enchuecar(se)	S. Am., Mexico	*Chile, Mex.* fam. Twist, bend.	*atacar*	7
Enchumbar	Lat. Am.	Dunk, saturate with water.	*cantar*	5
Encielar	S. Am.	*Chile.* Make a ceiling, roof or covering for something.	*cantar*	5
Encimar	S. Am.	**1**. *Col.* Give more than what is required, add. **2**. *Chile.* Reach the top of a mountain or hill.	*cantar*	5
Encobrar	S. Am.	*Chile.* Tie one end of a rope to a tree trunk, rock, etc., to hold fast an animal.	*cantar*	5
Encohetarse	Cent. Am.	*C. Rica.* Be infuriated, lose one's temper.	*cantar*	5
Encorselar(se)	Lat. Am.	Put on a corset.	*cantar*	5
Encuartar	Mexico	**1**. Get tangled in the harness. **2**. refl. fig. Get tied up in a deal and not know how to get out of it.	*cantar*	5
Encuerar(se)	Lat. Am.	*Col., Cuba, Mex., Peru, Dom. Rep.* Undress someone, leave someone naked.	*cantar*	5
Enditarse	S. Am.	*Chile.* Fall into debt, be indebted.	*cantar*	5
Endrogarse	Caribbean	*P. Rico, Dom. Rep.* Drug oneself, use narcotics.	*pagar*	6
Energizar(se)	S. Am.	**1**. *Col.* Work with energy, act with vigor and vehemence. **2**. *Col.* Stimulate, give energy.	*cruzar*	8

Spanish Verb Manual

VERB	REGION	MEANING	MODEL	TABLE
Enfiestarse	Lat. Am.	*Col., Chile, Hond., Mex., Nicar., Venez.* Be in a festive mood, have fun.	*cantar*	5
Enflautar	S. Am.	*Col.* fam. Hurl an insult, say something inappropriate or bothersome to someone.	*cantar*	5
Enfunchar(se)	Caribbean	*P. Rico.* Anger, infuriate.	*cantar*	5
Enfurruscarse	S. Am.	*Chile.* fam. Be infuriated.	*atacar*	7
Engaratusar	Cent. Am., Mexico	*Guat., Hond., Mex., Nicar.* Get around someone, wheedle.	*cantar*	5
Engarzarse	Lat. Am.	Get mixed up or involved in something.	*cruzar*	8
Engavetar	Cent. Am.	*Guat.* Store something in a drawer for an indefinite period (see *desengavetar*).	*cantar*	5
Engorrar	S. Am.	*Venez.* Upset, bother.	*cantar*	5
Engrillarse	Caribbean, S. Am.	*P. Rico, Venez.* Hold its head too low [a horse].	*cantar*	5
Engringarse	Lat. Am.	Take on the customs and lifestyle of *gringos* or foreigners.	*pagar*	6
Engualichar	S. Am.	*Argent.* Bewitch, cast a spell on.	*cantar*	5
Enguaraparse	Lat. Am.	See *aguaraparse*.	*cantar*	5
Enguitarrarse	S. Am.	*Venez.* Dress like a Levite or use other ceremonial garments.	*cantar*	5
Enhorquetar(se)	S. Am., Caribbean	*Argent., Cuba, P. Rico, Urug.* Saddle, sit astride.	*cantar*	5
Enlajar	S. Am.	*Venez.* Cover the ground with thin, flat stones.	*cantar*	5
Enlatar	Cent. Am.	*Hond.* Cover a roof or build a fence using wooden tiles.	*cantar*	5
Enlozar	Lat. Am.	Cover with a layer of earth or vitreous enamel.	*cruzar*	8
Enmaniguarse	Caribbean	**1**. *Cuba, P. Rico.* Become a tropical forest, swampy and impenetrable [a plot of land]. **2**. *Cuba, P. Rico.* fig. Get accustomed to rural life.	*averiguar*	11

regional use

VERB	REGION	MEANING	MODEL	TABLE
Enmonarse	S. Am.	*Peru.* Get sloshed, drunk.	*cantar*	5
Enmontarse	Lat. Am.	Become covered with weeds [a field].	*cantar*	5
Enmontunarse	S. Am.	*Venez.* Become a hick; become rude, uncouth.	*cantar*	5
Enmugrar	S. Am., Mexico	*Col., Chile, Mex.* Cover with filth or dirt.	*cantar*	5
Enrejar	Lat. Am.	**1**. *Col., Cuba, Guat., Hond., Venez.* Place rope on or hobble an animal. **2**. *Col., Cuba, Hond.* Tie a calf to a cow's leg to milk the mother cow.	*cantar*	5
Enrielar(se)	S. Am., Mexico	**1**. *Chile, Mex.* Put on a rail track. **2**. *Chile.* fig. Get on track, guide.	*cantar*	5
Enrostrar	Lat. Am.	Throw into the face of someone.	*cantar*	5
Ensabanarse	S. Am.	*Venez.* Rise up, rebel, revolt.	*cantar*	5
Ensartar(se)	Lat. Am.	*Chile, Mex., Nicar., Peru, Urug.* fig. Make someone fall for a lie or a trap.	*cantar*	5
Enserenar	S. Am.	**1**. *Ecuad.* Leave (food, clothes) in the open air at night to keep them cool or air them out. **2**. *Ecuad.* refl. Stay outside in the cool of the night [a person].	*cantar*	5
Enseriarse	Caribbean, S. Am.	*Cuba, Peru, P. Rico, Venez.* Become serious, showing displeasure or disagreement.	*cantar*	5
Ensimismarse	S. Am.	*Col., Chile.* Enjoy oneself, be conceited, be arrogant.	*cantar*	5
Ensopar(se)	S. Am.	Soak; prepare a soup.	*cantar*	5
Entablar(se)	S. Am., Lat. Am.	**1**. *Argent.* Accustom cattle or horses to walk in a herd. **2**. *Lat. Am.* Equal, tie.	*cantar*	5
Enterar	Lat. Am.	*Col., C. Rica, Hond., Mex.* Pay, hand over money.	*cantar*	5
Enterciar	Mexico	Pack, make up loads with merchandise.	*cantar*	5

Spanish Verb Manual

VERB	REGION	MEANING	MODEL	TABLE
*Enterrar	Lat. Am.	Nail or puncture with a sharp, penetrating tool.	*pensar*	13
Entilar	Cent. Am.	**1**. *Hond*. Stain with soot, ashes or other similar materials. Used also with refl. **2**. *Hond*. Stain as with soot to change a substance's color. Used also with refl. **3**. *Hond*. fig. Tarnish, darken or stain the fame or reputation of someone.	*cantar*	5
Entisar	Caribbean	*Cuba*. Cover a vase with netting.	*cantar*	5
Entrabar	S. Am.	*Col., Peru*. Impede, disturb.	*cantar*	5
Entreverarse	S. Am.	**1**. *Argent., Peru*. Mix (persons, animals or things) indiscriminately. **2**. *Argent*. Collide while their riders fight each other hand-to-hand [two horses].	*cantar*	5
Entroncar(se)	Lat. Am.	**1**. *Mex*. Match two horses or mares with the same colored coat. **2**. *Cuba, Mex., Peru, P. Rico*. Join together two lines of transportation.	*atacar*	7
Entropillar	S. Am.	*Argent., Urug*. Accustom (horses) to living in a herd.	*cantar*	5
Envegarse	S. Am.	*Chile*. Become swampy, have excessive humidity [land].	*pagar*	6
Envelar	S. Am.	*Chile*. Hide, flee.	*cantar*	5
Enyerbar	Mexico	Give someone a poisonous drink.	*cantar*	5
Erogar	S. Am.	*Bol*. Spend money.	*pagar*	6
Erupcionar	S. Am.	*Col*. Erupt [volcano].	*cantar*	5
Escarapelar(se)	S. Am., Cent. Am.	**1**. *Col., C. Rica, Venez*. Shell, peel, crack. **2**. *Col*. Crumple, handle. **3**. *Peru*. refl. Get goose bumps.	*cantar*	5
Escarcear	S. Am.	*Argent., Urug., Venez*. Turn circles [a horse].	*cantar*	5
Escobillar	Lat. Am.	Tap shoes softly as if sweeping the floor (in some traditional dances).	*cantar*	5

VERB	REGION	MEANING	MODEL	TABLE
Escollar	S. Am.	*Argent., Chile.* fig. Fail, not carry out a goal because of a hindrance.	*cantar*	5
Escorar	Caribbean, Cent. Am.	**1**. *Cuba.* Prop up, shore up. **2**. *Cuba, Hond.* refl. Place oneself where one's entire body is hidden.	*cantar*	5
*Esmorecer(se)	Lat. Am.	*C. Rica, Cuba, Venez.* Faint, get out of breath.	*obedecer*	33
Espaldear	S. Am.	*Chile.* Back up, protect, defend someone.	*cantar*	5
Espelucar(se)	Lat. Am.	See *despeluzar.*	*atacar*	7
Espernancarse	Lat. Am.	Open one's legs.	*atacar*	7
Estacar	Lat. Am.	**1**. *Lat. Am.* Hold down, nail with stakes, especially of leather when stretched out to dry. **2**. *Col., C. Rica.* Be punctured, get a splinter.	*atacar*	7
Estaquear	S. Am.	**1**. *Argent.* Stake, stretch out leather, holding it taut with stakes. **2**. *Argent.* By extension, to torture by tying down with leather strips stretched between four stakes.	*cantar*	5
Estribar	S. Am.	*Argent.* Place a foot in a stirrup [a rider].	*cantar*	5
*Expedirse	S. Am.	*Urug.* Manage, go it alone, fend for oneself in life.	*pedir*	60
Expensar	S. Am., Mexico	*Chile, Mex.* Pay the costs of a financial action or a business deal.	*cantar*	5
F				
Fajar(se)	Lat. Am.	**1**. *Argent., C. Rica, Cuba, Chile, Peru, Urug.* Hit or strike someone. **2**. *P. Rico, Dom. Rep.* Ask to borrow money. **3**. *Cuba.* Court a woman, dishonestly causing her to fall in love. **4**. *C. Rica, P. Rico, Dom. Rep.* Work, dedicate oneself intensely to a job.	*cantar*	5
Farrear	S. Am.	*Argent., Chile, Peru, Urug.* fam. Go on a binge or spree, have fun.	*cantar*	5

VERB	REGION	MEANING	MODEL	TABLE
Farsantear	S. Am.	*Chile.* Speak or deal as a charlatan.	*cantar*	5
Felpear	S. Am.	*Argent.* fam. Reproach a person harshly.	*cantar*	5
Figurear	Caribbean	*Dom. Rep.* Try to play the role of protagonist or a main character.	*cantar*	5
Fintear	Lat. Am.	Behave falsely.	*cantar*	5
Fletar	Lat. Am.	**1.** *Lat. Am.* Rent an animal or a vehicle to transport people or freight. **2.** *Chile, Peru.* fig. Express, spit out, let loose words or actions that are inappropriate or aggressive. **3.** *Argent., Chile, Urug.* Send someone to a place against his/her will. **4.** *Argent., Chile, Urug.* Fire someone from a job or employment. **5.** *Cuba.* refl. Go away, leave quickly. **6.** *Argent.* Gate-crash, go to an event without being invited. **7.** *Mex.* Be in charge of a hard job, unwillingly. **8.** *Mex.* Lean.	*cantar*	5
Fletear	Cent. Am., Caribbean	**1.** *C. Rica, Nicar.* Transport freight from one place to another. **2.** *Cuba, C. Rica.* Walk through the streets looking for customers [a prostitute].	*cantar*	5
Florear	S. Am., Lat. Am.	**1.** *Chile.* Choose the best of a thing. **2.** *Lat. Am.* Bloom.	*cantar*	5
Fondearse	Lat. Am.	Accumulate funds, become rich.	*cantar*	5
Fotutear	Caribbean	*Cuba.* Blow the horn in an insistent and aggravating way.	*cantar*	5
*Fregar(se)	Lat. Am.	fig., fam. Pester, bother, get on someone's nerves.	*negar*	14
Fritar	S. Am.	*Col.* Fry.	*cantar*	5
Fundir	Lat. Am.	fig., fam. Be destroyed, sunken.	*vivir*	51
Fungir	Caribbean	*Cuba, P. Rico.* Act like one is something (conceited).	*dirigir*	52

VERB	REGION	MEANING	MODEL	TABLE
		G		
Gafarse	S. Am.	*Col.* Have sore feet or hooves from walking too much [especially unshod horses].	*cantar*	5
Galuchar	S. Am., Caribbean	*Col., P. Rico, Venez.* Gallop.	*cantar*	5
Gargarear	Lat. Am.	Gargle.	*cantar*	5
Garuar	Lat. Am.	impers. Drizzle.	*actuar*	10
Gauchear	S. Am.	*Argent., Urug.* Adopt the customs of *gauchos* (see *agauchar(se)*).	*cantar*	5
Golletear	S. Am.	*Col.* Grab someone by the neck.	*cantar*	5
Gorgorear	S. Am.	*Chile.* Make warbling sounds, especially when singing.	*cantar*	5
Guachapear	S. Am.	*Chile.* Steal, rob, snatch.	*cantar*	5
Guachinear	Caribbean	*Cuba.* fig. Be unable to choose between two options.	*cantar*	5
Guantear	Lat. Am.	Slap, insult.	*cantar*	5
Guapear	S. Am.	*Urug.* Show off, boast, brag.	*cantar*	5
Guataquear	Caribbean	**1**. *Cuba.* Clear the land of undergrowth with a hoe. **2**. *Cuba.* fig. Praise systematically and prompted by vested interests.	*cantar*	5
Guayar	Caribbean	**1**. *Dom. Rep.* Grate, break into small pieces with a grater. **2**. *P. Rico.* refl. Get drunk, get intoxicated.	*cantar*	5
		H		
Halar	Caribbean, Cent. Am.	*Cuba, Nicar.* Draw something toward oneself.	*cantar*	5
Hamacar(se)	S. Am., Cent. Am.	**1**. *Argent., Guat., Par., Urug.* Rock, swing. **2**. *Argent.* By extension, sway. **3**. *Argent.* fig., fam. Confront a difficult situation with vigor.	*atacar*	7

VERB	REGION	MEANING	MODEL	TABLE
Hamaquear(se)	Lat. Am., Caribbean	**1**. *Lat. Am.* Rock, swing, especially in a hammock. **2**. *Cuba.* fig. Make dizzy, keep someone on the go [especially a mischievous child].	*cantar*	5
Harinear	S. Am.	*Venez.* impers. Rain in small drops.	*cantar*	5
Harnear	S. Am.	*Chile.* Sift, clean wheat with a sieve.	*cantar*	5
Hijuelar	S. Am.	*Chile.* Divide a rural ranch into smaller ranches.	*cantar*	5
Historiar[30]	Lat. Am.	fam. Complicate, confuse, muddle.	*cantar*	5
Hormiguillar	Lat. Am.	Mix powdered silver ore with magistral and common salt for smelting.	*cantar*	5
Hornaguearse	S. Am.	*Chile.* Move a body from one side to the other.	*cantar*	5
Horrarse	Lat. Am.	*Col., C. Rica.* Die [the young of cows and horses].	*cantar*	5
Hostigar	Lat. Am.	**1**. *Col., Chile, Ecuad., Mex., Nicar., Peru, Venez.* Be sickening [food or drink]. **2**. *Col., Peru.* fam. Bother or weary someone.	*pagar*	6
Huachar	S. Am.	*Ecuad.* Plough, make furrows.	*cantar*	5
Huaquear	S. Am.	*Peru.* Excavate in pre-Hispanic cemeteries to extract the contents of Indian tombs.	*cantar*	5
Humear	Lat. Am.	Fumigate, disinfect using gases.	*cantar*	5
Hurguetear	Lat. Am.	Rummage in, snoop, ferret out.	*cantar*	5
		I		
Imprimar	S. Am.	*Col.* Cover the surface of an unpaved road with asphalt to avoid dust and erosion.	*cantar*	5
Improbar	Lat. Am.	Disapprove, condemn something.	*contar*	16
Incursionar	Lat. Am.	fig. Create a work in an unorthodox genre [a writer or plastic artist].	*cantar*	5
Invernar	S. Am.	*Argent., Bol., Chile, Par., Peru, Urug.* Pasture cattle in winter quarters.	*cantar*	5

VERB	REGION	MEANING	MODEL	TABLE
		J		
Jalar	Lat. Am., Cent. Am.	**1.** *Lat. Am.* fig. Run or walk very quickly. **2.** *Cent. Am.* Maintain loving relations.	*cantar*	5
Jeremiquear	Lat. Am.	Whimper, whine.	*cantar*	5
Jinetear	Lat. Am.	**1.** *Lat. Am.* Break wild horses. **2.** *Argent.* Mount colts, showing one's ability and skill as a rider. **3.** *Mex.* fig. Delay payment in the hope of increasing profits. **4.** *Col., Mex.* refl. Be safely mounted in a saddle.	*cantar*	5
Jocotear	Cent. Am.	**1.** *C. Rica, Guat.* Go out to the country to cut down and eat *jocotes* (a plum-like fruit). **2.** *C. Rica, Guat.* fig. Annoy very much, do harm.	*cantar*	5
Joropear	S. Am.	**1.** *Col., Venez.* Tap dance (popular Venezuelan dance). **2.** *Col., Venez.* Have fun.	*cantar*	5
Julepear	S. Am., Caribbean	**1.** *Argent., Urug.* Frighten, scare someone. **2.** *Col.* Annoy, mortify. **3.** *Col.* Insist, urge. **4.** *P. Rico.* Annoy, bother.	*cantar*	5
Jumarse	Lat. Am.	vulg. Get intoxicated, get drunk.	*cantar*	5
		L		
Lacear	S. Am.	*Chile, Peru.* Hold an animal with a rope or lasso.	*cantar*	5
Ladear	S. Am.	*Chile.* fig., fam. Fall in love with a woman.	*cantar*	5
Lagartear	S. Am.	*Chile.* Grasp someone by the biceps (with some tool or both hands), immobilizing him/her for torture or conquest.	*cantar*	5
Lampear	S. Am.	*Chile, Peru.* Remove earth with a hoe.	*cantar*	5
Laquear	S. Am.	*Chile.* Catch or fell an animal with the use of the *bolas.*	*cantar*	5
Leñatear	S. Am.	*Col.* Pick up firewood in the country.	*cantar*	5

VERB	REGION	MEANING	MODEL	TABLE
Lerdear	Cent. Am., S. Am.	**1**. *Cent. Am., Argent.* Be late, do something slowly. **2**. *Cent. Am., Argent.* Move with heaviness or awkwardness. **3**. *Cent. Am., Argent.* Get delayed, arrive late.	*cantar*	5
Llapar	S. Am.	Add, give a bonus.	*cantar*	5
Llavear	S. Am.	*Par.* Lock.	*cantar*	5
		M		
Macanear	Lat. Am.	**1**. *P. Rico, Dom. Rep.* Hit someone with an Indian club. **2**. *Nicar., Venez.* Clear land (see *desmalezar*). **3**. *Hond.* Work hard and assiduously. In *Nicar.,* used with refl. **4**. *Argent., Bol., Chile, Par., Urug.* Say foolish things or lies.	*cantar*	5
Machetear(se)	S. Am.	**1**. *Argent.* fig., fam. Use a cheat sheet. **2**. *Argent.* fam. Use a cheat sheet during an examination.	*cantar*	5
Magancear	S. Am.	*Chile.* Avoid work, be lazy.	*cantar*	5
Majaderear	Lat. Am.	**1**. Bother or annoy another person. **2**. Insist, in a tiresome and stubborn way, that certain things be done and others not.	*cantar*	5
***Maltraer**	S. Am.	*Argent.* Offend, reprove severely.	*traer*	47
Manejar	Lat. Am.	Drive, direct a car.	*cantar*	5
Manguear	S. Am.	**1**. *Argent., Chile.* Herd cattle, horses, sheep, etc. into a corral. **2**. *Argent.* Corral.	*cantar*	5
Manojear	Caribbean	*Cuba.* Bunch tobacco leaves together.	*cantar*	5
Mantearse	S. Am.	*Chile.* Become part of the mantle of the earth [a metal vein].	*cantar*	5
Mañerear	S. Am.	**1**. *Argent., Urug.* Work or proceed with bad skills. **2**. *Chile.* Show poor technique [an animal].	*cantar*	5

regional use

VERB	REGION	MEANING	MODEL	TABLE
Mañosear	S. Am.	*Chile, Peru.* Act, proceed with skill.	*cantar*	5
Marranear	S. Am.	*Col.* Deceive.	*cantar*	5
Matear	S. Am.	*R. Plate.* Drink more and more *mate*.	*cantar*	5
Matrimoniar	S. Am.	Unite in matrimony, get married.	*cantar*	5
Mezquinar	S. Am.	**1**. *Argent.* Avoid, separate, put to one side. **2**. *Col.* Free someone from a punishment.	*cantar*	5
Mordacear	S. Am.	*Argent.* Soften, rub leather with a *mordaza* (cylindrical tool).	*cantar*	5
Mulatear	S. Am.	*Chile.* Start to blacken or darken [fruit that is black when ripe].	*cantar*	5
Muñequear	S. Am.	**1**. *Chile.* Begin to produce ear or cob [corn or similar plants]. **2**. *Argent., Bol., Par.* fig. Use influence to obtain something.	*cantar*	5
N				
Nalguear	Cent. Am., Mexico	*C. Rica, Mex.* Spank someone.	*cantar*	5
Nancear	Cent. Am.	**1**. *Cent. Am.* Harvest *nances* (small, aromatic fruit). **2**. *Hond.* Reach.	*cantar*	5
Neblinear[12]	S. Am.	*Chile.* impers. Drizzle.	*cantar*	5
Ñ				
Ñangotarse	Caribbean	**1**. *P. Rico., Dom. Rep.* Crouch. **2**. *P. Rico.* Humble oneself, submit. **3**. *P. Rico.* Lose heart.	*cantar*	5
O				
Ofertar	Lat. Am.	**1**. Offer, promise something. **2**. Offer, give something voluntarily. **3**. Offer, dedicate or consecrate something to God or to the saints.	*cantar*	5
Opacar(se)	Lat. Am.	Become dark, cloudy.	*atacar*	7

VERB	REGION	MEANING	MODEL	TABLE
Orejear	S. Am.	*Argent.* fig. Lose one's bearings; show cards little by little.	*cantar*	5
		P		
Pajarear	Lat. Am.	**1.** *Lat. Am.* Frighten horses. **2.** *Lat. Am.* Shoo away, frighten away (birds). **3.** *Mex.* Try to hear or find out about something slyly.	*cantar*	5
Palanganear	S. Am.	*Argent., Chile, Peru.* Show off.	*cantar*	5
Palanquear	S. Am.	*Argent., Urug.* fig. Use one's influence so that someone may obtain a desired goal.	*cantar*	5
Palenquear	S. Am.	*Urug.* Tie animals to a stake stuck in the ground.	*cantar*	5
Pallaquear	S. Am.	*Peru.* See *pallar.*	*cantar*	5
Pallar	S. Am.	Improvise stanzas, over or against another singer.	*cantar*	5
Paluchear	Caribbean	*Cuba.* fam. Chatter, prattle.	*cantar*	5
Pampear	S. Am.	Travel through the *pampa.*	*cantar*	5
Pantallear	S. Am.	*Argent., Par., Urug.* Circulate air with a fan.	*cantar*	5
Pañetar	S. Am.	*Col.* Cover walls, roof, etc. of a building with plaster.	*cantar*	5
Papachar	Mexico	See *apapachar.*	*cantar*	5
Paporretear	S. Am.	*Peru.* Repeat something without understanding it.	*cantar*	5
Paquetear	S. Am.	*Argent.* Show off, show others how well one is dressed.	*cantar*	5
Parar(se)	Lat. Am.	Stand up.	*cantar*	5
Parquear	Lat. Am.	Park.	*cantar*	5
Pasmar	S. Am.	*Peru.* Decline in health, become weak.	*cantar*	5
Patriar	S. Am.	*Argent.* Cut the middle of the right ear of a horse to indicate that it belongs to the State.	*cantar*	5

Spanish Verb Manual

regional use

VERB	REGION	MEANING	MODEL	TABLE
Payar	S. Am.	*Argent., Chile, Urug.* Sing improvised songs like those of traveling minstrels.	*cantar*	5
Pechar	Lat. Am.	Sponge, scrounge, swindle.	*cantar*	5
Pelar	Mexico	Leave, escape, flee all of a sudden.	*cantar*	5
Pelotear	S. Am.	**1**. *Bol.* Cross a river in a cowhide raft. **2**. *Argent.* Mistreat someone, treat someone without consideration.	*cantar*	5
Peluquear(se)	S. Am., Cent. Am.	*Col., C. Rica, Par., Urug., Venez.* Cut someone's hair.	*cantar*	5
Pendejear	S. Am.	*Col.* fam. Do or say foolish or silly things.	*cantar*	5
Pepenar	Cent. Am., Mexico	Pick up off the floor, search thoroughly.	*cantar*	5
Perimir	S. Am.	*Argent.* Expire [time limit for a process] because the parties involved did not bring the case forward.	*vivir*	51
Peticionar	Lat. Am.	Present a petition or request, especially to the authorities.	*cantar*	5
Pialar	Lat. Am.	Throw a lasso on an animal to bring it down, hobble.	*cantar*	5
Picanear	S. Am.	Make oxen walk faster.	*cantar*	5
Pichulear	S. Am.	**1**. *Chile.* Deceive. **2**. *Argent., Urug.* Search fervently for advantages and small profits in purchases or business dealings.	*cantar*	5
Pifiar	S. Am.	**1**. *Argent., Chile, Peru.* Make fun of, scoff at, make jokes in bad taste. **2**. *Chile, Ecuad.* Whistle insistently. Make fun of someone to extreme; mock or ridicule.	*cantar*	5
Pircar	S. Am.	Close off a place with a dry-stone wall.	*atacar*	7
Pirquinear	S. Am.	*Chile.* Work free of conditions, with all expenses paid by the employer [a worker].	*cantar*	5
Pispar o pispiar	S. Am.	*Argent.* Investigate, listen or observe, prying into someone else's business.	*cantar*	5

Spanish Verb Manual

VERB	REGION	MEANING	MODEL	TABLE
Pitar	S. Am.	**1**. *S. Am.* Smoke cigarettes. **2**. *Chile.* Deceive, play a joke on, make fun of someone.	*cantar*	5
Plagiar	Lat. Am.	Seize someone for a ransom.	*cantar*	5
Politiquear	Lat. Am.	Engage in politics based on intrigues and vile deeds.	*cantar*	5
Pololear	Lat. Am., S. Am.	**1**. *Lat. Am.* Bother, importune. **2**. *Chile.* Flatter someone in order to have sex with them.	*cantar*	5
Premunir(se)	Lat. Am.	Provide something as a prevention or precaution against some goal.	*vivir*	51
Prosear	S. Am.	*Urug.* Converse.	*cantar*	5
Provocar	S. Am.	*Col., Venez.* fam. Whet the appetite, crave, be pleasing.	*atacar*	7
Puntear	S. Am.	**1**. *Argent., Chile, Urug.* Remove the topsoil layer using the tip of the shovel. **2**. *Argent., Col., Peru, Urug.* March at the head of a group of people or animals.	*cantar*	5
Putear	Lat. Am.	Insult, use vulgar words with someone.	*cantar*	5
Puyar	Lat. Am.	**1**. *Col., C. Rica, Guat., Hond., Nicar., Mex., Pan.* Injure with the goad of a lance. **2**. *Col., Chile, Pan.* Get someone to do something by insisting.	*cantar*	5
Q				
Quedar	S. Am.	*Argent., Urug.* Die.	*cantar*	5
Quinchar	S. Am.	Cover or enclose with reed binding.	*cantar*	5
Quiñar	S. Am., Cent. Am.	**1**. *Chile, Ecuad., Pan., Peru.* Hit with the tip of the cone-like tool used to enlarge pipes. **2**. *Peru.* Chip, splinter.	*cantar*	5
R				
Rajar	Lat. Am.	Speak badly of someone, discredit someone.	*cantar*	5
Rasmillar	S. Am.	*Chile.* Scratch softly.	*cantar*	5

275

regional use

VERB	REGION	MEANING	MODEL	TABLE
Rasquetear	S. Am.	Clean the coat of horses with a currycomb.	*cantar*	5
Rastrillar	S. Am.	*Argent.* Reconnoiter urban or unpopulated areas to examine or search them [the military, police].	*cantar*	5
Recargarse	Mexico	Lean on.	*pagar*	6
Recesar	Lat. Am.	**1.** *Bol., Cuba, Mex., Nicar., Peru.* Cease activities temporarily [a corporation]. **2.** *Peru.* Adjourn a legislative chamber.	*cantar*	5
Reciprocar	Lat. Am.	Respond to an action with a similar one.	*atacar*	7
*Recordar(se)	S. Am., Mexico	*Argent., Mex.* Awaken someone who is sleeping.	*contar*	16
Reencauchar	S. Am.	*Col., Peru.* Retread with rubber.	*cantar*	5
Refaccionar	Lat. Am.	Restore or repair.	*cantar*	5
Refundir	Cent. Am., Mexico	Lose, mislead.	*vivir*	51
Regresar	Lat. Am.	Return or restitute something to its owner.	*cantar*	5
Relievar	S. Am.	**1.** *Col., Peru.* Paint in relief, make something prominent. **2.** *Col., Peru.* fig. Stand out, exalt, enlarge.	*cantar*	5
Rematar	S. Am.	*Argent., Bol., Chile, Urug.* Buy or sell in a public auction (in *Argent.,* only sell).	*cantar*	5
*Remoler	Cent. Am., S. Am.	**1.** *Guat., Peru.* Bother. **2.** *Chile.* fig. Go on a binge, make merry, have fun.	*mover*	30
Repelar	Mexico	Grumble, moan.	*cantar*	5
Reportear	Lat. Am.	**1.** Interview someone important to write a report [a journalist]. **2.** Take photographs for a pictorial report.	*cantar*	5
Repuntar	Lat. Am., S. Am.	**1.** *Lat. Am.* Rise again [the waters of a river]. **2.** *Lat. Am.* Begin to manifest itself [disease, change of weather, etc.]. **3.** *S. Am.* Appear unexpectedly.	*cantar*	5

VERB	REGION	MEANING	MODEL	TABLE
		4. *Argent.* Bring together animals dispersed across a field. **5**. *Argent.* Recuperate a favorable position.		
Requintar	Lat. Am.	**1**. *Argent.* Fold or lift up the brim of a hat. **2**. *Col.* Charge the cavalry. **3**. *Cent. Am., Col., Mex., R. Plate.* Make a rope taut.	*cantar*	5
Restear(se)	S. Am.	*Venez.* Bet all the money one has on the table.	*cantar*	5
Retacear	S. Am.	*Argent., Par., Peru, Urug.* fig. Be stingy about something given to another, materially or morally.	*cantar*	5
Retobar	S. Am., Mexico	**1**. *Argent., Urug.* Cover certain objects with leather, like *bolas* or the end of a whip. **2**. *Chile.* Wrap up bundles with leather or sackcloth, oilcloth, etc. **3**. *Mex.* Grumble, respond. **4**. *Argent., Urug.* refl. Become unpleasant and excessively reserved. **5**. *Argent.* Rebel, get angry.	*cantar*	5
*Retribuir	Lat. Am.	Respond to the favor or gift that one receives.	*concluir*	59
Retrucar	S. Am.	*Argent., Peru, Urug.* Answer with skill and energy.	*atacar*	7
Revirar	S. Am., Mexico	*Col., Mex.* Double the opponent's bet (in certain games).	*cantar*	5
Revolear	S. Am.	*Argent., Urug.* Make a circular motion with a belt, lasso, etc. or any object.	*cantar*	5
Reyar	Caribbean	*P. Rico.* Go out in groups to solicit a small monetary Christmas gift.	*cantar*	5
Rochar	S. Am.	*Chile.* Surprise someone doing something illicit.	*cantar*	5
Rodajear	Cent. Am.	*El Salv., Guat., Nicar.* Cut into slices.	*cantar*	5
Rodear	Lat. Am.	*Argent., Col., Cuba, Chile, Nicar., Peru.* Bring in cattle, horses, and mules from where they are grazing.	*cantar*	5

regional use

VERB	REGION	MEANING	MODEL	TABLE
Rosquear	S. Am.	*Chile.* Look for trouble or fights.	*cantar*	5
Rumbar	S. Am.	*Chile.* Take the route or direction.	*cantar*	5
Rumbear	Lat. Am.	**1.** *Lat. Am.* Head for, walk toward, direct oneself to. **2.** *Nicar.* Head toward; make patches. **3.** *Cuba.* Go on a *rumba* or a binge.	*cantar*	5
Rumorar	Lat. Am.	Disseminate a rumor.	*cantar*	5
Rustir	S. Am.	*Venez.* Stand, put up with patiently (jobs or punishments).	*vivir*	51
		S		
Sabanear	Lat. Am.	Cross the savanna where a herd is located to round up or watch the cattle.	*cantar*	5
Salar(se)	Lat. Am.	**1.** *Cuba, Hond., Peru.* Stain, dishonor. **2.** *C. Rica, Guat., Nicar., Peru, P. Rico.* Ruin, spoil. **3.** *C. Rica.* Give or cause bad luck.	*cantar*	5
*Salir	S. Am.	**1.** *Col.* Harmonize one thing with another. **2.** *Col.* Adjust something to an established model.		79
Semblantear	Lat. Am.	*Argent., Chile, El Salv., Guat., Mex., Nicar., Urug.* Look at someone eye to eye to discern the person's feelings or intentions.	*cantar*	5
*Sentar	S. Am.	*Argent., Chile, Ecuad., Peru.* Jerk sharply on the reins of a horse, causing the horse to rear up on its hind legs.	*pensar*	13
Serenar	S. Am.	**1.** *Col.* Drizzle. **2.** *Col., Venez.* refl. Be exposed to the cool of the night (see *enserenar*).	*cantar*	5
Sobar	S. Am.	**1.** *Argent.* Give a massage, rub. **2.** *Argent.* Tire a horse, demanding a huge effort from it.	*cantar*	5
Socapar	S. Am., Mexico	*Bol., Ecuad., Mex.* Cover other people's faults.	*cantar*	5

Spanish Verb Manual

VERB	REGION	MEANING	MODEL	TABLE
Solapear	S. Am.	*Col.* Shake someone, grabbing him/her by the coat lapel.	*cantar*	5
*Sonar	S. Am.	**1**. *Argent., Urug.* vulg. Die or suffer from a deadly disease. **2**. *Argent., Chile, Par.* fam. Fail, lose, have a bad end. **3**. *Chile.* Suffer the consequences of some act or change.	*contar*	16
Sufragar	Lat. Am.	Vote for a candidate, proposal, report, etc.	*pagar*	6
		T		
Taimarse	S. Am.	**1**. *Chile.* Become obstinate. **2**. *Chile.* Be sullen, obstinate.	*cantar*	5
Tallar	S. Am.	*Chile.* Talk of love [a man and a woman].	*cantar*	5
Talonear	Mexico, S. Am.	**1**. *Mex.* vulg. Practice prostitution in the street; by extension, work. **2**. *Argent., Chile, Mex.* Spur a horse by kicking it with one's heels.	*cantar*	5
Tapiscar	Cent. Am.	*C. Rica, Hond., Nicar.* Harvest corn, removing the kernels from the cob.	*atacar*	7
Tascar	S. Am.	*Ecuad.* Break with one's teeth food that is hard, like a cookie.	*atacar*	7
Taucar	S. Am.	*Bol.* Place some things on top of others, pile up.	*atacar*	7
Tejer	S. Am.	*Chile.* fig. Intrigue, sow discord.	*beber*	24
Temperar	Lat. Am.	*Col., C. Rica, Nicar., Pan., P. Rico, Venez.* Move temporarily to a different climate for pleasure or health.	*cantar*	5
Templar	S. Am.	Fall in love.	*cantar*	5
Tempranear	Lat. Am.	Get up early.	*cantar*	5
Terciar	Lat. Am.	**1**. *Argent., Col., Mex., Venez.* Carry something on one's back. **2**. *Col., Cuba, Chile, Ecuad., Guat., Mex.* Mix liquids, especially with wine and milk, to adulterate them.	*cantar*	5

regional use

VERB	REGION	MEANING	MODEL	TABLE
Tertuliar	Lat. Am.	Have a get-together; converse.	*cantar*	5
Tijeretear	Lat. Am.	fig. Murmur, criticize.	*cantar*	5
Tincar	S. Am.	**1.** *Argent.* Snap one's fingers. **2.** *Argent.* Shoot marbles with the thumbnail. **3.** *Argent.* Hit one ball with another.	*atacar*	7
Tinquear	S. Am.	*Argent.* See *tincar.*	*cantar*	5
Tirar	S. Am., Caribbean	*Col., Cuba, Chile.* Drive, transport, haul.	*cantar*	5
Topar	Lat. Am.	Make roosters fight each other in preparation for the real fight.	*cantar*	5
Torear	S. Am.	**1.** *Argent.* Bark several times as a sign of alarm and attack [a dog]. **2.** *Argent.* fig. Provoke, express insistently to people words that may bother or irritate them. **3.** *Chile.* fig. Set a dog on someone, provoke.	*cantar*	5
Tornar	S. Am.	*Col.* Swing one's arm in an arc to throw a bird into the air.	*cantar*	5
Tortear	Cent. Am.	*Guat.* Make *tortillas.*	*cantar*	5
*Tostar	S. Am.	*Chile.* fig. Reprove someone severely.	*contar*	16
Trabar	Lat. Am.	Be tongue-tied, stutter.	*cantar*	5
Transar(se)	Lat. Am.	Compromise, give in, arrive at a transaction or agreement.	*cantar*	5
Trapear	Lat. Am.	Clean the floor with a mop or scourer.	*cantar*	5
Trasbocar	Lat. Am.	Vomit, throw up what is in the stomach.	*atacar*	7
Trepidar	Lat. Am.	Vacillate, doubt.	*cantar*	5
Trincar	Cent. Am., Mexico	Tighten, squeeze.	*atacar*	7
Trompar	Lat. Am.	Play with a top.	*cantar*	5
Turnar	Mexico	Send a communication, certificate or act to another department, court, tribunal, official, etc.	*cantar*	5

Spanish Verb Manual

VERB	REGION	MEANING	MODEL	TABLE
Tusar	Lat. Am., S. Am.	**1**. *Lat. Am.* Shear an animal. **2**. *Argent.* Cut a horse's mane according to a certain model.	*cantar*	5
		U		
Ubicar	Lat. Am.	Locate or install in a certain space or place.	*atacar*	7
Ultimar	Lat. Am.	Kill.	*cantar*	5
		V		
Vaquear	S. Am.	*Argent.* Practice cattle-raising or the hunting of wild steers.	*cantar*	5
Varar	Lat. Am.	Be immobile because of a breakdown [a car].	*cantar*	5
Varear	S. Am.	*Argent.* Exercise a competition horse to maintain its good physical condition.	*cantar*	5
Ventajear	S. Am., Cent. Am.	*Argent., Col., Guat., Urug.* Finish ahead, obtain the advantage.	*cantar*	5
Viborear	S. Am.	*Argent., Urug.* Slither, move by undulating like a snake.	*cantar*	5
Vichar	S. Am.	*Argent., Urug.* fam. Spy on, watch.	*cantar*	5
Vistear	S. Am.	*Argent.* Simulate a knife fight, as a show of ability and skill.	*cantar*	5
Vivar	Lat. Am.	Acclaim, cheer.	*cantar*	5
Voltear	S. Am., Caribbean	**1**. *Argent.* Knock down. **2**. *Col., Chile, Peru, P. Rico.* refl. Change from one political party to another one.	*cantar*	5
		Y		
Yapar	S. Am.	**1**. *S. Am.* Add quicksilver. **2**. *Argent.* Add to one object another of the same material or one that can be put to the same use.	*cantar*	5
Yerbear	S. Am.	*R. Plate.* Have a drink of *mate* (a medicinal herbal drink).	*cantar*	5

regional use

VERB	REGION	MEANING	MODEL	TABLE
		Z		
Zafar	Lat. Am.	Dislocate a bone.	*cantar*	5
Zampar(se)	Lat. Am.	Throw, propel something with violence.	*cantar*	5
Zanquear	Lat. Am.	*C. Rica, Mex., Dom. Rep.* Go out looking for someone or something.	*cantar*	5
Zaragutear	S. Am.	*Venez.* Lead a vagrant life.	*cantar*	5
Zarandearse	S. Am., Caribbean	*Peru, P. Rico, Venez.* Sway one's hips.	*cantar*	5
Zarpear	Cent. Am.	*C. Rica, Hond.* Sprinkle with mud, fill with claw marks or spatters of mud.	*cantar*	5
Zonificar	S. Am.	*Col.* Divide a property into zones or parcels.	*atacar*	7
Zoquetear	Lat. Am.	Act like a half-wit or blockhead.	*cantar*	5
Zorrear	S. Am.	*Chile, Urug.* Chase or hunt foxes with a pack of dogs.	*cantar*	5
Zurdear	Lat. Am.	Do with the left hand what one usually does with the right hand.	*cantar*	5

Spanish Verb Manual

appendix

regional use of *ustedes* and *vos*

1   The loss of *vosotros* as 2nd person plural

Across all of Latin America the *vosotros* form (second person plural) has been lost, both in spoken and written expression, and **ustedes** has taken its place.

Ustedes is used as the plural form of *tú* and *usted* (*ud.*). It takes the Third person plural form of the verb.

Although students in Latin America continue to learn that there are six persons to the verb, in reality they have been reduced to only five.

		Castilian Spanish (Spain) 6 persons	**Latin-American Spanish** 5 persons
S	**1st**	yo	yo
I	**2nd**	tú	tú/*vos*
N G.	**3rd**	él/ella/ud.	él/ella/ud.
P L	**1st**	nosotros/-as	nosotros/-as
U	**2nd**	vosotros/-as	**ustedes**
R A L	**3rd**	ellos/ellas/uds.	ellos/ellas/uds.

2   The use of *vos* (*voseo*) and *tú* (*tuteo*)

Another feature that is common in a large part of Latin America is called *voseo*. It is the use of **vos** instead of *tú*.

The areas where *vos* is most used are the River Plate (Rio de la Plata) region, especially Argentina and Uruguay; in Central America; and in the Mexican state of Chiapas. It is used with the following construction:

vos + second person plural (accent change),

but there are two other forms of *vos* that are also used, though less frequently:

– change of the personal subject pronoun only: **vos + second person singular:**
    vos cantas, vos tienes, vos vienes

– change of the verb only: **tú + second person plural (modified):**
    tú cant-ás, tú ten-és, tú ven-ís

The following Spanish verb tables illustrate the form of *vos* used in the major tenses:

A. PRESENT Indicative (presente de indicativo)

	Castilian Spanish		Latin-American Spanish	
2nd pers. sing.	tú	cant -as	**vos**	**cant -ás**
	tú	tien -es	**vos**	**ten -és**
	tú	vien -es	**vos**	**ven -ís**

B. Preterite (pretérito indefinido)

	Castilian Spanish		Latin-American Spanish	
2nd pers. sing.	tú	cant -aste	**vos**	**cant -aste(s)**
	tú	tuv -iste	**vos**	**tuv -iste(s)**
	tú	vin -iste	**vos**	**vin -iste(s)**

C. IMPERATIVE (imperativo)

	Castilian Spanish	Latin-American Spanish
2nd pers. sing.	cant -a	**cant -á**
	ten	**ten -é**
	ven	**ven -í**

D. Present subjunctive (presente de subjuntivo)

	Castilian Spanish		Latin-American Spanish	
2nd pers. sing.	tú	cante -s	**vos**	**cant -és**
	tú	teng -as	**vos**	**teng -ás**
	tú	veng -as	**vos**	**veng -ás**

E. Imperfect and future tenses

The same verb form as *tú*:

tenías, vinieras, cantarás, etc.

F. SER

	Castilian Spanish	Latin-American Spanish
Present, 2nd pers. sing.	eres	**sós**

appendix: *ustedes* and *vos*

3   The use of pronouns with *vos*

The *vos* form uses the same reflexive pronoun and direct/indirect object pronoun as *tú* (that is, *te*), except when the pronoun is the object of a preposition (when *vos* is used, instead of *ti*).

<u>Castilian Spanish</u>   <u>Latin-American Spanish</u>

¿Tú te marchas ya?   *¿Vos **te marchás** ya?*
Voy contigo.   *Voy **con vos.***

4   Other characteristics of Latin-American conjugation

The following points illustrate some of the more common tendencies in Latin-American verb use. Although they should not be generalized to include every single Spanish-speaking country on the continent, these points do represent grammatical choices frequently made in the region in terms of the use or the elimination of certain verb forms. Linguistic features that relate only to limited regional or local areas are not included here.

● More prevalent use of the preterite (préterito indefinido) than the present perfect (pretérito perfecto).

● Preference for the **-ra** ending for the imperfective subjunctive (pretérito imperfecto de subjuntivo), almost totally eliminating the use of the **-se** ending.

● Use of the imperfective subjunctive (pretérito imperfecto de subjuntivo) **-ra** ending to express the same meaning as the past perfect in the indicative (pluscuamperfecto de indicativo):

     llegara   for   *había llegado.*

● Frequent use of the following forms:

     ***ir + a* + infinitive** instead of future,
     ***estar* + gerund** instead of present, etc.

● Abundant use of verbs in their reflexive form:

     enfermarse, tardarse, etc.

● Loss of the future subjunctive (futuro de subjuntivo) and past anterior (pretérito anterior) tenses.

Spanish Verb Manual

● Conjugation of some of the impersonal forms of the verb:

Habían *muchos niños.*   There were many children.
Hacen *meses que vine.*   It is months since I came.

5   A brief history of *voseo*

● *Vos* was an ancient personal pronoun for the second person singular that was used as a term of respect and courtesy in Spain in the sixteenth century.

● *Tú* was the personal pronoun for the second person singular that was used as a term of familiarity and indicated equality of position.

● As **usted** (*Vuestra Merced* > *Usted*) began to be used more frequently in Spain, it soon occupied the position of *vos*, and *vos* began to be used in the more colloquial expressions formerly reserved for *tú*.

● In summary, we can say that:

• The *tú* form became the norm in Spain and in the regions of Latin America most influenced by the Spanish court, eliminating *vos*; this is the case in Mexico, the Antilles, and almost all of Peru and Bolivia.

• Nevertheless, *vos* is the most common form of familiar address in Argentina, Uruguay, Paraguay, Central America, and the Mexican state of Chiapas.

• There is vacillation between the use of *tú* and *vos* in Panama, Colombia, Venezuela, Ecuador, Chile, and the southern regions of Peru and Bolivia.

● Therefore, in Latin America, the Castilian norm of peninsular Spanish is not the preferred form, and we find zones of *voseo*, zones of *tuteo*, and zones of mixed forms.

● Evaluation of the correctness of using *vos* has changed according to eras, countries, and social classes, from its total acceptance as norm all the way to its rejection as something that is uncultured and should be avoided.

appendix: *ustedes* and *vos*

● However, throughout recent years the enormous cultural diffusion of *voseo* all over the world has caused it to be accepted as a standard substitute for *tuteo*. Its use by famous contemporary authors such as Miguel Ángel Asturias (1997 Nobel prize winner), Jorge Luis Borges, Julio Cortázar, Ernest Sábato, and others, and its appearance in the renowned cartoon series of the adventures of the little girl Mafalda, drawn by Quino of Argentina, have contributed greatly to its acceptance all over the world.

Spanish Verb Manual